| DATE | | | |
|---|---|---|---|
|  |  |  |  |
|  |  |  |  |
|  |  |  |  |
|  |  |  |  |
|  |  |  |  |
|  |  |  |  |
|  |  |  |  |
|  |  |  |  |
|  |  |  |  |
|  |  |  |  |
|  |  |  |  |
|  |  |  |  |

# THE NATURE OF INTELLIGENCE

*1*

# THE NATURE
# OF INTELLIGENCE

EDITED BY

## Lauren B. Resnick
*University of Pittsburgh*

LEA LAWRENCE ERLBAUM ASSOCIATES, PUBLISHERS
1976    Hillsdale, New Jersey

Lawrence Erlbaum Associates, Inc., Publishers
62 Maria Drive
Hillsdale, New Jersey 07642

84767333

**Library of Congress Cataloging in Publication Data**
Main entry under title:

The nature of intelligence.

  Based on papers presented at a conference held
March 1974 at the Learning Research and Development
Center, University of Pittsburgh.
    1. Intellect–Congresses.   I. Resnick, Lauren B.
II. Pittsburgh. University. Learning Research and
Development Center.
BF431.N38   153.9   75-37871
ISBN 0-470-01384-2

Printed in the United States of America

To my colleagues
at the Learning Research
and Development Center

# Contents

# Preface

In the past several years, converging scientific and social movements have generated increasing concern over the meaning of the term intelligence. Traditional definitions, rooted in the history of intelligence testing and school selection practices, have come under challenge as experimental psychology has turned increasingly to the study of human cognitive processes and as our understanding of the influence of culture on patterns of thinking has grown.

For several decades prior to our own, intelligence has been the almost exclusive concern, in America, of that branch of psychology often called differential psychology. Differential psychologists, using largely correlational methods, had sought through the development and analysis of tests to further our understanding of differences in intellectual capacity and performances among human beings. During most of this period, experimental psychology ignored individual differences, while differential psychology failed to take seriously the methodology or findings of experimentalists. Nor did either branch of psychology take much account of other approaches to the study of cognition, such as the structuralist–developmental and ethological movements of Europe. In the 1970s this picture began to change, perhaps partly as a result of social pressure for a new look at intelligence. In light of the converging interests of psychologists of many persuasions, a critical examination of the possibilities for redefining and studying intelligence seemed appropriate.

The chapters included in this book are based on papers that were originally presented and discussed at a conference held in March, 1974, at the Learning Research and Development Center, University of Pittsburgh. The contributors are cognitive psychologists and psychometricians, representing varied viewpoints, who were invited to come together to address the question of the nature of intelligence. The theme of the book is an examination of cognitive and adaptive processes involved in intelligent behavior and a look at how these processes might be related to tested intelligence. The book contains sections on intelligence from the psychometric viewpoint, computer simulations of intelligent behavior, studies of intelligence as social and biological adaptation, and intelligence analyzed in terms of basic cognitive processes. In a number of the chapters the constructs and methods of modern information-processing psychology are used in their analyses of intelligence. As the reader will discover, the divisions of the book do not necessarily represent competing viewpoints, but rather multiple windows on the phenomenon of human intelligence. Discussion at the conference ranged freely across the topical divisions. This mingling of concerns is reflected in certain individual chapters, in the discussion chapters at the close of each section, and most strongly in the general discussion chapters at the end of the book. The thematic content of the various chapters and of the book as a whole is described in some detail in the introductory chapter.

The conference on intelligence was the sixth in a series of conferences sponsored by the Learning Research and Development Center. These conferences are held on topics of significance for the psychology of instruction. At each conference, outstanding scholars have come together to present and discuss reviews of theory, research, and applications, and to ascertain areas of agreement and challenge. The objective of these conferences is to report and analyze scientific progress in a field at a time when current developments make such discussion particularly useful and when important new issues and concerns can be brought into focus. The conference on intelligence, and subsequent preparation of this volume, were supported by the National Institute of Education, through Contract OEC-4-10-158 with the Learning Research and Development Center at the University of Pittsburgh.

As chairwoman of the conference and editor of the volume, I would like to thank the many individuals who contributed to the conference itself and to preparation of this volume. Phyllis Blumberg, Mary Beth Curtis, Thomas Hogaboam, Thomas Holzman, Timothy Mulholland, Robert Palmer, and Joseph Shimron prepared detailed summaries of the conference and discussions that were of great help in preparing the manuscripts for publication. Cathlene Hardaway and John Magee assisted in the many details of planning and running the conference and in initial editing. The figures and tables for all but Chapters 5 and 13 were prepared for publication by Donna Rottman. Wendy W. Ford acted as my assistant in bringing this volume into its final form; her suggestions and editorial work were invaluable.

LAUREN B. RESNICK

# THE NATURE OF INTELLIGENCE

# 1
# Introduction: Changing Conceptions of Intelligence

Lauren B. Resnick

*University of Pittsburgh*

For many years, the term intelligence has been used by psychologists in a particular and very pragmatic sense to refer to the level of performance on tests designated intelligence tests. Beginning with Binet's work in France, intelligence tests were designed to predict performance in European and American schools, and they do predict this performance with considerable accuracy and consistency. In fact, the measurement of intelligence for purposes of prediction has generally been considered one of psychology's major success stories. Highly talented people have been involved in the design, construction, standardization, administration, and interpretation of tests, and steady progress has been noted in measurement technique and in the psychometric definition and understanding of intelligence.

American psychologists' belief in the promise of testing as both a social and technical advance was at its height in the 1920s. Binet's tests had been successfully translated—a more than merely linguistic task—for use in the American setting. During World War I the United States Army had provided the trial ground for the first large-scale use of group tests of intelligence. Standardized testing of many kinds was about to become a routine tool of the educator for sorting and classifying students and assigning them to the kinds of programs in which it was thought they could perform best. Optimism was abundant, both in the possibilities for a social order based on merit and in the power of the new psychometrics to provide one of the technological tools needed to bring about such a social order. The spirit of the period is well expressed by the following quotation from Goddard (1920):

> With this army experience it is no longer possible for any one to deny the validity of mental tests, even in case of group testing; and when it comes to an individual

examination by a trained psychologist, it cannot be doubted that the mental level of the individual is determined with marvelous exactness.

The significance of all of this for human progress and efficiency can hardly be appreciated at once. Whether we are thinking of children or adults it enables us to know a very fundamental fact about the human material. The importance of this in building up the cooperative society such as every community aims to be, is very great. The mechanical engineer could never build bridges or houses if he did not know accurately the strength of materials, how much of a load each will support. Of how infinitely greater importance is it then when we seek to build up a social structure that we should know the strength of our materials. Until now we have had no means of determining this except a few data on the physical side such as a man's strength, ability to bear burdens, and so forth, and on the mental side a rough estimate born of more or less experience with him. How inadequate all this has been is indicated by the large proportion of failures that are continually met with in society [pp. 28–29].

Amidst the optimism, however, as Sheldon White (1975) has pointed out in an essay on the social implications of definitions of intelligence, there remained a curious contradiction. A technological tool—the intelligence test—of apparently enormous practical validity and social utility had been invented. Yet the basis of the invention was unclear. Little consensus could be found on what the tests measured, even among psychologists who were active in developing and promoting the use of the tests. This lack of consensus, and lack of even the terms in which a consensus might be sought, was evident in a landmark symposium that appeared in 1921, in the *Journal of Educational Psychology* (Intelligence, 1921).

Leading investigators of the time contributed to the symposium. Each was asked to comment on a central question: "What do you conceive intelligence to be and by what means can it best be measured?" Little doubt was expressed by the contributors about the possibility or wisdom of testing intelligence. Yet the authors' conceptions of intelligence ranged widely. Intelligence was defined variously as: the ability to "carry on abstract thinking" (Lewis Terman); "the power of good responses from the point of view of truth or fact" (E. L. Thorndike); "learning or the ability to learn to adjust oneself to the environment" (S. S. Colvin); "general modifiability of the nervous system" (Rudolf Pintner); a "biological mechanism by which the effects of a complexity of stimuli are brought together and given a somewhat unified effect in behavior" (Joseph Peterson); an "acquiring capacity" (Herbert Woodrow); and a "group of complex mental processes traditionally defined ... as sensation, perception, association, memory, imagination, discrimination, judgment, and reasoning" (M. E. Haggerty).

In the ensuing decades, intelligence tests, and their close cousins, the various differential aptitude tests, became more technically sophisticated and were depended upon increasingly as potential sources of a definition of intelligence. The growth of a new psychometric methodology, factor analysis, expanded the hope that measurement itself might be a means for identifying and relating the major abilities that together comprise intelligence. This line of investigation included Thurstone's (1938) work on Primary Mental Abilities and has seen its most elaborate statement in Guilford's long program of research (see Guilford, 1959, 1967).

During most of the period in which the technology and theory of differential aptitude and intelligence testing was developing, another major branch of psychology was bent on pursuits of quite a different kind. Experimental psychologists paid almost no attention to individual differences in the behavior of their subjects, and in their reports and discussions the term intelligence almost never arose. It was, until recently, as if intelligence "belonged" entirely to one branch of psychological research—the differential, or "correlational" as Cronbach (1957) has called it—while experimental psychology turned its attention elsewhere. This historical division, and its negative effects on the development of both a true science of human abilities and an effective applied psychology, was noted by Lee Cronbach in his 1957 Presidential Address to the American Psychological Association (Cronbach, 1957):

> I shall discuss the past and future place within psychology of two historic streams of method, thought, and affiliation which run through the last century of our science. One stream is *experimental psychology;* the other, *correlational psychology* [p. 671].
>
> It is not enough for each discipline to borrow from the other. Correlational psychology studies only variance among organisms; experimental psychology studies only variance among treatments. A united discipline will study both of these, but it will also be concerned with the otherwise neglected interactions between organismic and treatment variables. Our job is to invent constructs and to form a network of laws which permits prediction of the situation and of the present state of the organism. Our laws should permit us to predict, from this description, the behavior of the organism-in-situation [p. 681].

The theme of uniting experimental and individual difference approaches in the study of mental abilities was also developed by Arthur Melton (1967) in his comments on a conference on learning and individual differences, and by Estes (1970) in a review of the contributions of learning theory to an understanding of mental retardation. Nevertheless, reviewing the state of the emergent field of instructional psychology a few years ago, Glaser and Resnick (1972) could find few instances in which successful experimental analysis of individual differences had taken place, or in which individual difference variables were being taken into serious consideration in studies of learning and cognitive performance. One indicator of how little we had progressed along these lines was the failure of research on "aptitude-treatment interactions" (ATIs) to identify situations in which one instructional treatment was best for individuals of one type, as measured by aptitude or ability tests, and a different treatment best for individuals of another type (see reviews by Bracht, 1970, and Cronbach & Snow, 1969). What still seemed needed was a way of defining both aptitudes and treatments in terms of a common set of dimensions that described the actual mental processes involved in particular tasks. Neither the traditional definitions of instructional treatments nor the traditional tests provided such descriptions.

If we knew which cognitive processes the treatments called upon and if we knew which processes individuals were capable of using, then perhaps an effective blending of experimental and differential psychology might be brought about.

## THE PROCESSES OF INTELLIGENCE

The need, then, seems clear enough. There must be a joining of psychometric and experimental psychology in order to determine the kinds of basic processes that underlie intelligent performance. This volume is a direct response to this need. The chapters included here are papers that were originally presented and discussed at a conference on the nature of intelligence held in March, 1974. The contributors are cognitive psychologists and psychometricians representing varied viewpoints. The issues addressed in these pages differ quite sharply from those that have dominated most recent discussions of intelligence and intelligence testing. There is no central concern, for example, with the question of proper or improper uses of tests, or with how to build tests. There is concern, however, for what tests of intelligence might measure. The long accepted definition by default—"intelligence is what the intelligence tests measure"—is rejected quite explicitly. Further, the contributors are not concerned with the heritability debate or with differences between racial and social classes. Rather, a more basic question is asked concerning intelligence—what *is* it, rather than who *has* it.

The theme of this book, broadly stated, is the explication of the cognitive and adaptive processes involved in intelligent behavior, and how these processes might be related to tested intelligence. Leona Tyler's opening chapter provides a brief history of intelligence testing. She concludes:

> We have gone as far as we are going to be able to go. . .with psychometric procedures designed for precise, quantitative evaluation of an individual's place in a norm group. . . . [T]o understand intelligence as a mental process and the ways individuals differ in their endowments we must launch out in new directions, freeing ourselves from some of the psychometric fetters we have forged. . . [Tyler, Chapter 2, p. 25].

Tyler's conclusion sets the occasion for the chapters that follow, all of which, in one form or another, constitute attempts to provide increased precision of meaning for the term intelligence.

Since the issue itself—defining intelligence—is hardly a new one, one might well wonder why we should have greater expectations for success at this time than in the past. The great successes of intelligence testing came, after all, when pretenses of measuring "basic" or "underlying" processes were dropped. Binet's essentially atheoretical work succeeded. Earlier efforts, including Galton's and some of Binet's own early work, that attempted to differentiate among successful and unsuccessful individuals on the basis of simple sensory and physical capacities of various kinds had failed. If the nineteenth and early twentieth century approaches to defining intelligence in terms of simple processes were unsuccessful, why expect current searches for underlying processes to fare any better?

There seem to be two important reasons for optimism, both having to do with developments in psychology since Binet's time. These developments are quite recent, at least in their impact on the American research scene. One is a change in the nature of experimental psychology, especially in that segment of it that is now comfortable with the label "cognitive" or "information processing." It is once again proper for experimental psychologists to study internal processes. Even more important, quite rigorous experimental methods are now being applied to the study not only of simple sensory processes but also of complex cognitive tasks. Methodologies for relating simple processes to the complex tasks in which they are embedded are being developed. For these reasons, it appears that we are now in a position to study a rather different set of "basic processes" than were psychologists in Binet's time, and it seems at least possible that the processes we can now study will prove to be useful ones in developing descriptions of intelligent behavior and thereby providing the basis for a new theory of intelligence. Several chapters in this book explore these possibilities.

*Information-processing conceptions.*   Among those attempting to account for intelligence in information-processing terms, Carroll (Chapter 3) and E. Hunt (Chapter 13) tie their work most closely to psychometric tests, although in quite different ways. Carroll's theoretical chapter seeks to reinterpret factorially identified aspects of tested intelligence in terms of the memory constructs that are current in many of today's information-processing theories. Hunt reports on a series of empirical studies that have been charting the relationships between measured intelligence and such fundamental functions as the speed with which information is processed in short-term memory or the kinds of conceptual encoding used in memory tasks. Other chapters using information-processing approaches ignore tests as a starting point for analysis but nevertheless remain close to the problem of defining intelligence. Simon (Chapter 5), for example, analyzes a variety of specific tasks, seeking for common elements of processing that might be the basis for what we call "general intelligence." Klahr (Chapter 6) describes the early stages of a research program that is attempting to build formal simulation models for how transitions in intellectual competence, including the passage from one Piagetian stage to another, might occur. Resnick and Glaser (Chapter 11) use problem solving and invention tasks as a vehicle for examining some of the processes involved in intelligent behavior, defined as learning in the absence of direct or complete instruction. These chapters illustrate some of the ways in which the constructs and methods of information-processing psychology may be used in elucidating intelligence in modern cognitive terms.

*Developmental conceptions.*   A second reason for optimism concerning new conceptions of intelligence comes via developmental psychology. Although there is no separate chapter on Piaget's theory of cognitive development in this volume—largely because it seemed safe to assume that we were all familiar with the basic outline of Piaget's work—many of the authors have been deeply influenced by Piaget. This influence is reflected in Klahr's and in Resnick and Glaser's concern for transitions in cognitive competence; in both contributions, an underlying assumption is that the acquisition of new competence, particularly when not brought about by direct instruction, is a major task of intelligence. The discussions by Flavell (Chapter 12) and by J. McV. Hunt (Chapter 18) are also developmental in their approach. Hunt, in particular, suggests ways in which concepts of cognitive structure and development, derived quite explicitly from Piagetian analyses, may lead to clarified conceptions of the nature of intelligence.

*Biological and cultural conceptions.* Whether or not one is convinced by Piaget's particular claims concerning sequences of cognitive competence, there is little doubt that the general notion that intelligence can be thought of in terms of cognitive structures that permit species, and therefore individuals, to adapt to their environments has permeated many psychologists' thinking. The section of this book on Intelligence as Adaptation (Part III) highlights this general way of looking at intelligence. Charlesworth (Chapter 8), drawing on the ethological tradition of the study of animal behavior, considers intelligence as a form of biological adaption to the demands of the environment. Goodnow (Chapter 9) examines the ways in which cultural expectations and definitions of intelligence interact. Olson (Chapter 10) extends the notion of intelligence as cultural adaptation to a consideration of the relationship between cognitive demands and technological tools (particularly the tools of written language) available at various times in the development of a particular society. The general conception of intelligence as a form of adaption to the cultural environment informs many of the chapters in this volume. This is particularly clear in Neisser's (Chapter 7) reactions to Simon and Klahr, and it finds some expression, as well, in Flavell's discussion of Resnick and Glaser. Both of these authors suggest that the range of tasks and problems thus far studied by the information-processing analyst may be unnecessarily restricted, relative to the full range of situations important in life outside of the laboratory or school.

*The role of language.* A few years ago any consideration of the nature of intelligence would undoubtedly have included rather heavy debate on the relative primacy of thought versus language, as for example in the long-distance and time-delayed discussion between Vygotsky and Piaget (see Piaget, 1962; Vygotsky, 1962) over whether language sets the occasion for the development of concepts or only expresses already developed cognitive structures. To a certain degree this issue is reflected in Huttenlocher's work (Chapter 14), with its emphasis on the independence of knowledge structures and conventional encodings of that knowledge in the form of language. On the whole, however, language is treated in this volume as simply one of several possible aspects of intelligence. Perfetti (Chapter 15) notes that language is given particular weight in studies of intelligence such as E. Hunt's because the intelligence tests give so much weight to verbal abilities. Perfetti suggests a natural extension of Hunt's contrastive analyses of good and poor performers on intelligence tests to analyses of good and poor performers on other verbal tasks, such as reading. The clear implication is that many forms of verbal behavior, whether or not they appear on aptitude tests, can be viewed as aspects of intelligence and can be subjected to process analyses of the kind reported in many of the chapters of this volume.

*General intelligence.* Threaded throughout the volume, in a kind of recurring counterpoint to the discussion of specific processes that might comprise intelligence, there is concern with what has surely been the most active debate within the psychometric tradition of research on intelligence, namely, the relationship between general intelligence and specific abilities. Tyler (Chapter 2) provides a brief history of past discussions and research on the issue. Cooley (Chapter 4), however, first calls attention to the question as a current and still important one. He points out that whenever a battery of cognitive tests is given to a sample of subjects from a reasonably heterogeneous population there will result a set of positively correlated scores. It is this recurrent finding that virtually forces attention to the question of general intelligence. Although separate abilities can be identified through factor analysis, and a variety of laboratory and natural environment tasks can be defended as involving intelligent behavior, the phenomenon of correlation among all of these separate tasks remains one of the most stable findings of psychology. Humphreys (Chapter 19) emphasizes this point, and adds to it further evidence that some form of general intelligence, rather than any highly specific aptitude, is probably what plays the most important role in such social phenomena as assortative mating, selection into educational institutions, and the like. Estes (Chapter 16), in his discussion of preceding chapters of the book, suggests the "attractive possibility" that experimental analysis of cognitive processes involved on various tests may eventually show that a relatively small number of basic mental processes are tapped, in different combinations, by these tests. Such an explanation for the recurring finding of communalities in test scores is what Humphreys, too, appears to find a promising outcome for the combined efforts of experimentalists and psychometricians.

## THE FUTURE OF INTELLIGENCE

This book provides a kind of "snapshot" of intelligence at a time of transition in the development of the concept. Past conceptions are seen to be lacking in specificity; new ones are just now being formed. When a concept is in transition, one naturally wonders about its future form. What will psychologists mean when they use the term intelligence in a decade or two? Strong predictions concerning a concept in the process of transformation are risky at best. Nevertheless, the authors of the final chapters of this book, each in a somewhat different way, address themselves to this question of the future of intelligence as a scientific concept. Each of these chapters was originally a general discussion of the proceedings of the conference. Each picks up on one or more of the threads of the conference and highlights it, looking at possibilities for the future as much as at achievements of the past.

Estes (Chapter 16) and Voss (Chapter 17) see the very concept of intelligence receding as descriptions of the processes involved in what we now label intelligent acts become more viable. Each foresees the emergence of a new differential psychology based on theories of cognitive functioning. Estes urges the extension of research on the experimental analysis of tasks, particularly those tasks that have appeared in intelligence tests in the past. He expects explanation of individual differences, rather than their measurement, to become the major concern of research on cognitive functions. Voss expects that measurement will remain a concern of psychologists interested in individual differences, but that its character will shift. Tests will be based upon experimentally identified cognitive processes, and will yield profiles of individuals' abilities that will provide diagnostic bases for instruction in basic skills.

Humphreys (Chapter 19) is much more optimistic about the future viability and visibility of intelligence as a construct and of the science of psychometrics as an important contributor to further knowledge concerning intelligence. Humphreys' chapter constitutes something of a brief textbook on problems of bias inherent in all measurement, including measurements taken in the laboratory. He suggests that experimental psychologists need more rather than less concern with these issues if their findings are to have generality beyond the particular occasion of the experiment reported. Thus, as if to balance the expectation that experimental analysis will yield the definition of the future, Humphreys looks to measurement theory to inform future experimental practice. At the same time, he shares with Estes and Voss the belief that constructs drawn from experimental psychology may be what are needed to give substantive meaning to the persistent concept of general intelligence.

Like Voss, J. McV. Hunt (Chapter 18) suggests that, in the future, normative predictive testing will be replaced by more diagnostic tests. Hunt describes work already underway on what he calls "ordinal scales"—that is, scales that allow observation of behaviors indicative of an individual's position in a hierarchically sequenced, and developmentally regular, set of capabilities. Ordinal scales, as envisaged by Hunt, differ in two important ways from the normed tests that have constituted our measures of intelligence in the past. First, they are based explicitly on a theory of what specific competencies are important in intellectual development. Second, they are designed to describe individuals in terms of these specific competencies, rather than in terms of their general ability relative to other people. Ordinal scales, like Voss' process-based profile batteries, are close in spirit to what others have called "criterion-referenced tests" (Glaser, 1963). Because they are tied to specific competencies, and because items are selected to make judgments about these competencies possible, such tests can be used as the basis for intervention designed to enhance the level of cognitive functioning. By knowing exactly where an individual stands in an established developmental sequence, or in a description of basic cognitive abilities, one can match instructional interventions to individual intellectual status.

These concluding chapters suggest an emerging consensus concerning future study of intelligence. The particular tests on which our past conceptions of intelligence have been based will probably become less central to our definitions. At the same time, however, many principles drawn from measurement theory will probably remain important as work proceeds toward uncovering basic intellectual processes. With respect to practical uses of tests, a shift in focus from prediction to diagnosis is envisaged, a shift made possible by the use of theoretically and experimentally derived conceptions of cognitive functioning as the basis for test validation. In this context, possibilities for enhancing intelligence through instruction, and adapting to it in education, take on new meanings.

In the concluding chapter of this volume, Glaser (Chapter 20) considers the implications of these new views of intelligence for the organization of schooling. Several models of education are considered, ranging from the traditional one, in which initial assessment of ability is used primarily to weed out those unlikely to succeed, to a complex system in which multiple instructional environments are made available for individuals with different capabilities and in which provision is made for teaching the specific abilities necessary for success. In the most complex system, multiple attainments as well as multiple routes to attainment are rewarded, in an implicit recognition of the cultural relativity of accomplishment and success. Since Binet's time, our definitions of intelligence have been rooted in our practices of schooling and related conceptions of social success. Glaser's alternative scenarios for the educational future suggest how new scientific conceptions of intelligence may give us the power to change traditional conceptions of schooling. Equally important, changed educational practices may provide the social environments in which future conceptions of intelligence can be validated.

## REFERENCES

Bracht, G. H. Experimental factors related to aptitude-treatment interactions. *Review of Educational Research,* 1970, **40,** 627–645.
Cronbach, L. J. The two disciplines of scientific psychology. *American Psychologist,* 1957, **12,** 671–684.

Cronbach, L. J., & Snow, R. E. *Individual differences in learning ability as a function of instructional variables.* (Final Report, Contract No. OEC-4-6-061269-1217, US Office of Education). Stanford, California: Stanford University, School of Education, 1969.

Estes, W. K. *Learning theory and mental development.* New York: Academic Press, 1970.

Glaser, R. Instructional technology and the measurement of learning outcomes: Some questions. *American Psychologist,* 1963, 18, 519–521.

Glaser, R., & Resnick, L. B. Instructional psychology. In P. H. Mussen & M. R. Rosenzweig (Eds.), *Annual review of psychology.* Vol. 23. Palo Alto, California: Annual Reviews, 1972. (Also University of Pittsburgh, Learning Research and Development Center Publication 1972/6.)

Goddard, H. H. *Human efficiency and levels of intelligence.* Princeton, New Jersey: Princeton University Press, 1920.

Guilford, J. P. The three faces of intellect. *American Psychologist,* 1959, 14, 469–479.

Guilford, J. P. *The nature of human intelligence.* New York: McGraw-Hill, 1967.

Intelligence and its measurement: A symposium. *Journal of Educational Psychology,* 1921, 12, 123–147, 195–216.

Melton, A. W. Individual differences and theoretical process variables: General comments on the conference. In R. M. Gagné (Ed.), *Learning and individual differences.* Columbus, Ohio: Merrill, 1967.

Piaget, J. Comments on Vygotsky's critical remarks concerning *The language and thought of the child,* and *Judgment and reasoning in the child.* Cambridge, Massachusetts: MIT Press, 1962.

Thurstone, L. L. *Primary mental abilities.* Chicago: University of Chicago Press, 1938.

Vygotsky, L. S. *Thought and language.* Cambridge, Massachusetts: MIT Press, 1962.

White, S. H. Social implications of IQ. In IQ: The myth of measurability, *National Elementary Principal,* 1975, 54(4), 2–14.

# Part I

## COGNITION AND INTELLIGENCE IN THE PSYCHOMETRIC TRADITION

# 2

# The Intelligence We Test—
# An Evolving Concept

Leona E. Tyler

*University of Oregon*

Until a decade or so ago, the measurement of intelligence was generally considered to be one of psychology's major success stories. Large numbers of tests had been designed, built, standardized, and placed on the market. Tests were available for the assessment of mental ability in persons of all ages, all levels of education, many languages, and many special kinds of sensory or psychiatric disability. The interpretive information publishers made available to the users of tests had constantly increased and improved. Training programs for psychologists and other test users had turned out thousands of practitioners skilled in the administration and interpretation of tests, and knowledgeable about the ethical principles governing their use. Each year millions of tests were administered—in schools, in the Armed Forces, in business and industry, and in government. While there were still some areas where experts were not in complete agreement about what was being measured, most of us believed that steady progress along this front made it only a matter of time until research would settle the remaining issues.

However, the climate of opinion has changed drastically in recent years, in this as in so many other areas of American life. Intelligence testing is under attack from many directions. Diatribes appear regularly in magazines and newspapers. Not only psychologists but also specialists in related fields are proposing that we discontinue testing entirely. Doubts about the validity and utility of intelligence measurement are widespread, and public statements about hereditary differences in intelligence can lead not just to argument but to vilification and outright persecution (Jensen, 1973; Herrnstein, 1973). Now would seem to be a particularly appropriate time for us to stand back and look at the course we have been steering. What have we really accomplished? Where, if at all, did we go wrong?

## THE ORIGINS OF INTELLIGENCE TESTING

Every school child knows that it all began with Alfred Binet. We can now see that the social milieu in which he and the other pioneer intelligence testers worked at the turn of this century may have had a good deal to do with their efforts. It was a period in which people really believed in progress. They saw all around them what they interpreted as evidence that civilization was advancing and that human societies were becoming more enlightened, more concerned about human welfare. The new psychological laboratories had demonstrated the feasibility of quantitative research. Through the efforts of Quetelet and Galton, statistical techniques had been made available for distilling meaning from measurements. Psychiatrists in France where Binet worked had come a long way toward differentiating the various kinds of abnormality. New methods of diagnosis and treatment for mental difficulties were being proposed.

These events and trends have been cited many times in historical introductions to mental testing. There is, in addition, another fact that so far has received very little attention, but one that I think may have been even more important in setting the stage for intelligence tests. During the late 19th and early 20th centuries, in most European countries and in all American states, systems of universal *compulsory* education were being set up. The only major text on testing in which I have found any reference to this point is Goodenough's (1949), and there it is mentioned only in a footnote (Goodenough, 1949, p. 14). Theta Wolf, in an excellent new biography of Binet (Wolf, 1973), mentions in the course of a rather extended discussion of efforts to help retarded children that " . . . retarded children had raised difficult questions for the schools ever since the administrative decision to enforce universal education in 1881 [pp. 160–161]." Books about the history of education apparently have neglected to pay much attention to the drastic difference it must have made in schools when laws were passed compelling *all* children to attend. Edwards and Richey (1963), for example, say only in passing, "Legislation excluding children from gainful employment was accompanied by statutory enactments requiring compulsory school attendance. In 1852 Massachusetts passed the first law to be enacted in this country requiring children to attend school. In time other states took similar action and by 1918 all the states had some kind of compulsory attendance provisions on their statute books [p. 490]."

The historical fact is that demand for intelligence tests arose everywhere in the period after school attendance was made compulsory. Obviously what the legislation did was to assemble in one place, probably for the first time in human history, almost the full range of human intellects, and to make it necessary for educators to struggle with this diversity. Society has not yet met this challenge. People still blame the schools or tests for the magnitude of the variation that compulsory attendance reveals. The first mental-test developers and their successors were at least attempting to cope with the problem.

As we think about current controversies, it is useful to remind ourselves of some other features of the period in which intelligence tests began. It was a time in which differences in the general quality and worth of individuals, classes, and races were assumed without question. Most people could be trusted to "know their place." It is instructive to return to 19th-century novels like those of Anthony Trollope to see how all-pervasive this attitude was. A Miss Adelaide Palliser, in *Phineas Rex*, for example, just naturally knew that Mr. Spooner, who was proposing to her, was "beneath" her. Servants knew that they belonged in the servants' quarters, not in the drawing room  The recent television series, "Upstairs, Downstairs," makes this point clear. On a broader scale, few questioned the rightness of a world order in which the "superior" peoples were bringing the advantages of good government, religion, and "civilized" ways to the "lesser breeds without the law." Furthermore, it was generally assumed at that time that these differences between classes and races were hereditary in origin.

Critics today sometimes imply that mental testing has itself produced class distinctions. This view fails to recognize the preexistence of class distinctions. Similarly, the early mental testers did not originate the idea of hereditary differences in intelligence; they simply accepted it. Assuming that innate differences existed, they saw their job as one of measuring the differences as accurately as possible. It is quite possible that the testing movement accelerated the breakdown of classes by identifying able individuals from the "lower" strata who might otherwise have gone unnoticed.

Of all the ideas that were circulating during the late 19th century probably the most influential were those derived from Darwin's theory of evolution, as interpreted at that time. Biological determinism, the survival of the fittest, adaptation, and eugenics were concepts that 19th-century intellectuals found tremendously exciting. These were concepts that influenced the search for psychological tools to employ in identifying persons more or less fit to survive. Herrnstein's (1973) book considers in some detail this influence and its current effects on our thinking about testing.

Before Binet the concept of intelligence was primarily a philosophical one. Intelligence was not clearly differentiated from other concepts about human functioning, such as mind, soul, consciousness, intellect, and reason. These concepts, growing out of associationist philosophy and structuralist psychology, had little or nothing to do with individual differences, as Matarazzo (1972) has pointed out. Nevertheless, their influence still persists in theoretical discussions of intelligence, and leads still to confusion in definitions.

It was Alfred Binet's great achievement to weld together many of the diverse pieces, discarding the useless ones and developing a set of tasks, arranged in order of difficulty, which identified different levels of mental ability in children. As Wolf's book shows, Binet was a broad, tolerant, and humane sort of person. He was interested in facilitating optimal development in each child, whether retarded, normal, or superior, and simultaneously increasing his own understanding of complex mental phenomena. Quantification was not very important to him. Contrary to statements often made about his contributions to mental testing, Binet himself never used the term "mental age," preferring the more qualitative, noncommittal term "mental level" (Wolf, 1973, pp. 202–203). The use of IQ as a precise numerical indicator of some hypothetical entity would have struck him as highly objectionable. Wolf's interviews with Simon in 1959–60 revealed that this eminent co-worker of Binet's had "continued to think of the use of the IQ as a betrayal (trahison) of the scale's objective" (Wolf, 1973, pp. 202–203).

After Binet's death, mental testing could have developed in any number of possible directions. We tend to forget this when we think about what actually did happen, as we always do when we assume the inevitability of a particular historical trend. World War I occurred, and psychologists conceived the idea of simultaneously testing large numbers of army recruits. This required that they select tasks and questions that would force respondents to give definite scorable right or wrong answers. Because testers weren't going to be communicating directly with individual testees, they weren't going to be able to learn how these people were thinking by analyzing their wrong answers. Qualitative differences would have to be ignored. Score became all important. After the war the exclusively quantitative emphasis continued, as group testing techniques were adapted for use in schools at all levels. Psychologists who produced the major theories about the nature of intelligence worked with scores, not people. As tests were improved, their administration was more and more in the hands of nonpsychologists who had neither the background nor the interests that would lead them to new insights. However, with the growth of clinical psychology, some psychologists continued the Binet tradition of exploring qualitative potential in individuals. Matarazzo (1972) has analyzed the ways in which the two separate streams, academic theoretical research on the nature of intelligence and clinical work on assessment, developed and occasionally interacted. David Wechsler is the most outstanding example of such interactional thinking. Unfortunately, there are not many others.

I think it was a great pity that this total shift from qualitative to quantitative thinking in the decade following Binet occurred. It closed out possibilities that were more promising than those it left open, possibilities to which we are just now returning. It directed attention to products rather than processes. It generated explanations about why some persons succeeded and others did not, rather than generating plans for adapting environments to individual differences. It intensified competitiveness rather than development in diverse directions. The clinical use of tests, as Matarazzo points out, mitigated these consequences to some degree, but did not really neutralize them. Before World War II most clinicians engaged in assessment were psychological technicians rather than fully-trained psychologists, and after 1940 assessment procedures were applied mainly to abnormal or deviant individuals. At present, clinicians' interest in assessment has declined. Thus, most of what we know about intelligence has appeared through the academic, large-scale testing channel.

We shall return to a consideration of present trends that appear to be picking up some of the loose ends Binet left and presenting us with new insights about intelligence itself rather than intelligence test scores. But first let us look at some of the important facts researchers did find out about what the tests do and do not measure and the issues that they have been able to resolve in a fairly satisfactory way.

## TESTS AND DEFINITIONS OF INTELLIGENCE

### Intelligence: Singular or Plural

The most conspicuous focus for research has been the question as to whether intelligence should be thought of as singular or plural. Quite consistently the answer has turned out to be "both." To begin with it was assumed to be a unitary quality, and Spearman's early correlational research seemed to demonstrate conclusively that all tests measured "*g*" to a greater or lesser degree. But it soon became apparent to applied psychologists that verbal and performance tests, while correlating positively, were not similar enough that they could be used interchangeably. In the 1930s Thurstone (1938) demonstrated that correlations between tests could be accounted for by postulating several primary mental abilities rather than a single "*g*." More recently Guilford (1967) has undertaken this line of investigation and discovered the important "structure of intellect" theory, postulating more than a hundred separate abilities, classified along three dimensions representing content, operation, and product. In all of this effort to separate intelligence into its components, "*g*" has not, however, been entirely lost. Separate measures of abilities and factors still correlate positively, and one or more general factors always appear at the second order level.

There have been attempts to break the amorphous concept of intelligence down in other ways. The distinction Thorndike made (Thorndike *et al.*, 1926) between *altitude* (referring to the degree of difficulty of the tasks that the individual can do successfully), *width* (referring to the number of tasks of a given difficulty that the individual can accomplish), and *speed* (referring to the amount of time required to produce the correct response to a task) is still as important to keep in mind as it was when first proposed. Many of the current arguments about test bias and compensatory education, for example, seem not to be taking into consideration the fact that the real issue is whether altitude, or level, can be raised. If there is a sizable fraction of the population whose intellectual level is not high enough to enable them to comprehend abstract principles in the sciences and humanities, then it would seem to be a mistake to encourage the attendance of such individuals at academically-oriented secondary schools and colleges. I believe that recently we have not been honestly facing a considerable body of evidence that individuals do differ in altitude as well as width. (Let me hasten to add emphatically that I am talking about *individual*, not race or class differences. The question is whether it is really possible to give 50% of the population the same kind of higher education that the top 5 or 10% used to receive.) Hierarchical theories about the organization of intelligence have generally been preferred by British authorities, such as Burt and Vernon. Such theories incorporate the concept of intellectual level into their total structure more easily than the American theories of Thurstone and Guilford do.

Another important attempt to differentiate kinds of intelligence is to distinguish between *fluid* and *crystallized* intelligence (Cattell, 1963; Horn, 1968). Fluid ability, measured by so-called "culture-fair" tests, made up of tasks requiring a grasp of complex relationships in nonverbal material, is thought to be largely determined by heredity, to reach its peak in early adulthood, and to decline thereafter. Crystallized intelligence, as well as many kinds of special abilities and aptitudes, comes into existence through the "investment" of fluid ability in particular kinds of skill valued by the culture. Crystallized intelligence, in contrast to fluid, may increase throughout life.

## Hereditary and Environmental Determinants of Intelligence

As Cattell's and Horn's formulation suggests, a second issue, the perennial nature—nurture question, repeatedly surfaced during the post-Binet decades. As previously mentioned, the investigators during the beginning of this century were conditioned by the general culture to assume that differences in intellectual quality were innate. However, collective research has generated incontrovertible evidence that environmental factors, especially education, influence intelligence test scores. Thus, it is now generally agreed that both heredity and environment influence the individual's performance. But the conclusion is one that society finds difficult to accept. There are always articulate spokesmen for extreme positions. Also, the argument has shifted somewhat from period to period. Now the focus is on the meaning of heritability coefficients. Overton (1973) has produced a clear analysis of the differing assumptions that underlie the argument about the legitimacy of heritability coefficients. What we have here, he says, is a paradigm clash. Those who consider any phenomenon in nature to be a linear function of independent variables continue to seek more precise heritability coefficients. Those who follow a developmental-organismic paradigm reject such computations as meaningless, assuming instead that at all stages of development hereditary and environmental factors are intertwined in such a way that it is impossible to separate them. Personally, I should like to see us abandon this nature—nurture controversy once and for all, since paradigm conflicts are not likely to be resolved through argument. But I suspect that it will continue to flare up in the future as it has in the past.

## Other Issues in the Nature and Measurement of Intelligence

Several other questions that have generated much controversy and considerable research in the past have been resolved, although they too sometimes reappear as new generations of psychologists not familiar with the old evidence take their places on the scene. One of these is the matter of the constancy of the IQ. Longitudinal studies have demonstrated that individual IQs do change as development proceeds. Some of them change quite drastically. However, at least from approximately age six on, changes are likely to be less frequent and pronounced than many people think they are. Correlations between one age level and another are high; large shifts are rare. Bright children tend to remain bright, dull children tend to remain dull. The effects of marked improvements in environment, such as occur when poor children are adopted into affluent homes, are to raise the general level or the mean score of the group undergoing the favorable change, rather than change the relative positions of individuals within the group.

Another of these settled issues is the relationship of intelligence to learning. The common practice of defining intelligence as "learning ability" should probably be discontinued. From Woodrow in the 1930s to Guilford in the 1960s, evidence has continued to accumulate that the concept of general learning ability is false. Different people learn different things quickly and well. Furthermore, intelligence test scores do not predict how quickly individuals will master a new skill or how much verbal material they will assimilate in a given period of time. Why then have intelligence tests predicted school achievement at all levels as well as they have? What seems to be involved is the *altitude* aspect, which we have tended to ignore. Throughout the elementary school years, the curriculum for each grade is more difficult than that for the preceding grade. The secondary school curriculum is more difficult than the primary school cirriculum, and certainly college is more difficult than high school. A child who grasps the more difficult, complex ideas presented each year achieves higher grades and accelerates faster than his neighbor who may actually be learning more of the material they are both capable of comprehending. Thus, the schools reward ability to learn material at a higher level of complexity. Similarly, measured intelligence is related less to the speed or efficiency of learning, than to the complexity of what can be learned at all.

There is now a good deal of evidence proving that even the retarded are not deficient in all sorts of learning ability. Low-IQ children, classified as mentally retarded on the basis of both test scores and school achievement, manage to perform fairly well in meeting the demands of the world outside the schoolhouse. Longitudinal studies reported by Baller (1936), Charles (1953), and Baller, Charles, and Miller (1967) indicate that about 83% of one such group succeeded in supporting themselves and keeping out of trouble well into their middle years. The results of this long-range Nebraska study have been corroborated in other parts of the country.

One other perennial question has never been answered to everybody's satisfaction. It is whether intelligence is a purely cognitive characteristic or has motivational–temperamental components. Here academicians and clinicians tend to part company, academicians preferring cognitive formulations, clinicians preferring global definitions with both cognitive and motivational aspects included (Wechsler, 1950).

Cattell's comprehensive theoretical book (1971) is probably the most successful attempt so far to weld together what almost seventy years of psychometric research have taught us about intelligence. His triadic theory of abilities differentiates between three kinds of ability components:

1. *capacities* ($g$s)–general powers operating through all brain action to affect all cognitive performance. In addition to $g_r$, the ability to grasp relationships and correlates, there are at least two other $g$s: $g_s$, speed, and $g_f$, fluency or retrieval facility.
2. *provincials* ($p$s)–powers having to do with the functioning of particular sensory and motor systems.
3. *agencies* ($a$s)–aids or acquired cognitive skills based on education and training, and proficiencies based on particular interests.

While Cattell still classifies what he has been calling fluid intelligence as a $g$, he now considers crystallized intelligence to be an $a$, a sort of average of the abilities a given culture prizes and encourages. While he recognizes the importance of motivational factors in achievement, he differentiates them from abilities.

## PSYCHOMETRIC TESTS AND COGNITIVE PROCESS

Having completed this rapid survey of individual differences as revealed through psychometric research since Binet, I should now like to shift to some different research directions, suggested by Binet but not followed up until recently. One of these is the idea that a child's growth from infancy to maturity can be divided into distinct stages—stages that differ from one another qualitatively rather than just quantitatively. If one assumes this, the whole concept of intelligence as a single trait or dimension is called into question, at least for children. As I mentioned before, Binet himself was uncomfortable about the assumption that there is a unitary, quantitative dimension, and did not like the idea of using mental age as a score.

Testing of Cognitive-Developmental Stages

Jean Piaget, a young assistant in Simon's laboratory in Paris, had as his first assignment to develop a French version of some English reasoning tests. Piaget was a man whose background and general orientation resembled Binet's in many ways. He discovered the notion of qualitative stage differences and began to investigate it (Matarazzo, 1972, p. 59). In the fifty years since that decision a steady stream of books, papers, and reports flowed from Geneva, where Piaget lived. They have delineated more and more clearly what these qualitative stages are and how they come into existence.

It naturally occurred to many people, as this research program unfolded, that its findings might constitute the groundwork for a superior sort of intelligence test, free from the ambiguities about what is being measured that have plagued the mental-age scales and their progeny through the years. It seemed that tests grounded in a clear, well-supported theory of mental development might escape from the tyranny of norms. It would not be necessary to compare a child's performance with that of others of his age. One could simply state what stage in his own developmental process he had reached by ascertaining what mental structures had emerged. Efforts to produce such a testing instrument, however, were slow in getting started, perhaps partly because Piaget himself has never been interested in individual differences. But in several places such efforts are now being made, and it is possible to evaluate their potential contribution.

In 1969 a conference on Ordinal Scales of Cognitive Development brought together measurement and child development specialists, including Piaget himself and his principal co-worker, Barbel Inhelder. The published report of this conference (Green, Ford, & Flamer, Eds., 1971) provides the best available summaries of what had been done up to 1969, along with critical accounts of the problems and difficulties encountered in these efforts.

There are three principal research projects concerned with the production of Piaget-type tests. One, not reported at the conference, has been going on for several years at the University of Montreal (Pinard & Sharp, 1972). Twenty-five of Piaget's experiments, conducted in a semistandardized way, using as subjects French-Canadian children between the ages of four and twelve, have been combined into a scale. Another research program under the direction of Tuddenham at the University of California in Berkeley is a continuing attempt "to convert Piagetian experiments into test items meeting strictly psychometric criteria, while conserving, insofar as we could, the essence of the original problems" (Tuddenham 1971, p. 64). At the time of the 1969 report, the five-year undertaking had involved more than 40 of the Piaget experiments, using as subjects about 400 children in kindergarten and the first four grades of Bay Area schools, a population that includes a wide range of economic levels and at least three racial groups. The third major attempt is the work on the new

British Intelligence Scale. One feature of this instrument will be that on some of the subscales, a report will be possible about the qualitative level of the testee's thinking, preoperational, concrete operational, or formal operational (Lovell, 1971). So far as I have been able to ascertain, this is the only attempt to develop tests for the higher Piaget stages.

One other major research effort ought to be mentioned here, although its purpose is somewhat different from that of the programs just mentioned. J. Mc V. Hunt and his co-workers at the University of Illinois have put together for use in their research some ordinal scales of the development of particular cognitive processes, inspired, as they say, by Piaget (J. McV. Hunt & Kirk, 1971; Paraskevopoulos & J. McV. Hunt, 1971). The average age at which a group of children in a particular sort of environment reaches each of these "landmarks" becomes in this research an indicator of the "goodness" of the environment. J. McV. Hunt's discussion chapter in this book (Chapter 18) includes a detailed description of a part of this research program.

It has turned out that the task of psychometrizing Piaget's experiments is more difficult than it was expected to be. The main problem is what the Swiss researchers call *décalage* or time lag. All evidences of the structures characterizing a particular stage do not show up at the same time. An example Piaget cites has to do with inclusion. A child of about eight, given a bunch of flowers some of which are primroses, will answer the question, "Are all of the primroses flowers?" correctly. The child will also answer the more difficult question, "Are there more flowers or primroses in this bunch?" correctly. Younger children answering the second question compare the number of primroses and nonprimroses, but are not able to compare two classes one of which includes the other. Where the décalage shows up is in the finding that when identical questions are asked with regard to birds and seagulls instead of flowers and primroses, the eight-year-old makes the same error that younger children make with the flowers. We are left in doubt as to whether he has the structures required for this sort of reasoning or not. Somehow, Piaget says, flowers that one can take in one's hand or lay out on the table are easier to handle mentally than birds than cannot be manipulated. Décalage of this sort is characteristic of all the Piaget tasks. Thus the decision as to whether the structures characteristic of, say, the concrete operational stage are present in a child being tested cannot be clearcut. It depends upon which questions you ask him. The psychometric solution to this problem is obvious, simply use multiple items involving content of various kinds and score the person according to the number he answers correctly. But would such a score tell us any more about the qualitative features of the individual child's thinking than present intelligence tests do? One alternative would be to have each variety of content separately scaled. But this would be cumbersome to administer and not easy to interpret to teachers, parents, and others.

The same sort of inconsistency between different kinds of evidence about what stage each child has reached shows up in correlations Tuddenham has computed between items. Such correlations tend to be low, mainly in the 10s, 20s, and 30s. This is not unusual for ordinary intelligence tests, but it does somewhat dim the hopes for a more precise qualitative characterization through the use of Piaget-type items. Tuddenham (1971) concludes, " . . . the evidence thus far obtained has about extinguished whatever hope we might have had that we could place each child on a single developmental continuum equivalent to mental age, and from his score predict his performance on content of whatever kind [p. 75]." Ward (1972) reports similar scaling difficulties with the ingenious material at the formal operations level tried out for the British Intelligence Scale.

Considered simply as test materials, not as qualitative indicators of structures underlying stages, tests made up of Piaget tasks correlate fairly highly with ordinary intelligence tests and with school achievement. Kaufman (1971), for example, reports correlations in the .60s, based on a group of kindergarten children, between a Piaget-type battery and both the Lorge-Thorndike and the Gesell tests. Kaufman and Kaufman (1972) report also that for the same group of children both the Piaget and the Lorge-Thorndike correlate in the .60s with first-grade achievement a year later. Thus, it seems to me that the effort to produce a test made up of Piaget's experiments is still worthwhile, even though it will not perhaps revolutionize the testing movement. Such a test would do what present tests do, and at the same time allow the examiner to observe interesting qualitative aspects of a child's thinking. In order for this to happen, tests would have to be given individually and scored by hand. I see no prospect for tests of this kind to replace tests designed for large-scale group surveys.

One question that I have not been able to find evidence that anyone is working on is whether or not everybody attains the formal operations level, or whether a sizable fraction of the population is limited to concrete operations. This, of course, is related to questions raised earlier about the significance of altitude as distinguished from breadth. The answer could be very important for education. Perhaps data obtained with the British Intelligence Scale will provide some information about it.

### Aptitude—Treatment Interactions and Cognitive Processes

I should like to consider now another problem that looked important to Binet, was largely ignored for several decades, and is now coming into prominence. It is the problem of aptitude—treatment interaction, often abbreviated ATI. For many years it has seemed obvious to some people that it would be a great boon to education if different teaching methods could be linked to individual differences in aptitudes. The best teachers intuitively attempt something like this, providing reading material at various levels of difficulty, encouraging independent activities in some children, supervising others closely. The trouble is that so far the tests we have developed have given them very little assistance in this endeavor. It would be a useful contribution to develop techniques for sorting out groups of individuals suitable for clearly specified kinds of treatment. To what extent is this possible?

The most comprehensive review of the "state of the art" was brought out by Cronbach and Snow (1969). According to their findings the art is not very advanced. Some interactions of treatment with general intelligence have appeared, but attempts to relate different learning strategies to different patterns of primary mental abilities or factor scores have generally been unsuccessful, as have attempts to relate learning strategies to personality characteristics.

Nevertheless Cronbach and Snow do not advocate giving up the search for aptitude–treatment interaction patterns. What they see as necessary is a more thorough analysis of processes rather than the use of test scores and crudely classified teaching methods. More attention must be given to the actual mental activity of persons taking tests and to learning what is presented in school, so that aptitude specification will grow out of an understanding of these processes. This links up with the research growing out of Piaget's theory. If we could be sure, for example, which boys and girls in an eighth-grade class had reached the stage where they could employ formal operations, and which were still limited to concrete operations, appropriate teaching strategies could be designed for the two groups and results of the differentiation evaluated. The burgeoning research on cognitive style may also have something to offer. Koran's (1969) doctoral dissertation cited by Cronbach and Snow suggested that persons low on Hidden Figures, a measure of field independence, improved most under audiovisual, fixed-pace, attention-restricting procedures, whereas those high in field independence improved most under verbal, self-paced, unrestrictive, articulate treatment. Studies of this sort should be extended.

## INTELLIGENCE AS A REPERTOIRE OF ABILITIES

In my own thinking about human abilities over the last few years, I have been considering one further extension of our concepts. Like the topics we have been discussing, it requires that we pick up Binet's emphasis on process, and on direct observation of how individuals think. My new assumption is that a person with several years of complex development registered in his or her neural tissue probably possesses several abilities he or she can bring to bear in any particular situation, a set of tools from which he or she chooses rather than an amount of something to which he or she is limited. Perhaps some of the unreliability that we have never been able to exorcise arises from actual shifts individuals make in thinking processes they bring to bear on different parts of a test or on the same items on different days. If this assumption holds, what we need to evaluate by testing procedures is the individual's *repertoire,* his portfolio of assets, as it were. Ironically, the more carefully we have standardized our testing procedures, the less likely we are to observe such alternative cognitive processes. All along we have insisted on only one answer to each test item when perhaps we could have elicited several by simply asking for them. What I should like to see now is a loosening up of some of our rigid testing procedures: asking children, as Binet did, how they arrived at their answers; noting, as Piaget does, the nature of errors as well as correct responses; and seeing what happens if we follow the first response, right or wrong, with the remark, "Now see if you can do it another way."

We have gone as far as we are going to be able to go, I believe, with psychometric procedures designed for precise, quantitative evaluation of an individual's place in a norm group. If this kind of evaluation is what we want, we now have the tools to make it. But to understand intelligence as a mental process and the ways individuals differ in their endowments we must launch out in new directions, freeing ourselves from some of the psychometric fetters we have forged. I hope that we have already begun to do this.

## REFERENCES

Baller, W. R. A study of the present social status of a group of adults who, when they were in the elementary schools, were classified mentally deficient. *Genetic Psychology Monographs,* 1936, 18, 165–244.

Baller, W. R., Charles, D. C., & Miller, E. L. Mid-life attainment of the mentally retarded: A longitudinal study. *Genetic Psychology Monographs,* 1967, 75, 235–329.

Cattell, R. B. Theory of fluid and crystallized intelligence: A critical experiment. *Journal of Educational Psychology,* 1963, 54, 1–22.

Cattell, R. B. *Abilities: Their structure, growth, and action.* Boston: Houghton Mifflin, 1971.

Charles, D. C. Ability and accomplishment of persons earlier judged mentally deficient. *Genetic Psychology Monographs,* 1953, 47, 3–71.

Cronbach, L. J., & Snow, R. E. *Individual differences in learning ability as a function of instructional variables.* Stanford: School of Education, Stanford University, 1969.

Edwards, N., & Richey, H. G. *The school in the American social order.* (2nd ed.) Boston: Houghton Mifflin, 1963.

Goodenough, F. L. *Mental testing.* New York: Rinehart, 1949.

Green, D. R., Ford, M. P., & Flamer, G. B. (Eds.). *Measurement and Piaget.* New York: McGraw-Hill, 1971.

Guilford, J. P. *The nature of human intelligence.* New York: McGraw-Hill, 1967.

Herrnstein, R. J. *IQ in the meritocracy.* Boston: Little, Brown, 1973.

Horn, J. L. Organization of abilities and the development of intelligence. *Psychological Review,* 1968, 75, 242–259.

Hunt, J. McV., & Kirk, G. E. Social aspects of intelligence, evidence and issues. In R. Cancro, *Intelligence genetic and environmental influences.* New York: Grune & Stratton, 1971.

Jensen, A. R. *Genetics and education.* New York: Harper & Row, 1973.

Kaufman, A. S. Piaget and Gesell: A psychometric analysis of tests built from their tasks. *Child Development,* 1971, 42, 1341–1360.

Kaufman, A. S., & Kaufman, N. L. Tests built from Piaget's and Gesell's tasks as predictors of first-grade achievement. *Child Development,* 1972, 43, 521–535.

Koran, M. L. The effect of individual differences on observational learning in the acquisition of a teaching skill. Unpublished doctoral dissertation, Stanford University, 1969.

Lovell, K. Some problems associated with formal thought and its assessment. In D. R. Green, M. P. Ford, & G. B. Flamer (Eds.), *Measurement and Piaget.* New York: McGraw-Hill, 1971. Chapter 5.

Matarazzo, J. D. *Wechsler's measurement and appraisal of adult intelligence.* Baltimore: Williams & Wilkins, 1972.

Overton, W. F. On the assumptive base of the nature-nurture controversy: Additive versus interactive conceptions. *Human Development,* 1973, **16**, 74–89.

Paraskevopoulos, J., & Hunt, J. McV. Object construction and imitation under differing conditions of hearing. *Journal of Genetic Psychology,* 1971, **119**, 301–321.

Pinard, A., & Sharp, E. IQ and point of view. *Psychology Today,* 1972, **6**, 65–68, 90.

Thorndike, E. L., Bregman, E. O., Cobb, M. V., & Woodyard, E. *The measurement of intelligence.* New York: Teachers College, Columbia University, 1926.

Thurstone, L. L. Primary mental abilities. *Psychometric Monographs,* 1938, No. 1.

Tuddenham, R. D. Theoretical regularities and individual idiosyncracies. In D. R. Green, M. P. Ford, & G. B Flamer (Eds.), *Measurement and Piaget.* New York: McGraw-Hill, 1971, Chapter 4.

Ward, J. The saga of Butch and Slim. *British Journal of Educational Psychology,* 1972, **42**, 267–289.

Wechsler, D. Cognitive, conative, and non-intellective intelligence. *American Psychologist,* 1950, **5**, 78–83.

Wolf, T. H. *Alfred Binet.* Chicago: University of Chicago Press, 1973.

# 3
# Psychometric Tests as Cognitive Tasks: A New "Structure of Intellect"

John B. Carroll[1]

*Educational Testing Service*

From its beginnings, psychometrics has had a split personality. On the one hand, it has been concerned with practical means of measurement and prediction, including not only the construction of instruments but also the mathematical and statistical bases for obtaining reliable and valid measurements—or what is commonly called "test theory." On the other hand, the very notion of validity— particularly the notion of "construct validity" (Gulliksen, 1950)—implies that one be at least somewhat bothered by the problem of *what* a test measures. Tests of "intelligence" have always been the most prominent type of psychometric instrument. However great their interest in practical matters, all the leading figures in psychometrics—Binet, Spearman, Thurstone, and Guilford (to name but a few)—have had an abiding concern for the nature of intelligence; all of them have realized that to construct a theory of intelligence is to construct a theory of cognition. It is not without significance that one of Spearman's (1924) major works bore the title *The Nature of Intelligence and the Principles of Cognition.* The same theme was carried by the titles of books by Thurstone (1924) and Guilford (1967).

We could say, then, that the first "cognitive psychologists" (in this century at least, for we must remember the efforts of 19th century psychologists, particularly in Britain) were the psychometricians. Perhaps because of the seemingly "soft" nature of the data on which their theories were based, but also for many other reasons, psychometrics has increasingly lost contact with the mainstream of psychological theory and experimentation. Theories of intelligence developed by psychometricians have never found favor among radical behaviorists nor

[1] Since July 1974, the author is Kenan Professor of Psychology and Director of the L. L. Thurstone Psychometric Laboratory at the University of North Carolina, Chapel Hill, N.C. 27514.

among experimental psychologists—even those concerned with "verbal learning," and psychometricians have, for their part, paid little attention to work going on in experimental laboratories. Psychometric and experimental psychology have proceeded along largely independent paths.

Recently what has come to be known as cognitive psychology has experienced a rebirth among experimental psychologists and theorists (Miller, Galanter, & Pribram, 1960; Neisser, 1967). Cognitive psychologists are willing to talk about such "mental events" as plans, sets, covert thought, imagery, rehearsal, stimulus codings, and memory stores, and they are sometimes able to make precise predictions of experimental phenomena by assuming the operation of such events (e.g., Atkinson & Shiffrin, 1968). Along with the development of cognitive psychology there has been the formulation of a "human information processing" viewpoint (e.g., various papers in Chase, 1973; Hunt, 1971; Newell & Simon, 1972; Reitman, 1965), in which the performance of cognitive tasks is described as the operation of integrated "programs" for the processing of information available from sensory channels and from memory stores assumed to exist in the central nervous system.

A few cognitive theorists have already sensed the possibility of forging a link between psychometric data and cognitive information processing theory. Green (1964)—himself both a psychometrician and a cognitive theorist—proposed that computer simulations of intelligence test performance should be attempted. Such computer simulations have in fact been performed; for example, Reitman (1965) described a program for solving analogies items, and Williams (1972) developed a program which he calls Aptitude Test Taker (see Simon, Chapter 5 for a fuller description) that develops its own rules for solving inductive tasks when presented with worked examples.

One of the most interesting developments, however, was contained in a recent paper by Hunt, Frost, and Lunneborg (1973). These workers—the first two being experimentalists and the last a psychometrician—sought relationships between psychometric tests scores and the parameters of performances in certain learning and memory tasks studied by experimentalists. Although their $N$s were relatively small, and the psychometric data they employed were composite scores of verbal and quantitative ability that a factor analyst would regard as too global, fairly consistent trends emerged. Verbal ability appeared to be correlated with the speed with which a person enters information into a short-term memory store, and quantitative ability appeared to be related to resistance to interference in memory tasks. Hunt, Frost, and Lunneborg (1973) made a strong argument that their results suggested that psychometric and cognitive theorists should unify their efforts.

Meanwhile, "back at the psychometric farm," things have been stirring quite actively, but not too vigorously in the directions suggested by Hunt, Frost, & Lunneborg. Various new theories of intelligence have been fashioned, but largely in the traditions established by Spearman and Thurstone, i.e., based on speculative interpretations and classifications of "factors" revealed in correlational studies. Guttman (1970) has presented a new model of intellect based on a distinction between three major facets: (1) the language of communication (verbal, numerical, or figural); (2) the type of task imposed on the subject (rule inferring or rule applying); (3) school achievement. Somewhat more attention is paid to cognitive theory in Cattell's (1971) model, whereby cognitive abilities are organized according to three major dimensions: (1) action phases, (2) content, and (3) process parameters, and then further into types of action phases, contents, and processes. For example, there are thought to be three action phases: (a) involvement of input, (b) involvement of internal processing and storage, and (c) involvement of output. The two content dimensions are: (a) experiential-cultural (with various subdimensions), and (b) neural-organizational. The seven process dimensions refer to task demands such as complexity of relations to be educed, memory storage, retentivity, retrieval, and speed.

Certainly the most prominent of the recent psychometric models is the Structure of Intellect (SI) model developed by Guilford (1967; Guilford & Hoepfner, 1971). As is well known, this is a three-way classification of factors according to four kinds of contents, five kinds of operations, and six kinds of products. This is a classification that seemed to emerge from consideration of the variety of factors found in a major program of research on "higher-level cognitive abilities." In his book, Guilford (1967, pp. 255 ff) adapts a model of perception and memory processes given by Crossman (1964) for the interpretation of his SI model. One has the impression, however, that the SI model came first, only to be followed by a kind of Procrustean fitting of one model into the other. Guilford deserves much credit, nonetheless, for his thorough and careful explorations of the literature of experimental psychology for possible relationships with his model. Still, as I (Carroll, 1968, 1972) and others (Horn, 1970; Horn & Knapp, 1973) have complained, Guilford's SI model seems too pat and rigid, and not sufficiently well supported either by theoretical considerations or by the empirical facts, to stand for all time as a final model for the "structure of intellect" or of cognition. Probably not even Guilford intended it to be. Charitably, we may say that Guilford's model was a brilliant attempt, but premature, certainly not adequate for the extrapolations that have been made from it, e.g., Meeker's (1969) application of it to school learning problems.

Almost parenthetically, one may note that Guilford uses the term *cognition* in a rather narrow sense, as *one* of his "operations," concerned with "awareness, immediate discovery or rediscovery, or recognition of information in various forms; comprehension or understanding" (Guilford, 1967, p. 203). "Cognition" thus stands apart from Guilford's other operations of memory, divergent production, convergent production, and evaluation. Whatever Guilford's "operations" may be, surely they are all included in the purview of a psychology of cognition, which in Neisser's (1967) terms would be concerned with "all the processes by which the sensory input is transformed, reduced, elaborated, stored, recovered, and used [p. 4]," including such processes as "*sensation, perception, imagery, retention, recall, problem solving,* and *thinking,* among many others." It is from this broad perspective that I view cognitive psychology.

What still seems needed is a general methodology and theory for interpreting psychometric tests as cognitive tasks, and for characterizing (but not necessarily *classifying*) factor-analytic factors (hereafter, FA factors) according to a model of cognitive processes. In this chapter I will attempt to provide such a methodology and theory, but necessarily only sketchily. My procedures are still largely subjective—like those of other "structure of intellect" modelers. What I believe is new in my approach is that I *start* from a model of cognitive processes suggested by recent theories and experimental findings, and only then attempt to interpret and characterize FA factors according to this model. I avoid the assumption that FA factors can be classified according to some *n*-way taxonomic system, believing, rather, that the cognitive tasks used in FA studies are necessarily complex from an information-processing point of view and that FA factors simply tend to feature or highlight certain aspects of information processing in which there are prominent individual differences (there being many other aspects in which individual differences may exist, but are not salient for a given set of tasks). Avoiding the *n*-way classification notion will undoubtedly make my "structure of intellect" model less immediately appealing, and harder to comprehend readily, than previous models, but one must confront the fact that cognition is a complex matter.

This chapter is addressed both to cognitive theorists and psychometricians. At the same time it is offered to those who, in the current mood of skepticism about intelligence tests and the meaning of individual differences, are complaining that cognitive tests do not measure anything well-defined or important. I shall not say anything about the importance of intelligence or the social import of individual differences, for these are matters of one's values, but I do believe that a new structure of intellect model based on cognitive theory can contribute to a better definition of what intelligence tests actually measure, and thus to a firmer basis on which to judge their social implications.

## THEORIES OF COGNITIVE PROCESSES

I said that my procedure was going to be to *start* from a theory of cognitive processes and *then,* on this basis, to attempt to characterize FA factors and, by implication, what the corresponding FA tests measure. To my knowledge, such a procedure has never been seriously followed by students of factor analysis, who have usually employed precisely the reverse approach—to try to develop a theory of cognitive processes starting from FA results.

At this point in the history of psychology, one has a good deal to choose from in selecting or formulating a theory of cognitive processes. Many cognitive theorists have attempted to build models or partial models of memory processes, relying on the considerable amount of evidence that it is useful to distinguish among various forms of memory and storage elements. These include sensory "buffers" in which iconic storage of material from sensory receptors takes place, and "memories" of different "terms" (short-term memory, intermediate-term memory, long-term memory, permanent memory—terminology differs from one theorist to another). Information of different kinds (according to sensory modality, or different types of memory coding) gets passed from one kind of buffer or memory storage to another, often becoming transformed or recoded in some way in this process, or sometimes fading away or dropping out of existence completely. Processes of storing items in memory, searching for items in memory, and retrieving items from memory through some form of "addressing" are assumed to occur. The analogy of an electronic computer is often appealed to. Some cognitive theorists (e.g., Neisser, 1967, pp. 292–296) also believe it desirable to postulate an "executive process" or simply "executive" that somehow controls all this information flow.

Nobody seriously believes that the mind is made up of a series of separate storage boxes (although brain studies have demonstrated that there is indeed some kind of partitioning of cortical function), and nobody has been able to find an exact location for an "executive process" in the brain (though there are some interesting speculations about even this). Nevertheless, a model of cognition that accepts the idea that information exists, and that it gets processed in the brain (i.e., is coded, transformed, stored, retrieved, etc.), is justified in assuming, for convenience, that it passes from one set of neural components to another. The assumption of an executive process also seems an intuitive necessity if one is going to get the system in operation. Whether memory stages are in fact distinctly separated by "term" (short-term, intermediate-term, etc.) does not have to be decided, but it is clear that the inputs for memorial information occur at different times (from moment to moment, and in the total life history of the individual) and it may indeed be convenient and even necessary to classify memories with reference to the more or less distinct periods of relative time-depth implied by the terms *short-term, long-term,* etc. We do not even have to decide whether memories can indeed be "permanent"; it is only necessary to accept the fact that some memories are relatively long enduring.

To start from something concrete and rather well elaborated, I adopt the "distributive memory model" proposed by E. Hunt (1971), the overall architecture of which is shown in Fig. 1. A detail of the model as Hunt supposes it to operate in connection with inductive problem solving or concept learning is shown in Fig. 2. Briefly, the model depicts information coming from the environment through a series of sensory and iconic buffers into a short-term memory, and then through an intermediate-term memory into a long-term memory. Hunt's equivalent of an "executive" appears in Fig. 1 as "conscious thought" (as shown next to the box for "short-term memory") or, better, as a

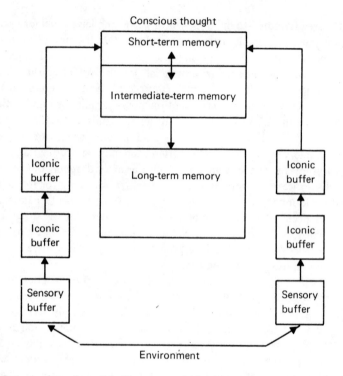

FIG. 1   A schematic model of human cognitive processing. (From Hunt, 1971.)

separate box (Fig. 2) for a "conscious memory processor" that has access to other memories. In concept learning, for example, the "conscious memory processor" utilizes "current hypotheses" and "guesses about attributes" drawn from intermediate-term memory, as well as a Concept Learning System (CLS) program (and/or related programs) drawn from long-term memory.

I need to make, however, one major extension of E. Hunt's model—one that I believe is thoroughly in the spirit of the model but that did not happen to receive attention by Hunt in his presentation of it. This is the concept of a "program" or a "production system" (Newell, 1973) that is assumed to be stored in memory and that controls the flow of information.

According to Newell (1973):

> A production system, starting with an initially given set of data structures, operates as follows. That production whose condition is true of the current data (assume there is only one) is executed, that is, the action is taken. The result is to modify the current data structures. This leads in the next instant to another (possibly the same) production being executed, leading to still further modification. So it goes, action after action being taken to carry out an entire program of processing, each evoked by its condition becoming true of the momentarily current collection of data structures. The entire process halts either when no condition is true (hence nothing is evoked) or when an action containing a stop operation occurs [p. 463].

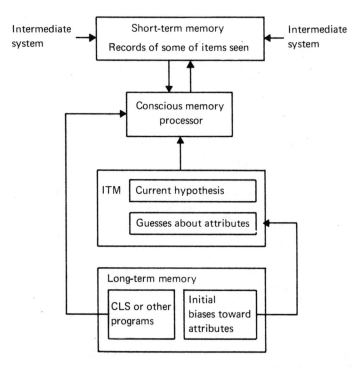

FIG. 2 The model of human cognitive processing as it may be supposed to operate in inductive concept formation. (From Hunt, 1971.)

For my present purposes, I borrow from Newell only the general concept of a production system, not any particular realization of it. What strikes me as important and useful about the concept of a production system, in the present context, is that it provides a sophisticated way of specifying the "program" for any given cognitive task. The various condition–action statements incorporated in a production system specify not only the task itself, but also the rules and strategies by which the subject performs the task. The production system also specifies the data available to the subject as he starts performing the task, and the changes in "data" that occur as he carries out the operations that are required, or that seem to him to be required, to complete the task. These changes in "data" are, in the main, changes in internal memory states, although they could be changes in the external environment that develop as the task is performed (either as the result of the subject's actions or as the result of other circumstances, such as new stimuli presented by the tester or experimenter). Also, every action is assumed to take a certain amount of time, i.e., actions have temporal parameters (often they are to be specified in milliseconds).

Since a production system includes a specification of the task, it should be possible to encode in it the instructions that are given to the subject or examinee. The instructions for a cognitive task (e.g., "Find the word whose meaning is closest to that of the key word," "Find the word whose meaning is opposite to that of the key word," and "Find and mark all instances of the letter *a* on this sheet," etc.), when fully comprehended by the subject, constitute a task set which is then to be applied to each item in a test, to each item or stimulus in a series of learning trials, or the like. One of the most unstudied problems in psychology is the nature of these task sets. As Newell (1973) remarks, "The interaction of the instructions with the task performance program is as much central to control as the internal part of the performance program. It is predictable that a full fledged theory of task instruction will be required [p. 522]."

In Hunt's (1971) model, a place must be found for these instructions or task sets. The task instructions have to be comprehended by the subject—if not from verbal statements, then from experiences in working sample problems—and the resulting "programs" have to be integrated with elements of production systems already resident in permanent memory. Just how all this happens has to be explained, but let us ignore this problem by assuming, in our analyses of cognitive tasks, that the subject comes to us already well instructed, that is, he has already developed the production system that he will use to perform the task.

The instructions to the subject, or the task set, will hardly be enough to specify the full production system in detail. For one thing, we will need to know much more about the cognitive processes, and their parameters (temporal and otherwise), that would be entailed in the production systems for different tasks. For example, we could explore the possibility, as argued by Posner (1973), that a stimulus may evoke multiple codes, visual, auditory, lexical, and semantic. Each such coding would constitute a separate action in a production system for a particular task situation. The more important reason for saying that a production system cannot be specified solely from the task instructions is that in order to do so we must know something about the individual. The production systems of different individuals may differ, from very little to quite a lot, depending upon the characteristics of those individuals and their past experiences. Most likely, the production systems of a representative sample of individuals will have many common elements (identical or nearly identical condition–action statements), but they may differ with respect to the particular strategies and kinds of data available to, and employed by different individuals.

Let us state this point in more detail. Individual differences among $S$s in their production systems would arise through:

1. differences in the composition and ordering of the sets of condition–action rules incorporated in the system; and
2. differences in the temporal parameters associated with these condition–action rules.

There would, however, be further sources of individual differences in the actual performance of a task, arising from differences in individuals' success in applying their production systems. These differences in application might be a result of differences in the processing capacity of the "executive" and its associated memory stores, or of differences in the contents of long-term or permanent memory stores. For example, a person might have a perfectly effective production system for responding to a vocabulary test, but he would fail a particular item if his permanent memory did not contain the meaning of a word presented in the item.

There is one more extension of E. Hunt's model that needs to be made. I am sure it was simply an oversight, or a matter so obvious that it was unworthy of attention, that Hunt did not include provision for a *response* in his system. When the central processor or executive recognizes that it has achieved some result from its application of the production system, it must activate some motor system to make that result manifest. At least, this would be true in a test or task-oriented situation. It might not be the case if the individual is merely storing information by reading, or "thinking of" a name without uttering it even subvocally. In the analysis of psychometric tests as cognitive tasks, we must reserve a place for the specification of the kinds of responses to be made, and any other requirements in the task, such as the instruction to give "as many different responses as possible."

I have given here only a very brief and sketchy account of the type of theory of cognitive processes that I propose to use in analyzing and characterizing the nature of FA factors and the psychometric tests that presumably measure those factors. I have emphasized the role of individual differences in this theory because, of course, individual differences are what FA factors are all about. What I hope to do is to identify particular sources of individual differences on tests in the cognitive domain with particular aspects of information processing behavior as it is described in the theory. For the moment, I regard the description of the theory as adequate for what follows. Some details will be filled in as we proceed.

ANALYSIS OF A REPRESENTATIVE SERIES OF
PSYCHOMETRIC TESTS AND FACTORS IN THE
COGNITIVE DOMAIN

As of the publication of their most recent book (Guilford & Hoepfner, 1971), Guilford and his associates had claimed identification of at least one factor (occasionally, two or three) to occupy each of 98 out of the 120 possible cells in their SI model. It would be too large a task, one impossible to report here, to analyze each of these SI factors and each of the approximately 520 tests described by Guilford and Hoepfner as having been used in their Aptitudes Research Project. Instead, I have selected as a representative sample of cognitive psychometric tests the 74 tests, presumably measuring 24 different FA factors, that were assembled by French, Ekstrom, and Price (1963) to constitute a *Kit of Reference Tests for Cognitive Factors.*

This sample has a number of virtues, and also some limitations. Its virtues are: it includes a large number of test types that are found in various omnibus intelligence tests such as the Otis, the Wechsler tests, and the CEEB Scholastic Aptitude Test, etc.; it contains a variety of test types that have been used repeatedly in FA studies and that, from the evidence available to French *et al.* (1963), could be regarded as "good" tests of the 24 factors (each test, with items that are highly homogeneous in type, was selected as being most probably a "pure" test of a given factor); and the kit is readily available (though at present a new edition is in preparation at ETS). Its limitations are: nearly all the tests involve a time limit, introducing an unknown speed component; they are all paper-and-pencil tests (except for three memory-span tests) and thus tend to emphasize information presented visually; they are suitable mainly for college-age and adult populations and thus permit little consideration of developmental aspects of cognitive processing; all but three tests of "Associative (Rote) Memory" are conventional tests requiring performance on a series of tasks presented one at a time (rather than with a temporal structure such as to require delayed recall); and finally, there is now evidence (Ekstrom, 1973) that not all the factors are as distinct and well-defined, from a statistical point of view, as was originally thought.

I deal with the time-limit problem by considering the task requirements for performance of a single "item" at a time (including specification of any temporal parameters that may be involved in such a performance). I define an item as any stimulus, or group of stimuli considered as a unit, on the basis of which one or more responses are to be made. In the case of a standard multiple-choice item, or the like, the item is the "lead" stimulus and the alternatives from which the subject is to make his selection. For certain of the "fluency" tests, an item would be the stimulus that is supposed to evoke a series of responses. The extreme case, in terms of complexity of response, would be the "Theme" test where the item is the topic specified for a theme that is to be written—one or more paragraphs.

In attempting to characterize the tests and the factors in terms of cognitive theory, I started by developing a uniform system for coding the characteristics of the task represented by the items of each test. Developing this system required much drafting and redrafting, and much consulting and review of the tests themselves. The complete coding system (which even now needs further revision and reorganization) is given in Table 1. The task characteristics that were coded included the types of stimuli presented (Section I), the kinds of overt responses that were required to demonstrate performance (Section II), any relevant aspects of sequencing of subtasks within the task (Section III), and the elements in the production systems that I conceived a subject (at least, myself)

3. TESTS AS COGNITIVE TASKS   37

would employ in performing it. The latter elements referred to the types of operations and strategies that would probably be employed in a central processor or executive element (Section IV), the probable ranges of the relevant temporal parameters (Section V), and the types ("term" and contents) of memory stores that would probably be addressed in storage, search, and retrieval operations (Section VI).

After the coding system was worked out, it was programmed to operate on an interactive computer (using FOCAL with the PDP-8) in such a way that the program would successively demand my codings for a given test, and then print out my codes in a format convenient for analysis. I selected 48 of the tests (a randomly selected two for each of the 24 factors) and coded them according to the system, considering them in a randomly determined order such that no two tests of the same factor were considered unless separated by tests of at least two other factors.

The bases and justifications for my codings cannot be described here in detail. I tried to lay aside, and be unbiased by, any knowledge I had of the empirically determined "factor structure" of each test, or of its classification according to Guilford's or anyone else's system. I did try to rely on what knowledge of cognitive information processing theory I have acquired through a fairly extensive acquaintance with its literature, as represented by books such as those of Neisser (1967), Reitman (1965), Kintsch (1970), and Chase (1973), and journals such as Cognitive Psychology, the Journal of Verbal Learning and Verbal Behavior, and others. I have not yet been able to determine anything about the intercoder reliability of the system, because that would take a good deal of time on the part of a cognitive psychologist.[2]

The resulting codings for the tests could be regarded as raw materials, as it were, for constructing "production systems" for the test tasks. I have not attempted, however, to construct an actual production system for any of the test tasks. This would require decisions about the detailed ordering of processes and their exact specifications, as well as assumptions about the strategies that particular individuals are likely to employ.

Instead, I next turned to a detailed analysis of the codings made for the 48 tests. In this analysis, it was assumed that the factors supposedly represented by the tests were sufficiently well established and factorially distinct, and that the tests were sufficiently representative of their respective factors, to justify using the assignment of tests to factors as a basis for finding common elements in the codings and isolating distinctive patterns of codes for given factors. Attention was first directed to pairs of tests that had similar codes for operations and

[2] Thanks are due to Dr. John Frederiksen, Brandeis University, who in a session lasting about four hours worked through the codings of two tests with me, on the basis of an early version of the system. Dr. Frederiksen and I seemed to agree on our codings most of the time, but no formal check of agreement was made. My own coding of 48 tests took a total of about 14 hr, an average of about 17 min per test, with a considerable standard deviation.

## Table 1

## A Provisional Coding Scheme for Cognitive Tasks Appearing in Psychometric Tests

I STIMULUS MATERIALS  (as provided at outset of task)

1A  Number of stimulus classes
    1  One stimulus class (a word, picture, etc.)
    2  Two stimulus classes (as in many types of MC items, PA learning, etc.)

Description of the ith stimulus class:
1B  Completeness
    1  Complete
    2  Degraded (with visual or auditory "noise")

1C  Interpretability
    1  Unambiguous (immediately interpretable)
    2  Ambiguous (codable several ways)
    3  Anomalous (not immediately codable)

Memory to be addressed in interpretation:
6A  Term (see list 6A)
6B  Contents (see list 6B)
6C  Relevance of individual differences (in this memory store) (see list 6C)

II OVERT RESPONSE TO BE MADE AT END OF TASK

2A  Number and type
    1  Select response from presented alternatives
    2  Produce one correct answer from operations to be performed
    3  Produce as many responses as possible (all different)
    4  Produce a specified number of responses (all different)

2B  Response mode
    1  Indicate choice of alternative (in some conventional way)
    2  Produce a single symbol (letter, numerical quantity)
    3  Write word
    4  Write phrase or sentence
    5  Write paragraph or more
    6  Make spoken response
    7  Make line or simple drawing

2C  Criterion of response acceptability
    1  Identity
    2  Similarity (or nonsimilarity) with respect to one or more features
    3  Semantic opposition
    4  Containment
    5  Correct result of serial operation
    6  Instance (subordinate of stimulus class)
    7  Superordinate
    8  Correct answer to verbal question ("fill in wh-")
    9  Comparative judgment
    10 Arbitrary association established in task
    11 Semantic and/or grammatical acceptability ("makes sense")
    12 Connectedness of lines or paths

III TASK STRUCTURE

3A  1  Unitary (each item completed on a single occasion)
    2  There is a temporal structure such that stimuli are presented on one occasion, responses are made on another occasion (as in memory and learning tasks)
      [This coding would have to be extended greatly to include many types of experimental cognitive tasks]

## Table 1 (continued)

**IV OPERATIONS AND STRATEGIES**

4A  Number of operations and strategies coded for the task

Description of the ith operation:

4B  Type or description
    1   Identify, recognize, interpret stimulus
    2   Educe identities or similarities between two or more stimuli
    3   Retrieve name, description, or instance from memory
    4   Store item in memory
    5   Retrieve associations, or general information, from memory
    6   Retrieve or construct hypotheses
    7   Examine different portions of memory
    8   Perform serial operations with data from memory
    9   Record intermediate result
    10  Visual inspection strategy (examine different parts of visual stimulus)
    11  Reinterpretation of possibly ambiguous item
    12  Imaging, imagining, or other way of forming abstract representation
        of a stimulus
    13  Mentally rotate spatial configuration
    14  Comprehend and analyze language stimulus
    15  Judge stimulus with respect to a specified characteristic
    16  Ignore irrelevant stimuli
    17  Use a special mnemonic aid (specify)
    18  Rehearse associations
    19  Develop a special search strategy (visual)
    20  Chunk or group stimuli or data from memory

4C  Is the operation specified in the task instructions?
    1   Yes, explicitly
    2   Implied but not explicitly stated
    3   Not specified or implied in instructions
4D  How dependent is acceptable performance on this operation or strategy?
    1   Crucially dependent
    2   Helpful, but not crucial
    3   Of dubious effect (may be positive or negative)
    4   Probably a hindrance, counterproductive

Memory involved in this operation:

6A  Term (see list 6A)
6B  Contents (see list 6B)
6C  Relevance of individual differences (in this memory store) (see list 6C)

**V TEMPORAL ASPECTS OF THE OPERATION OR STRATEGY**

    (if 5A = 0 ["irrelevant"] 5B pertains to the probability that the S
    will adopt a strategy)
5A  Duration (range of average duration)
    0   Irrelevant or inapplicable
    1   Very short (e.g., < 200 msec )
    2   Middle range (e.g., <1 sec )
    3   Long (e.g., 1 - 5 sec )
    4   Longer (e.g., >5 sec )

5B  Individual differences in duration (or probability of strategy)
    1   Probably inconsequential
    2   Possibly relevant
    3   Probable wide individual differences (in likely test populations)

5C  Criterion for termination of operation
    0   Irrelevant
    1   Upon arrival at recognizably correct solution (self-terminating)
    2   Not self-terminating in sense of (1). (That is, the solution may
        be a guess, or S may be satisfied with what is actually an
        incorrect solution.)

# Table 1 (continued)

## VI MEMORY STORE INVOLVED

### 6A Term
1  Sensory buffer
2  Short-term memory (STM) (a matter of seconds)
3  Intermediate-term memory (ITM) (a matter of minutes)
4  Long-term or permanent memory

### 6B Contents
0.5  Non-specific
1.0  Visual (general, non-specific)
1.1  Points, positions of points
1.2  Lines (one-dimensional)
1.3  Lines and curves (2-dimensional)
1.4  Geometric patterns and shapes
1.5  Pictorial (objects, etc.)
1.51  - - Subcategory (e.g., tools)
1.6  Real 2-dimensional items
1.7  Maps, charts, grids
1.8  Representations of 3-dimensional geometric shapes
1.85  - - Pictures of 3-dimensional objects or situations
1.86  - - Faces
1.9  Real objects in 3-dimensions
2.0  Auditory (not further specified here)
3.0  Graphemic, general
3.1  Letters
3.2  Words (apart from their semantic information)
3.5  Alphabetic order information
4.0  Linguistic, general (of native language)
4.01  - - Subcategories (e.g., terminolgy and expressions in a special field)
4.1  Lexical
4.11  - - Subcategories
4.2  Syntactic
4.21  - - Lexicogrammatical (e.g., grammatical classifications of words)
4.3  Grammatical rules and features, general
4.4  Semantic (meanings of words, syntactic features, etc.)
4.5  Non-verbal semantics (e.g., meanings of pictorial symbols)
5.0  Numerical, mathematical, general
5.1  Digit symbols with meanings
5.2  Elementary number operations and symbols
5.3  Algorithms for dealing with quantitative relations
6.0  Logic, general
6.1  Various abstract patterns (alternation, sequence, etc.)
6.2  Attributes in which stimuli could vary
7.0  Movements, kinesthetic "concepts"
8.0  "Real world" experiences and learnings, situations, facts, information
8.1  - - Subcategories (e.g., mechanical and electrical information)
9.0  Arbitrary, new codings and associations established in the task situation

### 6C Relevance of individual differences in this store
1  Most Ss will have required store
2  Doubtful that most Ss will have required store
3  Wide individual differences in this memory store are likely

strategies carried on by the central processor and for the types of memory stores presumably addressed by them, especially when the coding indicated that substantial individual differences (in samples of people likely to be administered these tests) existed either in the contents of the relevant memory stores or in the temporal parameters of the operations. It was found that nearly all pairs of tests from the same factor had one or more codes in common (with associated individual differences) and that the patterns of these codes were generally distinct from factor to factor. In a few cases, where no such codes were in common between the tests representing a factor, I managed to convince myself that I had inadvertently missed some opportunities to code, perhaps through insufficient definition of the codes themselves (for example, sometimes I used the operation "retrieve name or instance" and the operation "retrieve association" alternatively to code essentially the same process).

I then considered similarities between test-factor pairs with respect to the types of stimuli and overt responses involved. In a few cases, individual differences in certain parameters of item response seemed to account for the test pairings.

The essential results of this study are in fact the cognitive processes identified as being characteristic of each of the 24 FA factors and the tests that represent them. It turns out that these processes are quite diverse with respect to type, memory store involved, temporal parameters, and other details. Furthermore, most of the FA factors differ markedly from one another. In the few instances in which they do not, there is a suggestion that further empirical study by conventional FA methods might show them not to be statistically distinct (we will examine some evidence of this sort in a later section in which the factors will be discussed in detail).

In many cases, it may appear that the characterizations of the factors made here are not very different from the sorts of characterizations made, for example, by French et al. (1963) when they assembled the *Kit of Reference Tests for Cognitive Factors*. I would claim, however, that the added element is the orientation with respect to a unified cognitive theory based on recent findings in cognitive psychology. Rather than saying that a given factor appears to involve some presumed mental process drawn, as it were, from thin air, a theory-oriented characterization identifies the role of that process in a total matrix of cognitive operations, drawing attention to the role of individual differences in well-defined aspects of the process.

Presentation of my results poses a problem. I could simply list the factors in some arbitrary order and give their characterizations, and in some ways that ought to be sufficient. Clarity demands, however, that the list ought to be organized in some principled way. But any "principled way" implies what would appear to be taxonomic classification, and I do not believe that taxonomic classification is justified in the case of a series of FA factors that are presumably distinct and uncorrelated specimens, which have common elements, if any, quite by accident. The problem of classifying factors is somewhat like that of classifying the letters of the alphabet. We could classify letters on the basis of whether they have only straight lines, or only curves, or some mixture of straight lines and curves, or we might classify them by the number of strokes needed to write them, or by the number of serifs they have in a particular font of print; all such classifications would, however, be ad hoc. It is with some misgiving, therefore, that I present the factors and their characterizations in a somewhat organized manner, first in a table (Table 2) and then in a series of verbal descriptions that give explanations of entries in the table.

The *vertical* organization of Table 2 reflects:

1. the type of memory (STM, ITM, or LTM) in which some aspect of individual differences is regarded as being predominant; and
2. the modality (in the case of STM factors) or contents (in the case of ITM and LTM factors) of memory.

The *horizontal* organization of the table concerns the specification of operations and strategies ("control processes") in which individual differences are assumed to be prominently involved in specified FA factors. The distinction between an operation and a strategy is only that *operations* are control processes that are explicitly specified, or implied, in the task instructions and fore-exercises and that must be performed if the task is to be successfully completed, while *strategies* are control processes that are not specified in the task instructions, but may or may not be used (discovered) by a particular subject. Strategies may or may not be helpful in performing the task; some may even be counterproductive.

### Memory Aspects of the Factors

Of the 24 factors, there seem to be eight for which individual differences appear to be most prominently associated with operations and strategies that address either a short-term memory (STM) or some kind of sensory buffer. Put otherwise, there is little or no involvement of individual differences with either an intermediate-term or a long-term memory store. For seven of these factors, the modality of the sensory buffers and the STM is visual; for the eighth factor, the modality is regarded as nonspecific, since the contents of sensory buffers and STM could be either visual or auditory.

It should be emphasized at this point that Table 2 indicates *only* the operations, etc., in which individual differences are identified as of great magnitude. The coding scheme (Table 1) contains codes for all operations and strategies that were perceived as possibly functioning in the performance of a given task, but these codes are reflected in Table 2 only when individual differences were thought to be relevant either to the temporal parameters ($T$) of a process, to the capacity or contents (*C*) of a relevant memory store, or to the probability (*P*) that a particular strategy would be employed by a subject (the symbols *T, C,* and *P* are used in Table 2). Thus, every factor in the table involves addressing of sensory buffers (that is, perceiving stimuli presented in the task), and it is often the case that these stimuli have to be interpreted by reference to either ITM or LTM. But for the STM factors, it is believed that individual differences are not likely to pertain to contents of ITM or LTM. For example, in the case of the Perceptual Speed factor any likely test takers would be thoroughly familiar with, or be readily able to interpret, the digit symbols or other stimulus elements presented in tests of P.

Only one factor, Ma (Associative Rote Memory), is assigned to ITM, for insofar as a memory store is concerned, individual differences appear to arise mainly in storage and retrieval operations with ITM. The contents are non-specific as to modality, on the present evidence.

The remaining 15 factors are assigned to LTM because (so far as a memory store is involved) individual differences are associated mainly with search and retrieval operations with LTM. Usually, they depend upon the contents of LTM or some particular portion thereof. That is, individual differences in these factors will be a function of the contents of particular kinds of LTM stores, i.e., what the individual has learned in his previous history and stored in his permanent memory. The major types of LTM contents may be classified for our present purposes as:

1. Visual-representational (images or other abstract representations derived from visual perceptions).
2. Auditory-representational (analogous to visual-representational, but in the auditory mode).
3. Lexicosemantic information (abstract representations of words, and their semantic and grammatical features and rules). Lexicosemantic information is usually cross-referenced to visual-representational and auditory-representational contents. It is assumed that this information pertains to the English language. (The French *et al.* tests are in English, not French!).
4. Quantitative information (abstract representations of numbers, number operations, and algorithms for dealing with quantitative information). Much of this is cross-referenced to visual-representational and to lexico-semantic information.
5. Abstract concepts and "general logic" information (representations of various concepts, principles, and rules having to do with implication, inference, causality, sequencing, attributes, patterning, etc.).
6. Experiential information (relating to the individual's general store of information about himself and his environment, and his past experiences). Some of this information would result from special learning experiences such as schooling and reading.

Table 2

Individual Differences in Cognitive Processes and Memory Stores
Associated with 24 FA Factors [a]

| FACTOR | PRINCIPAL MEMORY INVOLVED | COGNITIVE PROCESSES | | | STRATEGIES | RESPONSE RENDERING |
|---|---|---|---|---|---|---|
| | | OPERATIONS | | | | |
| | | Addressing Sensory Buffers | Addressing ITM or LTM | Manipulations in executive and STM | | |
| Ss Spatial Scanning | STM (visual) | Visual search for connectedness of lines and paths (T,C) | | | Search from goal rather than start (P) | |
| Le Length Estimation | STM (visual) | | | Compare distances (T,C) | | |
| P Perceptual Speed | STM (visual) | Visual search for specified items (T) | | | | |
| Cf Flexibility of Closure | STM (visual) | | | Image figure-in-ground (T,C) | | |
| S Spatial Orientation | STM (visual) | | | Mentally rotate spatial configuration (T,C) | | |
| Vz Visualization | STM (visual) | | | (1) Mentally rotate spatial configuration (T,C) (2) Perform serial operations (T) | | |
| Xa Figural Adaptive Flexibility | STM (visual) [LTM, general logic] | | Search hypotheses in LTM (T,C) | (1) Image figure-in-ground (T,C) (2) Perform serial operations (T) | | |
| Ms Memory Span | STM (non-specific) | | | (1) Store in STM (T,C) (2) Retrieve from STM (T,C) | Chunk or group stimulus items (P) | |
| Ma Associative Memory | ITM (non-specific) | | (1) Store in ITM (T,C) (2) Retrieve from ITM (T,C) | | (1) Find mediators in LTM (P,C,T) (2) Rehearse associations (P) | |
| Cs Speed of Closure | LTM (visual-representational) | | Search for match of cue (T,C?) | | (1) Search hypotheses in LTM (P, C) (2) Search different portions of LTM (P) (3) Restructure perception (P) | + Writing Speed ? |
| Fw Word Fluency | LTM (lexico-graphemic) | | Search for instances (T,C) | | (1) Search different portions of LTM (P) (2) Use alphabet as mnemonic (P) | + Writing Speed |
| Fe Expressional Fluency | LTM (lexico-grammatical) | | Search for instances (T,C) | | (1) Search different portions of LTM (P) (2) Use grammatical mnemonics (P) | ++ Writing Speed |

[a] Individual differences in: (C) contents or capacity of memory store involved; (T) temporal parameters of the process; (P) probability of a strategy.

Table 2 (continued)

| | | | | | | |
|---|---|---|---|---|---|---|
| Fa<br>Associational<br>Fluency | LTM<br>(lexico-<br>semantic) | | Search for instances<br>(T,C) | | Search different<br>portions of LTM<br>(P) | + Writing<br>Speed |
| V<br>Verbal<br>Comprehen-<br>sion | LTM<br>(lexico-<br>semantic) | | Retrieve word<br>meanings (C) | | | |
| N<br>Number<br>Facility | LTM<br>(numbers<br>& numeri-<br>cal opera-<br>tions) | | Retrieve number<br>associations and<br>algorithms (C) | Perform serial<br>operations with<br>algorithms (T,C) | (1)Chunk inter-<br>mediate results<br>(P)<br>(2)Record inter-<br>mediate results<br>(P) | |
| I<br>Induction | LTM<br>(abstract<br>logical) | | Search hypotheses<br>(C,T) | | Serial operations<br>to construct new<br>hypotheses (P,T) | |
| Rs<br>Syllogistic<br>Reasoning | LTM<br>(lexico-<br>semantic,<br>abstract<br>logical) | | Retrieve meanings &<br>algorithms (C,T) | Perform serial<br>operations (T,C) | Attention to<br>stimulus<br>materials (P) | |
| R<br>General<br>Reasoning | LTM<br>(abstract<br>logical,<br>algorithms<br>for quanti-<br>tative<br>relations) | | Retrive algorithms<br>(C,T) | Perform serial<br>operations (T,C) | | |
| Fi<br>Ideational<br>Fluency | LTM<br>(experien-<br>tial,<br>general) | | Search for<br>associations (C,T) | | Search different<br>portions of LTM<br>(P) | ++ Writing<br>Speed |
| O<br>Originality | LTM<br>(experien-<br>tial,<br>general) | | Search for "unusual"<br>instances (C,T) | | Search different<br>portions of LTM<br>(P) | + Writing<br>Speed ? |
| Re<br>Semantic<br>Redefinition | LTM<br>(experien-<br>tial, uses<br>of objects) | | Search for<br>associations (C,T) | | Search different<br>portions of LTM<br>(P) | + Writing<br>Speed |
| Xs<br>Semantic<br>Spontaneous<br>Flexibility | LTM<br>(experien-<br>tial) | | Search for<br>associations (C,T) | | Search different<br>portions of<br>LTM (P) | + Writing<br>Speed |
| Sep<br>Sensitivity<br>to Problems | LTM<br>(experien-<br>tial, abstract<br>logical) | | Retrieve<br>associations (C,T) | Perform serial<br>operations (T,C) | Search different<br>portions of LTM<br>(P) | ++ Writing<br>Speed |
| Mk<br>Mechanical<br>Knowledge | LTM<br>(mechanical<br>knowledge) | | Retrieve<br>associations (C,T) | | | |

Some tests and factors seem to draw upon further subcategories of LTM contents; for example, factor Fw (Word Fluency) emphasizes lexicographemic information (orthographic characteristics of words), and factor Fe (Expressional Fluency) draws upon the individual's stock of knowledge about syntactic rules and grammatical classifications of words.

The classification of the contents of LTM is to a large extent arbitrary and solely a matter of convenience. It should not mislead one to the impression that cognitive tests and FA factors are concerned *only* with some particular type of contents. Most cognitive tasks involve at least some elements of LTM, and those elements may be sampled from any portion of it. Further, because of the large amount of cross-referencing and interconnectedness that may be presumed to exist in LTM, for example between the lexicosemantic store and the visual, auditory, and other kinds of storage to which lexicosemantic elements "refer," we must assume that the whole of LTM may be involved in a cognitive task. Our designation of certain factors as being addressed to certain portions of LTM implies only that certain portions are *featured* in that involvement. For example, factor V (Verbal comprehension) is primarily concerned with the richness and variety of the lexicosemantic store.

### Cognitive Control Aspects of the Factors

Control processes are of three general types: (*a*) attentional processes addressing sensory buffers, (*b*) processes addressing longer-term memories (ITM or LTM), and (*c*) processes operating primarily within an "executive" and an associated STM, usually with contents that arrive in STM as a result of control processes (*a*) or (*b*), or both.

Attentional processes (with associated individual differences) are exemplified in the French *et al. Kit of Reference Tests* primarily by visual search operations and strategies (e.g., controlling eye movements to access different parts of a visual display). In a more diversified collection of cognitive tasks, these attentional processes could include attending to particular features of stimuli in various modalities.

Operations addressing ITM or LTM are of three major types: (1) storing an element in ITM or in LTM, (2) searching for an element with given attributes in ITM or LTM, and (3) retrieving an element from ITM or LTM by some process of "addressing." We cannot yet specify what parameters of a storage operation are associated with individual differences. It can only be said that there *are* apparently individual differences in the efficiency and success of such storage. Individual differences in search operations would seem to be associated with the time spent in such searches and the rate of search. A search operation may or may not eventuate in a successful retrieval. Individual differences in direct retrieval operations may be associated with their temporal parameters, but most often they are associated with the contents of the memory being searched (and thus with the probability that a given item is present in ITM or LTM and can in fact be retrieved).

A special remark must be made concerning the way in which certain tests of "fluency" factors involve LTM search operations. Many of these tests require the subject to retrieve "as many [different] items as possible," usually in a portion of LTM that may be assumed to contain items of the type being searched (so that it is not a matter of the richness of the store). Since the tests are administered under a time limit, the scores are a function primarily of the rate of search (but also of any special search strategies adopted by the subject). Some tests, however, require only *one* item to be retrieved. Such unusual constraints may be placed on this one item, however, that we may assume that the subject may have to spend much time searching for it, so that the probability of success may still be assumed to be a function primarily of rate of search.

So far as their association with individual differences is concerned, control processes in an executive and its associated STM are exemplified by such things as:

1. Simple judgments of stimulus attributes such as to reveal identity, similarity, or differences between two stimuli.

2. Certain manipulations of STM contents, such as "imaging" or otherwise abstractly representing an item, imaging a figure-in-ground, and mentally rotating a visuospatial configuration.

3. "Serial" operations using algorithms from the general logic store (or, more generally, a production system that includes such algorithms). That is, certain elements are operated on, producing new elements. These in turn are operated on, producing still further elements, and so on until the process is terminated (either successfully or unsuccessfully). Individual differences concern the ability to perform these operations efficiently and correctly with whatever algorithm or algorithms are being used. (Of course, individual differences also arise from whether appropriate algorithms are in fact being used, but such differences are assigned to differences in contents of relevant LTM memory stores.)

## Response Aspects of the Factors

A final column of the table notes whether individual differences may be presumed in the temporal parameters of "response rendering." This applies to the particular tests offered in the French *et al. Kit of Reference Tests for Cognitive Factors.* Many of these tests (usually, all tests of a given factor) require the subject to render his or her response by writing words, phrases, or sentences, rather than simply selecting a response. We know that there are individual differences in writing speed (Carroll, 1941) that enter into test correlations. The table notes factors in which such individual differences may play a role, although it may not be that such a role is essential to their measurement.

## CHARACTERIZATIONS OF THE FACTORS IN TERMS OF COGNITIVE PROCESSES

In the following "characterizations," I must emphasize again that the descriptions address only aspects of tasks that involve individual differences. The factors are arranged roughly in terms of the type of memory and the number of cognitive processes that are involved. (This is also the order in which the factors are presented in Table 2.)

*Factor Ss (Spatial Scanning)* requires addressing sensory buffers to make a visual search for the connectedness of lines and spaces (paths). Both the temporal parameters, and the capacity of STM and the visual sensory buffer, are involved. In at least two of the *Kit* tests (Maze Tracing Speed and Choosing a Path) *S*s may differ in their probabilities of discovering a possibly helpful special strategy, namely, scanning from the goal rather than from the start.

*Factor Le (Length Estimation)* requires simply a comparison of distances, a comparison which may be assumed to take place in the executive and an associated STM. Both capacity and temporal aspects may be involved.

*Factor P (Perceptual Speed)* involves primarily the temporal parameters of a visual search through a field for specified elements. This search occurs by addressing sensory buffers.

*Factor Cf (Flexibility of Closure)* involves a process occurring in STM whereby a figure is imaged in relation to a surrounding visual-representational field. Both capacity and temporal aspects may be involved.

*Factor S (Spatial Orientation)* involves essentially the ability (capacity of STM) and rate (temporal parameters) of a process occurring in STM whereby a spatial representation is "mentally" rotated.

*Factor Vz (Visualization)* involves the same process as Factor S but *in addition* requires the performance, in executive and STM, of serial operations upon the results of mental rotations.

*Factor Xa (Figural Adaptive Flexibility)* requires the same process as in Factor Cf (Flexibility of Closure), i.e., imaging a figure in relation to a surrounding visual-representational field. In addition, it requires the performance, in STM, of serial operations, and also a search for relevant hypotheses in a LTM logic store. [I would not expect it to be a "pure" factor, and the evidence assembled by Ekstrom (1973, pp. 64–65) tends to confirm this suspicion.]

*Factor Ms (Memory Span)* involves storage and retrieval of information (nonspecific as to modality) in STM. The capacity of STM for this operation is the primary individual difference determiner. Strategies of chunking or grouping stimulus elements may be helpful to some subjects.

*Factor Ma (Associative Rote Memory)* is similar to Memory Span except that the storage and retrieval operations are with respect to ITM. Usually, the time allowed for this test permits *S*s to use special strategies, such as rehearsal in STM, and finding "mediators" in lexicosemantic and/or experiential LTM stores. Thus, individual differences may also appear in the probability and success of using such strategies.

*Factor Cs (Speed of Closure)* requires a search of a LTM visual-representational memory store for a match for a partially degraded stimulus cue. Individual differences appear primarily in the rate of this search, but the probability of certain special strategies may also be involved: (1) searching and utilizing hypotheses drawn from associations in LTM, (2) (consciously) searching in different portions of LTM, and (3) restructuring the perception of the stimulus (an operation involving the addressing of a sensory buffer, and similar to the alternation of the perception of ambiguous figures such as the Necker cube).

*Factor Fw (Word Fluency)* requires a search of a "lexicographemic" portion of a LTM store for instances fitting certain orthographic requirements; the temporal parameters of this search, and the contents of the LTM, figure in individual differences. A special strategy that undoubtedly many subjects adopt is to use the alphabet as a mnemonic, i.e., systematically testing memory store with different letters. Also, some subjects may "consciously" search different portions of memory, such as (for the test requiring words beginning with RE-) searching memory for verbs for which RE- is a prefix meaning "back" or "again."

*Factor Fe (Fluency of Expression)* involves search of lexicosemantic memory, with special attention to the grammatical features of lexical items and different syntactical patterns of phrases and sentences. Special strategies include the "conscious" search of different portions of memory, and the use of "grammatical mnemonics" (such as deliberately considering different grammatical classifications in searching for words).

*Factor Fa (Associational Fluency)* entails search of a major portion of a LTM lexicosemantic store, with special attention to its semantic and associational aspects. A special strategy that some subjects will doubtless use is a conscious search of different portions of LTM, trying different categorizations of the stimulus word or words. In many cases such a strategy might be helpful.

*Factor V (Verbal Comprehension)* is almost exclusively dependent upon the contents of the lexicosemantic LTM store, i.e., upon the probability that the subject can retrieve the correct meaning of a word. (In the French *et al.* (1963) *Kit,* only conventional multiple-choice vocabulary tests are offered as reference tests. A more diversified set of tests of this factor would probably call on other aspects of the lexicosemantic store, particularly its grammatical feature portions.)

*Factor N (Number Facility)* involves (1) retrieving appropriate number associations and algorithms from LTM and (2) performing serial operations on the stimulus materials using these associations and algorithms. Individual differences could appear in both content and temporal aspects of these retrieval and manipulative operations. Special strategies possibly contributing to individual differences might be special ways of "chunking" numerical materials (e.g., mentally adding two-digit numbers both digits at a time rather than by the more "elementary" one-digit-and-carrying methods).

*Factor I(Induction)* entails searching for relevant hypotheses in a LTM "general logic store." Success would depend primarily on whether the contents of this store are adequate to yield the solution to the problem. Some subjects, however, might adopt the possibly helpful strategy of performing serial operations with STM contents to construct new hypotheses.

*Factor Rs (Syllogistic Reasoning)* involves both retrieval of meanings and algorithms from relevant portions of LTM and performing in STM serial operations on materials retrieved. Individual differences could appear in content and temporal aspects of both these types of operations. They could also occur in the probability that the subject will give adequate attention to details of the stimulus materials.

*Factor R (General Reasoning)* is very similar to Factor Rs (Syllogistic Reasoning) in that it involves both retrieval and serial operations. It would be distinguished from Factor Rs only with respect to the precise types of contents in LTM that are required to be retrieved and utilized in the serial operations. In the case of Factor Rs, these contents have to do with logical characteristics of certain linguistic quantifiers (*all, some, no,* etc.) whereas in Factor R the contents are more general algorithms concerned with concrete quantitative relations (time, rate, cost, etc.), and in addition, the same types of number associations that are involved in Factor N (Number Facility).

We will deal with factors *Fi (Ideational Fluency), O (Originality),* and *Re (Semantic Redefinition)* as a group. All involve memory search for certain types of associations and instances in an "experiential" store. They differ only in terms of the particular portions of this LTM store that are to be searched. For Factor Fi (Ideational Fluency), a rather wide spectrum of experiences and concepts is to be searched. For Factor O (Originality), special constraints are introduced—the instances are to be somewhat unusual, or dependent upon special "physiognomic" associations of visual shapes. For Factor Re (Semantic Redefinition), experiences related to uses or possible uses of objects are searched. All three factors may elicit a special strategy of consciously searching different subportions of the relevant memory store (it should be noted that the response phases of many of the tests involve writing words or phrases, and thus individual differences in writing speed may partially account for FA results).

*Factor Xs (Semantic Spontaneous Flexibility)*, if it exists at all, would also depend upon search for associations in a LTM experiential store, especially that portion concerned with possible goals and uses for objects. Considering the fact that its tests are often scored in terms of the number of "category changes" in the responses, it would also depend upon the probability that the subject will use the strategy of examining different portions of memory. According to Ekstrom (1973), the factor is in any case not well supported by empirical data.

*Factor Sep (Sensitivity to Problems)* is another factor for which empirical evidence is slim. If it exists, I would interpret it as involving retrieving associations from a general experiential store concerned with properties and uses of objects, and then performing serial operations with these associations using algorithms from a "general logic" LTM concerned with causality, consequences of actions, and the like. Subjects could adopt special strategies in searching memory for appropriate associations.

*Factor Mk (Mechanical Knowledge)* obviously involves a special portion of a LTM experiential store concerned with mechanical and electrical devices and their properties (a cross-referenced lexicosemantic store is also involved, but individual differences are probably centered in the experiential or knowledge store rather than in the lexicosemantic store).

I have not mentioned a special strategy that may apply in the case of almost any test that requires search and/or retrieval of memories, in fact with nearly all the factors and tests, namely, forming an image of some item in STM in order to help in the elicitation of associations. It can be asserted with reasonable confidence that there are large individual differences in the capacity and predisposition to form such images (Anderson, 1973; Di Vesta, Ingersoll, & Sunshine, 1971; Hollenberg, 1970; Paivio, 1970; Posner, 1973). Because this facet of individual differences is so universal it has not seemed efficient to mention it in connection with every factor characterized above.

## IMPLICATIONS AND FURTHER STEPS

The characterizations of factors given above are admittedly speculative; however, they are given mainly in order to demonstrate the *kinds* of characterizations that I believe ought to be made as the result of theory-oriented research in factor analysis and in experimental psychology.

It is rare to find in Table 2 a factor in which individual differences are ascribed to a single aspect of a cognitive task. Nearly all cognitive tasks are complex, in the sense that they involve a number of different kinds of memories and control processes. (Yet, as Herbert Simon's analyses in Chapter 5 of this book suggest, they are fundamentally simple, in the sense that they are constructed out of fundamentally simple operations.) Each kind of memory, and each kind of control process, may have a number of different parameters. These considerations lead to the conclusion that it may be impossible, in principle, to identify "pure" factors of individual differences—probably not, at any rate, through the application of typical group-administered tests. Possibly methods for measuring "pure" factors of individual differences could be devised for use in an experimental laboratory (E. Hunt, Chapter 13, describes attempts to study individual differences in this way). The often-noted observation that all psychometric tests in the cognitive domain tend to be more or less positively correlated probably reflects the multifaceted nature of the tasks sampled in these tests.

The multifaceted nature of psychometric tasks also further supports the conclusion that it is impossible, in principle, to construct a "structure of intellect" model containing an $n$-way classification of tasks such that a "factor" can be found for each cell in the classification. Nevertheless, the model of intellect that I have tried to present here may have an heuristic value in the sense that further factor-analytic investigations could examine certain components and component combinations of the model in greater detail. I would think, however, that these investigations would have to rely on tests conducted under much more carefully controlled experimental conditions than has been generally true in the past.

Table 3

Examples of Cognitive Processes Under Study by Psychologists

---

Visual search (as in factors Ss and P):  Neisser, 1967, pp. 66ff.

Mental rotation of spatial configuration (as in factors S and Vz):
    Shepard and Metzler, 1971; Cooper and Shepard, 1973.

Serial operations in STM (as in many of the factors):
    Trabasso, Rollins, and Shaughnessy, 1971; Newell and Simon,
    1972; Groen and Parkman, 1972.

Memory storage and retrieval in STM (as in factor Ms):  Winzenz
    and Bower, 1970; Sternberg, 1969.

Memory storage and retrieval in ITM (as in factor Ma):  for references,
    see Goss and Nodine, 1965; Melton and Martin, 1972.

Memory storage and retrieval in LTM (as in factor Fa):
    Bousfield and Barclay, 1950; Freedman and Loftus, 1971.

---

Some of the cognitive processes postulated here are being intensively investigated by experimental psychologists. Table 3 gives a number of examples, but this list, and the citations, are only illustrative. Note that most of the investigations cited are concerned only with one kind of process, and little attention is being paid to individual differences, let alone correlations among individual difference variables.

The obvious next step would be to extend experimental investigations of this kind to include attention to individual differences and to possible linkages with psychometric tests that tap individual differences in cognitive processes. Such a step would lead to more precise specifications of cognitive processes, and it might yield some surprises. The individual difference linkages with learning parameters that are reported by Hunt, Frost, and Lunneborg (1973), and by E. Hunt in Chapter 13 of this book are somewhat suprising, to me at least, because I see little involvement of these particular processes in the actual performance of verbal and quantitative ability tests of the type used by these workers. Perhaps these correlations say something, not about how verbal and quantitative ability tests are performed, but about how verbal and quantitative abilities get developed in the first place. That is, for example, if it is the case that people with a high rate of entry of items into STM are likely to be high in verbal ability, perhaps verbal ability (that is, a large vocabulary and language store) is acquired most readily by people with a characteristically high value of $\alpha$ in Atkinson and Shiffrin's (1968) model of memory processes.

### Further Comments on the Nature of Intelligence

Let us return to the original theme of this book, remembering all those "people out there" who argue that intelligence is not well-defined, and that whatever the tests measure has no significant role in school success, and still less in life success.

I have tried to show, first, how the tasks on many types of psychometric tests in the cognitive domain are indeed cognitive tasks whose structure, contents, and control processes can be identified. Many of the control processes that I have found in these cognitive tasks can be operationally defined through the techniques of experimental psychology. It appears that there are wide individual differences in people's ability to perform these control processes efficiently, and certainly there are substantial differences in the contents of people's long-term memories.

But do these individual differences have any clear relevance to achievement in school or in life? We do know that certain types of "intelligence tests"—particularly those of Factors V (Verbal Comprehension) and R (General Reasoning)—have substantial correlations with measures of school success, despite the less than perfect reliability of school grades and other measures of school achievement. In accounting for what correlations we have, I would draw upon the model of intellect proposed here to identify elements and operations that are in common between psychometric tests and school performance. As we have seen, Factor V depends mainly on the individual's LTM stores of lexicosemantic information. Such stores not only are produced by school and school-related experiences, but also are prerequisite for many varieties of later learning. Factor R involves LTM stores of algorithms for reasoning, and the efficiency of serial operations in STM for applying these algorithms to problems requiring them. These algorithms and operations are also present in school learning tasks. Similar remarks could be made about various other factors in relation to school performance—Factors S (Spatial Orientation), Vz (Visualization), and Fi (Ideational Fluency), for example. The idea that there are mental operations in common between psychometric tests and school performance is not at all new. Such an assumption has in fact underlain the thinking of mental testers ever since Binet, if not before. I mention it here only because it seems in need of reiteration, in the face of allegations that "intelligence tests" do not measure anything important. Also, it seems to me that the clarification of what it is that cognitive tests measure—along the lines of a "structure of intellect" such as is proposed here—provides additional scientific support for this notion.

We could undoubtedly find elements in common between psychometric tasks and cognitive tasks in everyday life. Writing a letter, planning a route, understanding the operation of a machine, thinking of candidates for committee membership, learning a list of prices or ZIP codes—these are cognitive tasks which involve operations and strategies applied to various types of memory stores. These tasks are considered socially important. Is it not important also to study the cognitive processes that underlie them?

There have been complaints about the uses to which "intelligence tests" have been put, and the very notion of individual differences in intellectual abilities and capacities has become colored with a certain measure of opprobrium— opprobrium which, however, does not seem to attach to the notion of individual differences in, say, musical, artistic, or athletic abilities. This is not the place to comment on the proper uses of tests or to speculate about the role that individual differences in intellectual capabilities should play in the functioning of a free society. What I have tried to do in this chapter is to point out that the study of individual differences in cognitive task performances may lead to better understanding of the formation of individual differences in general, as well as to fundamental knowledge about the nature of the underlying cognitive processes.

## ACKNOWLEDGMENTS

Preparation of this chapter was supported in part by Office of Naval Research Contract N00014-17-C-0117, NR 150 329 with Educational Testing Service, and in part by general research funds of Educational Testing Service.

# REFERENCES

Anderson, R. Individual differences in the use of imaginal processing. Unpublished doctoral dissertation, University of California at San Diego, 1973.

Atkinson, R. C., & Shiffrin, R. M. Human memory: A proposed system and its component processes. In K. W. Spence & J. T. Spence (Eds.), *Advances in the psychology of learning and motivation: Research and theory.* Vol. II. New York: Academic Press, 1968. pp. 89–195.

Bousfield, W. A., & Barclay, W. D. The relationship between order and frequency of occurrence of restricted associative responses. *Journal of Experimental Psychology,* 1950, **40,** 643–647.

Carroll, J. B. A factor analysis of verbal abilities. *Psychometrika,* 1941, **6,** 279–307.

Carroll, J. B. Review of Guilford's *The nature of human intelligence. American Educational Research Journal,* 1968, **5,** 249–256.

Carroll, J. B. Stalking the wayward factors: Review of Guilford and Hoepfner's *The analysis of intelligence. Contemporary Psychology,* 1972, **17,** 321–324.

Cattell, R. B. *Abilities: Their structure, growth, and action.* Boston: Houghton Mifflin, 1971.

Chase, W. G. (Ed.) *Visual information processing.* New York: Academic Press, 1973.

Cooper, L. A., & Shepard, R. N. Chronometric studies of the rotation of mental images. In W. G. Chase (Ed.), *Visual information processing.* New York: Academic Press, 1973. pp. 75–176.

Crossman, E. R. F. W. Information processes in human skill. *British Medical Bulletin,* 1964, **20,** 32–37.

Di Vesta, F. J., Ingersoll, G., & Sunshine, P. A factor analysis of imagery tests. *Journal of Verbal Learning and Verbal Behavior,* 1971, **90**(5), 471–479.

Ekstrom, R. B. Cognitive factors: Some recent literature. Princeton, N.J.: Educational Testing Service Project Report 73–30, July 1973.

Freedman, J. L., & Loftus, E. F. Retrieval of words from long-term memory. *Journal of Verbal Learning and Verbal Behavior,* 1971, **10**(2), 107–115.

French, J. W., Ekstrom, R. B., & Price, L. A. *Kit of reference tests for cognitive factors.* Princeton, N.J.: Educational Testing Service, 1963.

Goss, A. E., & Nodine, C. F. *Paired-associates learning: The role of meaningfulness, similarity, and familiarization.* New York and London: Academic Press, 1965.

Green, B. F. Intelligence and computer simulation. *Transactions of the New York Academy of Sciences,* 1964, Ser. II, **27,** 55–63.

Groen, G. J., & Parkman, J. M. A chronometric analysis of simple addition. *Psychological Review,* 1972, **79,** 329–343.

Guilford, J. P. *The nature of human intelligence.* New York: McGraw-Hill, 1967.

Guilford, J. P., & Hoepfner, R. *The analysis of intelligence.* New York: McGraw-Hill, 1971.

Gulliksen, H. Intrinsic validity. *American Psychologist,* 1950, **5,** 511–517.

Guttman, L. Integration of test design and analysis. In *Proceedings of the 1969 Invitational Conference on Testing Problems.* Princeton, N.J.: Educational Testing Service, 1970.

Hollenberg, C. K. Functions of visual imagery in the learning and concept formation of children. *Child Development,* 1970, **41,** 1003–1005.

Horn, J. L. Review of J. P. Guilford's *The nature of human intelligence. Psychometrika,* 1970, **35**(2), 273–277.

Horn, J. L., & Knapp, J. R. On the subjective character of the empirical base of Guilford's structure-of-intellect model. *Psychological Bulletin,* 1973, **80,** 33–43.

Hunt, E. What kind of computer is man? *Cognitive Psychology,* 1971, **2,** 57–98.

Hunt, E., Frost, N., & Lunneborg, C. Individual differences in cognition. In G. Bower (Ed.), *The psychology of learning & motivation: Advances in research and theory*. Vol. 7. New York: Academic Press, 1973.

Kintsch, W. *Learning, memory, and conceptual processes*. New York: Wiley, 1970.

Meeker, M. N. *The structure of intellect: Its interpretation and uses*. Columbus, Ohio: Merrill, 1969.

Melton, A. W., & Martin, E. (Eds.) *Coding processes in human memory*. Washington, D.C.: Winston, 1972.

Miller, G. A., Galanter, E., & Pribram, K. H. *Plans and the structure of behavior*. New York: Holt, Rinehart & Winston, 1960.

Neisser, U. *Cognitive psychology*. New York: Appleton-Century-Crofts, 1967.

Newell, A. A theoretical exploration of mechanisms for coding the stimulus. In A. W. Melton & E. Martin (Eds.), *Coding processes in human memory*. Washington, D.C.: Winston, 1972. pp. 373–434.

Newell, A. Production systems of control processes. In W. G. Chase (Ed.), *Visual information processing*. New York: Academic Press, 1973. pp. 463–526.

Newell, A., & Simon, H. A. *Human problem solving*. Englewood Cliffs, N.J.: Prentice-Hall, 1972.

Paivio, A. On the functional significance of imagery. *Psychological Bulletin*, 1970, 73(6), 385–392.

Posner, M. I. Coordination of internal codes. In W. G. Chase (Ed.), *Visual information processing*. New York: Academic Press, 1973. pp. 35–73.

Reitman, W. R. *Cognition and thought: An information-processing approach*. New York: Wiley, 1965.

Shepard, R. N., & Metzler, J. Mental rotation of three-dimensional objects. *Science*, 1971, **171**, 701–703.

Spearman, C. *The nature of intelligence and the principles of cognition*. London: Macmillan, 1924.

Sternberg, S. The discovery of processing stages: Extensions of Donders' method. *Acta Psychologica*, 1969, **30**, 276–315.

Thurstone, L. L. *The nature of intelligence*. New York: Harcourt, Brace, 1924.

Trabasso, T., Rollins, H., & Shaughnessy, E. Storage and verification stages in processing concepts. *Cognitive Psychology*, 1971, **2**, 239–289.

Williams, D. S. Computer program organization induced from problem examples. In H. A. Simon & L. Siklóssy (Eds.), *Representation and meaning: Experiments with information processing systems*. Englewood Cliffs, N.J.: Prentice-Hall, 1972. pp. 143–205.

Winzenz, D., & Bower, G. H. Subject-imposed coding and memory for digit series. *Journal of Experimental Psychology*, 1970, **83**, 52–56.

# 4
# Who Needs General Intelligence?

William W. Cooley

*University of Pittsburgh*

Leona Tyler (see Chapter 2) traces some of the history of intelligence testing, emphasizing the shift to quantification following Binet's pioneering efforts. She then calls for a return to Binet's original concern for relating intelligence to cognitive processes. What Carroll (Chapter 3) has done is provide us with an example of how this reunion of quantitative, psychometric method and models of cognitive processes might be achieved. He does this in the rather novel way of starting from a model of cognitive processes and then attempting to interpret and characterize psychometric results in terms of this model.

It seems reasonable that any effort to develop an understanding of the nature of intelligence could profit from the large body of facts that have accumulated since psychometricians began studying individual differences in intelligence about 100 years ago. Unfortunately, as Travers (1967) has observed, psychometricians and psychonomers have been plowing different fields, so it is not surprising that their furrows have not crossed. As is generally recognized today, the psychometricians' efforts to develop theory out of this vast aggregation of facts by turning the job over to a factor analysis computer program have not been particularly enlightening. Perhaps Carroll's new approach will provide a "cognitive map" of the psychometric fields!

Tyler also reminds us that the concept of general intelligence (whether it be called $g$, or altitude, or intellectual level, or the principal factor that explains the inevitable correlations among any set of cognitive tasks) has persisted in spite of efforts to make the notion inoperative. There are several features of this general intelligence phenomenon that make it particularly interesting, yet it seems to be so frequently dismissed as being uninteresting. Here are some of the reasons why I think general intelligence is an important phenomenon:

1. Any battery of cognitive tasks given to a sample of subjects from some reasonably heterogeneous population results in a set of positively correlated

scores, the principal component of which accounts for at least one-fourth of the variance in the original measurements. This principal component, or general intelligence factor, is a measure of an individual's current profile level on that set of tasks. This is true whether one is talking about a battery of "differential aptitude" tests or a battery of school achievement tests. It is the current altitude of a child's intellectual development.

2. If one administers two different batteries of cognitive tests, the principal component from one battery will generally correlate at least .8 with the principal component from the other battery, hence "the indifference of the indicator" to which Spearman (1904) referred. The general factor continues to reappear, and scores on one general factor usually explain over 60% of the variance on any other general factor.

3. This general factor, when measured at one educational level, is by far the best predictor of academic performance at the next level. The reason for this is obvious. What one is able to learn today is in very large part a function of what one has already learned to date. This is why the general factor has been critically important in efforts to sort out the effects of different school programs in evaluation studies. It is also why significant program effects have been so difficult to establish. The other side of the coin is that although the general factor explains about 50% of the variance in future performance, half of it is left unexplained. We are now beginning to develop measures of school experiences that explain some of that previously unexplained variance in general intelligence.

4. The most important reason to be interested in the general factor is because it is by far the best predictor of what happens to youth upon leaving school. It is the best single predictor of the quality of the vocational prizes that one achieves. One may argue, as McClelland (1973) recently did, that the predictive effectiveness of the general factor is due to its role as a selection variable and that it is not necessarily assessing relevant competencies. It is not easy to deal with McClelland's argument in any direct empirical fashion, but if we can achieve a better understanding of the nature of general intelligence, that understanding may reveal that its predictive validity is not simply an artifact of current societal selection strategies. This understanding will certainly help if it includes showing how an individual's altitude is affected by his or her school experiences.

The correlational data available to date are consistent with the proposition that as children develop, there is a dependency relationship among specific cognitive abilities. A particular cognitive ability does not develop much in advance of the others. A model of cognitive processes that purports to explain available psychometric findings must be able to explain this basic psychometric phenomenon. Although Carroll did not deal with the general factor in his scheme, he will certainly have to if it is to be comprehensive. Either that or our experimental colleagues will have to disabuse us of the inevitableness of the correlations.

My main reason for dwelling on the general factor is that Paul Lohnes and I are arguing elsewhere as to its central importance in evaluating the relative merits of different educational programs (Cooley & Lohnes, in press). The general factor, when estimated from the abilities of children in school subject matters as they begin a school year, is the single most important predictor of end-of-year school performance. The challenge is to identify variations in school practices that will explain variance in end-of-year school performance not explained by initial abilities. Very little information is lost and considerable parsimony is gained if a single general measure of school abilities is used for both the fall and spring assessments. The information that one educational program raises children to a higher intellectual level than some other program is clearly useful in helping to decide among programs whose purpose it is to promote intellectual development. General intelligence is clearly a concept that educational policymakers are willing and able to use, which further supports its utility in evaluation studies.

Tyler indicated that one important issue is whether there is a ceiling to the altitude that any given person can attain. It is likely that some students would appear to have reached a ceiling simply because their educational program did not adapt to their entering capabilities and consequently did not provide the necessary background which would have allowed them to achieve at a higher level. The ceiling effect is most likely observed if an institution has developed an educational program for students who have achieved a particular altitude and then starts admitting students who are currently operating at a somewhat lower altitude, without adjusting the available programs for that lower general ability level. What needs to be tested is whether or not an individual's apparently absolute ceiling can be raised if the program is continually adaptive to the level at which he is currently operating.

Let me offer just one more reason for being interested in understanding the nature of general intelligence. It is clearly the key to the current controversy regarding the amount of influence that environmental changes can have in eliminating differences among racial groups in general academic achievement. It seems to me that showing how much various educational environments can affect development of the general factor will be far more convincing in demonstrating the importance of environmental factors than heritability coefficients can be in emphasizing the importance of genetic factors.

In the search for an understanding of the mechanisms of intelligent behavior, general intelligence, defined in terms of a general factor that explains the inevitable positive correlations among cognitive tasks, is probably not a useful construct. No one expects general intelligence to be a function of any single mechanism, but rather the tasks that compose its measurement draw upon the same composite of mental mechanisms. Thus, any explanation of general intelligence will only be indirect. The point of injecting general intelligence into consideration here is to remind you that it is still a very useful construct in studies of educational practices, and to express the hope that models of intelligence currently under development will, at least indirectly, shed further light on why general intelligence is so pervasive and so useful in practical affairs such as education and work.

## REFERENCES

Cooley, W. W., & Lohnes, P. R. *Evaluation research in education.* New York: Irvington Publishers, in press.
McClelland, D. C. Testing for competence rather than for "intelligence." *American Psychologist,* 1973, **28**, 1–14.
Spearman, C. E. General intelligence, objectively determined and measured. *American Journal of Psychology,* 1904, **15**, 201–292.
Travers, R. M. W. Learning measures and psychometric variables. In R. Gagné (Ed.), *Learning and individual differences.* Columbus, Ohio: Charles E. Merrill, 1967.

## SUPPLEMENTARY COMMENT: CARROLL'S RESPONSE TO COOLEY

Professor Cooley has raised the question of how a "general" or "g" factor (as often found in factor analyses either at the initial level of analysis or at a second- or higher-order level) would be handled by my analysis. In answering that question, I will omit any discussion of the technical problems associated with the specification of a g factor—problems having to do, for example, with whether orthogonal or oblique rotations are made, whether data are to be represented by a series of hierarchical, orthogonal factors whose number may be greater than the reduced rank of the correlation matrix, or whether the finding of a general factor is a function of the ways in which individuals and variables are sampled. Let us reduce the question of a general factor to its simplest form: how can we explain the fact that tests of cognitive factors tend generally to be positively correlated? To that question I would offer the correspondingly simple (and possibly oversimplified) reply that most cognitive tasks tend to involve a common pool of cognitive operations and strategies and of memory stores. According to the analyses offered in my Table 2 (page 45), most of the factors involve such cognitive operations as searching and retrieving some kind of information from some kind of memory; it is likely that the temporal parameters of such operations are similar (i.e., they tend to be correlated over individuals). Also, it is likely that on the basis of common environmental and educational experiences, individuals who have rich stores of items in one kind of memory will have rich stores in other kinds of memory. We have also noted that memory items are likely to have manifold interconnections. Merely on the basis of these assumptions we would expect factors to have generally positive intercorrelations. The factors represented in the *Kit of Reference Tests* must be regarded (to use Spearman's terminology) as "group" factors that feature particular cognitive operations, strategies, and memory stores (or combinations thereof). Few if any of them are so unrelated to the others as to merit description as "pure" factors.

I would also remark that I regard the attempt to identify the "essence" of a $g$ factor as hopeless. Spearman and his followers made such an attempt, to be sure, but their $g$ factor was undoubtedly so much a function of unspecified pools of genetic and environmental influences, or of ad hoc test selection procedures, that any specification of essential cognitive operations accounting for it (such as "eduction of correlates") was gratuitous or at least highly problematical. One is reminded of the fact that Godfrey Thomson (1951) was able to account for a $g$ factor on the basis of a wholly different type of theory, namely, his "sampling" theory of intelligence.

## REFERENCE

Thomson, G. *The factorial analysis of human ability.* (5th ed.) Boston: Houghton Mifflin, 1951.

# Part II

## COMPUTER SIMULATION
## IN THE STUDY OF INTELLIGENCE

# 5

# Identifying Basic Abilities Underlying Intelligent Performance of Complex Tasks

Herbert A. Simon

*Carnegie-Mellon University*

This chapter is listed under the heading of "computer simulation approaches in the study of intelligence." Another section of the book is labelled "basic processes in intelligence." This division of labor is only pragmatic, for computer simulation of intelligence is simply a particular technique for identifying and studying basic processes in intelligence.

In fact, this chapter is not restricted to simulation techniques either, because these techniques are used most profitably in close conjunction with experiementation and with observation of human behavior. A simulation is just one phase in a cycle of observing and experimenting, building and testing theories. The simulation is both a formal expression of the theory and a means of inferring consequences that can be tested empirically.

## INTELLIGENT PERFORMANCE

"Intelligent performance of complex tasks" means doing the tasks correctly, with little or no waste motion—with few or no mistakes or detours along the way. Let us jump to the end of the story, and suppose that we had a valid process theory for performance of a complex task, that is, a complete model describing the processes that are used to perform the task, and the way those processes are organized. For completeness, the model would also have to include a description of the knowledge, stored in memory, that was drawn upon for the task performance, and the way that knowledge was represented in memory so as to be available to the processes. If the model described the processes in sufficient detail, then we might say that we had identified the basic abilities underlying performance of that task. In this world view, "basic abilities" may take the form of knowledge, or processes, or both.

Can we bring it off? Can we construct such a valid process theory for any task of interest? How will we test its validity? How will we judge whether the abilities we are describing are "basic"? How will we know what is knowledge and what is process? Will our description be unique? If it is based on observation of the behavior of a small number of persons, or a single one, can it be extrapolated to other persons capable of performing the same task? Can it be used to predict transfer of abilities from one task to another? Can it be used to design efficient learning procedures for acquiring new knowledge and skills?

These are all appropriate questions to raise about a computer simulation of intelligent performance—or indeed about a theory in any form purporting to explain intelligent performance of tasks. The ethos of the computer simulation approach maintains that such questions are to be answered by writing and testing computer programs. The moment of truth is a running program.

The questions listed above give us more than enough agenda. The best strategy will be to proceed by example—describing a number of complex tasks which have been analyzed with the help of simulation techniques, and seeing what answers these analyses give to the questions we have raised.

## EXTRAPOLATION OF SEQUENTIAL PATTERNS

Patterned sequences of letters, numbers, or geometric shapes have been widely used as ingredients in nonverbal tests of intelligence and aptitudes (the letters ABMCDMEFM are a simple example of such a sequence). There are large individual differences in performance on such tasks, and items can be constructed at levels of difficulty appropriate to a wide range of ages and abilities. In the past decade or so, these tasks have also attracted considerable attention from experimental psychologists. For all of these reasons, they provide an attractive task environment for the analysis of intelligent performance.

A computer program describing the processes that human subjects use to perform these tasks was constructed by Simon and Kotovsky (1963), and subsequently tested in some detail (Kotovsky & Simon, 1973) by comparing the program's behavior in sequence extrapolation tasks with the behavior of human subjects. The theory embodied in the simulation program appears to be fully consistent with the findings of other investigators (e.g., Restle, 1970; Vitz & Todd, 1969) who have used a range of experimental techniques to study these same tasks.

### Constructing the Simulation Program

Constructing such a program is, like any other job of theory building, a relatively unstructured inductive undertaking. Ideas for the program may be derived from a detailed analysis of the task environment (abstracted from the specific characteristics of the human subject), from casual or systematic observation of subjects performing the task (including introspection about one's own methods of doing it), from theories of the human problem solver constructed and tested in other task environments, and from the current state of the art in artificial intelligence. The partly completed program itself becomes a rich source of ideas to guide the next steps of the induction by, first, revealing gaps in the theory (an incomplete program will not run, or if it runs, will not do what you expect it to do), and second, revealing discrepancies between the predictions of the theory (the program's behavior) and the actual behavior of human subjects.

In many respects, constructing such a program proceeds in the same way as making a task analysis of the sort that Gagné (1968) has introduced for the purpose of describing learning hierarchies. The differences between the two analyses are not qualitative, but are differences of degree. Hence, the computer simulation technique may be viewed as an extension of earlier, more pragmatic, forms of task analysis that takes advantage of some important technological innovations: computers and computer languages, tape recorders, videotape cameras, and eye-movement cameras. It permits processes to be analyzed down to units of a few hundred milliseconds duration, and perhaps further. It can be used in conjunction with any of the more standard methods of observation or experimentation, and in employing it, we are not faced with either-or dilemmas. The simple question to be asked before using it in any instance is whether the greater precision and detail it offers are worth the effort.

## Outline of the Simulation Model

Figure 1 describes the broad features of a simulation model for sequential pattern problems. The problems are solved in two stages. First, the solver *discovers the pattern* that is implicit in the sequence, and represents this pattern somehow in memory (the "somehow" will be discussed later). Then, he uses the stored pattern to *perform the extrapolation*, i.e., to infer what symbols should come next in the sequence, and to produce them.

Figure 1 also shows that the first, or discovery, stage can be broken down into three substages. Initially, the solver tries to *detect the periodicity* of the sequence. Then he or she seeks to *determine the rule* that generates each symbol in the period from symbols that have occurred previously. Finally, he or she tests each inferred rule by seeing whether it predicts correctly over the remainder of the sequence that has been presented to him or her.

With minor modifications, the program organization of Fig. 1 describes the behavior of all the subjects we have observed performing serial pattern extrapolation tasks.

## The Relational Structure of the Patterns

The analysis of Fig. 1, however, is still extremely gross. A process like "detect period" is itself a complex performance, often extending over seconds, or even

```
┌─────────────────────────────────┐
│                                 │
│        Discover pattern         │
│         Detect period           │
│      Determine the rules        │
│         Test the rules          │
│      Extrapolate pattern        │
│                                 │
└─────────────────────────────────┘
```

FIG. 1  General organization of processes for serial pattern extrapolation.

tens of seconds. It certainly does not qualify as a basic ability. To identify such abilities, we must carry the analysis down into lower levels of detail.

Consider the letter sequence

ABMCDMEFM---

Most subjects will discover rather quickly that this sequence has a period of three letters. That is, it is built on an underlying repeating pattern that is three letters long. What are the clues that could lead to this discovery? First, a single letter, M, is repeated at every third location in the sequence. Second, if we take every third letter in the sequence, starting from the first and second positions, respectively, we get the regular sequences, ACE- and BDF-. These latter two sequences are "regular" in the sense that each letter is the successor of the successor, in the Roman alphabet, of the letter that precedes it. Undoubtedly, it is the repetition of M in every third position that reveals the period of three to most subjects. Thus, the detection of periodicity in a pattern like this one calls upon one or both of two underlying abilities: the recognition that two letters are the *same*, and the recognition that one letter is *next* to (succeeds) another in a familiar alphabet.

The second main phase in extrapolating a letter sequence—determining the rules that generate the symbols in each period—involves the very same two relations—"same" and "next"—that must be perceived in order to detect the periodicity of the sequence. Thus, the rules that generate ABMCDM---are that: (*a*) the first letter in each period is next in the alphabet to the second letter of the previous period (C is next to B), (*b*) the second letter in each period is next to the first letter in that period (B is next to A, and D to C), and (*c*) the third letter in each period is the same as the third letter in the previous period (M in each case). The subject who has detected one or more of these relations in discovering the period of the sequence is already well on his or her way to describing the entire pattern.

The rules of the sequence, once discovered, can be tested simply by using them to predict succeeding letters. The same process can be used to extrapolate the sequence beyond the letters given in the problem statement. Thus, the rules given above for generating the sequence, ABMCDM, can be tested by predicting the next three letters (EFM). Since the prediction coincides with the actual sequence, the extrapolation can now be continued to GHM, and so on.

For this example of a letter sequence, the relations of "same" and "next" suffice to describe the pattern. What is perhaps more surprising is that the same pair of relations suffice to describe the patterns in all of the letter sequences that are used in intelligence tests, as well as the patterns used in letter analogy tests (A:B::M:?).

Only a few elements have to be added to the system to encompass the larger world of number sequences, sequences of geometric stimuli, and figural analogies:

1. Discovering the pattern of number series sometimes involves differencing successive elements. Thus, the sequence:

$$3 \ 6 \ 11 \ 18 \ 27 \ldots$$

becomes, by differencing:

$$3 \ 5 \ 7 \ 9 \ldots$$

which can be described (among other ways) as generated by the relation of "next" on the sequence, or alphabet, of the odd numbers. Division and multiplication, as well as subtraction and addition, may be involved in the construction of number sequences, but the relations of "same" and "next" remain central to the pattern discovery process.

2. A third basic relation, "complement," is used in constructing some patterns. Consider the sequence 162534. We can describe this sequence as having a period of two. The first digit in each period is the successor of the first digit in the previous period. The second digit in each period is the 7s complement of the first digit (7 − 6 = 1, 7 − 5 = 2, and so on). Complementation defines a symmetry, so that each digit is paired with its complement.

3. A pattern may be hierarchical in structure. The last example already embodies a simple hierarchy. We can think of each member of the simple sequence, 1234, being expanded into a pair—the original digit followed by its 7s complement. A statement of a melody in a piece of music, followed by that same melody transposed upward by a fifth is best described as a two-level hierarchy. Restle's (1970) research on number sequences has been especially concerned with patterns that involve complementation and multilevelled hierarchies.

4. The elements in a sequence may be multidimensional, with different rules governing the sequence of relations in each dimension. Consider the figural

analogy: a small red square is to a medium-sized blue circle as a medium-sized red square is to a _____. Applying the relation "same" to the dimensions of color and shape, and the relation "next" to the dimension of size, with values "small," "medium sized" and "large," we might venture the answer: large blue circle. With this extension, the scheme can solve problems like the Raven Progressive Matrices.

A case can be made for the proposition that the elements identified here are sufficient to handle almost any kind of task that can be characterized as pattern detection. Simon and Sumner (1968) have examined the case, for example, with respect to musical patterns. A number of first-order scientific discoveries (e.g., the periodic table of the elements, Balmer's formula for the hydrogen spectrum) involve patterns that fall within the scope of this scheme.

In summary, among the basic abilities required for intelligent performance of the sequence extrapolation task is the ability to perceive any of a small number of relations (same, next, and complement) among pairs of symbols or pairs of dimensions or symbols.

## Memory Requirements for the Task

Memory, as well as sensation and perception, is required for the detection of relations among symbols. The determination that two symbols are instances of the same letter takes place against the background of knowledge, stored in memory, of the set of shapes called "letters." What constitutes an identity depends on the nature of that background set—as becomes obvious if we consider handwritten instead of printed letters.

To determine that one symbol is "next" to another requires that the set containing them be ordered. A Chinese, untutored in the Roman alphabet, would be unable to detect the pattern in ABMCDM--- or to extrapolate this sequence. Pattern in music makes use of the successor relation on a number of musical "alphabets": the diatonic and chromatic scales, the cycle of fifths, and others. Thus, the sequence extrapolation tasks, while abstract in a certain sense, are not, by any means, culture free. Process (detection of relations) and substance (stored knowledge of orderings) are both essential to task performance.

Extrapolating patterned sequences places demands not only upon long-term memory, but upon short-term memory as well, where "short-term" refers to the store, limited to four or five "chunks," that subjects use in performing an immediate recall task. The symbols in the sequence must be scanned to detect the relations that are present. When a relation is detected, it must be held in memory for future use in building the pattern. To avoid cycling, some information must be kept about searches that were tried and failed (e.g., unsuccessful searches for a "same" relation). Information about the various components of the pattern must be stored in some orderly way as a basis for the extrapolation.

This information falls into two main categories: (1) information about the relations that define the pattern, which cumulates gradually as the search process proceeds, and (2) information to keep track of goals and subgoals, to remember what has been tried, and what hasn't. Information in the first category, once discovered, generally remains unchanged, and could presumably be gradually fixated and transferred to long-term memory. Information in the second category, however, is changing continually as the problem-solving process proceeds; hence it has to be held in some kind of short-term memory whose contents can be altered rapidly—in times of the order of a 100 msec, say.

Nothing has been said up to this point about the basic kinds of structures that permit pattern descriptions to be stored in memory—whether short-term or long-term. Almost all simulations that have been attempted make approximately the same assumptions about the nature of these structures. The memory (at least the long-term memory) is assumed to be associative, that is, to consist of a network of relations, or stated otherwise, a network of nodes and links.[1]

In storing an alphabet in such a relational memory, a node would correspond to each letter of the alphabet, and a link labelled "next" would connect each letter with its successor. The relational memory would be connected, in turn, with the sensory system by means of a recognition mechanism. When a particular letter is presented to the senses and noticed, a recognition process gives access to the node representing that letter in the relational memory. The recognition memory, which can also be represented as a relational structure, is sometimes called a "discrimination net," or "EPAM net." The latter term refers to the earliest cognitive simulation, due to Feigenbaum (1963), that made use of this organization (the acronym, EPAM, stands for Elementary Perceiver and Memorizer). EPAM was designed initially for the simulation of rote learning behavior, but its basic mechanisms are now seen to be a relatively general recognition device whose significance extends beyond the original application.

Metaphorically, a relational memory with a discrimination net can be viewed as an encyclopedia with an index. The node—link structure is the (cross referenced) text of the encyclopedia, while the discrimination net is the index. A

[1] This basic form of organization has received a number of different names in the literature of artificial intelligence and cognitive simulation, including: "list-structure memory," "description list memory," "directed colored graph," "relational memory," "associative memory," and others. It is logically equivalent to a system of binary asymmetric relations. The idea first appeared in psychology as the "directed associations" of Ach (1905) and Selz (1913). It first appeared in computing with the description lists incorporated in the IPL series of list processing languages, which in turn are called "property lists" in LISP. To a first approximation, all of these phrases are labels for variants of a single basic idea for memory organization. (See Newell & Simon, 1972; Anderson & Bower, 1973.)

particular item in the encyclopedia can be accessed either from an index entry to it (recognition), or by cross reference from another item (association).

How would the pattern for a sequence like ABMCDM--- be represented in a memory of this kind? Figure 2 shows a possible representation. Associated with the node representing the sequence is information about its period (ABM--- has a periodicity of 3), the number of subsequences it contains (two, ABCD--- and MMM--), the description of each symbol in the period (the first two symbols in each period are "next" in the alphabet to their predecessors; the third symbol is simply "M"), and the initial values for the subsequences (the first subsequence begins with "A," the second with "M"). Figure 2 makes explicit the memory requirements for the task of extrapolating (not the task of discovering) the pattern. M1 and M2 are place-keepers for the subsequences, which keep track of the last symbol produced in each subsequence. In addition, short-term memory is needed to keep place within the period, cycling among the components of the description node.

## Summary: Sequence Extrapolation

The sequence extrapolation task has served as an example of how simulation techniques can be used to identify basic abilities and capabilities needed for task performance. A computer program was written in a list-processing language, capable of performing the task. The performance of the program was compared with the behavior of human subjects performing the same tasks and the similarities and differences in behavior noted. In this case, the correspondences were close, so that the program could be taken as an approximate description of what the subjects knew and did.

Analysis of the anatomy and operation of the simulation program reveals that at least the following abilities and capabilities are needed to perform the sequence extrapolation tasks.

1. Ability to detect relations of same, next, and complement between pairs of symbols.
2. Familiarity with the symbols used, and knowledge of their alphabets, stored in long-term memory.
3. Ability to hold and accumulate in relational structures newly–acquired information about the sequence, and finally to represent the pattern of the sequence in a relational structure, stored in memory.
4. Ability to keep one's place in a system of processes (a program), and to keep track in short-term memory of information needed as inputs to processes.

All of these abilities and capabilities are described much more fully and precisely, of course, by the program itself and by the memory structures it creates, than by our account here.

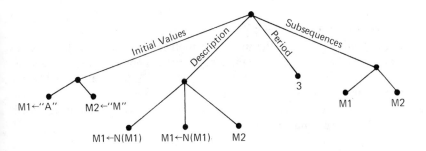

FIG. 2 Memory representation of the pattern for the letter sequence ABMCDM - - -.

Finally, a few words about individual differences. All of the sequence extrapolation tasks draw upon essentially the same set of underlying abilities, yet some of the tasks are much more difficult than others, and some subjects are consistently more successful with them than are others. Far fewer subjects will solve DEFGEFGH-- correctly than will solve ABMCDM--. How does the theory account for these differences in difficulty, and how does it account for the differences among subjects in their success with them?

There are a number of ways of predicting the relative difficulty of a sequence for human subjects from its structure. One of the simplest predictors is the number of symbols contained in the relational structure that describes the pattern. The larger the description, the more difficult the sequence. It is not obvious, however, how size of description of a pattern translates itself into difficulty for human subjects in discovering or extrapolating the pattern. There are several possibilities.

We would expect size of pattern description to be correlated with the time required to discover the pattern. The probability that an error will be made while discovering or extrapolating it might then vary with the time. (The simulation program, however, makes no explicit provision for this kind of error.)

A second and more interesting possibility is that the program could handle patterns only up to some definite level of difficulty. For example, short-term memory might have capacity for only two subsequences. Then the pattern ABRSMBCTUM--- which calls for three would be beyond the capacity of the system. The empirical evidence does provide some support for this source of difficulty.

A third possible source of problem difficulty, not closely correlated with pattern size, is the presence in the sequence of "spurious" relations that are not part of the pattern. For example, the sequence KLMLMMMNM--- is more difficult than ABMBCMCDM--- although the two patterns are identical except for their initial values. The reason for the difficulty of the first of these is the accidental "same" relations and "next" relations between letters of the subsequence KLLMMN and the constant M. Similarly, because of the "same" relations in

DEFGEFGHFGHI, many subjects erroneously try to describe this sequence with a pattern of Period 3 instead of 4.

These are only hints as to the sources of problem difficulty, for the topic has not yet received a thorough examination. It appears, however, that the simulation technique offers promise for error analysis. It is possible to modify the program to make it sensitive to difficulties of the sorts we have just described, and hence to simulate subjects at various levels of skill, i.e., subjects with different "programs" and memory stores.

## ALGEBRA WORD PROBLEMS

As a second example for studying task analysis, we take the domain of word problems or story problems in algebra (Paige & Simon, 1966). For example:

Don had twice as many nickels as quarters. The total value of his nickels was $4.20 more than the total value of his quarters. How many nickels and quarters did he have?

Word problems are often used in intelligence and aptitude test batteries. They are also prototypes for one of the central tasks in all applied mathematics: to take a verbal description of a situation, and translate it into a formal mathematical problem. Skill in this task is presumably important in most technical and scientific occupations. There is also some indication that word problems discriminate sensitively (more sensitively than arithmetic manipulation tasks) between persons who handle mathematics rather easily and those, of otherwise comparable intelligence, who have great difficulty with mathematics.

One hypothesis about the abilities required to solve word problems is that the task is one of translating from one language (English) to another ("algebra"). Bobrow (1969) has constructed a translation program, STUDENT, that is based on a relatively simple syntactical analysis of the English sentences. We can see roughly how the scheme works, without going into details.

The deep structure of "Don had twice as many nickels as quarters" could be something like

Equals (number-of-nickels, 2 × (number-of-quarters)).

Assigning literal names to variables, this becomes

$$x = 2y.$$

Similarly, the deep structure of the second sentence could be something like

Equals (value-of-nickels, 420 + value-of-quarters)

or

$$z = 420 + w.$$

Now, to reduce the number of variables to the number of equations, some factual knowledge must be supplied about nickels and quarters:

value-of-nickels equals 5 × (number-of-nickels)
value-of-quarters equals 25 × (number-of-quarters)

Presumably, this factual knowledge is already available in the problem solver's semantic memory. Using it allows $z$ to be replaced by $5x$ and $w$ by $25y$, changing the second equation to

$$5x = 420 + 25y.$$

This is roughly the procedure that Bobrow's program would follow to set up the equations for this problem. What basic abilities are required?

1. The program must be able to extract the deep structure from the kinds of English sentences that occur in word problems. To do this, it must have syntactical rules, and must understand the meanings of some of the words ("twice," "as many . . . as," "had" and so on), but not of others ("Don").
2. The program must have semantic information—in this case about the relation between the numbers and values of nickels and quarters, but need not know anything else about the meanings of "nickel" and "quarter."
3. The program must be able to substitute the appropriate algebraic equivalents for components of the natural-language structures: "=" for "equals," $x$ and $y$ for specific names of variables, and so on.
4. As with the program for sequential patterns, this program must be able to keep track of what it is doing, and must be able to build up and hold new symbol structures (for example, the deep structures of the sentences) in memory.

Comparison with Behavior of Human Subjects

There are even more obvious variations in human behavior with word problems than with sequential patterns. A problem like the one we have been using as our example, however, reveals a particularly interesting dimension of individual difference. If the reader will examine the problem closely, and solve the equations derived from it, he will see that the answer is −21 nickels!

When "impossible" or "contradictory" problems like this are given to subjects, with the instruction to set up the equations but not to solve them, at least three distinct kinds of behavior are observed: (a) some subjects proceed just as the STUDENT program would, and write down the "impossible" equations; (b) some subjects write down some related equations, but make a change that removes the "impossibility" (for example, $z + 420 = w$ or $z = 420 - w$ may be written instead of $z = 420 + w$); (c) some subjects say, "Isn't there a contradiction?" or words to that effect, calling attention to the difficulty. Other subjects, of course, quite numerous even among persons who have had a year or more of high-school algebra, never succeed in setting up any equations at all, or set up completely meaningless ones, but we will not be concerned with them here.

This experiment shows that different persons may use entirely different processes to solve the same problem. The subjects in Class (a) appear to be using mainly syntactic processes—they carry out a literal translation of the sentences. The subjects in Class (b) appear to make a less thorough syntactic analysis of the sentences, but are guided in part by some kind of semantic representation of the real-world problem that tells them that the 420 needs to be added to the nickels instead of the quarters if the problem is to make sense. The subjects in Class (c) appear to be guided both by syntactic and by semantic cues, which they find to be inconsistent with each other. Notice that there is nothing contradictory about the problem statement itself; it is only when the subject supplies additional real-world semantic information that the inconsistency arises.

What is the nature of the semantic processes used by the subjects of Classes (b) and (c) to replace the stated problem by one with real-world meaning? A possible scheme, that is easily programmed, might work as follows: if it be noted that a quarter is worth five times as much as a nickel, but that there are only two times as many nickels as quarters, a rather simple inference concludes that the value of the quarters must be greater than the value of the nickels. Since the difference between them is 420, we get the equation $w = 420 + z$. No direct evidence is available that this is actually the process used by subjects in such problems; it is described here simply to indicate the general nature of the abilities (knowledge and processes) a person would have to have in order to behave as these subjects did.

In summary, attempts to simulate the processes used to solve algebra word problems have led, first, to a deeper understanding of how meanings are extracted from natural language; second, to an assessment of the semantic information that must be stored to make syntactic analysis of language possible; and third, to the insight that semantic processes may be an alternative to syntactic ones for extracting meanings. By the use of "impossible" problems it becomes possible to detect the extent to which subjects are depending upon syntactic and semantic cues, respectively, in problem interpretation. Thus, the research on algebra offers potentially valuable suggestions for the investigation of individual differences, and for the diagnosis and characterization of individual problem solving styles.

## THE TOWER OF HANOI

None of the task environments discussed so far has received as much attention in research as has been given to puzzle-like well-structured problems. In our book, *Human Problem Solving* (Newell & Simon, 1972), Allen Newell and I have discussed three problem domains at length: cryptarithmetic, a class of logic problems, and chess. This paper will not retrace the path followed there, or summarize our findings, but will use a different task as an example of this general class of problems.

The Tower of Hanoi is a familiar puzzle that consists of three upright pegs and a number of disks, graded in size, that can be impaled on the pegs (Fig. 3). At the outset, all the disks are arranged in a pyramid on one peg. The task is to move them all to another peg, with the two constraints that: (a) only one disk may be moved at a time, and (b) a larger disk may not be placed on top of a smaller disk. With $n$ pegs the minimum-solution path requires $2^n - 1$ moves—thus, with 3 pegs 7 moves, with 4 pegs 15 moves, and with 5 pegs 31 moves.

Consider a subject who has learned how to solve the Tower of Hanoi problem with three disks. We ask the classic question: "What has he or she learned?" In what form is the solution, or solution strategy, stored in his or her memory? There are many possible answers to this question. Corresponding to the different answers are different basic abilities he or she is using to solve the problem, with different consequences for the transferability of his or her skill to other problems, and perhaps also for retention of the skill. Let us examine some of the different possibilities.

1. *Rote method.* The subject may have memorized the specific solution steps; for the three-disk problem there are only seven of these. To move the pyramid from peg A to peg C, move from A to C, A to B, C to B, A to C, B to A, B to C, and A to C. If the solution is stored in precisely this form—as this sequence of specific moves—then it is not transferable, without additional problem solving, even to the task of moving the pyramid from peg A to peg B. However, suppose that the subject names the pegs: source peg (S), target peg (T), and other peg (O). Then the solution may be stored in such a way as to apply to moving the pyramid from any source to any target: S–T, S–O, T–O, S–T, O–S, O–T, S–T. This solution, however, gives no direct clue as to how to solve the four-disk problem or any larger problem.

2. *Recursive method.* The subject may have analyzed the problem structure, and stored the solution in terms of his or her analysis: "To move three disks from S to T, move two of them off S to O, then move the third from S to T, and finally, move the other two from O to T." This solution is easily generalized to

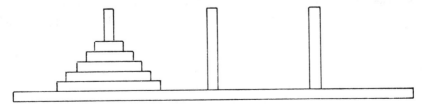

FIG. 3    The tower of Hanoi puzzle.

handle any number of disks: "To move a pyramid of $N$ disks from S to T, move the pyramid of $N - 1$ from S to O, then move the largest disk from S to T, and finally, move the pyramid of $N - 1$ from O to T."

To achieve this solution, or even to understand it if it is explained to him, the subject must be able to handle a number of concepts. First, he or she must have the idea of moving a pyramid. The rules of the puzzle allow only one disk to be moved at a time. It is not immediately evident that the problem of moving three disks can be solved by solving several problems of moving two disks. In fact, to conceptualize the task this way, the subject must have the concept of a *recursion,* that is, to solve a problem with the parameter $N$, reduce it to one or more problems of the same form with parameter $N - 1$.

3. *Perceptual method.* The subject may have analysed the problem structure in a somewhat different way from the previous scheme: "Always seek to move the largest disk not yet on T. If it can be moved to T, move it. If other disks rest on top of it, set up the goal of moving the largest of these, and proceed in the same way. If other smaller disks rest on its target, set up the goal of moving the largest of these, and proceed in the same way."

This solution also handles any number of disks. It requires certain perceptual discriminations to be made. The subject must be able to find the largest disk not on T. He or she must be able to find the largest disk resting on a given disk, and the largest disk obstructing the move of a given disk to a target disk. He or she must be able to formulate goals in terms of these concepts, and keep track of the goals and subgoals he or she has established and not yet realized.

4. *Pattern method.* The subject may have detected and learned a pattern in the moves themselves. (*a*) On odd-numbered moves, the smallest disk is moved. If $N$ is odd, it always moves in the cycle S → T → O → S; if $N$ is even, it always moves in the cycle S → O → T → S. (*b*) On even-numbered moves, some disk other than the smallest is moved (there is always exactly one such legal move). It is not obvious why this pattern of moves will solve the problem, but it will; and the subject may learn the solution without knowing why it works. This solution, too, handles any number of disks. It requires the subject to keep track of the parity (odd or even) of the move, and of the direction of cycling of the smallest disk (or, equivalently, of the parity of $N$).

Here, then, are four quite distinct strategies for solving the Tower of Hanoi problem. They call on different information stored in long-term memory, on different perceptual discriminations to be made, and on different sets of information to be held in short-term memory. If we only know that a subject can solve the three-disk Tower of Hanoi problem, we cannot tell which of these strategies (or some other) he has. If we wish to predict what will happen when we ask him to solve the four-disk problem, we will need to know more about what he knows. If he has Strategy 1, we would not expect him to be able to solve it without additional search. If he has Strategy 2, we might expect him to solve it without much difficulty. If he has Strategy 3, it can be shown that his ability to solve it will depend on the size of his short-term memory. If he has Strategy 4, he should have little difficulty in solving it.

To derive these predictions with any rigor, we would, of course, have to describe in detail the programs that implement each of the four methods. Space does not permit that description to be presented here. The actual programs have been written as *production systems,* a scheme of organization that is described in greater detail in Klahr's chapter (Chapter 6).

The four methods that have been described are not peculiar to the Tower of Hanoi problem but resemble closely processes that arise frequently in other task environments. The Rote Method could be implemented as part of a rote learning mechanism like EPAM. The Pattern Method draws upon essentially the same capabilities as the programs for discovering and extrapolating sequential patterns, discussed earlier.

The Recursive and Perceptual Methods are instances of means–ends analysis like that incorporated in the General Problem Solver (Newell & Simon, 1972). In the Recursive Method, the task of moving a pyramid is broken down into three subtasks, and this process is repeated until a task is reached that can be executed. In the Perceptual Method, the next action is determined by comparing the actual problem situation with the desired goal situation, detecting the most important difference between them (the largest unmoved disk), and attempting to take action to reduce this difference.

Thus, writing programs to solve the Tower of Hanoi problem gives us new insights into the abilities that are required to solve this problem. We find that there is a rote strategy that is executable by a very simple program, but which is not generalized to the $N$-disk problem. For other strategies, there are tradeoffs between keeping track by maintaining a goal stack in short-term memory, and keeping track by making perceptual tests on the current problem situation. To some extent, the ability to use one of these control methods is a functional substitute for the ability to use the other. The efficiency of particular strategies depends on the sophistication and appropriateness of the perceptual tests the solver has available—a perceptual component of ability to handle these kinds of problems. Two of the principal strategies applicable to this problem turn out to be variants of the General Problem Solver.

The variety of strategies that are available for handling the problem, and the important differences in the abilities that each of these depends on, shows that there is no unique answer to the question of which abilities are required for intelligent performance of this task.

## PERCEPTION IN CHESS

All of the tasks we have discussed thus far make rather modest demands upon long-term semantic memory. The situation is different with the task of playing chess. Since the facts of the matter have been reviewed in detail in several papers published recently (Chase & Simon, 1973, 1974; Simon & Gilmartin, 1973), they need only be mentioned briefly here:

1. A chess master or grandmaster, on seeing a chess position from a game for five seconds (with about 25 pieces on the board), can reconstruct the position from memory with 80 or 90% accuracy. A weaker player will be able to remember the positions of only some half dozen pieces.

2. If the same pieces are placed on the board at random, chess master and duffer will perform equally badly—neither will be able to recall the positions of more than about half a dozen pieces.

3. A strong chess player can play at a speed of ten seconds or so per move with only a moderate loss in playing strength. To put the matter in extreme form, there are probably not a hundred players in the world who could beat Bobby Fischer if they were permitted the usual time for a move (say 20 moves per hour) while Fischer was limited to 10 seconds per move.

The second of these three facts permits us to conclude that there is nothing unusual about the general capabilities of chess masters for visual imagery. The surprising visual memory revealed by the first fact is specific to chess. The first fact is most readily explained by the hypothesis that the short-term memory of a chess master has the same capacity, measured in chunks, as the short-term memory of a duffer, but that the duffer's chunks consists of individual pieces, while the master's chunks consist of configurations of pieces, averaging three or four pieces each, that have become thoroughly familiar and recognizable from their frequent recurrence in the tens of thousands of chess positions he has seen. The master's ability to remember the positions of 25 pieces then becomes no more mysterious than a reader's ability to recall a sequence of 25 Roman letters after a brief exposure—provided that the letters are arranged as four or five familiar English words. Both phenomena follow from the postulate that short-term memory has a fixed capacity in chunks, and that any familiar, recognizable visual (or auditory) pattern constitutes a chunk (Simon, 1974).

If we accept this explanation, then we can use it to arrive at some estimates of the number of familiar configurations of chess pieces that are stored in the long-term memory of a chess master. Such estimates can be made from consideration of the variety of chess positions that occur in games, and the size of the "vocabulary" of chunks that would be required to generate this variety. Estimates can also be made by writing a computer program that simulates the chunking process and measuring its recall performance as a function of the number of familiar chunks it has acquired in long-term memory.

Figure 4 describes a computer program, MAPP, devised by Simon and Gilmartin (1973) to simulate human performance in the recall experiment. In the pattern-learning phase, the program is presented with a large number of configurations of chess pieces, of the sorts that occur frequently in game positions. The program familiarizes itself with these patterns by growing a discrimination

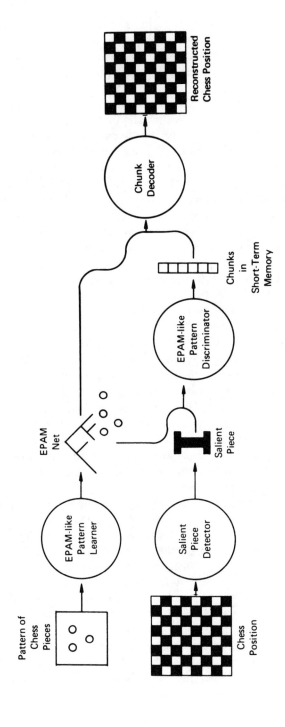

FIG. 4 Principal processes of MAPP (the learning component is shown in the upper half of the figure, the three parts of the performance component in the lower half).

net in memory containing tests for sorting out the different patterns, and holding the information about each pattern at the terminal node to which the tests sort it. The discrimination net is essentially identical with the EPAM net mentioned earlier, which has been used to simulate the phenomena of verbal rote learning.

The performance component of MAPP scans a chess position for configurations that are stored in its discrimination net. When it finds one, consisting of one or more pieces, it stores its label in short-term memory. When short-term memory is full, MAPP undertakes to reconstruct the position by using the labels in short-term memory to recover from long-term memory the information about each of the patterns of pieces it has recognized. Thus, the entire simulation model postulates an EPAM-like learning system, a simple short-term memory of fixed capacity (in chunks), and an ability to decode the chunk labels in short-term memory by accessing the information stored in the discrimination net. The perceptual component of this system assumes that the basic components of the patterns, the chess pieces, are already familiar units that can be recognized in terms of their perceptual features.

Let us return now to the amount and kind of chess information stored in the discrimination net. Different methods of estimating the number of patterns of chess pieces that are familiar to a chess master all yield numbers in the neighborhood of 50,000. This number is of the same order of magnitude as the natural language reading vocabularies of educated adults. This seems reasonable when we observe that a chess master has typically spent as many hours examining chess positions as the rest of us have spent reading books.

How do these findings relate to the third fact mentioned earlier—the ability of a chess master to play very rapidly at a good level of skill? This ability is most evident in demonstrations of simultaneous play—where the master may play as many as a hundred opponents, winning most of the games, drawing a few, and losing almost none. Ability to recognize configurations of pieces would not appear, by itself, to explain such a performance.

To explain how the chess master can accomplish this, we postulate that an important part of his chess knowledge is embodied in a production system, which itself is incorporated in his recognition net for configurations. When he recognizes a familiar configuration of pieces, there is evoked a move that is worth *considering* whenever that configuration occurs on the board. Thus, to a chess player of even modest ability, an open file (a column of empty squares) suggests a move of a rook to command the file. Danger of an attack on the King's position suggests the special move known as castling the King, and so on.

Under the normal conditions of tournament or match play, the moves suggested by the recognition of configurations and the evocation of the actions associated with them would be subjected to careful analysis before an actual move was selected. Under the conditions of rapid or simultaneous play, the master would simply make standard strategic moves (developing his men, controlling the center, bringing pieces into cooperation with each other) until a feature was recognized on the board (usually resulting from a weak move by the opponent) that was associated with a strong tactical move. Since the standard strategic moves can usually be associated with simple features of a position, play based on these principles could be expected to do quite well against players who were likely to make obvious mistakes ("obvious" in terms of the recognition net of the master!), and who were unlikely to be able to lay deep traps.

There is no reason to suppose that the perceptual and memory component of skill that has been documented in chess is totally different from skill in other expert performances—making administrative decisions, cooking, engineering design, or carpentry. The expert detects important and familiar features in the situations that confront him. He has rapid intuitive "gut" reactions that permit him to respond to situations quickly, if not always correctly. He has spent many hours in the acquisition of his expertness working in the task environment, and encountering a large number of situations. It remains to discover exactly how these skills are stored in memory, and whether an organization of the sort we have postulated for chess can account for them.

## PROGRAMMING ONESELF TO PERFORM A NEW TASK

An important human ability is to be able to assemble various components into a program for performing a new task. The information about the nature of the new task may come, for example, from written or oral instructions, or from worked-out examples of the task. This information must be capable of guiding the assembly of the new program.

Suppose that a person, or a program, were endowed with the following elementary abilities: to represent and process strings and groups of symbols; to detect that two symbols are the same or that one is next to another in an alphabet; to add, subtract, multiply, and divide integers; to remove a symbol from a group or string, or to replace a symbol; and to recognize symbols of the Roman alphabet, and the integers. We have already seen how a program possessing these abilities is capable of doing letter series and number series problems, as well as letter and number analogies. The same basic abilities are required for problems like:

"Identify the out-of-place element in 1 2 3 3 5 6," or
"Which of the following groups doesn't belong with the others:
    AABC  ABCD  AACH  AAYZ?"

Now it is not plausible to suppose that a subject appears in the psychological laboratory possessing specific programs for handling each one of these particular kinds of test items (or other similar ones we could invent). It is plausible to suppose that he has all or most of the basic abilities listed above. The question is how these abilities, in the face of a particular kind of test item, become organized into a program for taking the test.

Successive steps toward answering this question have been taken by T. G. Williams (1972), D. S. Williams (1972), and Hayes and Simon (1974). T. G. Williams constructed a programming language (General Game Playing Program) encompassing the basic concepts used in card and board games ("move," "deck," "square," "suit," "piece," and so on), and showed that the instructions for most of the card and board games described in Hoyle were readily translated into a program written in this language.

### Induction of Task from Examples

D. S. Williams constructed a program (Aptitude Test Taker, or ATT) which, upon being presented with one or more worked-out examples of a particular kind of test item, builds a program for handling items of that kind, and proceeds to take the test. Three ideas are central to ATT: the notion of inducing the nature of a task from an example; the notion of defining the task in terms of the differences between a test item and its answer; and the notion of using its abilities to solve various kinds of test items in order to define the task item before it. The ATT program, while strongly influenced by what we know of human performance, "does not try to simulate exactly the processes used by human beings; its development has been based both on computer models of human performance and on artificial intelligence research [D. S. Williams, 1972, p. 143]." Suppose that ATT is presented with the following array of symbols:

Problem:  AABC  ACAD  ACFG  AACG
Answer:  ACFG

A Test Form Analyzer constructs a representation of this task, called the Task Form Specification. The Analyzer notes that the problem consists of four groups of Roman letters, and the answer of just one of these groups. From this it infers that the task is to find the exceptional group—the one that is "different" or "doesn't belong." More concretely, the exceptional group is the group that lacks some property shared by the others. Hence, the Analyzer assembles a program to search for properties of the original groups (properties expressible in terms of relations of same and next among letters). If it finds a property shared by all groups save the exceptional one, it takes this as confirmation of its analysis, and uses the program it has assembled to take the test. This program will be sufficiently general and powerful to find the exceptional group in sets like:

1. XURM  ABCD  MNOP  EFGH (all but the first are sequential)
2. KABC  KEFG  LOPQ  KUVW (all but the third begin with K)

D. S. Williams' Aptitude Test Taker program demonstrates that the task of inducing a program to take a test is itself a problem solving task calling upon the same general kinds of symbol-analyzing and symbol-manipulating abilities that are required for other problem solving tasks.

## Understanding Task Instructions

A program called UNDERSTAND has been constructed by Hayes and Simon (1974) to investigate how a task can be understood from written instructions. The initial task, "The Himalayan Tea Ceremony," to which the program was applied, shown in Fig. 5, is an isomorph of the Tower of Hanoi problem, disguised in the form of a story. The UNDERSTAND program is built on the assumption that the problem solver already has available a set of basic problem-solving processes equivalent to the General Problem Solver (GPS) (Ernst & Newell, 1969). Therefore, understanding task instructions means translating those instructions into a form that would be acceptable as an input to GPS. If the instructions could be translated, then the GPS could go to work on the problem.

The main requirements for the input to GPS are: a representation for the initial problem situation, the goal situation, and intermediate situations that may be reached during the solution process; and a definition of the legal move operator in such a form that it can actually operate on the representation of the situation. Thus, in order to attempt to solve the Tea Ceremony problem, GPS would need a representation of the initial situation with the host performing all five tasks, the goal situation with the elder guest performing all the tasks, and other situations with arbitrary allocations of tasks among the guests. It would also need a move operator that would transfer a task from one participant to another, observing the restrictive conditions stated in the problem.

These are not a complete set of inputs for GPS. The General Problem Solver would also need for its operation (a) a set of differences for comparing pairs of situations, and (b) a set of associations from differences to operations relevant for removing them. However, it is known that learning programs can be devised that will induce sets of differences and difference—operator associations from the other task information. The UNDERSTAND program, in its present form, does not concern itself with these additional induction tasks.

The UNDERSTAND program falls into two main parts. The first part takes the natural language text as input, and extracts deep structure from it, primarily by syntactic means. In a rough way, it resembles Bobrow's STUDENT program for analyzing word problems, although UNDERSTAND employs a somewhat fuller syntax than does STUDENT. The second part of the UNDERSTAND program uses the transformed text to construct the problem representation and the operator.

UNDERSTAND is only one of a substantial number of programs that are able to extract meanings from some range of natural language text. (A dozen or so of

## A Tea Ceremony

1. In the inns of certain Himalayan villages is practiced a most civilized and refined tea ceremony.

2. The ceremony involves a host and exactly two guests, neither more nor less.

3. When the guests have arrived and have seated themselves at his table, the host performs five services for them.

4. These services are listed below in the order of the nobility which the Himalayans attribute to them:

    stoking the fire,
    fanning the flames,
    passing rice cakes,
    pouring tea,
    reciting poetry.

5. During the ceremony, any of those present may ask another, "Honored Sir, may I perform this onerous task for you?"

6. However, a person may request of another only the least noble of the tasks which the other is performing.

7. Further, if a person is performing any tasks, then he may not request a task which is nobler than the least noble task he is already performing.

8. Custom requires that by the time the tea ceremony is over, all of the tasks will have been transferred from the host to the most senior of the guests.

9. How may this be accomplished?

FIG. 5   Statement of the tea ceremony problem.

such programs are surveyed in Siklóssy & Simon, 1972, Chapter 2, and others by Simmons, 1965.) Not one of these programs will handle anything like the full range of English, in large part because to do so would require storing an enormous amount of lexicographic information. For a long time it appeared that the syntax, too, would have to be enlarged indefinitely to handle the whole gamut of acceptable English constructions, but as a result of new insights that have been gained, largely during the past five years, it now seems that a very elaborate syntax is unnecessary for processing everyday natural language.

The principal new insight is that if a program has good semantic capabilities—if it can make use of information about the meanings of the situations that are being communicated—then it may need only a relatively unsophisticated syntactic processor. The UNDERSTAND program, for example, gets along with a fairly simple set of syntactic productions, primarily because its specific task gives it processing direction and a target. Since the task is to produce a problem representation and an operator, it can search actively in the input instructions for sentences or parts of sentences that show promise of contributing to those structures. It has no obligation to translate all of the language of the instructions, or to translate literally.

Later stages of the syntactic and semantic analysis extract from the text several important kinds of information: in particular, the sets and lists of objects that are mentioned and the relations between objects that are mentioned. Thus, the program discovers a set of participants, and a list of tasks, the latter ordered by nobility. It identifies the relation of a participant doing a task, a participant asking another for permission to do one of his tasks, and a task being transferred from one participant to another. Since the arguments of the latter two relations have the same types, they are interpreted as different ways of speaking about the same relation.

Beyond its language processing, the principal abilities that UNDERSTAND uses are abilities to create list structures, of kinds we have already considered in other contexts, and abilities to match information extracted from the instructions against "templates" already stored in long-term memory. Using the sets and relations it discovers in the Tea Ceremony instructions, UNDERSTAND generates the representation of the initial situation shown in Fig. 6. Associated with the node "Host," a member of this list, is a list of his Tasks. The node for each task, in turn, has associated with it its type, "Tasks," whereas the node for "Tasks" has associated with it the Order "Nobility."

We have also seen that, from the Tea Ceremony instructions, the UNDERSTAND program is able to induce that an operation is performed in the ceremony of passing a task from one participant to another participant, or more abstractly:

PASS (Task, from Participant, to Participant)

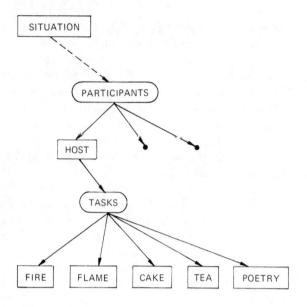

SITUATION = " : ,PARTICIPANT L1,"

L1 = " HOST GUEST.1 GUEST.2 : ,TYPE SET,"

HOST = " : ,TYPE PARTICIPANT,TASK L2,"

L2 = " FIRE FLAME CAKE TEA POETRY : ,TYPE LIST,ORDER NOBILITY,"

FIG. 6   Representation of the initial situation in the tea ceremony problem generated by UNDERSTAND.

In semantic memory there are stored a number of operators, together with programs for executing them in the context of particular representations. The operators are characterized by the number of operands they have, and the identity or difference of the sorts of things that can serve as the various operands. For example, EQUALS $(X1, X2)$ is an operator with two operands, both of the same sort. DELETE $(X, \text{from } Y)$ is an operator with two operands of different sorts—$X$ might be a symbol, for example, and $Y$ a list. TRANSFER $(X, \text{from } L1, \text{to } L2)$ is an operator with three operands, two of one sort (designating locations), and one of another sort (designating the object to be transferred).

Now it can be seen (and can be detected by a simple matching process) that the PASS operator extracted from the Tea Ceremony instructions is of the same type as the TRANSFER operator, for it also has two operands of one sort (participants), and one of another sort (tasks). The UNDERSTAND program thereby interprets PASS as a transfer operation, and uses the processes associated in memory with the transfer to execute the operation of passing tasks from one participant to another in the internal representation of the problem situation. Thus, to transfer the task of stoking the fire from the host to the elder guest in the representation of Fig. 6, the symbol "fire" would be deleted from the list of tasks of the host, and inserted on the list of tasks of the elder guest (creating that list if it did not already exist).

In this way, the UNDERSTAND program becomes relatively independent of the precise terms used in the Tea Ceremony instructions to name things. If "participants" in the ceremony were called "members," or "therbligs" for that matter, it would make no difference; the instructions would be interpreted correctly. Nor does it matter whether the term "transfer" is used or not to refer to the operation. What matters is that the operation be recognized as a relation having two operands of one sort and one of another. Moreover, the matching process that recognizes an operator as a transfer gives the system access to the programs needed to execute transfers, which are already stored in long-term memory.

These programs are sufficiently flexible to handle the transfers, whatever representation of the problem situation has been generated by other components of the program, operating independently on the problem instructions. The match process in UNDERSTAND is a way of assimilating new task instructions to things the system already knows how to do. Since the program does this by abstracting from the concrete detail of the language of the instructions, a relatively small number of powerful general structures (like the transfer process) can handle the operations needed in a large number of different specific tasks.

## Summary

In this section two aspects have been explored of the ability of an intelligent system to program itself to perform a new task. One set of abilities, exemplified by D. S. Williams' ATT system, allows the program requisite for performing a task to be induced from one or more worked-out examples of the task. The component abilities used by ATT look remarkably similar to the abilities required to perform pattern induction tasks like the letter sequence extrapolation tasks.

A second set of abilities, exemplified by the UNDERSTAND program, assembles the program for performing a task by reading and understanding a set of task instructions written in natural language. Central to the capabilities needed to process natural language is a syntax processor. In addition, capabilities are needed of abstracting relational structures from the transformed text, and matching these against generalized operators that are stored in semantic memory together with programs for executing them.

## SPELLING ENGLISH WORDS

The final task to be examined is a school subject, and the discussion will be pointed at the possible implications of task analysis and simulation for the improvement of instruction. Simon and Simon (1973) have written a program to simulate the way in which a writer of English spells words. The program, when tested against empirical data, does a good job, qualitatively and quantitatively, of predicting children's spelling mistakes. It predicts that most mistakes will involve double consonants and schwas; it predicts that errors will generally be in the direction of spelling words more phonetically than is correct; and it predicts quantitatively the observed variation of the serial location of spelling errors within the word (few errors at ends of words, most in the middle).

The general flow diagram of the program is shown in Fig. 7. The particular method used to spell a specific word depends on the information about that word the subject has stored in long-term memory. This information may include: (a) the complete spelling of the word; (b) enough visual information about the word to recognize it in reading, but not necessarily complete information about all its letters; (c) associations from particular phonemes to one or more possible spellings for those phonemes; (d) contextually dependent rules that select particular spellings for phonemes from among the larger set in (c); (e) procedures for extracting morphemic elements from words, and using these to suggest spellings. The present program includes only items (a) through (c), but some comments will be offered below on the extent to which inclusion of (d) and (e) would affect spelling skill.

The program assumes that if the subject already has the complete spelling stored in memory he or she will simply use it. If he does not, he will begin to sound out the word, using the information in item (c) to generate possible spellings for phonemes, but checking these against the partial visual information in (b). If the generated spelling agrees with the visual information, or if the visual information for the part of the word in question is missing, the generated spelling is accepted. If there is a contradiction between the spelling generated from the phoneme, and stored visual information about the word, then another possible spelling for the phoneme is generated from the list of associations in item (c). It is assumed that the probability distribution of missing letters in the visual recognition words of item (b) will correspond in shape to the usual serial position curve of errors in nonsense syllable learning. Under these assumptions, misspellings will occur when two conditions are satisfied: (1) the visual informa-

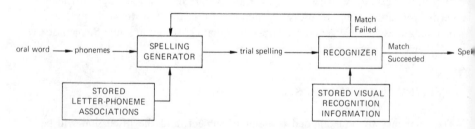

FIG. 7   Spelling by means of a generator-test process.

tion is missing, and (2) the phoneme is ambiguous—there are several plausible spellings for it.

A second computer spelling program has been constructed by Rudorf (1965) on the basis of a system of spelling rules (about 200 rules) developed by Hanna, Hanna, Hodges, and Rudorf (1966). This program depends entirely on information of type ($d$) contextually dependent spelling rules for phonemes, organized as a system of productions.

The Rudorf program spells substantially less accurately than normal fourth-grade children. From this it can be concluded that a program to teach spelling by teaching a very large number of spelling rules cannot overcome the great irregularity of English spelling, in the absence of stored visual information. Or, to put the matter in another way, it may be futile to teach children to spell words that they have not seen a large number of times, and which are not in their recognition vocabularies.

How well the Simon and Simon program spells depends entirely on how much visual information of categories ($a$) and ($b$) is provided to it. By making plausible assumptions about the information that children have stored about words they have learned to recognize in reading, it can be made to simulate the spelling of children at various grade levels. The performance of the program depends critically on its having not just one possible spelling associated with each phoneme, but several, so that the subject can try various alternatives until he finds one that is consistent with the visual information available to him.

Consideration of the performance of the program leads to some conjectures about effective methods of teaching spelling. It suggests that the teaching of large numbers of spelling rules is probably not warranted, although a few rules of very common application may be useful (for example, dropping the final silent "e" or doubling the consonant of an accented short vowel before adding "ing," as in "make" "making," or "drop" "dropping"). It suggests that children should be taught to generate a number of alternative spellings for a phoneme, those used most commonly first, and to test conjectured spellings by writing them out. Some estimates have also been made of the possible contribution of morphological information to spelling, with the conclusion that it is likely to be only marginally useful for those words that are most frequently misspelled.

None of these pedagogical proposals has been tested. They are cited here not as recommendations, but as indications of how a task analysis in the form of a computer program might be used as a guide to pedagogical design and experimentation. The analysis might also be used as a basis for diagnosing individual spelling difficulties. By comparing the performance of the program (calibrated to a particular reading level) on a set of words with the performance of individual students, the nature of their difficulties becomes clearer. For example, a small number of students exhibit not only poor spelling, but quite atypical patterns of errors that may point to specific difficulties in their use of information of either type ($b$) or type ($c$).

These ideas are hardly revolutionary, for informal task analysis has long been a basis for pedagogical design and diagnosis of learning difficulties in such subjects as reading and spelling. Simulation techniques place such analysis on a more formal and systematic basis, however, and hold promise for carrying the analysis down to a lower level of detail than has been possible without it.

## CONCLUSION

It has been the aim of this paper to analyze the basic abilities underlying intelligent performance of a number of complex tasks that have been studied by laboratory and simulation techniques.

Six task domains have been selected as examples: the extrapolation of patterned sequences, algebra word problems, the Tower of Hanoi puzzle, perception in chess, understanding task instructions, and spelling. Even with such a heterogeneous collection of tasks, there is more commonality than diversity in the basic abilities required for their performance.

Matters are really a little more complex than this comment would suggest. Whether the programs for performing these tasks look similar or quite different depends on the level of detail we look at. At the grossest levels—the programs as wholes—they are of course quite different, else the programs would not perform different tasks. A program for solving the Tower of Hanoi puzzle does not spell English words, and vice versa. As soon as we dig a level deeper, similarities begin to appear.

### The Basic Faculties

Let us start from the other end—examining the structures the central nervous system must provide as a basis for the storage and activity of the various programs we have considered. The programs all postulate some familiar basic components: a long-term memory, a perceptual system for recognizing and discriminating stimuli, and a short-term memory of limited capacity. Some of the specific properties attributed to these structures, however, are more or less peculiar to the information processing approach, having emerged from efforts to simulate the programs and to test the verisimilitude of the simulations.

The long-term memory is assumed, in these programs, to be organized as a combination of a discrimination net and a semantic memory organized as a node-link structure. The node-link organization is common to substantially all simulations of long-term memory that have been constructed, not just those discussed in this chapter.

The programs discussed in this chapter do not simulate the early stages of sensory and perceptual encoding. They assume, in some cases, that stimuli have been encoded as structures of features, in other cases, that the encoded familiar components of the stimuli have already been recognized and are consequently represented by internal "names" or labels, which can be identified with nodes in the node-link memory. Thus the programs postulate, but do not simulate, that the initial stages of reception of stimuli involve feature extraction processes.

In those programs that simulate the recognition of encoded stimuli, the recognition system is represented as a discrimination net (EPAM net), which tests the stimuli successively for the values of different features, and sorts them accordingly. The sorting process accesses the terminal node corresponding to the internal label of the stimulus in the node-link memory. Thus, the EPAM net can be viewed as an "index" to the content of semantic memory, and stimuli as information for evoking particular index items.

The simulation programs assume a short-term memory of limited capacity. The capacity is measured in chunks, where a chunk is a familiar item, i.e., the internal label of any stimulus that can be recognized through the discrimination net. The short-term memory is a way station not only for incoming sensory stimuli, after recognition, and outgoing motor signals, but also for the symbols that are the inputs and outputs of the system's information processes.

All of these faculties, it is postulated, are common to the programs for any person in any task environment. To explain the differences in abilities required for different tasks, therefore, or the differences in abilities among persons, more specific differential assumptions must be made about the information and programs that are stored in these facilities, and perhaps also, about specific parameters that affect their functioning (e.g., capacity of short-term memory, time required to access long-term memory, and so on).

Knowledge in Long-Term Memory

In order for a person (or a program) to be able to perform the tasks that have been sampled here, a great many kinds of information (and in some cases a great amount of information) must be available, stored in the node-link memory. In the sequence extrapolation tasks, the storage requirements are modest—the alphabet and the sequence of integers stored as lists. To extend the program for doing these tasks to musical analysis, additional lists (for example, the various musical scales) would have to be available.

For the algebra word problems, several kinds of information are needed in long-term memory. Information is needed about the meanings of words that are critical for the interpretation of sentences in such contexts, words like "equals," "times," "greater than," and so on. In addition, to the extent that syntactic are supplemented by semantic processes, information is needed that would allow the problem situation to be represented, and information setting constraints on physically possible situations (for example, that the nickels can be worth more than the quarters only if there are more than five times as many of them).

The Tower of Hanoi problem makes no specific demands on knowledge in long-term memory. Performance in the chess perception task, at the other extreme, depends almost entirely on how much knowledge is available. How well a player can reconstruct a briefly viewed position is mainly a function of how large a vocabulary of familiar configurations of pieces is stored in his long-term memory, and accessible through his discrimination net.

For inducing a program from worked-out examples to perform a task, little more information is needed than to perform the task. For inducing a program from written task instructions, a good deal of information is required about both vocabulary and syntax in the source language. The amount depends on the words used in the instructions, and the complexity of their grammatical construction.

The information requirements for the spelling task resemble most closely those for the chess perception task, with the added complication that some missing information may be supplied by the system of phonetic productions that allows plausible spellings to be tried when the complete spelling is not immediately available from the visual recognition system.

There is no sharp boundary between information stored in a passive link–node memory and information stored as the associational link between a perceptual test and an associated process or action. As a matter of fact, actions can be stored directly in the relational memory simply by treating the condition–action link as one of the relations that can be represented. There is little or no empirical evidence to tell us what part of human knowledge is stored in the form of passive node–link structures, and what part is stored in the form of active program structures.

Programs in Long-Term Memory

Keeping in mind the caveat that the data-program distinction is vague, we can now review the kinds of programs, stored in long-term memory, that were postulated for performing the six tasks. A central question is the extent to which the programs are specific to their respective tasks, or conversely, the extent to which general-purpose programs gain specificity by drawing upon task-specific information.

The pattern extrapolation program requires specific capabilities for organizing information about relations that have been detected among symbols into appropriate structures in memory (the pattern), and needs an interpretive process to read these memory structures and extrapolate the sequences with them. All of the components of the pattern extrapolation program are of a general-purpose nature: in particular, an EPAM-like system can handle the symbol-recognition tasks, and can learn new symbols and lists of symbols. Detecting relations require only simple programs for comparing two symbols for identity and finding the next symbol on a list of symbols. These are capabilities that are required for many other tasks. The specificity that is needed to deal with literal symbols, numerical symbols, or musical symbols, respectively, is mainly embedded in the EPAM net and node–link memory.

The program for solving algebra word problems requires an interpretive system to apply its syntactic and semantic knowledge to the input text, and, if it is to solve as well as to set up equations, some processes for algebraic manipulation.

In the systems that solve the Tower of Hanoi puzzle, there are few components that are specific to that puzzle. The "move" operator is a particular application of the "transfer" operator discussed in connection with the UNDERSTAND program. The programs embody a number of simple perceptual tests involving notions of above and beneath, larger and smaller, and the relation between a disk and the peg it is on. The organization of the two more complex systems is a simple application of the General Problem Solver organization.

The specificity in the chess task lies almost entirely in the content of the EPAM structure, as we have already noted. The faculties the system requires are: a process to scan the stimulus in order to initiate the recognition of familiar configurations; the EPAM structure and its interpreter, which accomplish the recognition; a process that stores labels of recognized chunks in short-term memory; another process that recovers from long-term memory the information about the configurations whose labels are held in short-term memory; a process that reconstructs the board by associating the information about the configurations with a representation of the board. T. G. Williams' (1972) work shows that even those parts of the program that relate directly to the representation of chess can readily be generated by a system that has general game-playing capabilities, or equivalently, that can read Hoyle with understanding. Finally, in its learning phase, the chess perception program requires a process for growing EPAM nets, which, again, is not specific to chess.

The spelling program requires processes for retrieving alternative graphemes associated with given phonemes, for retrieving word recognition information stored in a semantic memory, and for matching postulated spellings derived from phonemic information with the partial spellings stored in the visual word recognition memory. Thus, most of its program components are of a general-purpose nature.

The abilities required by the two task learning programs, the Aptitude Test Taker and the UNDERSTAND program, are also mainly general in their applicability. The Aptitude Test Taker uses processes very similar to those used by the program for extrapolating patterned sequences. The UNDERSTAND program has abilities to extract deep structure from natural language strings, then to map these deep structures onto templates that define inputs to a General Problem Solver system.

General Intelligence

This description of the processes required for intelligent performance in a half dozen disparate task environments sounds a bit like an argument for Spearman's *g*. A number of basic structures and processes show up again and again in the various programs. If we equate abilities with these kinds of structures and processes, then it appears impossible to construct any simple isomorphism between particular abilities and particular task environments (a result that is consistent, I think, with the experience with factor analysis).

If this be true, why does *g* account for only a modest part of the total variance in intelligence? First, we have seen that, while there is a great commonality of process, most tasks require also some very specific knowledge (words, perceptual tests, familiar chunks), and expert performance of some tasks calls for an enormous amount of such knowledge. Second, while the same basic processes show up in many different tasks, a given process may be employed more or less frequently in different task environments. Third, the basic processes may be combined in more than one way to produce a program for performing a particular task. In the case of the Tower of Hanoi problem, we described four different programs that draw to some extent upon different underlying abilities, and that may differ greatly in effectiveness. Proficiency in a task may depend on how the basic processes and relevant knowledge have been organized into the program for task performance.

Finally, it is not certain to what extent *g* is to be attributed to common processes among performance programs, or to what extent it derives from individual differences in the efficacy of the learning programs that assemble the performance programs. Suppose, to take an extreme "Guthriean" point of view, that a person learns if and only if he attends, and in amount proportional to the time that he attends. Suppose, further, that all persons learn at the same rate, per second of attention. Now a child with IQ of 150 has learned half again as much, up to a certain age, as a child with IQ of 100; and a child of IQ 70 only about two-thirds as much. Yet a ratio of only two to one in the time spent attending to learning the sorts of things tested in IQ tests could account for substantially the whole difference between the 70 and 150 score. This is not proposed here as "the" explanation of differences in ability, but as an indication of how wide a range of hypotheses about the causes of individual differences is consistent with the empirical evidence.

The evidence cited in this paper shows that valid process theories can be constructed for a wide range of complex tasks. We are steadily learning how to subject such theories, expressed as computer programs, to empirical testing. Through these theories, we are discovering and identifying a number of basic faculties provided by the central nervous system, and a number of basic processes that employ these facilities. We are learning also to build task-learning programs—programs that are themselves able to assemble programs for performing specific tasks.

Educational psychologists, developmental psychologists, and human factors specialists have always been attracted, rather more than their brethren in the profession, to the study of processes underlying human performance. Process analyses of reading skill, albeit at a rather gross level, have been with us for many years, as have been analyses of some perceptual and motor skills. In recent years Gagné has proposed a concept of learning hierarchies, and some techniques for analyzing them, that has influenced curriculum construction.

The limits of process analysis have been fixed by the limits on our conceptual apparatus for describing process, and the limits on our ability to devise empirical methods of observing and dissecting process. The development of computer simulation techniques has relaxed these limits considerably, and these techniques, combined with chronometric studies, eye-movement studies, and other new observational methods, have already greatly extended our understanding of the basic abilities underlying intelligent performance of complex tasks.

We have just begun, however, to exploit these new techniques, and have hardly begun at all to consider how we may apply them to the practical concerns of teaching, training, and child development. The results reported in this chapter should be regarded as hints of the potential of powerful new tools, not as predictions of what these tools will discover for us when we have learned to exploit them effectively.


## ACKNOWLEDGMENTS

This research has been supported by Public Health Service Grant MH-07722 from the National Institute of Mental Health, Department of Health, Education, and Welfare, and by the Advanced Research Projects Agency of the Office of the Secretary of Defense (F44620-70-C-0107) which is monitored by the Air Force Office of Scientific Research.


## REFERENCES

Ach, N. Über die Willenstätigheit und das Denken. Göttingen, 1905.
Anderson, J. R., and Bower, G. H. Human associative memory. New York: Halsted Press, 1973.
Bobrow, D. Natural language input for a computer problem-solving system. In M. Minsky (Ed.), Semantic information processing. Cambridge, Massachusetts: MIT Press, 1969.
Chase, W. G., & Simon, H. A. Perception in chess. Cognitive Psychology, 1974, 4, 55–81.
Chase, W. G., & Simon, H. A. The mind's eye in chess. In W. G. Chase (Ed.), Visual information processing. New York: Academic Press, 1973. Pp. 215–281.
Ernst, G. W., & Newell, A. GPS: A case study in generality and problem solving. New York: Academic Press, 1969.
Feigenbaum, E. A. The simulation of verbal learning behavior. In E. A. Feigenbaum & J. Feldman (Eds.), Computers and thought, New York: McGraw-Hill, 1963.
Gagné, R. Learning hierarchies. Educational Psychologist, 1968, 6, 1–9.
Hanna, P. R., Hanna, J. S., Hodges, R. E., & Rudorf, E. H., Jr. Phoneme-grapheme

*correspondences as cues to spelling improvement.* Washington, D.C.: U.S. Government Printing Office, 1966.

Hayes, J. R., & Simon, H. A. Understanding written problem instructions. In L. W. Gregg (Ed.), *Knowledge and cognition.* Hillsdale, New Jersey: Lawrence Erlbaum Associates, 1974.

Kotovsky, K., & Simon, H. A. Empirical tests of a theory of human acquisition of concepts for sequential patterns. *Cognitive Psychology,* 1973, 4, 399–424.

Newell, A., & Simon, H. A. *Human problem solving.* Englewood Cliffs, New Jersey: Prentice-Hall, 1972.

Paige, J. M., & Simon, H. A. Cognitive processes in solving algebra word problems. In B. Kleinmuntz (Ed.), *Problem solving.* New York: Wiley, 1966, Pp. 51–110.

Restle, F. Theory of serial pattern learning: Structural trees. *Psychological Review,* 1970, 77, 431–495.

Rudorf, E. H., Jr. The development of an algorithm for American-English spelling. Unpublished doctoral dissertation, Stanford University, 1965.

Selz, O. *Über die Gesetze des geordneten Denkverlaufs.* Stuttgart, 1913.

Siklóssy, L., & Simon, H. A. (Eds.) *Representation and meaning: Experiments with information processing systems.* Englewood Cliffs, New Jersey: Prentice-Hall, 1972.

Simmons, R. F. Answering English questions by computer: A survey. *Communications of the Association for Computing Machinery,* 1965, 8, 53–70.

Simon, D. P., & Simon, H. A. Alternative uses of phonemic information in spelling. *Review of Educational Research,* 1973, 43, 115–137.

Simon, H. A. How big is a chunk? *Science,* 1974, 183, 482–488.

Simon, H. A., & Gilmartin, K. A simulation of memory for chess positions. *Cognitive Psychology,* 1973, 5, 29–46.

Simon, H. A., & Sumner, R. K. Pattern in music. In B. Kleinmuntz (Ed.), *Formal representation of human judgment.* New York: Wiley, 1968. Pp. 219–250.

Simon, H. A., & Kotovsky, K. Human acquisition of concepts for sequential patterns. *Psychological Review,* 1963, 70, 534–546.

Vitz, P. C., & Todd, R. C. A coded element model of the perceptual processing of sequential stimuli. *Psychological Review,* 1969, 76, 433–449.

Williams, D. S. Computer program organization induced from problem examples. In H. A. Simon & L. Siklóssy, *Representation and meaning.* Englewood Cliffs, New Jersey: Prentice-Hall, 1972.

Williams, T. G. Some studies in game playing with a digital computer. In H. A. Simon & L. Siklóssy, *Representation and meaning.* Englewood Cliffs, New Jersey: Prentice-Hall, 1972.

# 6

# Steps toward the Simulation
# of Intellectual Development

David Klahr

*Carnegie-Mellon University*

## INTRODUCTION

My intent in this paper is to offer a view of the current state of the art in information processing (IP) approaches to the study of cognitive development. I will provide sufficient substance to indicate what this approach might yield in the way of insight or understanding about the nature of intelligence, although I will not attempt to explicitly define intelligence. It is clear that we are building models of systems which exhibit what is generally considered to be intelligent behavior. However, the fundamental nature of these models is still incompletely understood. Thus, the first order of business appears to be to describe their characteristics, and most of this chapter is directed to that task. Perhaps others can attempt the mapping between definitions of intelligence, either extant or new, and the components of these models.

Even within the IP framework, the scope of the work to be discussed is quite circumscribed: it is limited to the work I understand most thoroughly. The notion of the human as an information processor is so widely accepted in psychology now that an immense range of research could be classified as having an IP approach. So in lieu of a definition of intelligence, I will list a few characteristics of what is meant by an IP approach to the study of cognitive development.

*Tasks.* The tasks that elicit the behavior to be modeled are variants of the familiar Genevan battery for concrete operations. They include classification, simple quantification, transitivity, seriation, and class inclusion.

*Measures.* In addition to pass/fail scores, detailed recordings of the full range of motor and verbal behavior during task performance are obtained. These include all temporal information, except that in some cases only reaction times are measured.

99

*Subjects.* Children in the 4–10 year range are typically included in these studies. Some traditional group aggregation is done, but usually the unit of analysis is the individual child. The developmental inferences are derived from cross-sectional data.

*Models.* All the models to be described here are cast in the form of production systems. In later sections I will describe some of the important features of production systems, but at this point I want to emphasize the underlying view of the system architecture of human information processing that production systems adopt. The basic model is derived from the studies of adult problem-solving behavior presented by Newell and Simon (1972). The human cognitive system can be summarized as a parallel/serial/parallel processor: parallel, in the unselective response of the sensory system to its environment; serial, and quite limited, in capacity to attend to and encode that sensory information and to store it in long-term memory (LTM); and parallel, in the search through LTM for previously stored information.

The models consist of rules that determine which aspects of the environment and/or the limited capacity short-term memory (STM) will determine the next state of knowledge or overt action. The rules are usually stated with sufficient precision that they can be run on a computer. In this way the implications of the total rule set can be unambiguously derived and compared to the child's actual behavior.

All models describe distinct states of development. None contain any precisely stated transition mechanisms. In the next section, this important point will be elaborated.


## THE GLOBAL STRUCTURE OF A SELF-MODIFYING SYSTEM

During the course of development, the child's cognitive system goes through a sequence of state changes. Changes occur in the physical capacities and the processing rates, the "hardware," and in the content of organization of processes and data structures, the "software." Of course, we have no access to these states, and must infer them from behavior. Some of the changes over time in children's performance are so striking, so qualitatively different from Time 1 to Time 2, and so coherent across tasks presented within Time 1 or Time 2, that we say the child is in a *stage.* One can interpret the observed improvements in performance either as the result of a revolutionary reorganization of the system or as the final completion of an incremental process of relatively localized state changes. In either case, the scientific task for the developmental psychologist is to clarify the nature of both the different stages and the transition rule that causes the system to go from one stage to the next.

All of the IP analyses to be described here share the view that the more precisely one states his model of what a stage is, the more precisely can one state a theory of the transition process itself. Fig. 1 provides a nutshell summary of the state of the art. $S_1$ and $S_2$ represent simulation models of children at different stages on a specified range of tasks. $T_{1-2}$ represents the process that changes the $S_1$ model into the $S_2$ model.

We now have some very precisely stated $S_1$ and $S_2$ models for certain interesting, but limited, ranges of behavior. For example, Baylor and Gascon (1974) have constructed convincing models, in the form of computer programs which can simulate behavior of a preoperational ($S_1$) and a fully operational ($S_2$) child on a weight seriation task. However, their model of development, $T_{1-2}$, is stated only at the level of verbal description. Although these descriptions of transition are stated in terms of specific components and relations among components of the stage models, particularly in proposing some of the functional characteristics of the $T_{1-2}$ transition, there are no real theories of transition mechanisms.

Neither criticism nor pessimism is implied by this statement. It should be clear that my own strategic bet is that this is an appropriate direction in which to move, but we have a way to go yet. I would like to suggest what one of the next steps in the general approach might be.

As conceived thus far, the $S_1$ model could never develop into the $S_2$ model, for at every stage, and for every task, not only does the human system perform, but also it may learn something from that performance. No existing model has the capacity to represent this fact. A performance model that cannot simulate learning is as unsuitable for our purposes as a learning model that cannot simulate performance. We must extend our models so that a single system contains both the performance and the learning mechanisms.

Thus, the state models must be embedded in a much more powerful system— we call it the $D$ system, or Developing system—that could actually account for the $S_1$ to $S_2$ change. I have sketched this conception in Fig. 2, where the full system at Times 1 and 2 is represented by $D_1$ and $D_2$. The models constructed so far are silent on the nature of this larger system, but I believe that the next advances in this area will consist of specifications for the full $D$ systems in which the existing $S$ systems are embedded.

Of course, the capacity to learn itself develops over time, so that we might conceive of yet another system in which the $D$ system is embedded, but I believe

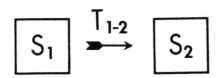

FIG. 1   A naive view of developmental simulation.

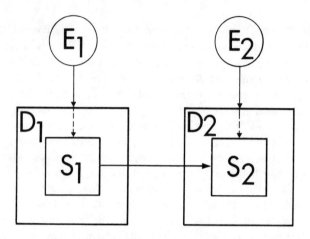

FIG. 2   Development of both $D$ and $S$ systems.

that this is unnecessary. As soon as we can specify a model whose task is the development and modification of some of its parts, that is, a $D$ that changes an included $S$, then within that same $D$ system we should be able to include self-modification capacity, that is, a $D$ that changes some parts of $D$.

It is important to bear in mind the distinction between the $D$ system and the $S$ system. All of the models to be reviewed are limited to $S$ systems. In a subsequent section I will return to the issue of development, focusing on self-modification, with a few speculative comments on what the $D$ system might need to do in order to develop.

## SOME EXAMPLES OF THE APPROACH

In this section I would like to describe some examples of computer simulation models of cognitive development. As I indicated earlier, I will limit myself to three lines of work with which I am most familiar. All are clearly descendants of the "Carnegie approach" of Newell and Simon (1972). Two of the lines of investigation to be described here are concerned with the ability of a child to pass a seriation task. The third is concerned with conservation and related quantification tasks.

George Baylor and his associates at the University of Montreal have studied weight seriation (Baylor & Gascon, 1974; Baylor, Gascon, Lemoyne, & Pothier, 1973; Gascon, 1969; Gascon & Baylor, 1973), and Richard Young, in his Ph.D. dissertation at Carnegie-Mellon University (Young, 1973) investigated length seriation. Seriation has been accorded great importance by the Genevans, and seriation of length, size, weight, and color represent Piaget's (1972) "addition of transitive asymmetric relations." In all its variants, the seriation task presents the child with an unordered collection of objects that vary along some dimension, and the child is instructed to construct a serial ordering based upon the dimension of interest. The child then generates a stream of behavior which is observed and recorded by the experimenter. The simplest datum is whether or not the child passes the task, i.e., produces the desired series. Of immensely more interest, to both Genevan and IP approaches alike, is the *way* that the child solves the problem: the stream of behavior during the task, the responses to variations in the task, and the differences between successful and unsuccessful paths to completion of the problem.

### Baylor and Associates' Studies of Weight Seriation

Baylor and Gascon's (1974) weight seriation task consisted of seven cubes, 2 in. on a side, indistinguishable to the eye except for an arbitrary letter painted on each one. The blocks weighed from 100 to 107 g, with about the same increment of weight between each adjacent pair. The blocks were presented in a line (not according to weight) and the child was instructed to arrange them by weight by using a two-pan balance. The instructions (as translated from the French) were, in part:

> Okay, do you understand what I want? I want you to find which one of the blocks is the heaviest, then the one that weighs a little bit less, and so on until the least, least, least heavy of all the blocks. And then when you are sure, put the heaviest block here (E points to a place on the table); the one that weighs a little bit less here; and so on until the least, least, least heavy block here. Do you understand? Can you repeat back to me what I just asked you? [Baylor & Gascon, 1974, p. 3]

The child was then allowed to work on the problem with little or no intervention from the experimenter. He was not encouraged to give a "thinking aloud" protocol. Instead, his behavior was video-taped. This record of his overt actions provided the raw data for analysis, which was described by Baylor and Gascon (1974) in the following way:

> The scientific task here is to induct from the protocol the underlying information processes that enabled S to generate the protocol in the first place. This leads to a *single-subject performance model* that reproduces or simulates S's behavior on this task. Such a model is purely descriptive and of limited scope. Its predictive value can only be assessed on new data for the same S on another weight seriation problem or, more generally, on a range of (seriation) tasks. One can try to broaden its scope . . . [but] in this quest for universality and developmental tractability, the trick is to maintain contact with the details of individual performance so that the model remains falsifiable [p. 4].

Given the incredible richness of a filmed record of 5 min of problem solving, how does one choose which aspects of the behavior to model? We have already mentioned one extreme: simply record "pass" or "fail" and ignore the rest. At the other extreme would be a model that could reproduce a precise time path of

all overt behavior: eye movements, hand coordination, head and trunk orientation, etc. The current state of the art falls between these two extremes. Baylor
and Gascon extract from the protocol information about the sequence in which
blocks are moved from their original position to the pan balance and to the final
configuration. The elements with which their models must deal are: symbols
which represent blocks, their positions, and the results of repeated weighings of
pairs of blocks. The reduced task for Baylor and Gascon is the following:
construct a model that simulates the sequence in which blocks were considered,
weighed in the pan balance, and placed in the final configuration for each child.

Table 1 shows the symbolic form of the behavior that Baylor and Gascon are
attempting to simulate. The three columns represent: (1) the initial positioning
of the blocks, in which they are not arranged according to weight; (2) the
position and relative weights of the blocks on the pan balance; and (3) final
positioning of the blocks, that is, the result of the attempted seriation. The
blocks in each position are designated by numbers corresponding to their relative
weights. Of course, the children did not see any such numbers; their blocks were
distinguished only by arbitrary letters. The first line in Table 1 describes the
following situation: Block 3, 6, and 4 are still in their original positions; Blocks 7
and 1 are on the balance, and the balance has tipped indicating that 7 is heavier
than 1; Blocks 5 and 2 have been positioned (correctly so far) in the final

Table 1

Segment of a Weight Seriation Protocol

| STATE | ORIGINAL POSITION | PAN BALANCE | FINAL POSITION |
|-------|-------------------|-------------|----------------|
| 1 | 3 6 4 | 7 > 1 | 5 2 |
| 2 | 3 6 4 | 7 | 5 2 1 |
| 3 | 3 6 4 | 7 > 5 | 2 1 |
| 4 | 3 6 4 | | 7 5 2 1 |
| 5 | 3 | 4 < 6 | 7 5 2 1 |
| 6 | 3 | | 7 5 2 1 4 6 |
| 7 | 3 | 4 < 6 | 7 5 2 1 |
| 8 | 3 | | 7 5 2 1 6 4 |
| | | 3 < 4 | 7 5 2 1 6 |

Adapted from "An Information Processing Theory of
Aspects of the Development of Weight Seriation in
Children" by G. W. Baylor and J. Gascon, *Cognitive
Psychology*, 1974, 6, 1–40, Figure 6.

configuration. The next line symbolizes the end result of a "move" by the child. At this level of analysis, what is recorded is a change in the state of the distribution of blocks. No finer "grain" (for example, which hand grasped which block) is attended to. Thus, the second line indicates that Block 1 was moved from the right end of the balance to the right end of the final line. The third line tells us that Block 5 was put back on the balance to be weighed with Block 7, and that the weighing indicated that Block 7 weighed more than Block 5. Next, both Blocks 7 and 5 are moved from the balance, and with their relative positions maintained, placed at the left end of the final position.

Now the child makes what turns out to be an important error. Rather than attempting to coordinate the unweighed blocks with those already weighed, he moves two blocks from the original position to the balance (State 5), and then to the final position (State 6). Then, apparently uncertain about whether he has maintained the ordering that was previously used, he returns Blocks 4 and 6 to the balance for a reweighing (State 7) and then puts them in the correct order (with respect to each other) back into the final position (State 8). And so it goes. (The full protocol for this child is presented in Baylor & Gascon, 1974, Fig. 6, p. 23.) The child makes eleven weighings in about 2 minutes, finally producing the ordering 7, 5, 2, 1, 6, 4, 3—a classic example of what Piaget calls "juxtaposed subseries."

In order to function in this task environment, the child needs to have some representation of both the external world and his own internal processes. The child is conceived of as passing from one state of knowledge to another. The full set of possible states of knowledge is called the problem space. For the weight seriation task, the problem space consists of information about the blocks, their positions, their relative weights while on the balance, and information about possible operations, e.g., moving blocks, setting and satisfying subgoals, and explicitly remembering what the system has just attended to.

The justification for these assertions comes from the attempt to build models that generate the observed behavior. In order to build such a model, one finds that this information and its internal accessing is crucial. It appears impossible to build a performance model at this level of detail without assuming access to this kind of information.

Using this kind of problem space, Baylor and Gascon have written a production system that accounts for the full protocol of which we saw a segment above. (They have also accounted for the protocols of several other children whose performance ranged from "juxtaposed couples" to "operational seriation." We will discuss these different systems below.) The production system for this child on this task consists of rules that deal both with the external environment, the configuration of blocks and the results of weighing, and with internal memory for goals and placekeepers within the collections of blocks. For example, the rule that is satisfied by the initial state shown in Table 1 says something like: "If the current goal is to get rid of a block, then move the lighter of the two blocks in the balance to the first (lightest) position in the final series." The rule also satisfies the goal that evoked it. The rule that makes the last move shown in Table 1, weighing Blocks 3 and 4, is stated like this in the actual computer simulation model:

P11:   WEIGH
( (PB = 0) (PO = 1) => (MOVE ( (PO) (PF1 RIGHT) ) ) PB) (SATISFIED WEIGH) )

The verbal equivalent of this rule is: "Production 11: If the current goal is to weigh some blocks, and the balance is empty, and there is only one block remaining in the original line, then move the block from the original line to the left pan in the balance, and move the rightmost block from the final series to the right side of the balance and satisfy (i.e., deactivate) the weighing goal." This precise statement can then be interpreted and executed by a computer program. The full set of such rules constitutes the performance model, and the trace of its behavior, i.e., its output, (in this case the sequence of block moves) can be compared with the subject's protocol.

*A complete production system.*    In this section a complete production system for weight seriation will be described. This will serve two purposes: first, the specific psychological assumptions and their dynamic interactions will become clear, and second, in subsequent comments about development we will be able to use this production system as an example.

The production system is shown in Table 2. It is taken from Baylor and Lemoyne (1974). First we will describe the details of the representation in Table 2, then we will describe the strategy that is effected by the system.

In Table 2, each row corresponds to a production rule. The conditions are on the left side of the table and the actions are on the right. The condition side can have three types of components: (*a*) tests for the current "top" goal; (*b*) tests upon the stimulus configuration; and (*c*) tests upon internal memory.

The goals are symbols that are placed in a stack. When a new goal is set, it gets placed upon the top of the goal stack, and all other goals are pushed down one "notch." When a goal is satisfied and "popped" from the top of the stack, everything below it moves up one notch, and the goal that was second in the stack becomes the top goal. All the tests on goals are tests for the value of the top goal.

The stimulus configuration consists of three positions: the original position (PO); the pan balance (PB); and the final position (PF), i.e., the series being constructed. The values of these positions are, for this system, rather simple: they are concerned with the presence or absence of all or some of the blocks.

There are two memory variables (in addition to the goal stack), that the system needs. One concerns remembering what block was just selected, the other

Table 2

Production System for Weight Seriation
Using "Insertion" Strategy

| | | Conditions | | | | | Actions | | | |
| | | Stimulus | | | Memory | | | Move Blocks | | |
| Prod. | Top Goal | PO | PB | PF | new | next | Goal manipulation | from | te | remember |
|---|---|---|---|---|---|---|---|---|---|---|
| P1 | SERIATE | not empty | | | | | Set INSERT | | | |
| P2 | SERIATE | empty | | | | | Pop | | | |
| P4 | INSERT | | not full | | | | Set COMPARE | | | |
| P5 | INSERT | | full | empty | | | Pop | PB Light / PB Heavy | PF / PF | |
| P6 | INSERT | | full | | PB LIGHT | | Pop | PB Light / PB Heavy | PFH / PFH | |
| P7 | INSERT | | full | | PB HEAVY | true | Set PUT-BACK | PB Light / PB Heavy | PF Right | next = PF R-OF-HOLE |
| P9 | INSERT | | full | | PB HEAVY | nil | Pop | PO Left / PO Left | PB / PB | |
| P10 | COMPARE | | | empty | | | Pop | | | |
| P11 | COMPARE | | empty | not empty | | | | PO Left | PB | next = PF Left / new = PO Left |
| P13 | COMPARE | | one block | not empty | | | Pop | PF next | PB | |
| P14 | PUT-BACK | | | | | | Pop | PB Light | PFH | |

Adapted from "Experiments in Seriation with Children: Towards an Information Processing Explanation of the Horizontal Décalage" by G. W. Baylor and G. Lemoyne, *Canadian Journal of Behavioural Science*, 1975, *7*, 4–29.

is a place keeper for what to do next. Every production tests for the value of the top goal plus some, but not all, of the stimulus and memory variables.

On the action side, there are three kinds of activities. The system can manipulate the goal stack by setting or popping goals. It can move blocks around and it can remember what is new or next.

Let us look at a few productions and restate them in English. P1 says: "*If* the top goal is SERIATE *and* there are blocks in PO, *then* set the INSERT goal." P5 says: "If the top goal is INSERT *and* the pan balance is full *and* the final position is empty, *then* pop the goal stack and move two blocks from the balance to the final position, preserving their light-heavy ordering."

*A trace of the system in operation.* The best way to understand both the interpretation and the function of the productions in Table 2 is to examine a trace of the program's behavior. Table 3 shows a segment of a trace of the system shown in Table 2. The column headed "stimulus" has a dual interpretation. It represents the program's effect upon the block configuration, and it also is the actual protocol from one of Baylor and Lemoyne's subjects (Pierre, age 8:1). For this segment of the protocol, Baylor and Lemoyne's production system (shown in Table 2) produced a perfect match with Pierre's behavior.

Pierre's strategy is one of systematic insertion. He constructs an ordered sequence of $n + 1$ blocks by finding where in a previously ordered sequence of $n$ blocks to insert the next block. He does this by weighing the new block with each of the blocks in the ordered set, starting with the lightest, until he finds one that is heavier than the new one. Then he inserts the new block in the line.

Table 3 shows a single insertion episode. The episode starts at state 29: the top goal is SERIATE; there are three blocks remaining in PO; the balance is empty; and PF contains the four blocks that have been seriated thus far. Referring back to the production system in Table 2, we see that the only rule satisfied by this set of circumstances is P1. Therefore it fires, and the action, "Set INSERT," is taken, producing state 30. The only difference between 29 and 30 is that the goal stack now contains two goals, with INSERT at the top. This state satisfies the conditions of P4, and so COMPARE is now put on top of the goal stack, producing state 31. P11 says: "*If* the top goal is COMPARE *and* the balance is empty *and* there are some blocks in PF, *then* move the leftmost block from PO to the balance, call it the "new" block and call the leftmost block in PF the "next" block. The conditions of P11 are satisfied by state 31, and its actions are taken: Block 4 is moved to the balance, it is marked "new," and Block 1 is marked "next." All of this produces state 32.

With this much explanation the reader should be able to follow the rest of the trace in Table 3. If we focus only upon the sequence of block moves (the stimulus columns in Table 3), we see that Blocks 4 and 1 are compared; Block 4 is found to be heavier, so 1 is put back, then 4 and 2 are compared, and 2 is put back. Then Blocks 4 and 5 are compared, whereupon 4, the new block, is

Table 3

Trace on Insertion Episode

| State | Production | Goal Stack | Stimulus | | | Memory | |
|---|---|---|---|---|---|---|---|
| | | | PO | PB | PF | new | next |
| 29 | P1 | SERIATE | 4 6 3 | – – | 1 2 5 7 | | |
| 30 | P4 | INSERT SERIATE | 4 6 3 | – – | 1 2 5 7 | | |
| 31 | P11 | COMPARE INSERT SERIATE | 4 6 3 | – – | 1 2 5 7 | | |
| 32 | P13 | COMPARE INSERT SERIATE | 6 3 | 4 – | 1 2 5 7 | 4 | 1 |
| 33 | P7 | INSERT SERIATE | 6 3 | 4 > 1 | 2 5 7 | 4 | 1 |
| 34 | P14 | PUT-BACK INSERT SERIATE | 6 3 | 4 > 1 | 2 5 7 | 4 | 2 |
| 35 | P4 | INSERT SERIATE | 6 3 | 4 – | 1 2 5 7 | 4 | 2 |
| 36 | P13 | COMPARE INSERT SERIATE | 6 3 | 4 – | 1 2 5 7 | 4 | 2 |
| 37 | P7 | INSERT SERIATE | 6 3 | 4 > 2 | 1 5 7 | 4 | 2 |
| 38 | P14 | PUT-BACK INSERT SERIATE | 6 3 | 4 > 2 | 1 5 7 | 4 | 5 |
| 39 | P4 | INSERT SERIATE | 6 3 | 4 – | 1 2 5 7 | 4 | 5 |
| 40 | P13 | COMPARE INSERT SERIATE | 6 3 | 4 – | 1 2 5 7 | 4 | 5 |
| 41 | P6 | INSERT SERIATE | 6 3 | 4 < 5 | 1 2 7 | 4 | 5 |
| | | SERIATE | 6 3 | – – | 1 2 4 5 7 | 4 | 5 |

Adapted from "Experiments in Seriation With Children: Towards an Information Processing Explanation of the Horizontal Décalage" by G. W. Baylor and G. Lemoyne, Canadian Journal of Behavioural Science, 1975, 7, 4–29.

discovered to be lighter than 5, and then both are placed, in the correct order, into the "hole" in PF (PFH) by P6.

It is worth a slight digression here to emphasize the clarity with which psychological assumptions can be stated in this form of modeling. In order for the cognitive system to determine the truth or falsity of its conditions, it must be able to have some rudimentary quantification ability. For example, it must be able to discriminate an empty pan balance from a nonempty one. How powerful must this quantification ability be for this task? Not very. The productions shown in Table 1 require only that the system be capable of discriminating between empty and nonempty PO and PF, and among full, empty, not full and one block in PB. Thus it is unnecessary to postulate any very general quantification operator.

*Goals and their interpretation.* We saw earlier that a production rule fires only when all of its conditions, both goals and predicates, are satisfied. We can loosely interpret the goal as a symbol that indicates what the system is attempting to accomplish, while the predicates describe the immediate state of the world. It is clear that cases can arise in which the predicates alone are insufficient information for deciding what action to take. The system needs to know where it is going as well as where it is, and goals provide this directionality.

In the Baylor and Gascon systems, goals serve another function. They permit a characterization of the problem-solving system one level removed from the stimulus-specific conditions of the production system. Baylor and Gascon call this representation a "base strategy":

> In order to try to account for the typically observed intrastage regularities across *Ss* . . .
> it appears necessary to introduce the notion of a *base strategy* or method . . . associated
> with each level of intellectual development on this task. Base strategies are written in
> terms of imperative statements: goals. Goals are inferred both from a logical analysis of
> the task demands and from the observed directionality in *S*'s actual behavior [Baylor &
> Gascon, 1974, p. 5].

A base strategy for a successful seriator is shown in Table 4. Two notational devices are used in this representation. The indenting indicates that one goal is subsidiary to the goal(s) less indented than it, and the asterisk indicates that the bracketed goal sequence may occur any number of times (including not at all).

Now we can interpret the base strategy in Table 4. It is a strategy which says, in effect, "If you want to seriate, then do repeated insertions in an already seriated subset." How should insertions be done? That's what the next set of indented brackets tells us. "To do an insertion, compare and put-back until you find where to do the insertion." Notice that this base strategy notation leaves out all of the specific detail about the task environment, and relates instead to its logical structure.

The base strategy concept is thus a useful means for comparing the global behavior of different children on the same task. It also provides a precise description of the similarities that underly performance variations across tasks

Table 4

Base Strategy for Insertion

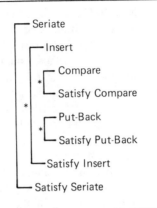

Adapted from "An Information Processing Theory of Aspects of the Development of Weight Seriation in Children" by G. W. Baylor and J. Gascon, *Cognitive Psychology,* 1974, **6,** 1–40, Figure 2.

for a single individual. In an exploration of some aspects of "horizontal décalage," Baylor and Lemoyne (1974) compared the production systems that simulated the behavior of a single child on three seriation problems: length seriation, weight seriation, and hidden-length seriation. In the latter task, the sticks to be seriated were enclosed in cigar tubes, so that their lengths were not immediately discernable. Only two sticks could be out of their tubes at any one time; thus the task provided an isomorph to the weight seriation situation. Baylor and Lemoyne demonstrated that by working from a single base strategy, one can construct three task-specific production systems that account for most of the subject's behavior on the three tasks.

The base strategies and the specific production systems are linked by the third component of the model: the compiler or interpreter. This is a processor that creates, from the task specification and the base strategy, the appropriate production system. It is similar in concept to the assembler in the Klahr and Wallace (1970) model, and needless to say, it is central to any theory of intelligent behavior. As Baylor and Gascon (1974) point out, "It seems highly unlikely that a child who has never before seriated weights comes into the experimental setting with such a specific representation in his head though he may well leave with it. . . . A child *is* postulated to come into the experiment with the components of a particular base strategy in his head [p. 38]." However,

Baylor and Gascon have no theory at present of how such a compiler or interpreter or assembler might operate, a question which becomes important in studying development. We will return to this issue in a later section.

What does seriation "mean" to the Baylor and Gascon child? We must be careful in answering this, for we have no good definition of meaning to guide us. In one sense the meaning of seriation is precisely the base strategy. It is the "deep structure" of seriation, stated as a series of imperatives. The task-specific production systems generate the surface structure, but the meaning must be inferred from them. One might postulate additional information that could evoke this meaning. Perhaps the system has associated with the base strategy a representation of the visual image of seriated lengths. This representation might be used both to evoke the base strategy, and to test for the correctness of the final product. Baylor and Gascon make no use of the form of visual representation, but Young's system, to be described below, does.

Thus, the meaning of seriation is a combination of: (1) the base strategies available to the system; (2) the memory of any task-specific production systems for task variants; (3) a representation of the final result, or desired state or "solution" to a seriation problem; and (4) links to other related terms in semantic memory. (We have had little to say about this form of representation, but include it for completeness.)

As for development, Baylor and Gascon are in the same boat as the rest of us. They have suggested a precise model of what might be changing in the base strategies and in the specific production system, but they are silent about how these changes take place. They suggest that: (1) the base strategies develop; (2) the "mechanism that translates the base strategy into a set of production rules" develops; and (3) the problem space gets richer with time. It is also likely that large numbers of task-specific production systems do get created and saved in memory.

## Young's Study of Length Seriation

In a recently completed Ph.D. dissertation at Carnegie-Mellon University, Richard Young (1973) studied the behavior of young children on a length seriation task. The general paradigm was similar to Baylor's: construction of production systems to account for the behavioral sequence abstracted from a video-tape recording of the problem-solving process. Several aspects of Young's work are quite distinct from any of the other IP approaches. I will mention only a few of them here.

Young used a repeating cycle of observation, modeling and modified observation *on the same child* for several different children. Thus, he would record the behavior on the basic task, construct a model that could account for that behavior, and, in the (several) cases where alternative interpretations—and hence different systems—could do the job, he would create a task variant that was designed to critically reject one or the other model. Young views this as an information-processing extension of Piaget's "revised clinical method" (Ginsburg & Opper, 1969). The strength of his approach lies in the fact that the final system that emerges for each child has accounted for more behavior than just the base task.

The productions in Young's systems are stated at a level of detail about midway between the base strategies and the running systems of Baylor and Gascon. They are silent on the details of STM structure and process and on the perceptual and linguistic encoding that accompanies the task performance. The principal component in the productions is an "operation," an internal symbol that "combines the properties of the 'goals' and 'operators' of other analyses of problem solving [p. 44]." The basic mechanism in the system is an operation stack: it functions like a goal stack. A typical production rule is

S2:   Seriate-one $\Rightarrow$ Get [suitable]

and its informal interpretation is

"If the current operation is to add a block to the line, then 'push it down' (in the operation stack) and set up the new current operation of getting a suitable block from the pool."

(The pool is the original scrambled pile of blocks, the line is the series that the child is constructing.)

Compared to the level of detail at which the models of Baylor and Gascon and Klahr and Wallace (see below) operate, there are some disadvantages to Young's approach. However, his work has produced an analysis that should be of great interest to those concerned with a mapping between traditional psychometric approaches to intelligence and information-processing analysis. Rather than attempt to describe any more of Young's productions, I will turn to his analysis of the "dimensions of seriation."

After completing the construction of production systems to account for the seriation behavior of about a dozen children, Young discovered that all the systems could be fashioned out of a basic "seriation kit" consisting of a handful of rules for each of four aspects of the task: Episodes, Selection, Evaluation, and Placement. The Episode rules provide a rudimentary control structure over the other three aspects. All of the children can sequentially move one block at a time from the pool to the line. The Episode rules account for that. What differentiates one child from another is the manner in which he or she functions at three crucial decision points: selecting the next block, evaluating it after (or immediately before) he or she places it in the line, and correcting any choice that appears to be inappropriate. The rules in the seriation kit represent different ways of reaching these decisions. The rules for one type of decision are independent of the rules for another. Thus, one could construct a system that had a "strong" selection rule and a "weak" correction rule (that is, a rule that changes a placement that is evaluated as incorrect). Such a system would generate a type of seriation behavior characteristic of one of the children studied by Young.

Young then suggests a three-dimensional space of seriation performance. The dimensions correspond to the decisions of selection, evaluation, and correction. There are three gross regions along each dimension. Table 5 illustrates the regions. Consider a child in the region S0, E1, C0. He would select a block without regard to size (probably the nearest one to him). Then, he would place it next in the line as long as it was larger than the previous one, without regard to incremental size differences. If it was out of order, he would return it to the pool (rather than leave a few "spaces" in the line). The end result of this approach would be an ordered series in the line, with blocks left over in the pool.

Now consider a child in S2, E0, C0. The child would always choose the correct block (the longest remaining in the pool). Even though his evaluation and correction rules are weak, he would succeed on the strength of his selection alone. This particular strategy illustrates a nice feature of Young's work. Suppose we want to determine how the child chooses the correct block. One approach would be for him to scan the pool for the largest. This requires no memory of anything in the line. Another possibility is that the child extrapolates from the series under construction and creates a target image which he then seeks in the pool. Several task variations used by Young enable him to decide the issue. In one variant, the line being constructed is hidden from the child. In another, some of the sticks in the series are initially missing from the pool. In a variant designed to separate selection from evaluation and correction, the experimenter gives the blocks to the child, thus keeping selection under experimenter control.

This dimensional representation is used by Young to discuss both individual differences—his subjects can be located in different regions—and development. Since the dimensions are ordered with respect to success on the task, one can consider cognitive development as progression through the space defined by the (orthogonal) dimensions. Young takes a strong position with respect to the notion of stages when he says: "Instead of distinct 'stages,' the various [production systems] to model children of different levels of ability have revealed a picture of cumulative progress along a developmental trajectory through the space of seriation structures [p. 209]." This is an interesting speculation, because it attempts to integrate two lines of attack that have traditionally been quite disparate: psychometric and information-processing. As with both Carroll and Simon (see Chapters 3 and 5), Young's analysis modifies the dimensional analysis of intelligence in such a way that the dimensions become well-defined basic processes, in this case productions, rather than factor loadings.

Table 5

Regions Along the Dimensions of Seriation

---

SELECTION

  S0    Proximate: Blocks are chosen in an order unrelated to their size

  S1    Weak: Some account is taken of size, but the correct block is not reliably chosen

  S2    Suitable: The correct block is usually picked

EVALUATION

  E0    None: Any block is accepted

  E1    Monotonic: A block is accepted provided the line remains in order

  E2    Precise: Only the correct block is accepted

CORRECTION

  C0    Reject: An unacceptable block is simply returned to the pool

  C1    Weak: Limited means are available for correcting a wrongly placed block

  C2    Strong: A block can usually be put where it belongs

---

Adapted from "Children's Seriation Behavior: A Production System Analysis" by R. M. Young, C. I. P. Working Paper No. 245, Carnegie-Mellon University, 1973.

## Klahr and Wallace's Studies of Conservation and Quantification

Now I will turn to some of the work that Iain Wallace and I have been engaged in for the past few years (a summary can be found in Klahr, 1973a, and an extended theoretical statement in Klahr & Wallace, 1976). To define precisely the particular variant of conservation under consideration, I will start with a quote from an earlier paper (Klahr & Wallace, 1973):

> The classic version of the Piagetian test for conservation of quantity starts with the presentation of two distinct collections of equal amounts of material (e.g., two rows of beads, two vessels of liquid, two lumps of clay, etc.). First the child is encouraged to establish their quantitative equality (e.g., "Is there as much to drink in this one as in that one?"; Is it fair to give this bunch to you and that bunch to me?"; etc.). Then he observes one of the collections undergo a transformation that changes some of its perceptual features while maintaining its quantity (e.g., stretching, compressing, pouring into a vessel of different dimensions, etc.). Finally, the child is asked to judge the relative quantity of the two collections after the transformation. To be classified as "having conservation" the child must be able to assert the continuing quantitative equality of the two collections without resorting to a requantification and comparison after the transformation. That is, his response must be based not upon another direct

observation, but rather upon recognition of the logical necessity for initially equal amounts to remain equal under "mere" perceptual transformations [p. 301].

What kinds of information processing ability must a child possess to demonstrate that he "has" conservation? The first level reply to this question consists of a simple task analysis. The child needs to be able to make the initial comparison, he needs to know something about transformations (i.e., that some preserve quantity and others don't), and he needs a "conservation rule," something that says: "If two things were equal to each other, and one of them underwent a certain kind of transformation, then they are still equal."

Now let us go down to a finer level. Consider the first requirement, the ability to make a quantitative comparison. In information processing terms, what is required here is the capacity to produce an internal symbol that represents the relative magnitude of two entities. The symbol itself might be represented in several forms: verbally, as an image, or as an abstract structure. Some process must produce this symbol. For example, what subprocesses would a child need in order to carry out a quantitative comparison?

First, the child would need some way of communicating with his environment—some way to respond to verbal and visual stimuli. He would also need to recall or generate information about each of the quantities he was trying to compare. Finally, he would need to actually generate the internal symbol representing the relative magnitudes of the items in question. Now we have a rough idea of the different kinds of processes required for quantitative comparison (QC), but things are still quite imprecise. We can refine this analysis by stating a series of conditionals for QC:

1. If you want to determine which is more, $X$ or $Y$, compare them.
2. If you want to compare two collections, determine the relative magnitude of their corresponding quantitative symbols.
3. If you want to do 2, but you don't have two symbols to compare, then generate the appropriate quantitative symbols.
4. If you want to generate a quantitative symbol for $X$, apply some quantification operator.

This conditional form of statement is obviously going to facilitate the recasting of this verbal model into a production system. But before we do that, we must consider the level of analysis or "grain" that the simulation model attempts to capture. Quantitative comparison is pervasive in tasks designed to test for Piaget's stage of concrete operations, and the model for QC should apply to at least this range of tasks. In questions about subclass comparison or class inclusion, the steps outlined above are sufficient. However in conservation, the idea is to avoid this entire process of quantitative comparison, relying instead upon the results of previous executions of QC and a conservation rule. Thus, we would need to modify the QC model above so that the first thing it tries to do is to use prior information to make an inference about the current situation. We also need to generalize it to deal with any relative magnitude term, not just "more." At the other end of the model, we would like to be as explicit as possible about the form of the processes that produce the quantitative symbols—the quantification operators. It appears that these operators and their development play a central role in the developing ability of the child to understand what are commonly termed "quantity concepts" (Gelman, 1972; Klahr, 1973c; Klahr & Wallace, 1973).

*Production system architecture.* Before describing the details of our model for QC, some additional comments about production systems are necessary. The psychological model that is implemented in our production systems is shown in Fig. 3. There are three principal components: LTM, where the production system resides; STM, which is the workspace for the system, and which controls the firing of production rules; and the Visual short-term memory (VSTM). Visual short-term memory is a surrogate in this model for a visual buffer whose contents can be tested by productions whose conditions refer to it, rather than to STM. The dashed lines indicate that VSTM and STM can both be interrogated by production rules, and the arrows indicate the direction of information flow. However, STM is the only buffer in this system whose contents can be changed, as indicated by the solid lines. Notice that LTM modification is not possible in this particular model. The model builder ($E$) can directly modify the contents of any of the buffers to provide a symbolic representation for the end result of processes that are not formally modeled at all. This usually includes processes at the boundaries of the model, that is, both encoding processes and internal subroutines. The cyclic operation of the system consists of repeated passes through the productions in LTM. The conditions of each production are compared with the contents of STM and/or VSTM, until a match is found. When a production fires, it usually takes actions that modify STM, and the cycle repeats, starting again with the testing of the first production in the production system. All symbolic processing in this model is contingent upon the state of either the world (represented by VSTM) or the STM. New information is added to the "front" of STM, old information may eventually get pushed out of STM, unless it is rehearsed. Rehearsal is automatic: whenever a production's conditions are met, all those STM elements that made it true are moved to the front of STM.

*A production system model for quantitative comparison: PSQC.* At some stage in development, the child performs successfully on quantitative comparison tasks including conservation of quantity. If our goal is the construction of a series of models representing progressively more successful performance in this area, then one such model must include the appropriate conservation rules, simple quantitative comparison, and some basic quantification processes. In this section we will describe such a model, written as a production system, called PSQC. Since the full model has been described elsewhere (Klahr & Wallace, 1976), we will present only enough to convey its general flavor. The main purpose of this description is to demonstrate how the general system architec-

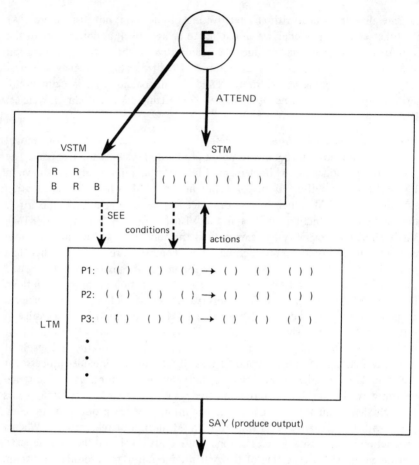

FIG. 3 Production system architecture.

ture of a production system—a modeling form that has proven so useful in explaining global adult problem-solving processes (Newell & Simon, 1972)—can be used to model important features of children's processes. A secondary purpose is to "demystify" the reading of production systems. Figure 4 shows parts of a production system for quantitative comparison, PSQC, and Fig. 5 shows part of a trace of PSQC in a typical conservation experiment. The excerpts are taken from the actual computer listings in order to indicate the level at which the models are stated. The full system for PSQC is about twice the size of this excerpt, containing about 30 individual productions.

One often gets a first impression of overwhelming complexity when faced with even a partial listing of this kind of model. But consider the task. We are attempting to construct a model of a process that takes a child only a few seconds to complete, but which at even the grossest level of formal analysis consists of several steps. A more thorough logical analysis reveals the necessity of at least a dozen substeps, all executed serially. For example, careful analysis of experimental data for the quantification processes indicates processes that tick over at the rate of 25–50 msec each (Klahr, 1973c). We seek to represent each of these elementary operations as one or two productions. Furthermore, the models must contain rules to account not only for what *did* happen on a given task, but also for what *might* happen on a task variant. PSQC is a model of the cognitive processes of an "operational" child on Class Inclusion, several kinds of Conservation, and a range of subclass comparison processes. It includes a rudimentary linguistic processor, the basic logic for quantitative comparison, and a model for subitizing (the very rapid process for quantifying small collections of discrete objects). All of these processes are coordinated. Although the full model is necessarily extensive, it is not really complex, as I will attempt to show in the discussion below.

The model is written in a language called PSG (Newell, 1973b). The model builder can construct a program which is then interpreted according to a specific set of rules about production systems—refinements of the general description of production systems presented in the previous section. A few details of the PSG interpretive rules will be presented here. For more complete descriptions see Newell (1973a, b) and Klahr (1973a).

First I will describe the rules from the production system excerpts in Fig. 4; then I will describe the actual behavior of the program, the trace in Fig. 5.

All the productions are written in the form

$$LL: (C1\ C2\ C3\cdots--\!>\!A1\ A2\cdots),$$

where LL is a label (the "name" of the production), the $C$s are condition elements that are to be matched against the contents of STM, and the $A$s are actions to take if all the $C$s are true, that is, if each one matches an element in STM.

It is impossible to describe the productions in their "static" form (e.g., the production system in Fig. 4) without referring to their dynamic effect (e.g., the trace in Fig. 5). The recommended way to read the following description is to first, skim this section on the general features of each production, and then look at the trace and its description, referring back to this section as necessary. The productions can be divided into four distinct functional groups. First, we will describe the general function of each group, and then we will describe each of the rules in detail.

1. *The goal manipulation productions (PA and PZ).* These enable the system to treat goals in the same manner as other elements in STM. The goal manipulation productions are:

PA:   $((*\ GOAL)\ (*\ GOAL)--\!>\!(*===\!>\!\%))$

```
                              Goal manipulation
    PA: ((* GOAL) (* GOAL) --> (* ===> %))
    PZ: ((* GOAL) ABS (% GOAL) --> (% ==> *))

                              Verbal encoding
    PDV1: ((RELWORD) (V1) (V2) --> (HEARD **) (X ===> HEARD X) (Y ====> HEARD Y)
                              (VALUE (V1)) (VALUE (V2)) (* GOAL GETREL V1 V2))

                              Quantification
    PDVS3: ((GOAL * SUBIT (XLM)) (SEE XLM) (SEE XLM) (SEE XLM) (SEE XLM) ABS --> SAT (QS THREE XLM))

                              Conservation
    PDCON11: ((* GOAL CON) (OLD (V1 QGT V2)) (TSUB V2 NEW V2) --> SAT (V1 QGT NEW V2))

                              Main quantitative comparison
    P1B: ((* GOAL GETREL Y X) (X QREL Y) --> SAT (NTG (X QREL)) (OLD **) SAYIT)
    P2: ((* GOAL GETREL) (TS) (- GOAL CON) ABS --> (* GOAL CON))
    P4: ((* GOAL GETREL X Y) --> (* GOAL COMP X Y))
    P6: ((* GOAL COMP) (X QREL Y) --> SAT)
    P7: ((* GOAL COMP X Y) (QS (X)) (QS (Y)) --> RELATE)
    P9: ((* GOAL COMP) (VALUE X) --> (VALUE ===> OLD VALUE) (* GOAL QUANT (X)))
    P10: ((* GOAL QUANT (X)) (GOAL + QUANTIFIER (X)) --> SAT)
    P11: ((* GOAL QUANT (X)) --> (GOAL * SUBIT (X)) )
    PQ: ((* GOAL) ABS (% GOAL) ABS --> ATTEND)
```

FIG. 4    Partial listing of production system for quantitative comparison.

"If there are two active goals in STM, then change the second of the two from an active state to an interrupted state." The most recent one—the first in STM—will remain active. The production works in the following way. First STM is scanned for an element that starts with the subelement (* GOAL) (our symbol for active goal). If such an element is found, the production then searches for another element that contains (*GOAL). Suppose STM contained: ( (* GOAL COMPARE BLUE RED) (* GOAL GETREL BLUE RED)......). Then PA would match on both of its condition elements. There is a single action for PA. It replaces the symbol * with the symbol % in the second element in STM. The symbol * is used to indicate an active goal. Other goal "tags" are: "%" (interrupted), "+" (satisfied), and "−" (failed).

PX:   ( (* GOAL) ABS (% GOAL) − − > (% = = >*) )

"If there are no active goals, and there is an interrupted goal, then change the interrupted goal to an active goal." The "ABS" symbol following a condition element means that the condition will not match unless the specified element is *absent* from STM.

2. *Verbal encoding.* This model has a single production which serves as a rudimentary model for the encoding of verbal input in the quantitative comparison task.

PDV1:   ( (RELWORD) (V1) (V2) − − > (HEARD **) (X = = = > HEARD X) (Y = = = = > HEARD Y) (VALUE (V1) ) (VALUE (V2) ) (* GOAL GETREL V1 V2 ) )

PVD1 fires if it finds a RELWORD, a V1, and a V2. Each of these is defined in this model as a *class variable.* That is, each can match on any of a small set of specific values in STM. RELWORD will match against relational terms such as MORE, LESS, BIGGER. V1 and V2 have been similarly defined to match on values such as RED, BLUE, WOOD, etc. Thus, an input to STM such as (MORE) (RED) (BLUE) will be sufficient to fire PDV1. The actions in PDV1 do two kinds of things. First, they tag the three elements that fired PDV1 so that they are essentially inhibited from firing it again. Each element is tagged with the symbol "HEARD." Then three new elements are added to STM. Two of them are tagged as VALUE elements, with whatever particular value V1 and V2 have at that moment. The third new element is an active goal of determining the relationship between the two values: (* GOAL GETREL RED BLUE). The psychological function of this production is to transform the auditory input from the question "Which is more, the reds or the blues?" into an imperative command to the system: "Get the relationship between the reds and the blues."

The use of condition elements that contain variables enables one to build models of extensive generality, since the variable definitions can themselves include other variables. The match between a condition element thus defined and an STM element could involve the search of a hierarchy of arbitrary extent.

3. *Quantification.* The quantitative comparison system must have the means to "look at" the external environment to determine certain required quantities. We know that both adults and children have at least three distinct quantification operators: subitizing, counting, and estimating (Chi & Klahr, 1975; Klahr, 1973c). Subitizing, defined above as a rapid process for directly quantifying small collections of discrete objects, is the only process that is included in this model, and in Fig. 4 only one representative production from the subitizing system is shown. The logic of subitizing is essentially a template match. Each of the productions seeks precisely $n$ elements of the desired type and the one that fires produces an appropriate quantitative symbol for the value of $n$.

The stimulus is represented by a list of elements in VSTM (described on page 117, in the section on production system architecture). There is a special condition element called SEE which tests for the presence of a specific element in VSTM. The production that would detect precisely three elements in VSTM is

PDVS3:  ( (GOAL * SUBIT (XLM) ) (SEE XLM) (SEE XLM) (SEE XLM)
        (SEE XLM) ABS − − > SAT (QS THREE XLM) )

"If there is an active goal of subitizing the XLMs, and you SEE three XLMs and no more, then satisfy the subitizing goal, and put a quantitative symbol in STM, indicating that you have seen three XLMs." XLM is a class variable that can take on values like RED, BIG, DOT, etc. When the goal is matched in STM, XLM is assigned one of these specific values. Thus, by the time the SEE operator starts looking for elements in VSTM,

XLM has become something specific like RED or BIG. Exactly three of the target XLMs must exist in DISP (the visual display presented to the child) to fire PDVS3. This is accomplished by seeking the presence of three elements and the absence (ABS) of a fourth.

A full subitizing system would consist of several such rules, for up to four or five elements. Beyond that numerical range, processes other than subitizing appear to operate, and production systems for counting, enumerating, adding or estimating (Klahr, 1973a, b) would be required to represent the full range of quantification abilities.

4. *Conservation.* The general form of the condition side of the conservation productions is a test for an initial quantitative relationship and some transformation of one of the quantities included in that relationship. If a match is found, then a new element, representing the appropriate quantitative inference, is added to STM. In Fig. 4, only one of 11 conservation rules is shown:

PDCON11:   ( (* GOAL CON) (OLD (V1 QGT V2) ) (TSUB V2 NEW V2)
              −−> SAT (V1 QGT NEW V2) )

"If the conservation goal is active, and there is old information that V1 was of greater quantity than V2, and V2 just underwent a quantity reducing transformation (TSUB) yielding a new V2, then satisfy the conservation goal, and add a new element to STM indicating that V1 is greater than the new V2." Several of the symbols in PDCON11 are defined as class variables. V1 and V2 have already been described. QGT could be any of several symbols for quantitative inequality: MORE, BIGGER, etc. TSUB could be any of several kinds of reducing transformations—transformations that reduce the quantity of a collection: SUBTRACT, TAKE, EAT, etc.

PDCON11 is actually an *in*equivalence conservation rule. The other conservation rules cover all the determinate outcomes of addition, subtraction, and perceptual transformations upon initially equal or unequal two-collection situations and upon single-collection situations.

5. *Quantitative Comparison.* The productions in this section of Fig. 4 serve to coordinate the goals necessary to implement the set of four conditional statements listed on page 116. Recall that all the productions in Fig. 4 are tested sequentially. Thus, in addition to the explicit conditions which state what must be *true* of the current state of STM, the location of a production implicitly adds on an effective condition "and if all preceeding conditions are unsatisfied."

P1B:   ( (* GOAL GETREL *Y X*) (*X* QREL *Y*) −−> SAT (NTC (*X*
        QREL) ) (OLD **) SAYIT)

"If you have an active goal of determining the relationship (GETREL) between *X* and *Y*, and you also have an element that describes such a relationship, then, since you have what you are looking for, do the following: satisfy the GETREL goal, and mark the QREL element as OLD. Finally, 'say' the result." $X$ and $Y$ are defined as variables—they can take on any value. This production is the last step in the temporal sequence taken by PSQC.

P2:  ( (* GOAL GETREL) (TS) (– GOAL CON) ABS – –> (* GOAL CON) )

"If GETREL is active, and some transformation has been noticed and conservation has not failed recently, then set up a conservation goal." This production makes conservation attempts contingent upon an STM element representing an observed transformation. If no such element exists, then since the system has no record of any transformation, it should not even attempt to apply any conservation rules. However, if it had already tried and failed conservation, then it shouldn't attempt it again. Thus, unless it detects the absence of (– GOAL CON), P2 will fail, and the next rule will be tested.

P4:  ( (* GOAL GETREL $X$ $Y$) – –> (* GOAL COMP $X$ $Y$) )

"If you are still trying to get a relationship between $X$ and $Y$, then establish a subgoal of comparing two quantities: $X$ and $Y$."

Both P2 and P4 add an active goal to the front of an STM that already has an active goal. As will be seen in the trace, this situation immediately fires PA, which interrupts the second goal. Thus, both P2 and P4, in conjunction with PA, have an effect similar to the *set* operation in the Baylor and Gascon (1974) models.

P6:  ( (* GOAL COMP) ($X$ QREL $Y$) – –> SAT)

"If your goal is comparison, and you have a relation, then satisfy the comparison goal."

P7:  ( (* GOAL COMP $X$ $Y$) (QS ($X$) ) (QS ($Y$) ) – –> RELATE)

"If the active goal is to compare $X$ and $Y$, and you have quantitative symbols for both $X$ and $Y$, then determine the relative magnitude (RELATE) of the two quantitative symbols." Recall that quantitative symbols (QS . . . ) are produced by the quantification productions. If the system is attempting to compare two collections, say RED and BLUE, and it discovers that it has two quantitative symbols corresponding to those two values, then it executes the action RELATE, which determines the relative magnitude of the two quantitative symbols and produces a relational element, e.g., (RED MORETHAN BLUE), in STM. The presence of such a relational element is necessary to satisfy P6 and P1B.

P9:  ( (* GOAL COMP) (VALUE $X$) – –> (VALUE = = => OLD VALUE) (* GOAL QUANT ($X$) ) )

"If your goal is comparison, and you have an element with the tag "VALUE" then mark the value OLD—so it won't be processed again—and add an active goal of quantifying that value." If STM had (VALUE RED), then after P9 fired, STM would get the new elements (GOAL * QUANTIFY (RED) ). The system only gets to P9 after P7 has failed, i.e., when it does not yet have two quantitative symbols with which to determine a relationship. Thus, P9 attempts to remedy the situation by establishing a quantification goal. If quantification is eventually success-ful, a new QS will be added to STM.

P10:  ( (* GOAL QUANT (X) ) (GOAL + QUANTIFIER (X) )  - - >
      SAT)

"If the active goal is quantification of X, and there is a satisfied quantifier of X, then satisfy the active quantification goal." QUANTI-FIER is a class variable which could take on values representing the various quantifiers with which the system might work: SUBIT, COUNT, ESTIMATE, etc.

P11:  ( (* GOAL QUANT (X) ) - - > (GOAL * SUBIT (X) ) )

"If the active goal is quantification, then establish the subitizing goal." This production directly specifies that the only quantification operator used by this model is subitizing. A more complete model would, at this point, need addition productions to determine which of several possible quantifiers to use.

PQ:  ( (*GOAL) ABS (% GOAL) ABS - - > ATTEND)

"If there are no active goals and no interrupted goals, then attend to the environment, that is, seek further input." When the "goal stack" is empty, then the system simply awaits further information.

*A trace of PSQC on a conservation task.*  Figure 5 shows an edited trace of the system's response to an inequivalence conservation trial. The top line shows the initial condition of STM and DISP. STM starts with three elements representing a gross simulation of the system's initial representation of the query "Which is bigger, the red collection or the blue collection?" DISP contains the representa-tion for a display containing a collection including two blue things and three red things.

The rest of Fig. 5 lists the production rules carried out and their results on STM. Each pass or cycle through the system is numbered consecutively (1–27). For each pass, the name of the production that fires is shown, followed by the contents of STM after all actions have been completed.

Given the initial conditions, the first production to fire is PDV1. It draws upon its knowledge that BIGGER is a symbol for a relational word, and that RED and

BLUE are symbols for value words. PDV1 also marks the elements that fired it to indicate that it has attended to them. PDV1 takes five actions: two that modify existing STM elements and three that add information to STM. The net result of all this is shown in the rest of the line. Next, on pass 2, P4 fires. Notice that P2 does not fire here because its conditions are not satisfied. In this case the GETREL goal simply generates a subgoal of comparison. This new element goes to the front of STM, pushing all else down one "slot."

Since there are two active goals in STM at this point, PA fires next, followed by P9, and then PA fires again. We can interpret STM contents in terms of what the system "knows" after the fifth pass:

| It wants to quantify the red things, | (* GOAL QUANTIFY (RED) ) |
| because it's trying to do a comparison, | (% GOAL COMPARE BLUE RED) |
| in order to determine a relationship; | (% GOAL GETREL BLUE RED) |
| it has already HEARD the terms | (HEARD BIGGER) |
| | (HEARD BLUE) |
| | (HEARD RED) |
| and it has used the value RED so far | (OLD VALUE (RED) ) |
| but not the value blue. | (VALUE (BLUE) ) |

P11 responds to the quantification goal by inserting a corresponding subitizing goal into STM. Once SUBIT is active (Pass 6), the system "glances" at DISP and does a template match to determine how many red things there are. PDVS3 SEES precisely three RED things. The net result of all this is the placement of a quantitative symbol (QS), whose value in this case is 3, in STM.

Thus, by Pass 7 the system has managed to create one of the two quantitative symbols it needs for the comparison. A sequence of goal satisfactions and interruptions now ensues (P10, PZ, P9, PA, P11, PDVS2, P10, PZ), but the STM listing following each of them has been omitted from Figure 5. We pick up the detailed trace again following Pass 15, after two quantitative symbols have been created. Notice that STM contains two satisfied (+) quantification goals and two satisfied subitizing goals. At last P7 has what it needs, and it fires, calling upon the operator RELATE to determine the relative magnitude of the two quantitative symbols. We have no program for RELATE in this model for QC. Instead, the simulation system waits for the experimenter to provide the hypothetical result from such a process. Thus, after Pass 16, the symbol (RED MORETHAN BLUE) is inserted into STM. A few more goal manipulations (P6, PZ) ensue, and finally P1B fires, "saying" the final result to the world after Pass 19. By Pass 20, nothing is active, all goals are satisfied, and the default production PQ responds to the absence of any active or interrupted goals by ATTENDing to the environment.

Thus far, the model has accounted for the first phase of a conservation experiment: the determination of the initial quantitative relationship between the two collections. In the case we have just simulated, this is an inequivalence

```
STM:((BLUE) (RED) (BIGGER) NIL NIL NIL NIL NIL)     DISP:((RED) (BLUE) (BLUE) (RED) (RED))

n   pd              STM contents after pd fires

1   PDV1  ((* GOAL GETREL BLUE RED) (HEARD (BIGGER)) (VALUE (RED)) (VALUE (BLUE)) (HEARD BLUE) (HEARD RED) NIL NIL NIL NIL NI
2   P4    ((* GOAL COMPARE BLUE RED) (* GOAL GETREL BLUE RED) (HEARD (BIGGER)) (VALUE (RED)) (VALUE (BLUE)) (HEARD BLUE)
          (HEARD RED) NIL NIL NIL NIL )
3   PA    ((* GOAL COMPARE BLUE RED) (% GOAL GETREL BLUE RED) (HEARD (BIGGER)) (VALUE (RED)) (VALUE (BLUE)) (HEARD BLUE)
          (HEARD RED) NIL NIL NIL NIL )
4   P9
5   PA    ((* GOAL QUANTIFY (RED)) (% GOAL COMPARE BLUE RED) (OLD VALUE (RED)) (% GOAL GETREL BLUE RED) (HEARD (BIGGER)
          (VALUE (BLUE)) (HEARD BLUE) (HEARD RED) NIL NIL NIL )
6   P11   ((GOAL + SUBIT (RED)) (* GOAL QUANTIFY (RED)) (% GOAL COMPARE BLUE RED) (OLD VALUE (RED)) (* GOAL GETREL BLUE RED)
          (HEARD (BIGGER) (VALUE (BLUE)) (HEARD BLUE) (HEARD RED) NIL NIL )
7   PDVS3 ((QS THREE (RED)) (GOAL + SUBIT (RED)) (* GOAL QUANTIFY (RED)) (% GOAL COMPARE BLUE RED) (OLD VALUE (RED))
          (% GOAL GETREL BLUE RED) (HEARD (BIGGER)) (VALUE (BLUE)) (HEARD BLUE) (HEARD RED) NIL)
8   P10
9   PZ
10  P9
11  PA
12  P11
13  PDVS2
14  P10
15  PZ    ((* GOAL COMPARE BLUE RED) (* GOAL QUANTIFY (BLUE)) (GOAL + SUBIT (BLUE)) (QS TWO (BLUE)) (OLD VALUE (BLUE))
          (* GOAL QUANTIFY (RED)) (GOAL + SUBIT (RED)) (QS THREE (RED)) (OLD VALUE (RED)) (% GOAL GETREL BLUE RED)
          (HEARD (BIGGER)))
16  P7    ((RED MORETHAN BLUE) (* GOAL COMPARE BLUE RED) (QS TWO (BLUE)) (QS THREE (RED)) (* GOAL QUANTIFY (BLUE))
          (GOAL + SUBIT (BLUE)) (OLD VALUE (BLUE)) (* GOAL QUANTIFY (RED)) (GOAL + SUBIT (RED)) (OLD VALUE (RED))
          (% GOAL GETREL BLUE RED))
17  P6    ((* GOAL COMPARE BLUE RED) (RED MORETHAN BLUE) (QS TWO (BLUE)) (QS THREE (RED)) (* GOAL QUANTIFY (BLUE))
          (GOAL + SUBIT (BLUE)) (OLD VALUE (BLUE)) (* GOAL QUANTIFY (RED)) (GOAL + SUBIT (RED)) (OLD VALUE (RED))
          (% GOAL GETREL BLUE RED))
18  PZ    ((* GOAL GETREL BLUE RED) (+ GOAL COMPARE BLUE RED) (RED MORETHAN BLUE) (QS TWO (BLUE)) (QS THREE (RED))
          (* GOAL QUANTIFY (BLUE)) (GOAL + SUBIT (BLUE)) (OLD VALUE (BLUE)) (* GOAL QUANTIFY (RED)) (GOAL + SUBIT (RED))
          (OLD VALUE (RED)))
19  P18   ((OLD (RED MORETHAN BLUE)) (+ GOAL GETREL BLUE RED) (+ GOAL COMPARE BLUE RED) (QS TWO (BLUE)) (QS THREE (RED))
          (+ GOAL QUANTIFY (BLUE)) (GOAL + SUBIT (BLUE)) (OLD VALUE (BLUE)) (+ GOAL QUANTIFY (RED)) (GOAL + SUBIT (RED))
          (OLD VALUE (RED)))
                    ******** "RED  MORETHAN  BLUE" ********
20  PQ    ((EAT BLUE NEW BLUE) (OLD (RED MORETHAN BLUE)) (+ GOAL GETREL BLUE RED) (+ GOAL COMPARE BLUE RED) (QS TWO (BLUE))
          (QS THREE (RED)) NIL NIL NIL)
21  PQ    ((RED) (BLUE) (BIGGER) (EAT BLUE NEW BLUE) (OLD (RED MORETHAN BLUE)) (+ GOAL GETREL BLUE RED)
          (+ GOAL COMPARE BLUE RED) (QS TWO (BLUE)) (QS THREE (RED)))
22  PDV1  ((* GOAL GETREL RED BLUE) (HEARD (BIGGER)) (VALUE (BLUE)) (VALUE (RED)) (HEARD RED) (HEARD BLUE)
          (EAT BLUE NEW BLUE) (OLD (RED MORETHAN BLUE)) (+ GOAL GETREL BLUE RED))
23  P2    ((* GOAL CON) (+ GOAL GETREL RED BLUE) (EAT BLUE NEW BLUE) (HEARD (BIGGER)) (VALUE (BLUE)) (VALUE (RED))
          (HEARD RED) (HEARD BLUE) (OLD (RED MORETHAN BLUE)))
24  PA    ((* GOAL CON) (% GOAL GETREL RED BLUE) (EAT BLUE NEW BLUE) (HEARD (BIGGER)) (VALUE (BLUE)) (VALUE (RED))
          (HEARD RED) (HEARD BLUE) (OLD (RED MORETHAN BLUE)))
25  PDCON11 ((RED MORETHAN NEW BLUE) (+ GOAL CON) (OLD (RED MORETHAN BLUE)) (EAT BLUE NEW BLUE) (% GOAL GETREL RED BLUE)
          (HEARD (BIGGER)) (VALUE (BLUE)) (VALUE (RED)) (HEARD RED))
26  PZ    ((* GOAL GETREL RED BLUE) (RED MORETHAN NEW BLUE) (+ GOAL CON) (OLD (RED MORETHAN BLUE)) (EAT BLUE NEW BLUE)
          (HEARD (BIGGER)) (VALUE (BLUE)) (VALUE (RED)) (HEARD RED))
27  P1A   ((OLD (RED MORETHAN NEW BLUE)) (+ GOAL GETREL RED BLUE) (+ GOAL CON) (OLD (RED MORETHAN BLUE)) (EAT BLUE NEW BLUE)
          (HEARD (BIGGER)) (VALUE (BLUE)) (VALUE (RED)) (HEARD RED))
                    ******** "RED MORETHAN  BLUE" ********
```

FIG. 5   Trace on conservation task.

trial, since the two collections are initially unequal. Next comes a transformation that is observed by the child. Let us assume that the child observes some of the blue things being eaten (perhaps they are soybeans, red soybeans, and blue soybeans). In a mathematical type of notation, we might represent this transformation of one of the collections as something like: $T(x) - \rightarrow x'$, that is, collection $x$ is transformed into a new collection $x'$ (see Klahr & Wallace, 1973, for extensive use of this kind of notation for the conservation paradigm). In the production system, we represent the end result of an observed transformation by a single element with three components. In this case (Pass 20), it is (EAT BLUE NEW BLUE). Once this information is inserted in STM, the system again cycles through all its productions until it reaches PQ, which again waits for further input (Pass 21).

Now "the" conservation question is posed; PDV1 fires again. But this time the system has information about a transformation in STM: instead of P4 firing as before, P2 detects it, and inserts a goal of attempting to conserve (Pass 23). On Pass 25, a conservation rule, PDCON11, fires, producing new relational information. Having applied the conservation rule, the system goes through a series of cleaning up operations, similar to those on the initial quantification effort, and, having "said" the result, it quits.

Although we have presented only excerpts of both the production system and the trace, it is worth emphasizing that this is intended to be a single comprehensive model. Under some conditions it actually needs to do an encoding of a visual simulus under control of verbal inputs; under other conditions it uses previous knowledge to apply a rule of inference to achieve the same end. Although we have not demonstrated it here, this same model can handle several variants of class inclusion tasks as well.

I have dwelt at length upon a description of our work because I wanted to give a very concrete example of the kind of target at which we are aiming. This is a model of some important aspects of the cognitive processes of a child in the stage of concrete operations. The developmental question is very clear with respect to this model: "How can we account for the development of this information processing system?"

## DESIGN ISSUES FOR A SELF-MODIFYING SYSTEM

In this section we return to the issue of self-modification raised earlier in this chapter (beginning on page 100). As I pointed out there, no one has yet constructed a simulation model for the transition process in cognitive development, although precisely stated stage models such as those described here should provide a solid point of departure. As Simon noted in the preceding chapter, these models enable us to ask "new questions—questions we did not even know how to ask, or did not know needed to be asked." In this final section, I will approach some of the questions that have been raised by the attempts to simulate developmental processes. These comments should be viewed as a set of tentative design specifications for those who seek to model a developing, or self-modifying, system.

### Systemic Principles

Every design needs to be guided by some general systemic principles. Piaget (see Piaget, 1952) speaks of assimilation and accommodation, and Werner (1948) of dedifferentiation, articulation, and integration. Although such characterizations are more poetry than science, particularly if that is as far as they go, they do provide a broad sketch of the kind of system to be designed. Wallace and I have proposed elsewhere (Klahr & Wallace, 1973) two systemic principles characteristic of a developing information-processing system. One is a principle of redundancy elimination:

> The developing system constantly searches for consistent sequences which enable it to eliminate redundant processing. A consistent sequence is an internal representation of environmental inputs and system processes that always yield the same result. It is not simply an environmental regularity, but rather regularity arising from the interaction between the environment and the system [Klahr & Wallace, 1973, p. 302].

The other is a principle of local search for regularities: "If, in a particular context, the system is unable to detect consistent sequences, it widens the basis of its search [p. 302]." Based upon these principles we can now attempt to state some of the functional specifications of the system.

## Functional Specifications: What Must the Self-Modification System Accomplish?

*What is innate?*   Since the age range with which we are dealing starts no earlier than one year, that question, at least in its starkest form, need not be answered. We do, however, want to start with a system that has little or no task-specific knowledge. The self-modifying system, which we have called the *D* system (see Fig. 2), must start with nothing more than a record of empirical regularities. The *D* system must start with the capacity to notice, store, and process the internal representations for these regularities.

*Coordination of local rationality.*   At some point the developing child, our *S* system, has an uncoordinated collection of rules that he has abstracted from empirical regularities. These rules take the form of simple productions with a few predicates as conditions and a few actions that essentially predict the next environmental input, or the next state of knowledge that an appropriate test might yield. But there is no global rationality to the rules. The system that produced the uncoordinated subseries in the Baylor seriation task is an example of this. The *D* system must provide a means of coordination and communication among subsystems that really should have access to each other. One way to achieve this coordination is through the appropriate addition of goals to critical productions. A careful look at the production systems described above reveals the fact that the goals are used in many cases like subroutine calls in a conventional programming system. That is, they ensure that following a given situation, only a specific subset of all possible productions will be given a chance to fire. By thus "blocking" undesired rules from firing, goals effect a tremendous degree of directionality, without compromising the basic homogeneity of the production system representation.

*Now you see 'em, now you don't: Goal elimination.*   Production systems, as a language for describing the human information processor, grew out of work focused upon adult problem-solving behavior. The tasks presented were such as to cause no disagreement when characterized as problems. Thus, construction of a logical proof, choosing a move in chess, or doing the Tower of Hanoi are all clearly and explicitly problems to be solved. In the developmental area, it is similarly reasonable to consider some tasks as problems to be solved by the child. The seriation task is clearly a problem to be solved: it has a well-defined initial state, a set of permissible operations, and a well-defined final state. However, in extending the range of phenomena to which production-system models apply, we are implicitly characterizing a much wider range of tasks as problems.

For example, our model for quantitative comparison views the external request for a statement about which of two quantities is larger as a problem to be solved. The system that solves this problem generates a series of subgoals that lead to the appropriate operations, which ultimately satisfy the sequence of goals that led to their evocation. All of the subgoals generated to work out quantitative comparison problems are themselves viewed as problems to be solved by the system. Such a view appears to be reasonable in a model of a child who is still a newcomer to quantitative comparison tasks. The same view holds for modeling classification, conservation, and transitive inference. The model also gives us some suggestions about where to look for sources of failure in the child who can't quite succeed. However, in the adult, it seems a bit farfetched to postulate such a sequence of goals and subgoals for quantitative comparison. It's just not a problem for an adult. Since the stimulus is the same, if a task changes from a problem to a nonproblem, then we must be referring to changes in the system that produces the solution.

One indication that such a change occurs is that certain goals are no longer utilized to control the evocation of productions. For example, in Baylor's production system (see Table 2), it seems reasonable to posit the goals utilized. However, a careful analysis of that system reveals that the goals are redundant in every one of the productions. If the goal stack were eliminated, if P1 and P2 were deleted, and if the actions associated with goal manipulation were deleted, then the system would exhibit precisely the same "external" behavior, that is, the block moving sequence. A goal-free system would run faster, since P1 and P2 would never fire, and since each production would have one less action. It would also place less demand upon memory, where a certain amount of space is taken up by the goal stack. Such a simplified system might well be a more appropriate representation for practiced performance on this task than the more elaborate problem-solving model in Table 2.

Perhaps this is the essence of the "logical necessity" issue as an indicator of children's "true" comprehension of some of the Piagetian concepts. If the child no longer sees the task as being problematical, then he cannot conceive of there being any question about its solution. Extinction attempts will fail, because there is no mechanism to even test for the intermediate results that are falsified on typical extinction trials. Only if the child still characterizes the task as a problem will his system contain the appropriate tests that will be sensitive to the falsified information. The developmental issue changes from "When can the child do the task?" to "When is the task no longer a problem?"

## What Changes?

Earlier in this chapter (see pages 101–102), a distinction was made between the $S$ system and the $D$ system. The argument was that the $S$ system generates the task performance that we observe, while the $D$ system contains the rules for development. Now that a few concrete examples of $S$ systems have been presented, we can elaborate our model of the $D$ system. The three basic $S$ system components, shown in Fig. 6 are the Knowledge system ($K$ system), the Understanding system ($U$ system), and the Performance system ($P$ system). In various forms, these three components have been mentioned both in this chapter and elsewhere (Klahr & Wallace, 1970; Klahr & Wallace, 1973; Baylor & Gascon, 1974; Baylor et al., 1973). The $K$ system contains what the child knows about the world before he enters the task. The $P$ system is the process that actually generates the behavior we observe. The $U$ system takes the task environment, including instructions and materials, and creates, from the $K$ system, an appropriate $P$ system.

Consider Baylor and Gascon's (1974) task. The child is not postulated to bring to the task a production system for weight seriation. Between instruction time and performance time, something happens that enables him to carry out the task. Baylor and Gascon characterize the $K$ system as a "base strategy" and the $P$ system as a task-specific production system that elaborates the goal sequencing in the base strategy.

There are some very difficult technical issues that are immediately raised by this conception. Many of them revolve around the relative richness and power of the $K$ system and the $U$ system. Should the $U$ system be cast as an interpreter, a compiler or an assembler? How shall the contents of the $K$ system be represented—as structure or as processes? These issues have been cogently presented by Newell (1972), and I will not attempt to resolve them here. The basic point here is that the target for our sought-after transition process is itself a complex entity. All that we can get a chance to "look at," in the sense that we can directly compare its predictions to actual behavior, is the final production system. But in most cases, there is little likelihood that the child brought such a system to the task (or that he takes it away). Rather, he brings the capacity to construct the $P$ system. This capacity is contained entirely within the $U$ system and the $K$ system.

Our conception of the $D$ system has thus moved another layer away from the highly specific production systems that we saw above. The self-modification must occur primarily in the $K$ and $U$ systems. Perhaps the nature of this task (the self-modification task) is in some respects similar to the short-run demands

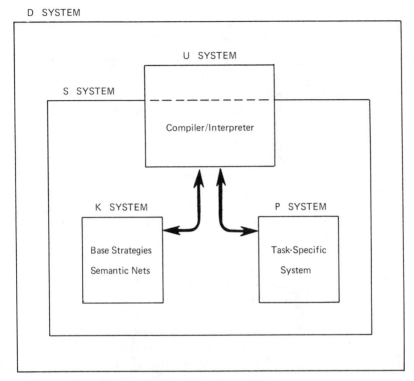

FIG. 6   Structure of the *D* system.

of a specific task. Thus, the *U* system may derive some of its power from the more fundamental processing ability of the *D* system. For this reason, the *U* system boundaries are extended in the diagram into the *D* system.

Having speculated to this extent, let me try one further flight of fancy. If indeed the *U* and *D* systems share some important processes, then this may account for much of the predictive validity of IQ testing. What we measure directly on such tests is the joint product of the *U* and *K* systems. However, what we are really after is a measure of the power of the *D* system. Clearly, if long-term self-modification (i.e., learning) ability derives from the same set of processes that facilitate short-term task assembly, then the two measures will be related.

### Information Requirements

What decisions must we make before we can design the *D* system? In Table 6, I have listed some of the issues that might be important. Such a list must be speculative, for until we have a convincing model of self-modification, we cannot know which questions were necessary and which were irrelevant.

Table 6

Information Requirements for Design of a Self-Modifying System

When does learning attempt occur ?
    What has just happened ? (Dynamic)
    What is the current state of knowledge ? (Static)

Why does learning attempt occur ?
    Why now ?
    Which variables are responsible ?
    What are their critical values ?

How will system be changed as a result of this learning ?
    Not at all; learning is a failure
    New productions
    New parameters
    New classes (semantic structure)
    New architecture

What information will be used to make the change(s) ?
    Information about current state of system
    Information about current state of environment

The performance models described in this chapter provide a concrete referent for our attempts to answer some of these questions. It would require another lengthy chapter to carry out such an exercise. However, it is clear that the kinds of answers one proposes are more likely to be meaningful if we have a wide variety of such performance models than if none exist. I have tried to indicate the direction of the first few steps toward the simulation of cognitive development, as well as some of the new questions raised by these efforts. It is clear that the designer of a convincing model of cognitive development faces formidable problems. It is also clear that such models will provide deep insight into one of the central problems of psychology: the nature of intelligence.

## ACKNOWLEDGMENTS

This work was supported in part by a grant from the Spencer Foundation.

## REFERENCES

Baylor, G. W., & Gascon, J. An information processing theory of aspects of the development of weight seriation in children. *Cognitive Psychology,* 1974, **6,** 1–40.

Baylor, G. W., Gascon, J., Lemoyne, G., & Pothier, N. An information processing model of some seriation tasks. *Canadian Psychologist,* 1973, **14,** 167–196.

Baylor, G. W., & Lemoyne, G. Experiments in seriation with children: Towards an information processing explanation of the horizontal décalage. Working Paper M. C. P. No. 15 (Rev.), Université de Montréal, 1974.

Chi, M., & Klahr, D. Span and rate of apprehension in adults and children. *Journal of Experimental Child Psychology,* 1975, **19,** 434–439.

Gascon, J. Modèle cybernétique d'une sériation de poids chez les enfants. Working Paper M. C. P. No. 2, Université de Montréal, 1969.

Gascon, J., & Baylor, G. W. BG manual. Working Paper M. C. P. No. 13, Université de Montréal, 1973.

Gelman, R. The nature and development of early number concepts. In H. Reese (Ed.), *Advances in child development and behavior.* New York: Academic Press, 1972.

Ginsburg, H., & Opper, S. *Piaget's theory of intellectual development: An introduction.* Englewood Cliffs, New Jersey: Prentice-Hall, 1969.

Klahr, D. An information processing approach to the study of cognitive development. In A. Pick (Ed.), *Minnesota symposia on child psychology.* Vol. 7. Minneapolis: University of Minnesota Press, 1973. (a)

Klahr, D. A production system for counting, subitizing and adding. In W. Chase (Ed.), *Visual information processing.* New York: Academic Press, 1973. (b)

Klahr, D. Quantification processes. In W. Chase (Ed.), *Visual information processing.* New York: Academic Press, 1973. (c)

Klahr, D., & Wallace, J. G. An information processing analysis of some Piagetian experimental tasks. *Cognitive Psychology,* 1970, **1,** 350–387.

Klahr, D., & Wallace, J. G. Class inclusion processes. In S. Farnham-Diggory (Ed.), *Information processing in children.* New York: Academic Press, 1972.

Klahr, D., & Wallace, J. G. The role of quantification operators in the development of conservation of quantity. *Cognitive Psychology,* 1973, **4,** 301–327.

Klahr, D., & Wallace, J. G. *Cognitive development: An information-processing view.* Hillsdale, New Jersey: Lawrence Erlbaum Associates, 1976.

Newell, A. A note on process-structure distinctions in developmental psychology. In S. Farnham-Diggory (Ed.), *Information processing in children.* New York: Academic Press, 1972.

Newell, A. Production systems as models of control structures. In W. Chase (Ed.), *Visual information processing.* New York: Academic Press, 1973. (a)

Newell, A. PSG manual. Carnegie-Mellon University, Computer Science Department, Pittsburgh, 1973. (b)

Newell, A., & Simon, H. A. *Human problem solving.* Englewood Cliffs, New Jersey: Prentice-Hall, 1972.

Piaget, J. *The origins of intelligence in children.* New York: International Universities Press, 1952.

Piaget, J. *Essai de logique opératoire* (2nd rev. ed.). Paris: Dunod, 1972.

Werner, H. *Comparative psychology of mental development.* New York: International Universities Press, 1948.

Young, R. M. Children's seriation behaviour: A production-system analysis. C.I.P. Working Paper No. 245, Carnegie-Mellon University, Pittsburgh, 1973.

# 7
# General, Academic, and Artificial Intelligence

Ulric Neisser[1]

*Cornell University*

My reactions to the chapters by Simon and Klahr (Chapters 5, 6) come out of a particular approach to the problem of intelligence and of thinking. I will try to make that approach clear before commenting on those chapters directly. More specifically, I will begin with some general remarks on intelligence as seen from a cross-cultural perspective. From this viewpoint I will consider both the "Academic Intelligence" which is measured by standard tests and the "Artificial Intelligence" achieved by machines. Only then will I turn to the chapters at hand.

## Intelligent Behavior

For some years, Michael Cole and his associates (Cole, Gay, Glick, & Sharp, 1971; Cole & Scribner, 1974) have been studying cognitive processes in a Liberian people called the Kpelle. They are an articulate people: debate and argument play an important role in their society. Many are entirely illiterate, having never gone to school. Like members of traditional societies everywhere, unschooled Kpelle get poor scores on tests and problems that seem easy to people with some formal education. The following example gives some idea of the reason why:

> EXPERIMENTER: Flumo and Yakpalo always drink cane juice (rum) together. Flumo is drinking cane juice. Is Yakpalo drinking cane juice?
> SUBJECT: Flumo and Yakpalo drink cane juice together, but the time Flumo was drinking the first one Yakpalo was not there on that day.

[1] This paper was prepared while the author was a Fellow at the Center for Advanced Study in the Behavioral Sciences, Stanford, California. The Center's support is gratefully acknowledged.

EXPERIMENTER: But I told you that Flumo and Yakpalo always drink cane juice together. One day Flumo was drinking cane juice. Was Yakpalo drinking cane juice that day?

SUBJECT: The day Flumo was drinking the cane juice Yakpalo was not there on that day.

EXPERIMENTER: What is the reason?

SUBJECT: The reason is that Yakpalo went to his farm on that day and Flumo remained in town on that day [Cole *et al.*, 1971, 187–188].

This example is not unusual. Cole *et al.* (1971) report that their subjects often respond by saying something like, "Yakpalo isn't here at the moment, why don't you go and ask him about the matter? [p. 188]" Such answers are by no means stupid. The difficulty is that they are not answers *to the question*. The respondents do not accept a ground rule that is virtually automatic with us: "Base your answer on the terms defined by the questioner." People who go to school (in Kpelleland or elsewhere) learn to work within the fixed limitations of this ground rule, because of the peculiar nature of school experience.

Scribner and Cole (1973) have described some of the characteristics of formal schooling which probably help to create this attitude. In school, a problem should be tackled in the same way no matter which teacher assigns it to you (teachers keep changing); numerical problems are worked out similarly regardless of whether apples or bombs are to be added (or without any specific numbers at all, as in algebra); geography is to be mastered whether or not one has any interest in traveling. The school child learns to use one particular skill or heuristic to solve many different puzzles, even if they differ in any details, simply because they share an abstract structure. He also learns to work on problems as they are presented, whether he cares about the solutions or not. It is the absence of these attitudes among the unschooled Kpelle that accounts in large part for the sorts of answers I have quoted.

Thinking like that of the traditional peoples is often called "concrete" as opposed to "abstract." If this terminology is taken to imply that they cannot work with abstractions, it is misleading. Very sophisticated manipulation of abstractions occurs in such societies. Cole *et al.* (1971) make this point repeatedly, as does Gladwin (1970) in his impressive study of Puluwat navigation. Nevertheless, it is clear that such subjects take their particular actual situation into account more fully than schooled people do, when they are presented with formal problems. This may seem to be a poor strategy, from the problemsetter's point of view. In general, however, it is an extremely sensible course of action. In the affairs of daily life it matters whom we are talking to, what we are measuring, and where we are. The environment is endlessly complex and surprising. We do well to be alert to its opportunities and dangers, both the continuing ones and those that reveal themselves unexpectedly.

Intelligent behavior in real settings often involves actions that satisfy a variety of motives at once—practical and interpersonal ones, for example—because opportunities to satisfy them appear simultaneously. It is often accompanied by emotions and feelings, as is appropriate in situations that involve other people. Moreover, it provides continual opportunities for cognitive growth of many kinds, because most situations turn out to have facets of which we were formerly unaware.

All this is different in school. We are expected to leave our life situations at the door, as it were, and to solve problems that other people have set. Notice also that problems on school tests are supposed to be "fair"—that is, all the information needed to solve them is typically given from the beginning. The pupil does not find out anything as he goes along that might have been otherwise. I will call problems of this kind "puzzles," because they are so different from the problems of ordinary human life. To solve "puzzles" like this requires particular skills, often skills of a high order. It is appropriate to call them *academic skills*. As a group they comprise *Academic Intelligence,* which can be abbreviated *AI*—a pair of initials familiar to computer scientists.

I do not mean to imply that academic skills are useful only in school; they are more and more in demand in many sectors of American society. Nevertheless, it is important to distinguish Academic Intelligence from intelligence in general. When Simon defines "intelligent performance of complex tasks" as "doing the tasks correctly, with little or no waste motion (page 65, this volume )" he mostly has Academic Intelligence in mind. His "complex tasks" are all set by other people, and accepted by subjects in an unemotional and conflict-free way. Most of them are puzzles, in which all the information needed for the solution is present from the first. "Intelligent performance in natural situations," in contrast, might be defined as "responding appropriately in terms of one's long-range and short-range goals, given the actual facts of the situation as one discovers them." Sometimes the most intelligent thing to do is to refuse a task altogether.

## Academic People and Academic Intelligence

Consider now the nature of "intelligence tests." In terms of the definition I have proposed, they measure primarily Academic Intelligence. This is obvious immediately if one looks at what they are and how they are typically administered. They consist largely of arbitrary problems with little intrinsic interest; they are administered in special sessions set up for the purpose. That is, the tests are deliberately disembedded from the child's or the testee's ordinary experience. Their academic nature is also evident from the manner in which they are validated—namely, against school performance. The correlations between test scores and nonschool indicators of achievement or success, by contrast, are relatively low (Jencks, 1972). As I learned from Leona Tyler's chapter in this volume (Chapter 2), even the history of testing indicates its close ties to the schools: the early French tests were developed to help teachers cope with the new problems created by the introduction of universal education. (For a related view of intelligence testing and much valuable cross-cultural material, see Good-now, Chapter 9.)

Not surprisingly, the tests are made up by academicians. By definition, their constructors are people who have done well in school. One might almost say that tests are devices for finding other people who resemble their creators. This is one reason why academic people are among the stoutest defenders of the notion of intelligence, and why the tests seem so obviously valid to us who are members of the academic community. All of us have the feeling that we can spot an intelligent person. Such a person is quick witted, finds the right argument, can follow a theoretical exposition, etc. We would think it essentially impossible to "sham" intelligence: a thief might convince others of his honesty, a coward might pretend to be brave, but no stupid person could fake intelligence for long.

Given our conviction that this quality exists and is easy to perceive in others, we have no reason to doubt that it can be measured. Indeed, IQ tests *do* correlate with our perceptions to a considerable extent. Thus, they have a kind of face validity for us. We regret, perhaps, that they are not more accurate instruments, but we cannot doubt them altogether. We admire, praise, and prefer to promote people who display this sort of intelligence, though we reluctantly admit other considerations (productivity, creativity, teaching skill) in judging someone's overall effectiveness. There is no doubt that Academic Intelligence is really important for the kind of work that we do. We readily slip into believing that it is important for *every* kind of significant work.

The view from outside the academy, however, is somewhat different. Even highly schooled people in American society have been known to express skepticism about the types they used to call "eggheads." We are not held in unqualified esteem. To put it bluntly, academics are often regarded as ineffectual, devoid of good sense, and preoccupied with trivia: stupid despite being intelligent. We have been doing our best in recent years to overcome this image. Many of us have been giving practical advice—to the military, to city planners, to government economic agencies, and so on. It cannot be said, alas, that our advice has been spectacularly successful.

Thus, academic people are in the position of having focused their professional activities around a particular personal quality, as instantiated in a certain set of skills. We have then gone on to *define* the quality in terms of this skill set, and ended by asserting that persons who lack these special skills are unintelligent altogether. We do this honestly, with considerable confidence, because we experience the validity of the concept in our own professional lives. We *know* about intelligence.

Working within a community where this all seems so clear, it is not easy to understand that any other perspective is even possible. An analogy may help. Other social groups have first valued, and then overspecified, other virtues. One enlightening example is the case of *courage*. It is an important quality in human life, taking many forms. One familiar form is the readiness to face death in battle. There are other types of courage, however, moral and social and spiritual forms of courage, that are by no means insignificant. To fully understand whether or not someone is being courageous, one would need to know a great deal about his life situation.

Soldiers at the front, however, tend to have a monistic view of courage. With their lives threatened every day, they can confidently tell whether someone is brave or not—just as we, who engage in academic activities every day, can tell if he is smart. Such men are impatient with other definitions of courage. They may give lip service to "moral courage" as we condescendingly admit "social intelligence," but they don't take it very seriously. They often argue that the country would be better off if it were led by men of courage, as intellectuals think it should be led by men of intelligence.

Probably brave men in this position would welcome a "courage test" as we welcome intelligence tests. Indeed, the phrase "a test of his courage" is often heard. It would not be very difficult to devise a courage test with substantial reliability and validity: the testee might be asked to run through an exploding minefield, for example. A few people would undoubtedly oppose such tests, especially since some population groups would (on the average) get low scores, but data supporting the validity of the tests would be easy to obtain. Scores on courage tests might tend to run in families; perhaps they might even be more closely correlated in identical than in fraternal twins. I can't resist pointing out that it would be rather easy to make a machine that demonstrated "Artificial Courage" and got high scores; easier by far than to make one Artificially Intelligent. When the chips were down, however, even soldiers might have their doubts about whether the machine would be a good thing to have at one's side in battle.

It has happened that whole societies have been organized around the narrowly-conceived virtue of courage in battle. Sparta was an outstanding example, and I think others can be found among native American Indian tribes. In such a society the leaders are chosen on the basis of courage, child training aims at inculcating courage, and people who lack courage by the generally agreed definition must be content with low social positions.

It may also happen, analogously, that our society will organize itself around the single virtue of Academic Intelligence. There is apparently a trend in this direction in business and in the governmental bureaucracy, for reasons I cannot go into here. If this were to take place, I would not welcome it. The fact is, academically intelligent people do often behave stupidly. The existing evidence does not suggest that they are markedly more successful than the unintelligent, in the conduct of their affairs or of the affairs of others. Nor is it clear that the quality of their lives is more enviable than that of other people. I am suspicious of attempts to extend the domain in which tests of Academic Intelligence are influential, as I would suspect the use of "courage tests" in more than a very narrow realm.

## Artificial Intelligence

Many years ago (Neisser, 1963) I called attention to some differences between human thinking on the one hand and then-existing computer programs on the other. As one who has borrowed many valuable metaphors from programming, I was not trying to deny the contributions that Artificial Intelligence would make to our understanding of the mind. Nevertheless, I was able to describe three aspects of thinking which contemporary programs seemed to lack. First, human thought undergoes cognitive development. It has a complex ontogenetic history, in which maturation, learning, and changing opportunities for experience all play a part. Second, human thinking is passionate, emotional, influenced by internal states that have both long- and short-run dynamics of their own. Finally, human beings have many motives simultaneously. They may play chess to bolster their egos, for esthetic pleasure, to maintain a personal relationship, and to symbolize unconscious wishes all at once. A computer program by contrast does not grow, has no emotional basis, and is monomaniacally single-minded. I see now that all three of these qualities arise because people develop and use their cognitive skills in a real environment; they are always in concrete situations with multiple opportunities.

In the 1963 paper I was contrasting Artificial Intelligence with human thinking as it naturally occurs in life, not with how people take intelligence tests. If I had been considering the latter, I would have been far less confident about its differences from "AI." To put it another way, the three properties lacking in Artificial Intelligence are also lacking in Academic Intelligence, though perhaps only in the ideal case. There is no room for multiple motives: the testee's only legitimate goal is to attain a high score. Emotions and feelings are irrelevant, except perhaps for the bittersweet glow that may accompany the "Need for Achievement." Cognitive development, my third discriminant, is less irrelevant: children are certainly expected to answer questions at age 9 that they failed at age 7. But their growth has little to do with the test itself. Until recently, cognitive development was of as little concern to test constructors as to programmers.

It is not only the testing profession which has taken a narrowly academic view of human intelligence, but experimental cognitive psychology as well. The subjects who flock into our laboratories in ever increasing numbers are given very particular test-like instructions. In fact, many college-student subjects habitually refer to experiments as "tests," though we try to persuade them otherwise. In such studies the subjects may be supposed to classify characters, report how many dots appeared, or say whether two forms are identical or different. They are *not* supposed to get bored, wonder if the experiment is worth doing, produce response sequences for their own amusement, or quit. Yet often these would be intelligent courses of action. We have all read of experiments (other people's) that seemed stupid enough to drop out of.

The behavior of subjects in such studies often can be (and sometimes has been) successfully simulated. Behavior on some intelligence tests has also been simulated, as have solution patterns on a wide variety of puzzles. These achievements are far from trivial. As a duffer at chess and as one profoundly out of tune with the Towers of Hanoi, I am enormously impressed with what, for example, Simon's programs can do. Nevertheless, I prefer to stress what they cannot do. My three favorite characteristics—development, emotionality, multiple motivation—are still missing. (For a contrary view and arguments against my 1963 paper, see Simon, 1967.) I now see, however, that the absence of these characteristics is no handicap if one's goal is to simulate Academic Intelligence alone, since it lacks them also.

## Comments on Simon's Chapter

I have few specific criticisms of Simon's chapter. As always, I am dazzled by the scope of his thinking and the ingenuity of his programs. In emphasizing that the programs model Academic Intelligence rather than intelligence in general, I do not mean to deny that it is being modeled well. It takes skills of a very high order to devise four different solutions to the Towers of Hanoi, to see that the Towers problem is isomorphic to the Himalayan Tea Ceremony, or to realize that a very wide class of patterns can be described with a group structure based only on "same," "next," and "complement."

One rather general objection to these programs may be worth raising. Like most other examples of Artificial Intelligence, they tend to describe mental activity in terms of two separate stages, operating independently and in succession. The first stage recognizes patterns; the second solves problems. Usually only one stage or the other is realized in a given program. This separation may not always be appropriate. Pattern recognition and problem solving are often interdependent in human thought—mutually embedded in each other. A person may look for certain patterns only because he is solving a particular type of problem. As Klahr points out, we are not always in a problem-solving attitude. For example one does not ordinarily notice, or take even half-seriously, the fact that the vowels in a given word occur in alphabetical order (as they do in HALF-SERIOUSLY). It would become relevant only if one were working with letter sequences. Simulation by two independent stages would be successful in this case only for subjects who were already working on the right problem with the right goals.

Simon's comment on the "small" magnitude of individual differences in IQ deserves some discussion. He notes the vast differences in chess memory between masters and inexperienced players—differences which are plausibly attributed to the amounts of time each has spent playing chess. Differences in IQ performance, by contrast, are much smaller. What we call a mental age of 12, for example (that is, the performance of the average 12-year-old on IQ tests) is reached by nearly everyone in America. A child with an IQ of 150 attains it when he is 8 years old; another with an IQ of 75 only when he is 16. One way of accounting for the difference between them, Simon argues, is to assume that both learn the same kind of things in the same way from their experiences, but the high-IQ child spends twice as much time in learning (e.g., he may be attentive for ten minutes out of every hour rather than five). For this reason, one may suppose, he takes only half as many years as his dull-witted school-fellow to reach any given mental age. Now since one rarely finds two persons whose IQs differ by more than a two-to-one ratio, everyone must have a good deal of opportunity to do the appropriate kind of learning. This argument leads Simon to conclude that test performance must depend primarily on abilities that pervade almost every kind of human performance and experience.

This argument is circular. It begins by *assuming* that IQ differences are created by differential attention to learning opportunities throughout life, and ends by *concluding* that these opportunities are indeed universally present. If increases in mental age above six are heavily dependent on school-based skills rather than life experience in general, for example, a learning ratio of two to one would no longer explain individual differences. Indeed, the differences may not be based on time invested at all. They may reflect variations in skill of some other kind, not unlike the sharp differences between two chess players that may remain even when both have devoted an equal number of hours to the game. Thus, the dependence of mental age on the time spent attending during the child's entire life is merely an assumption, and not a particularly plausible one. It is from this assumption alone, and not from any empirical observation, that Simon draws his conclusion about the pervasiveness of test-relevant abilities. The facts may be otherwise.

## Comments on Klahr's Chapter

I have stressed that human thinking undergoes cognitive development whereas computer programs generally do not. For this reason, Klahr's chapter was of particular interest to me. Klahr, and others whose work he describes, has tried to simulate children's performance on Piagetian conservation problems.

Piaget's conception of intelligence is by no means "Academic," in the sense I have been belaboring. Although some of his experimental tasks have a puzzle-like quality, he is not essentially interested in puzzles. For Piaget, intelligence is a matter of increasingly adequate adaptation to the world. The child's mental structure *accommodates* itself to the world by means of repeated encounters. Thus accommodated, he is better able to *assimilate* increasingly subtler aspects of reality. If the process of accommodation could be successfully modeled in a program, we might indeed understand cognitive development far better than we do now.

Unfortunately, Klahr's program does not actually simulate accommodation at all, and does not undergo cognitive change. Although it has something to do with "conservation of number," it does not *acquire* conservation. What is worse, perhaps, is that it does not even *have* conservation. It has what Klahr considers to be conservation, but I must disagree. What the program actually does is compare quantities $X$ and $Y$, using either of two methods. First, $X$ and $Y$ may be evaluated and compared directly. Second, the program may apply what Klahr calls a "conservation rule." This only means that the system will be guided by what it *remembers* about $X$ and $Y$. "In conservation, the idea is to avoid the entire process of quantitative comparison, relying instead upon the results of previous executions of QC and a conservation rule" (Klahr, Chapter 6, page 116).

To me, this is a caricature of what an adult, or a postconservation child, does when he sees water poured from a tall thin glass to a short fat one and says the quantity is unchanged, or when he insists that two rows of five coins have equal numbers regardless of their spacing. The adult could look at both glasses and estimate that they hold roughly equal amounts, without having seen any act of pouring at all! He has a notion of "volume," involving the reciprocity of height and width as well as a notion of reversible action, which the young child lacks. Similarly, he has a notion of "number," involving possible isomorphisms and matchings, which is a part of his understanding of the world. Correct performance on conservation tasks reflects these understandings themselves; it is not produced simply by a greater reliance on memory. Indeed, it is only *because* he has these notions that the child can rely more on memory! Remembering how big something was, or how many there were, is just one of several conservation devices available to the child who has gained this understanding.

A further example may help to clarify this point. Is memory really the basis of adult performance in conservation tasks? Suppose you saw water being poured from one glass to another of equal size and shape, and that the water did *not* fill the second glass as high as the first. Would you rely on memory, and announce that the amount of water had remained unchanged? Surely not; you would see that there was less and ask how the trick had been done. Did the second glass have a false bottom? The first a hollow core? Something must be wrong; liquids can't shrink like that! Thus, people can exhibit their understanding of conservation not only by rejecting perceptual information in favor of what they remember, but also by rejecting memory in favor of what they perceive. Klahr has made the mistake of treating the conservation task as if it were an academic puzzle, and he has come up with a heuristic solution. Children do not achieve conservation by acquiring a new heuristic, however; it is a part of their increasing understanding of the world itself.

The other main difficulty with the program has already been mentioned (by Klahr as well as by me). It does *not* undergo accommodation; it does not learn.

Klahr agrees that the issue of self-modification is central to the conception of intelligence, but neither his own system nor any of those reviewed by him meet this issue successfully. For better or worse, my 1963 claim that Artificial Intelligence has not modeled cognitive development remains valid. There is a reason for this. The development of human intelligence occurs in a real environment with coherent properties of its own. Many of these properties vary greatly from one situation to another; others remain invariant at a deeper level. As long as programs do not represent this *environment* systematically, in at least some of its complexity, they cannot represent cognitive growth either. They can only treat intellectual life as a series of puzzles, not as a sustained encounter with reality. By this measure, they must fall short of their goals.

One more general remark may be appropriate. Many chapters in this book report attempts to make the sophisticated resources of modern psychology bear on the problem of intelligence. In such an effort, one should be very sure of one's purposes. The general problem of intelligence—of how people choose the best course of action in problematic situations—is not only difficult but also *serious*. It has enormous political, social, and philosophical implications. Are we ready for it? Perhaps we are indeed prudent to settle for the lesser problem I have termed Academic Intelligence: How do people find the answers to test questions and school exercises? As academics, we are well fitted to undertake this task, and it is not unimportant. We have already made a good deal of progress with it, and will make more. Experimental and differential psychologists are joining forces for the first time in many years, and the techniques of Artificial Intelligence will reinforce and strengthen their enterprise. We must be careful not to expect too much, however. Academic Intelligence has a limited scope, and even the problems that surround testing and schooling in America run very deep. In addressing ourselves to them, we should strive to be modest as well as intelligent; otherwise we may deserve neither adjective in the long run.

## REFERENCES

Cole, M., & Scribner, S. *Culture and thought.* New York: Wiley, 1974.

Cole, M., Gay, J., Glick, J. A., & Sharp, D. W. *The cultural context context of learning and thinking.* New York: Basic Books, 1971.

Gladwin, T. *East is a big bird.* Cambridge, Massachusetts: Harvard University Press, 1970.

Jencks, C. *Inequality.* New York: Basic Books, 1972.

Neisser, U. The imitation of man by machine. *Science,* 1963, **139,** 193–197.

Scribner, S., & Cole, M. Cognitive consequences of formal and informal education. *Science,* 1973, **182,** 553–559.

Simon, H. A. Motivational and emotional controls of cognition. *Psychological Review,* 1967, **74,** 29–39.

# Part III

## INTELLIGENCE AS ADAPTATION

# 8
# Human Intelligence as Adaptation: An Ethological Approach

William R. Charlesworth

*University of Minnesota*

What follows is an attempt to apply ethology (the study of the habits and characteristics of animals in their natural habitats from an evolutionary viewpoint) to the phenomenon of human intelligence. Such an application cannot be optimal in the space permitted, nor totally professional. The author has not completed all the training needed to develop the full range of methodological and conceptual skills necessary to apply the ethological approach to something as complex as human intelligence. Nevertheless, a start in this direction must be made. The present state of our knowledge and the great personal and social implications of intelligence testing today make it necessary for psychologists to broaden their approach to intelligence. Opening their doors to other disciplines such as ethology, in the author's estimation, is one way to achieve this.

Ethologizing about human behavior has become a popular exercise, and, as most of us are aware, the results of this exercise have been quite mixed. The literature on human ethology is a confused collection of reckless speculations, clever insights, and respectable hypotheses backed by various admixtures of hard and soft data. This state of affairs is partially due to the fact that readers, writers, and even researchers at times, fail to distinguish between general working principles and hypotheses that guide research on one hand and generalizations that are the products of much detailed observation and experiment on the other. This can be particularly said about evolutionary arguments for the origins and evolution of intelligence. There has been much theorizing about it, but a vast amount of empirical work still has to be done before any evolutionary theory of intelligence can be said to have a solid basis in fact. While this chapter belongs to the class of speculation and quasi-theorizing, it also sketches out a methodological approach to obtaining facts on intelligence and its possible adaptive significance which will some day hopefully justify its existence.

By and large, psychologists have historically tended to focus upon what animals and humans *can do* when presented with test and laboratory situations. In contrast, the ethologist's emphasis has been primarily upon what animals *actually do* in response to the challenges of their natural habitats. Because of this difference in emphasis, two different approaches toward the nature and origin of intelligence are possible. While the ethologist historically has not tackled the problem of human intelligence, he has the conceptual and methodological tools to do so. The ethologist's main concepts derive from evolutionary theory and center around the notion that most major characteristics of animals, behavioral as well as morphological, are products of evolution and thereby represent the species' latest attempt at adaptation to its environmental niche. Intelligence can be viewed as representing one such adaptation.

The present discussion is ethological in the sense that it views intelligence as a mode of adaptation to everyday challenges. How this process of adaptation is carried on by individuals is not yet known. There is a method, though, employed by ethologists (as well as some psychologists), that gives us access to this process. This method involves prolonged observation of individuals in their natural habitats and is therefore in sharp contrast to psychometric testing which collects data from individuals under controlled conditions within a relatively short period of time. The main thesis of this chapter is that by observing how individuals deal with the problematic nature of their environments, it will be possible to obtain a better estimate of their intelligence or adaptive capacity. Once a detailed picture of the intelligent behavior of a large number of individuals is obtained, psychologists will be in a position to devise intelligence tests for general usage that more accurately reflect the demand characteristics of the environments in which the individual's intelligence has developed and to which the individual must respond on an everyday basis.

## DEFINITIONS

### Intelligence and Intelligent Behavior

For purposes of the present discussion intelligence is defined as a disposition to behave intelligently. The aim of this definition is to emphasize the importance of distinguishing between intelligence, which is an inferred property (disposition) of the individual, and intelligent behavior, which is an observable portion of the individual's overall behavior, behavior produced in the context of the everyday natural environment as well as in such contrived settings as test and laboratory situations. Intelligent behavior is viewed here as being elicited by problematic situations, but is, as such, not acquired or learned. What is acquired is intelligence, the disposition. The process of acquiring the raw material of intelligence (that is, the memory material derived from sensory stimulation) takes place during *ontogenesis* through the learning that results when the individual interacts with his environment. The process of acquiring the operations of intelligence (that is, the multitude of cognitive operations that make intelligent behavior possible) takes place during *phylogenesis* when the nervous system mechanisms responsible for the intelligent behavior of a particular species are "shaped" by the forces of natural and sexual selection that take place during the species' interaction with its environment. As a disposition, then, intelligence consists of sense knowledge and cognitive operations.

Intelligent behavior is viewed here as having two major characteristics: (1) it is behavior that generally aids individuals in their attempts to adapt to problematic situations resulting from imbalances in their interactions with the environment; and (2) it is behavior having certain characteristics which compel us to conclude that cognitive processes are organizing and controlling it.

## Adaptation to Problematic Situations

Adaptation has various meanings. In biology the term usually refers to a species' coping with environmental challenges successfully enough to insure its survival in subsequent generations. Such coping ultimately results in changes in the species' gene pool as a consequence of natural and sexual selection. Results of coping can be observed in the form of physical characteristics (e.g., morphological or physiological) or in the form of behaviors. Historically, the former have been viewed as constituting the main mode of an animal's adaptation. However, as Mayr (1970) points out, an animal's behavior rather than its physical characteristics may well be its most important mode of adaptation, in the sense that behavior is heavily implicated in the evolution of species. Reproductive success is frequently used as an index of successful coping. In the behavioral sciences adapting usually refers to a particular individual's coping successfully with environmental problems. The quality of the individual's life, his or her material, social, personal, and sometimes reproductive success are used as indices of successful coping. In the present discussion, adaptation by means of intelligent behavior is viewed in terms of the single individual. However, in doing so it should be stressed that the long-range, species-related determinants and consequences of such behavior cannot be overlooked. If they were overlooked, it would not be possible to argue the ethological position; such a position requires that behavior be viewed in terms of its possible long-range phylogenetic function as well as its immediate individual function.

As for problematic situations, they can be most generally described as imbalances or upsets in the equilibrium established between an individual (or species) and its environment, upsets which, if continued, could lead ultimately to injury or extinction. What is implicit in this definition is that the individual possesses built-in survival plans which specify in more or less general terms the kinds of environmental conditions he or she has to have in order to survive, as well as in terms of its immediate survival value and its implications for successful ontogenesis.
ways in which such conditions can be established or reestablished if they are lacking. The concept of physical, psychological, and social needs generally covers

what is meant here by built-in survival plans. The individual encounters a problem when the natural environment does not immediately meet the needs characterizing the plan, that is, when the environment makes unusual, atypical or unexpected demands upon the individual.

Stressing that the environment is the potential source of problems for the individual is crucial for the present thesis. As will be pointed out later, from the ethologist's viewpoint it does not make sense to talk about adaptation without something to adapt to. And if one designates intelligence as an important mode of adaptation, then intelligent behavior has to be viewed in terms of environmentally posed problems. Consequently, those measuring the potential for such behavior have to take the environment into consideration at one time or another. That this has conventionally not been done is a point that will be expanded upon later.

## Cognitive Control

The second property of intelligent behavior, namely that it is organized and controlled by cognitive processes, sets it off from such adaptive behavior as reflexes, taxes, tropisms, fixed action patterns, and overlearned habits that occur without any, or with very little, cognitive mediation. The attribution of cognitive processes to intelligent behavior presupposes at least three elements:

1. There are operations involved such as comparing, recalling, separating, combining, analyzing, conceptualizing, and counting. These operations, as noted above, are viewed here as inherent properties of nervous system functioning which are shaped by phylogenesis and hence in a loose sense inherited by the individual.

2. There is the raw material such as long- and short-term memory traces, immediate perceptions or sensations, and any other kind of information upon which cognitive operations operate. This raw material is viewed here as being acquired by the individual during his or her own lifetime.

3. There is an element of goal consciousness to intelligent behavior that sets it off from fortuitous behavior or behavior such as reflexes, fixed action patterns, and other instinctual acts which appear "blind" and compelled. Goal consciousness implies that the behavior is planned, hence capable of being altered depending upon external circumstances, and of being terminated once the goal is obtained.

In summary, then, intelligent behavior is defined here as behavior under the control of cognitive processes and employed toward the solution of problems which challenge the well-being, needs, plans, and survival of the individual.

Since problems are an ubiquitous property of every individual's environment at every level of his or her development, intelligent behavior, as the main mode human adaptation, is also ubiquitous. As a result such behavior can be observed and studied as the individual goes about the task of everyday living; it need not be studied or assessed only on the basis of tests aimed at eliciting it under controlled conditions. For this reason, and because it serves an adaptive function, intelligent behavior is a legitimate object of ethological research.

Before developing the main thesis further, it should be made clear that the ethological analysis of behavior incorporates within it questions concerning the possible origins and evolutionary history of the dispositions of the behavior under consideration. Intelligent behavior can be subject to this analysis in the same way as social, migratory, feeding, or any other behaviors that fall within the ethologist's purview. As will be seen in the next section, intelligence as a disposition has already been the focus of evolutionary analysis. It is this focus (labeled here as phylogenetic) which requires some attention.

## PHYLOGENESIS OF INTELLIGENCE

### Theory and Speculations

By the end of the nineteenth century there was a widespread conviction that intelligence, as inferred from fossil remains and other geological data, had gradually evolved over time in various species of animals (see Boring, 1950). Evidence for increases in the brain size of primates was used to argue that intelligence began accelerating (evolutionarily) in the primate order and within a relatively very short period of time reached its pinnacle in *Homo sapiens*. The dominant hypothesis underlying such a conviction was that animals with relatively large brains were better able in the long run to adapt to most new environmental challenges. The functions of the enlarged brains made themselves manifest in high levels of flexibility, planning, organization, and reality orientation in the everyday behavior required for adaptation.

It should be noted here that such a hypothesis is based on many inferences of events and processes, none of which can be subject to direct observation or experimental verification, simply because the phenomena they refer to are historically absent, irreversible, and novel (see Nogar, 1962). Such a hypothesis, therefore, is forced to depend for its credibility upon many kinds of knowledge obtained from outside of the realm of the fossil information available on brain characteristics. For example, knowledge of the various features of the environment (terrain, availability of food, predators, protection, etc.) under which the animal lived at the time is considered simultaneously with the animal's fossil brain characteristics in order to make estimates of its level of intelligence.

Apart from arguing that brain characteristics, behavior, and environmental characteristics are involved in evolution, it can also be argued that the intelligence level of any particular species at any point in time is a product of the evolutionary history of the species. Lorenz (1962), for example, made this point in his 1941 discussion of Kantian categories of thought and how such categories could be accounted for by evolutionary theory. He updated this point more recently (Lorenz, 1973) in a discussion of the natural history of human knowing ("Erkennen"). In capsule form, Lorenz's thesis is that those brain functions making perception and cognition (hence, intelligent behavior) possible are not coincidences, but products of millions of years of evolution during which environmental demands selected out, strengthened, and shaped basic nervous functions by acting directly upon the behaviors made possible by such functions. According to Lorenz, such a process, operating over many generations, led gradually to a greater and greater match between central nervous system function and the environmental demands upon the behavior served by such functions. Just as the horse's hoof became adapted to the physical properties of the steppe, the environment in which the horse evolved, so has the human brain come to match in its cognitive capacities the stable and recurring demand properties of the environment in which the human evolved. Donald Campbell (1966) argues a similar point when he defends the notion that in human evolution man made tremendous gains in adaptiveness by becoming increasingly able to represent "in stored templates" information which modeled useful invariances found in his environment.

Actually many early phychologists maintained a similar view. American functionalists, for example, such as James, Ladd, Hall, and Angell (see Boring ,1950), were convinced that mental processes including perceptions, thoughts, volitions, and emotions were biologically-given functions or evolutionary products, which aided the organism to adapt to and control its environment. Even Hull (1937), who concentrated heavily upon learning processes during ontogenesis, attributed man's preeminence in the world to his capacity for adaptive behavior which was controlled by that hypothetical entity called mind. However, unlike those with a biological orientation, most psychologists tended to view the adaptation conferred by intelligence pretty much *in vacuo.* That is, they did not concern themselves with examining the nature of the environment which required intelligent behavior for adaptation. As will be seen below, this lack of concern was also reflected in the psychometric approach which eventually came to dominate our current view of intelligence.

In passing, it should be pointed out that, although the biological view of human intelligence is plausible, it is not based on hard facts. That evolution of the brain (more accurately, the skull) took place is a certain fact. That the behavior controlled by the brain also evolved (became more adaptive, more organized, more complex, etc.) is *probably* a fact. The actual process by which evolution of the brain and behavior took place is not known and nowhere near being a fact. It is still only an assumption (most probably a correct one) that brain, behavior, and environment interacted over time to produce the higher levels of intelligence now seen in humans.

## Empirical Approaches

A distinctive characteristic of the phylogenetic view of intelligence is its reliance upon a cross-disciplinary commitment to clarify how and why intelligence evolved the way it did. This commitment is shared by ethologists in their approach to behavior in general, and distinguishes their approach from that which has historically been taken by many psychologists. In light of this, it is instructive to take brief cognizance of the kinds of empirical disciplines engaged in the phylogenetic analysis of intelligence.

At least five distinctive disciplines are committed to establishing an empirical basis for the assertion that intelligence is an evolutionary product. They are: (1) the brain evolutionists such as Jerison (1973), who view historical and species variations in brain size and morphology in terms of intellectual adaptation; (2) the archaeologist–ecologists such as Klein (1973), who study the adaptations of early man as inferred from his artifacts, the nature of his environment at the time, and the kinds of demands the environment placed upon him; (3) the comparative animal psychologists such as Rensch (1972, 1973), who conduct comparative studies of intellectual functioning in various species and attempt to link them to phylogenetic adaptations; (4) certain anthropologists such as Mason (1895/1966), who document preliterate man's intellectual accomplishments in terms of his inventions, tool-making, and general problem-solving skills, and the role they played in his adaptation; and (5) certain behavioral geneticists such as Thiessen (1972), who argue for the necessity of linking genetics and evolutionary biology via the concept of adaptation.

As I see it, a psychologist aspiring to understand intelligence from an ethological viewpoint would have to become familiar with these five disciplines, because it is intrinsic to ethology to concern itself both with an evolutionary–historical analysis of behavior and with a contemporary, environmental, comparative, and developmental analysis. The conventional psychometric approach to intelligence has tended to ignore both the historical phylogenetic dimension of intelligence as well as its contemporary role in meeting environmental demands. These omissions in the psychometric approach have been largely responsible, in my estimation, for the scientific malaise and social difficulty intelligence testing is currently in.

## PSYCHOMETRICS OF INTELLIGENCE

In light of the present definition of intelligence as adaptation, the psychometric approach will be examined in terms of two questions:

1. How much does the psychometric approach contribute to our knowledge of human adaptation in general?
2. How effectively does it measure this adaptation?

Intelligence: Measured, Not Observed

According to such writers as Murphy (1930) and Sattler (1974) mental testing developed in close connection with two nineteenth century traditions—that of general measurement psychology (Ebbinghaus, Weber, Fechner, and others) and that of differential psychology (Galton, Cattell, Wissler, and Binet). It is true that Galton's interest in identifying superior individuals (they and their families flourished, thus "proving" their adaptive superiority) developed as part of the Darwinian movement. But neither Galton nor those involved in general measurement psychology indicated interest in viewing intelligence as a natural everyday behavioral phenomenon in the way Darwin and his followers did. Nor was there any apparent interest amongst psychometricians in employing a naturalistic–observational–descriptive approach to intelligence, the approach that characterized Darwin's efforts as well as the efforts of the first ethologists, who followed in his footsteps—namely, Whitman, Heinroth, Craig, Spaulding, and Lorenz. In other words, there appears to be no historical evidence suggesting that mental testing developed out of the same tradition from which current ethology has developed. The dominant idea ruling psychometric circles at the period of its birth was that intelligence was a dispositional property of an individual which could be tapped and measured in controlled settings. It was not viewed as primarily something that could (or perhaps should) be observed in action in natural settings. Intelligent behaviors were presumed to be what intelligent persons engaged in, but were either not worth observing or at least very difficult or inconvenient to observe. The fact that early scientific psychology was very heavily laboratory-oriented reinforced this tendency.

This early emphasis on intelligence as a disposition to be measured rather than observed was not devoid, however, of some connections with biology. The early use of twins and relatives in intelligence studies is ample evidence that psychometricians did consider the role biological factors played in intelligence. Survival of the fittest (the most intelligent, among other things) was also studied, but evidence for survival was very grossly defined and usually based upon inferences drawn from such facts as achievement, profession, social rank, and income, many of which could have been consequences of chance social connections and historical factors rather than individual performance.

Piaget's (1952, 1960) theory of intelligence also has a biological dimension to it. He conceives of intelligence as an extension of biological adaptation. While biologically oriented, Piaget does not see himself as a descendant of Galton and the psychometricians who followed him. In fact, Piaget's work partly evolved as a reaction to the standard psychometric approach of the time. Not only did he begin his work by departing from standardized techniques of administering tests, he also ignored the main goal of psychometric testing, which is to discriminate quantitatively between individuals. Despite this, in the broad sense of the term, he still remains a psychometrician; his job has been primarily that of measuring cognitive traits and processes. Unlike most others, though, he concentrates on similarities between groups of individuals of the same age and differences between groups of different ages. In this regard Piaget is not a differential psychologist as the psychometricians are, but a developmental biologist–psychologist interested in universals and invariants that characterize adaptive behavior at various periods of development. But this orientation does not bring him in line with the ethological approach. Apart from observing his own children in their natural environment at home during their infancy, Piaget did the bulk of his work in controlled settings. Furthermore, Piaget's effort cannot be characterized as guided by evolutionary theory or sensitive to the importance, implied by the theory, of careful, detailed, and systematic observational records of behavior in natural surroundings.

In summary, then, despite the fact that biological considerations characterize two major movements within the study of intelligence, the kind of biological thinking that characterizes the ethologist's approach has not played any significant role in either. This, of course, does not lessen the significance of the efforts of both movements for understanding intelligence.

In spite of what was just said, it is nevertheless true that intelligence testing got its official start from a concern for problems of adaptation in the real world. The problem of detecting early differences in children's abilities to adapt to life and the school situation has been the major impetus to the development of intelligence testing. Alfred Binet was commissioned by the French government to study the intellectual capacities of children in order to determine their ability to profit from education. Special concern was shown for children identified as being retarded and consequently incapable of making a normal school adjustment. In Binet's mind, and in others' at the time, intelligence and adjustment were closely related, and adjustment was related to the kind of environment the child was in.

Although, as Binet and Simon (1905) pointed out, there were three methods for recognizing "inferior states of intelligence"—medical, pedagogical, and psychological (which was predominantly testing)—naturalistic observation was not among them. Some efforts were made to observe retarded children in their school and nonschool environments in order to determine what they could and could not do. Their performance was subsequently compared with that of normal children. To this extent Binet was within the Darwinian, biological, ethological tradition. However, as far as I can determine, Binet's observations and those of others he relied upon were not carried out in any systematic, exhaustive, and rigorous way. The methods used (not unlike those generally used at the time) were casual, intuitive, ad libitum, global, and void of attempts to obtain or quantify interobserver agreement or to produce frequency data which could be subjected to statistical analysis. This lack of rigor, which was definitely not the case with their approach to test construction and test data analysis, suggests that it was Binet's intention to know exactly what it was in the child's environment that required adaptation by means of cognitive skills and how frequently it occurred. Such knowledge, according to the present argument, would have been a good start toward identifying the abilities needed to do such adapting. The observational–ecological aspect of Binet and Simon's concern for adaptational differences between the normal and the retarded was greatly outweighed by the psychometric aspect, an aspect which they and those who followed them obviously developed very effectively on a massive scale.

## The Problem of External Criteria

*Intelligence tests and life "success."*   After the impact of Binet's effort was felt in the United States through the efforts of Terman and others, the editorial board of the *Journal of Educational Psychology* held a symposium in 1921 on intelligence and its measurement. Seventeen "leading investigators" were invited and produced a large corpus of ideas, definitions, facts, and hypotheses, some of which are relevant here because they show that many of the basic notions of the present thesis are not new. Thorndike (1921), for example, argued for defining intelligence (he used the word "intellect") as "the power of good responses from the point of view of truth or fact" and was interested in future research concentrating on establishing correlations of tests with "each feature of the intellectual work of the world." Terman (1921) followed up by arguing for the "continued search for outside criteria," although they must be discriminated with care. Colvin (1921) considered the most important concept of intelligence to be the one which emphasizes the ability of the individual to learn to adjust himself to his environment. And Pinter (1921) urged making "tests function in the school and life in general." In short, many of these scholars were clearly aware of the need for viewing intelligence as an important facet of everyday adaptation and hence the need for establishing external criteria for evaluating test results. In spite of this awareness, though, no concrete proposal was made to identify, define, and measure life adjustment (other than, of course, to use such global criteria as school achievement and job success).

The situation since 1921 has apparently not changed much. Nunnally (1967), in his monograph on psychometric theory, discusses ecological factors and points out that at present we "do not know to what extent our factors of human ability extend beyond the 'laboratory' to the things that people do everyday [p. 466]." Also Tyler (1971) notes that the IQ does not permit us to determine how flexible the person is in adapting to new situations, how he will adjust and learn in nonschool situations. More recently Jencks *et al.* (1972) point out that the IQ score is limited in predicting occupational success (although it is a better predictor than the kind of school experience the child had). And most recently, Sattler (1974) points out that IQ test scores ably predict educational achievement, but not nontest behavior and nonacademic ability, both of which certainly must constitute a large part of the individual's ability to adapt to life's problems after he leaves school. Terman's work with the gifted (Terman *et al.*, 1925–1959) demonstrates that it is possible to identify some of the major cognitive abilities that are implicated in successful life adjustment. The role of general intelligence (*g*) or of specific capabilities (*s*), such as number, verbal, spatial, reasoning, memory, or word fluency abilities, in everyday adaptation is most probably very significant. But obtaining measures of them, as well as of special talents, on the basis of test behavior does not constitute evidence that they are directly involved (that is, independent of other factors) in the process of everyday adaptation. That Terman and others in the testing tradition have made a very significant contribution to our understanding of the nature of intelligence and some of its correlates is, of course, indisputable. However, it must be admitted that one hundred years of intelligence testing have, at best, been only moderately successful in developing methods for effectively measuring the individual's ability to cope with life's problems.

How and why the psychometrics of intelligence developed the particular way it did is the job of historians to determine. One thing, though, is apparent. As is true of most of us, psychometricians have not been reluctant to do whatever comes most conveniently, namely collecting data on individuals in the shortest and materially most economical fashion possible. Using tests as the paradigm method, psychologists interested in individual differences quickly institutionalized an assessment procedure that very successfully began mapping out the cognitive abilities subjects possessed. But the procedure has not contributed substantially to our knowledge of what subjects actually did with such abilities or whether they employed them at all in nontest situations. As different tests began to proliferate at a rapid rate, testers became more and more preoccupied with determining how different test scores intercorrelated with each other or with school grades and achievement scores. Such criteria, however, as we know, are only indirectly relevant to the more important question of what is done in life outside of school. In short, the testing movement did not concentrate upon obtaining adequate criterion measurements (that is, based on field studies) against which to validate its vast amounts of data.

This is easy to understand. Measuring life success and observing how one actually goes about achieving it is obviously a much more difficult, value-ridden, and painstaking job than determining an individual's college grades or income. But as a consequence of not having developed better means of obtaining correction and validation from the outside (for example, by employing other measures of intelligence such as observation) the testing industry has come to appear in many public eyes as a vast, well-funded *folie à deux* in which test-giver and test-taker engage in mutually reinforcing behavior which may or may not lead to results which have a bearing on the test taker's outside behavior.

One argument underlying such a view of testing is as follows: The human brain is a superbly productive and accommodating organ which can produce as many answers to tests as there are tests or create as many tests as there are individuals to answer them. The brain is also constructed such that it insures that some test answers will inevitably correlate with others. In the presence of such a complex and hence versatile organ it seems more reasonable, therefore, to ask what it *normally* does than what it *can* do. In intelligence testing terms, it seems more reasonable to find out what individuals do that is intelligent and then, on the basis of what is found, determine ways to measure their abilities to do these intelligent things. It seems much more parsimonious to proceed this way than to test for all of an individual's abilities and then hope he or she employs some of them in outside test situations so that predictions are possible. It is true that testing has succeeded in identifying many cognitive operations which appear intuitively to be highly generalizable, highly usable, life-valuable operations that are responsible for intelligent behavior. But we actually know next to nothing about how (and how frequently) these operations function in everyday life. Hence we are in a very weak position to justify the practical value of much of the psychometrics of intelligence as it is now constituted. We are in a much weaker position when we attempt to base intervention programs upon test scores or make generalizations about groups of individuals.

*Adapting to specific environments.*    The consequences of this weakness in the psychometric approach are very apparent today. The crisis that intelligence testing is currently facing does not only reflect political and racial movements. The crisis would have developed without such movements, since it has become clear that the base upon which present intelligence testing has developed has been too narrow.

As many persons, especially anthropologists, have been arguing for years, adaptation for an American black, a poor Appalachian white, or a Peruvian peasant may be quite different from that of a middle-class American white. But it is interesting to note, as far as I can determine, that there is very little convincing data that has been produced to support this argument. Apart from the work of a few good novelists and a handful of scientists such as Barker (1963; Barker & Wright, 1955), Brunswick (1955), and Willems (1965), there is relatively little scientific concern for studying the nature of environments and determining whether environmental challenges for various subgroups of the population are basically different from those for other subgroups, and therefore require different modes of adaptation.

It should be mentioned in this vein that testing can profit from paying attention to the ethologist's stance in this matter. When an ethologist encounters an animal he does not know, he approaches the animal on the assumption that it is already more or less well adapted to its environment (Jolly, 1972). In other words, the ethologist assumes that the animal has already acted intelligently (or instinctively, i.e., without cognitive operations) under its environmental circumstances (otherwise it would not be alive), and that it most probably already has well-developed dispositions to continue to act that way. The ethologist will also expect to detect individual differences between animals the more he or she becomes acquainted with additional members of the species. Neither individual differences nor individual similarities are ignored by the evolutionary approach to behavior.

The same sets of assumptions made about animals can, of course, be applied to humans. If a psychologist or anthropologist goes into a lower socioeconomic section of town, into a ghetto, into the jungles of the Amazon, or even into the back wards of a mental institution, he or she should assume that the individuals in these places have already made their adaptations. These adaptations may be very different from the ones with which the researcher is familiar. But as ethologists must accept the often strange behavior patterns of the animals they observe, so must they accept those of unknown humans if they wish to understand why they act the way they do. It is fair to say that many psychologists have fallen into the very same trap they have condemned older, "less enlightened" ages for falling into—namely, that all things must be judged by the same measuring stick, the stick that conveniently turns out to be the one they themselves have constructed. The failures of most cross-cultural intelligence testing, for example, have testified to this (see Goodnow, Chapter 9).

However, knowing the nature of other *persons* is not enough. One must know what their *environment* requires of them to understand the nature of their abilities and how they use them. A psychometric measure of a person's abilities will not insure that the abilities tapped in this way represent those the person uses everyday. If a person performs poorly on a test it is reasonable to ask how much that test actually represents the common everyday environmental tests the individual has been put to and to which he or she has become adapted. In a discussion of the evolution of mind, Lashley (1949) insightfully noted that, "Unless the experimenter has wide experience with the animals he studies and adapts his questions to their modes of behavior, the results give little information about their true capacities [pp. 28–29]." Hinde (1966) makes a similar point and illustrates an important feature of the ethologist's approach: "If a species does appear to be deficient in some faculty, as defined by a particular type of test, we must still refer back to the natural situation to assess the extent to which this is compensated for by the development of other faculties [p. 422]." It is depressing to think of all the misunderstandings about subgroups of people that could have been avoided if this approach had been taken by test psychologists during the past century.

If the final arbiter of an intelligence test's value is how well it can predict and aid in explaining behavior outside of the test situation, then Hinde's point has to be taken with dead seriousness. Conventional testing, while superior to intuition and to much of common sense, still has no adequate foundation of information on the problematic nature of the individual's environment. Until it has such a foundation, the psychometrics of intelligence will continue in a hit–miss fashion, guided by convenience, intuition, tradition, or whatever it has been guided by that has brought it to its current crisis. A long and careful look at intelligent behavior in action in the field is, according to the present argument, the most effective way of building such a foundation. This is what is meant here by an ethological approach to the study of intelligence.

## AN ETHOLOGY OF INTELLIGENCE

In light of the foregoing, it is proposed here that we cease to emphasize the invention of new intelligence tests, or to strengthen relationships between different tests that have only weak connections with external criteria of human adaptation, and instead attempt to establish an empirical basis for adaptational criteria by studying intelligent behavior as it occurs in everyday life in the natural environment. The distinctively ethological feature of such a proposal is that it combines two heretofore separate methodological and conceptual approaches: (1) an approach that emphasizes intelligent behavior as a mode of adaptation to everyday environmental demands and hence requires naturalistic observation of such behavior relative to such demands; and (2) an approach that emphasizes both phylogenetic (historical) and comparative (cross-species contemporary) considerations in formulating research problems and interpreting results. Such a multidisciplinary approach is obviously unwieldly and more time consuming than conventional approaches, but it is the only way, in the author's estimation, of achieving a comprehensive and satisfying picture of the nature and role of intelligence in the human. Such an approach has been successfully employed in the area of children's play (see Smith, 1975) by such ethologists as Blurton-Jones (1967), Konner (1972), Loizos (1967), and Smith and Connolly (1972), and to date has proved very informative.

There are at least four mutually complementary ways ethological study of intelligence can proceed. Three will be discussed briefly: (1) a paleocomparative study of primate cognitive response to problematic environmental demands; (2) a conceptual and empirical analysis of common sense as it is implicated in everyday adaptive behavior; and (3) a study of the cognitive–behavioral mechanisms underlying the failure of human individuals to reach reproductive age or to reproduce, either because of accidents and injuries or because of severe mental retardation and other deviancies which limit reproduction. The fourth way—naturalistic observation of intelligent behavior—will be discussed in greater detail since it bears more directly upon the concepts of this chapter.

### The Paleocomparative Approach

The paleopsycho-comparative approach to cognitive behavior seeks to identify and clarify those cognitive structures or operations which underlie the construction of human and lower primate artifacts and social structures which have or have had survival value. A recent example of this approach can be found in the attempt of Omark, Omark, and Edelman (in press) to study the logical operations (à la Piaget) underlying social dominance hierarchies. These hierarchies characterize most higher-primate groups, including baboons and children. The originality of Omark's approach involves applying the ethological method (naturalistic observation and description as well as comparative analysis) directly to an important problem of human cognition that Piaget raised but that has not yet been attacked in any successful way to my knowledge. Piaget's theory of development does not specify which real-life experiences are directly involved in the process of cognitive change. Hence, there is an important gap that has to be filled in to give his theory more credibility. Omark's work is one of the first attempts to fill in this gap, by showing how everyday problems of social adaptation—namely one's position within a social hierarchy—are tied to the child's emerging logical cognitive structures. This interdisciplinary attempt (ethology and cognitive psychology) appears to be the first to reveal that Piaget's cognitive structures are "naturally expressed" in the life of the child and have adaptive significance. Increased knowledge of cognitive structures through this method would aid in specifying more exactly which cognitive operations "come naturally" to the child and would hence facilitate education of important cognitive functioning.

### The "Common Sense" Approach

The second approach, an analysis of common sense, is proposed here because common sense is a ubiquitous phenomenon of everyday experience which, strangely enough, has not been studied in any systematic and definitive way. Apart from a few writers, such as Baldwin (1967), and Heider (1958) who have pressed for a better understanding of the "naive theory" of human behavior (a subclass of common sense), there seems to be little scientific literature on the role of common sense in regulating everyday behavior. Common sense can be defined as a situation-specific, common (but not general), vernacular way of responding to problems as they arise in everyday life. It differs from fantasy, which is well studied by the psychoanalytically oriented, and from the precise and logically intact modes of hypothetico–deductive thinking studied by Piaget. Unlike fantasy and scientific thinking, common sense is reality oriented and practical on one hand, and unscientific and wish motivated on the other.

In an inquiry into the larger problem of insight, Lonergan (1957) discusses the importance of studying common sense in general and makes a good attempt at explicating its various meanings. For present purposes we go beyond the inferential and discursive approach of Lonergan and focus more upon the nature of actual problem-solving behavior in which common sense is recruited to participate. This can be achieved by using questionnaires, interviews, and, to a limited extent, observations to ferret out the cognitive steps people (usually adolescents and adults) employ to achieve solutions to their everyday problems.

## Studies of Failure to Adapt

The third approach, studying the failure of individuals to reach reproductive age or to reproduce, is based on the assumption that part of this failure is due to the lack (or inadequate use) of cognitive processes normally associated with intelligent behavior. The failure to engage in such cognitive activities as planning ahead, foreseeing consequences, calculating potential risks, or quickly remembering an important piece of information may result in death or injury during the prereproductive state of development. Childhood accidents, warfare, and other potentially lethal life situations may have a small, but permanent effect on the gene pool, although, as Mayr (1970) points out, prereproductive mortality most probably has much less effect on the gene pool than does unequal reproduction. Unequal reproduction is also related to cognitive functioning. As Reed (1965) has demonstrated, there is genetic selection against the severely retarded due to the fact that institutionalization plus other factors make marriage and reproduction very improbable or virtually impossible.

If intelligence is an orthoselective trait, then a great premium has been placed on it during the evolution of *Homo sapiens* and there is no reason to assume that such a premium (as subtle as it may be) is not being placed on it in the evolutionary scheme today. Knowing how mental deficiencies and abnormalities are reacted to by the everyday environment can aid in clarifying which intelligent acts in particular are being heavily challenged and which cognitive processes necessary for successful adaptation are lacking or malfunctioning.

## Naturalistic Observation

The fourth approach, more directly related to the main thesis of this presentation, requires the naturalistic observation of intelligent behavior. The scientific goal of such a program would be to achieve an accurate, comprehensive description of the individual's intelligent behavior as well as the cognitive demand characteristics of the environment, characteristics which not only daily challenge the individual to act intelligently but which also play a role in the development of his intelligence.

One practical goal of such an initially costly program is basically the same as that of conventional intelligence testing—namely, to identify basic cognitive skills or fundamental problem-solving processes that are significantly implicated in successful adaptation. Once such skills or processes are identified, it will be possible to construct "ecologically valid" test items or situations which tap them. Another practical consequence of having such a description is that environmental intervention programs would have something more than guess-work and unsubstantiated theory to go on in the development of relevant curricula. Unless the environment and environment—subject interaction are included in our formulation of intelligence, there is no sense in hoping for better predictions, interventions, or explanations of the nature and growth of intelligence. A view of intelligence based on testing in controlled situations will simply remain too far from the world to either explain or serve it.

The underlying rationale for the naturalistic observational approach has been alluded to earlier. By representatively sampling (using selected populations of individuals) environment–subject interactions involving intelligent behavior, it will be possible to identify more accurately what the factors and processes are that characterize the various degrees of success and failure the individual experiences in everyday life. Such a representative sample would lead to an expansion of the existing content domain of test items. It would identify major cognitive processes recruited to deal with recurring problems that require solution for survival. Further, it would point to factors other than those conventionally associated with intelligence (for example, contextual or emotional variables that directly influence task performance) which are, nevertheless, involved in the process of adaptation either as hindrances or aids. Test items generated from such a sample of known subject–environmental interactions should also have more predictive value than items generated from theories of cognition or guesses as to what the environment's requirements are.

An example of a naturalistic–observational study of intelligent behavior is a project started by Donna Spiker and the author (see Charlesworth & Spiker, 1975) and extended to a study of a normal child and a Down's Syndrome child (Charlesworth, Kjergaard, Fausch, Daniels, Binger, & Spiker, 1976). The study developed out of an earlier laboratory and home observational study of tool using in young children. The study's focus is upon problem-solving behavior in toddlers and young children in home and school situations. A problem is viewed as a relational term describing an imbalance in the relationship between an individual and some aspect of his environment. This imbalance may reveal a temporary or long-term failure of the individual to satisfy a need or continue a desired behavior because of a block placed in his way. In observational terms, an ongoing behavior is interrupted or an observable expression of a need is not satisfied. Both the ongoing behavior and need expression are replaced behaviorally by other behaviors, most of which are more related to the block than to the original goal. Such behaviors may involve variations on the original behaviors (persisting with variations to continue around the block) or totally different behaviors, which can range from very familiar behavior (common to the individual))to very novel behavior as in the case of a creative solution.

The observer records the context in which the problem episode takes place, the ongoing behavior that is blocked, the nature of the block, the subject's response to the block, and the consequences of the response. Distinctions are made between the various modes of solution behavior the child engages in. In the face of physical problems the child may seek help, use tools, apply greater strength, persist in manipulatory behavior, circumvent the barrier, or remove the barrier in some ingenious way. In the face of social problems he may use persuasion, force, or diversion, or he may yield, withdraw, seek help, or ignore the problem. These various modes obviously employ different kinds and different degrees of cognitive involvement, perceptual and motor skills, innovation, ingenuity, and novelty and yield different degrees of success and failure. To date, we have made no attempt to judge the adaptive value and ingenuity level of the various responses.

Criteria for separating problems from nonproblems are not yet sharply defined. Nonproblems are presently defined as subject–environment interactions that result in immediately available (usually overlearned) cognitive, verbal, perceptual, or motor behaviors characterized by facile movements, neutral and occasionally positive affect, and stereotypy. Problems, in contrast, are defined as interactions that may result first in no behavior, or in halting trial and error behavior, followed by the construction or employment of novel behaviors or the construction of new solutions through the synthesis of new or old behavior and object patterns. Problems are associated with delay to solution, frustration, persistence, neutral and occasionally negative affect, and novel behaviors.

Our naturalistic–observational study of intelligent behavior in the home involved on-the-minute category and episode observations of four toddlers for 30 hr each for 3 hr per day, for 10 days, sampled across a 35-day period. Below are four specimen samples of problem episodes.

1. *S* sits at the dining-room table, having dinner; tries to cut a frozen salad with his fork, but fails; *S* says "cut cut" as he hands his fork to mother (*M*) to cut the salad for him; *M* does this and *S* begins eating the salad.

2. *S* is in the kitchen in his high chair with the visiting girl; he stands in the high chair, and as he tries to sit down he gets his diaper caught on the arm of the chair; *S* says "uh oh" and the girl hears him and immediately comes and lifts him up so that he is loose again; *S* then proceeds to sit down in the chair, and this time does it successfully.

3. *S* is near the back garage with his sister (*F*), having just returned from the pool; when they get to the back door, *S* tries to put the key in the lock to open the door, but fails because he is using the key upside down; *F* tells him to turn it around; *S* does this and pushes the key into the lock, but has difficulty turning the key; *F* sees this and opens the door herself; they both enter the house.

4. Outside, *S* rides his trike on the sidewalk; pedals trike and comes to incline in sidewalk; tries to pedal up incline; begins to roll backward; climbs off of trike; pushes trike up incline; climbs back on trike; continues riding trike (ca. 15 sec).

Such specimens make it possible to obtain reliable data on: (*a*) the degree of "problematicity" of the child's environment, that is, how many problems he faces per unit time; (*b*) the nature of the problematicity; (*c*) his modes of dealing with the various problems; (d) the success–failure rate of his dealings; and (*e*) the extent to which those in his environment aid or hinder him in his problem solving. These data will provide us with a picture of the nature of the child's adaptive performance in his everyday dealings with his environment as well as allow us to evaluate his adaptive skills relative to others (including other primates) by applying some standard scoring system to his problem-solving behavior. The data can also serve a future psychometric function by the number and heterogeneity of existing tests for that particular age level. In addition to shedding light on individual performance, the data also provide us information on the child's experiences that are most heavily involved in the construction of his or her later intelligence. Such information could be useful in helping to account for IQ score changes (if there is any correlation between everyday intelligent behavior and the IQ score) that appear over time, as well as IQ differences between individuals from different environments. In short, to collect data in this manner, as time consuming and painstaking as it is at times, can serve a number of valuable functions.

As noted above, the present study developed out of a study of how young children use tools. The tool tasks and the methods for observing and recording behavior were constructed keeping the animal literature on tool use and problem solving in mind as well as the ethologist's emphasis (see Blurton-Jones, 1972) upon developing objective behavior and stimuli–event units. Hence the present study fits both methodologically and conceptually into the broad multidisciplinary scheme which characterizes the ethological approach.

## CONCLUSION

On the basis of the above, it is concluded that traditional intelligence testing has done about as much as it can with its present conceptualizations and techniques. It is now time for it to open itself to other disciplines, disciplines that deal with intelligence in terms of evolution, comparative animal studies, problem solving in various cultures, and just plain everyday behavior. While the historical–evolutionary comparative dimension of intelligence is important for helping us detect what the recurrent and important environmentally posed problems and modes for solving them are, the more immediate problem of making intelligence testing more ecologically valid and hence socially and personally more relevant has to be tackled.

To date, the environment has been almost totally left out of considerations of the origins, nature, and efficacy of human intelligence. Just as ecological factors are necessary to know in order to reconstruct historically the adaptational problems of animal species, so it is necessary to know what environmental factors shape and influence the human individual's potential for intelligence, a potential that he or she has inherited as being a member of the species *Homo sapiens*. We would not test a whale with the same intelligence test we would use on an Olympic swimming champion or on a crocodile because we know that these three species possess different kinds of intelligence. They have different kinds of intelligence because we are certain they have different neurophysiological systems and different evolutionary histories. We know too that an important dimension of each animal's evolutionary history is the kind and intensity of environmental demands made upon the species to which it belongs. The same reasoning can be applied to the testing of an individual. It is unreasonable to compare different individuals on a single test if there is reason to believe that they have different ontogenetic histories because they have grown up in different environments. Cross-cultural studies have shown how unreasonable this is. Different developmental-learning histories influence not only test-taking attitudes, problem-solving sets, etc., but also the kinds of basic cognitive processes that are employed to solve problems.

This is not to argue that there are no nonspecific cognitive abilities, or that intelligence, as a genetic trait, is totally unbuffered and limitlessly malleable. It is argued, rather, that the normal daily requirements of intelligent behavior involve many more aspects of the individual than are normally tapped in a conventional testing situation. It is also argued that the cognitive operations that humans inherit are subject from birth to environmental demands that act selectively upon them, strengthening some and weakening or totally suppressing others. Hence, it does not make sense to study these operations without studying the environment and how the individual interacts with it. For these reasons it is important that we shift our emphasis from intelligence, the disposition, towards intelligent behavior, the process of adaptation. To do this we have to deemphasize intelligence testing momentarily and emphasize the study of intelligent behavior in the natural environment.

## ACKNOWLEDGMENTS

Support for writing this paper was provided by Program Project Grant 1 P01 HD05027 from the National Institute of Child Health and Human Development and the Humanethologie Arbeitsgruppe, Max Planck Institut für Verhaltensphysiologie, Percha/Starnberg, West Germany. Thanks go to William Bart, John Flavell, Donna Spiker, and Irenaus Eibl-Eibesfeldt for their encouragement and stimulation and to Patty Rollins, super secretary A-1, and Lana Kjergaard, ultimate research supervisor from Lake Benton, Minnesota.

## REFERENCES

Baldwin, A. Theories of child development. New York: J. Wiley, 1967.
Barker, R. G. On the nature of the environment. Journal of Social Issues, 1963, 19, 17–38.
Barker, R. G., & Wright, H. F. Midwest and its children. New York: Harper & Row, 1955.
Binet, A., & Simon, T. The development of intelligence in children. L'Année Psychologique, 1905, 163–191. (Also in T. Shipley (Ed.), Classics in psychology. New York: Philosophical Library, 1961.)
Blurton-Jones, N. G. An ethological study of some aspects of social behavior of children in nursery school. In D. Morris (Ed.), Primate ethology. Chicago: Aldine Publishing Co., 1967.

Blurton-Jones, N. G. (Ed.) *Ethological studies of child behavior.* Cambridge, England: Cambridge University Press, 1972.

Boring, E. G. *A history of experimental psychology.* (2nd ed.). New York: Appleton-Century-Crofts, 1950.

Brunswick, E. Representative design and probabilistic theory in a functional psychology. *Psychological Review,* 1955, **62,** 193–217.

Campbell, D. T. Evolutionary epistemology. In P. A. Schilpp (Ed.), *The philosophy of Karl R. Popper.* LaSalle, Illinois: Open Court Publ., 1966.

Charlesworth, W. R., & Spiker, D. An ethological approach to observation in learning settings. In *Proceedings of the conference on systematic observation in school settings,* sponsored by Special Education, University of Minnesota, U.S.O.E., 1975.

Colvin, S. S. Intelligence and its measurement: A symposium. *The Journal of Educational Psychology,* 1921, **12**(3), 136–139.

Heider, F. *The psychology of interpersonal relations.* New York: Wiley, 1958.

Hinde, R. A. *Animal behaviour.* New York: McGraw-Hill, 1966.

Hull, C. L. Mind, mechanism, and adaptive behavior. *Psychological Review,* 1937, **44,** 1–32.

Jencks, C., Smith, M., Acland, H., Bane, M., Cohen, D., Gintis, H., Heyns, B., & Michelson, S. *Inequality: A reassessment of the effect of family and schooling in America.* New York: Macmillan, 1972.

Jerison, H. J. *Evolution of the brain and intelligence.* New York: Academic Press, 1973.

Jolly, A. *The evolution of primate behavior.* New York: Macmillan, 1972.

Klein, R. G. *Ice-age hunters of the Ukraine.* Chicago: University of Chicago Press, 1973.

Konner, M. J. Aspects of the developmental ethology of a foraging people. In N. Blurton-Jones (Ed.), *Ethological studies of child behaviour.* Cambridge, England: Cambridge University Press, 1972.

Lashley, K. S. Persistent problems in the evolution of mind. *Quarterly Review of Biology,* 1949, **24,** 28–42.

Loizos, C. Play behavior in higher primates: A review. In D. Morris (Ed.), *Primate ethology.* Chicago: Aldine, 1967.

Lonergan, B. J. F. *Insight: A study of human understanding.* New York: Longmans, Green, 1957.

Lorenz, K. *Die Rückseite des Spiegels: Versuch einer Naturgeschichte menschlichen Erkennens.* Munich: R. Piper Verlag, 1973.

Lorenz, K. Kant's doctrine of the apriori in the light of contemporary biology. In L. von Bertalanfly & J. A. Rapoport (Eds.), *General systems.* Vol. 7. Ann Arbor, Michigan: Society for General Systems Research, 1962.

Mason, O. T. *The origins of invention.* Cambridge, Massachusetts: MIT Press, 1966. (Originally published by Walter Scott, Ltd., London, 1895).

Mayr, E. *Populations, species, and evolution.* Cambridge, Massachusetts: Howard University Press, 1970.

Murphy, G. *An historical introduction to modern psychology.* New York: Harcourt, Brace, 1930.

Nogar, J. *The wisdom of evolution.* New York: New American Library, 1962.

Nunnally, J. C. *Psychometric theory.* New York: McGraw Hill, 1967.

Omark, D. R., Omark, M. D., & Edelman, M. S. Formation of dominance hierarchies in young children: Action and perception. In T. Williams (Ed.), *Psychological anthropology.* The Hague: Mouton, in press.

Piaget, J. *The psychology of intelligence.* Peterson, New Jersey: Littlefield, Adams, 1960.

Piaget, J. *The origins of intelligence in children.* New York: International University Press, 1952.

Pinter, R. Intelligence and its measurement: A symposium. *The Journal of Educational Psychology,* 1921, **12**(3), 139–143.

Reed, S. C. The evolution of human intelligence. *American Scientist,* 1965, **53**, 317–326.

Rensch, B. *Gedächtnis, Begriffsbildung und Planhandlungen bei Tieren.* Berlin: Verlag Paul Parey, 1973.

Rensch, B. *Homo sapiens: From man to demigod.* New York: Columbia University Press, 1972.

Sattler, J. M. *Assessment of children's intelligence.* Philadelphia: Saunders, 1974.

Smith, P. K. Ethological methods. In B. M. Foss (Ed.), *New perspectives in child development.* London: Penguin Books, 1975.

Smith, P. K., & Connolly, K. Patterns of play and social interaction in preschool children. In N. Blurton-Jones (Ed.), *Ethological studies of child behaviour.* Cambridge, England: Cambridge University Press, 1972.

Terman, L. M. Intelligence and its measurement: A symposium. *The Journal of Educational Psychology,* 1921, **12**(3), 127–133.

Terman, L. M. (Ed.) *Genetic studies of genius.* Stanford, California: Stanford University Press, 1925–1959. (5 vols.)

Thiessen, D. D. *Gene organization and behavior.* New York: Random House, 1972.

Thorndike, E. L. Intelligence and its measurement: A symposium. *The Journal of Educational Psychology,* 1921, **12**(3), 124–127.

Tyler, L. E. *Tests and measurements.* (2nd ed.). Englewood Cliffs, New Jersey: Prentice-Hall, 1971.

Willems, E. P. An ecological orientation in psychology. *Merrill-Palmer Quarterly of Behavior and Development,* 1965, **11**, 317–333.

# 9

# The Nature of Intelligent Behavior: Questions Raised by Cross-Cultural Studies

Jacqueline J. Goodnow

*Macquarie University*

Cross-cultural studies raise questions about the way we define intelligent behavior and the way we measure it. These are questions not only about the way other people behave, but also about the way we set goals for ourselves and our children, goals that affect the training we give and the criteria we use to distinguish "poor" from "good" performances.

## CROSS-CULTURAL RESULTS AND THEIR IMPLICATIONS

### Consistency of Performance

As a starting point, I wish to take a recurrent type of finding in cross-cultural work. The recurrent finding I have in mind deals with the consistency of behaviour: performances which go together, or are thought to go together, in our own culture, do not always do so in another culture. Roughly speaking, this lack of expected consistency occurs in four forms.

*Relation of thought to technology.* The first concerns the expectation that sophisticated thought is found only with sophisticated technology, to the extent that primitive technology has often led to the label "primitive man." We have been reminded many times, however, that people with simple technologies may have very complex ways of classifying their kin (see Lévi-Strauss, 1963). They may also display a keen concern for evidence and hypothesis testing, together with an ability to verbalize their reasoning, in functional situations such as tracking or hunting (see Tolkin & Konner, 1973).

*Relations among different tasks.* In a second form, the lack of expected cohesion involves a set of specific tasks thought to belong together because they are, in our culture, statistically tied to one another or, on theoretical grounds, regarded as tapping the same abilities. The fact that they often do not go together in the same way in other cultures has been commented on strongly by Heron and Simonsson (1969), by Olson (1970), and by Vernon (1967, 1969). The belief that they should go together, however, at least a little bit, is hard to discard. To use my own data as an example (Goodnow, 1962; Goodnow & Bethon, 1966), a number of Piagetian tasks, within the United States, discriminate equally well between a "dull" and a "bright" sample—"dull" and "bright" being based on IQ measures. The same tasks seem to hang together in much the same way when we deal with either Chinese or European boys in Hong Kong schools, that is, few boys perform beautifully on some tasks and dismally on others. That does happen, however, when the same tasks are given to Chinese boys with little or no schooling. These boys performed as well as the schoolboys on three conservation tasks—weight, area, and volume—but did very poorly on a task of combinatorial reasoning (find all the pairs you can make from a number of colors, without repeating pairs). The most striking discrepancy was between the last two tasks—conservation of volume and combinatorial reasoning. Success on these two tasks, in Western cultures, is usually achieved at much the same age. Moreover, the two tasks are thought to have the same theoretical base, i.e., they have both been proposed as measures of the achievement of formal operations in the Piagetian sense.

*Relations among different forms of the same task.* Perhaps it is not too surprising if a couple of very different tasks come apart. Worse, however, is to come. When we move into other cultures, even performances within a single task appear to vary more than we expect them to, shifting with the materials, the instructions, or the questions used. Performance may be good, for example, with familiar but not with unfamiliar objects, good with objects but not with photographs of objects (Glick, 1975).

For this third type of unevenness, I shall choose two particular examples. One comes from work by Bennett (1970) in Fiji. Bennett had devised three forms of a series continuation task. Indians in Fiji were adept on all three forms (materials were either numbers, letters of the alphabet, or symbols). Native Fijians, however, were adept with the first two, but often scored poorly on the third.

The other example is an incident cited by Glick (1975), discussing a variety of context effects in work by Cole, Gay, and Glick (1968a, 1968b) and Cole, Gay, Glick, and Sharp (1971). The investigators had carefully gathered a set of 20 objects, 5 each from 4 categories: food, clothing, tools, and cooking utensils. Both the objects and the names for the categories were familiar, i.e., all the proper spadework had been done. Despite the precautions, however, many of the Kpelle produced, when asked to put together the objects that belonged together, not 4 groups of 5 but 10 groups of 2. Moreover, the type of grouping and the type of reason given were frequently of the type we regard as extremely concrete, e.g., "the knife goes with the orange because it cuts it." Glick (1975) notes, however, that subjects at times volunteered " 'that a wise man would do things in the way this was done.' When an exasperated experimenter asked finally, 'How would a fool do it?' he was given back [groupings] of the type . . . initially expected—four neat piles with foods in one, tools in another [p. 636] ."

*Relations among performances at different ages.* A fourth and last form of variability consists of relationships among performances at different ages. We tend to assume, reminders such as Bayley's (1968) to the contrary, that behavior displayed early in life will be a fairly good predictor of behavior later on. From cross-cultural studies, however, come some strong indications that relationships to age may take more forms than we usually expect (Dasen, 1972). In the most striking cases, early "retardation" may give rise to later "normalcy" (Dennis & Najarian, 1957; Kagan & Klein, 1973). This area of experimentation is fraught with problems—problems, for instance, of the equivalence of tasks at different ages, the behavior expected at different ages by different cultures, and notions of irreversibility in behavior. Nonetheless, the existence of this complex type of inconsistency must be acknowledged.

## Consequences of Inconsistency

*The selection of tasks.* The several forms of unevenness have led first of all to a general concern about the best way to select tasks for cross-cultural work. Should we, for example, simply adapt our own tasks until some particular criterion, for example, an age change or a unimodal distribution, has been reached? Should we use only tasks that occur in all cultures, for example, tasks dealing with the acquisition of language? Should we look primarily at tasks already functional in a given culture, concentrating perhaps on Glick and Slobin's "mundane cognition" (Glick, 1975)? Or should we aim at a mixture, using first an analysis of tasks already existing in a culture and then devising experimental tasks to check hypotheses derived from signs of everyday effectiveness (Cole *et al.,* 1971; Feldman & Hass, 1970)?

In addition, unevenness has brought a revived interest in the effects of varying stimulus material. Two types of variation have been prominent: variations in the use of objects versus representations of objects, and variations in familiarity.

The analyses of *representational differences* have brought an awareness that, as experimenters, we often assume that objects and their pictured equivalents will be responded to in the same way by all individuals. In reality, it appears that some performances with pictured material—for example, matching a photograph or drawing to an object that is also present—are displayed by many cultural groups. Other performances—for example, determining relationships between pictured objects—are far more likely to vary across cultures. A survey and incisive analysis by Pick (1974) points up the need to know more both about cues offered by particular pictures and about the extent of an individual's knowledge of these cues, his or her willingness to take a pictorial hint (Gombrich, 1960). What we have begun to learn, in fact, is that we know relatively little about the nature of picture interpretation even in our own culture.

The effects of *familiarity* have sometimes been confused with the effects of representation, experimenters using, as Glick (1975) points out, objects for familiar stimuli and pictures for unfamiliar stimuli. This procedural point is now more sharply realized (see Deregowski & Serpell, 1971). In addition, we are acquiring some hypotheses about the ways in which familiarity may be defined. Work by Piaget and his colleagues, for example, suggests that familiarity may refer to the material itself (e.g., shapes), to an operation (e.g., grouping or counting), or to an operation applied to particular material (e.g., grouping or counting shapes) (Goodnow, 1969). Given such breakdowns, we can begin to ask about the presence of various kinds of effect, putting each into experimental form as Greenfield (cited by Glick, 1975) has apparently done. We can also begin to ask about the bases of different effects. We have, at present, for instance, hypotheses suggesting that familiarity is facilitating, perhaps because of a tie with language (Okonji, 1971), and hypotheses suggesting that negative effects may arise when the use of an operation with particular material is novel. In such cases, the individual may resist setting aside a way of looking at material that is well-entrenched and adequate for all purposes to date. The possible effects of such resistance in the face of a request to try and resort materials "in another way" have been raised especially by Glick (1975).

*Accounting for performance variability.* Over and above leading us to look again at the tasks and measures we use, cross-cultural results lead to the more theoretical question: How can we account for the apparent off-and-on appearance of skills? What general ways of looking at behaviour will best accommodate such phenomena?

One possibility is that in a number of cultures behavior is more context bound or more tied to specific skills than it is in our own. This kind of possibility underlies, for instance, Grant and Schepers' (1969) proposal that the concept of "*g*" may be especially inappropriate for African test performance, two or more factors being needed to account for the variance that in a European sample might be accounted for by one. It also underlies hypotheses to the effect that one function of Western schooling may be the extension of known techniques or concepts to new contexts (Cole, 1972; Greenfield & Bruner, 1966).

The alternate possibility is that behavior is no more specific in other cultures than it is in our own. The appearance of specificity may reflect early stages of learning or unfamiliarity, or the threads that bind situations or performances together may not be the same as in our culture and may not be represented in the tasks we assemble. They may, in fact, not be known to us.

These two general possibilities mask a number of finer possible responses to the appearance of specificity or unevenness. The responses all deal with the underlying models we use for analyzing the nature of intelligence, the nature of experience, and the nature of development. All of them, I think, offer novel and useful ways of looking at differences between cultures, as well as differences within a culture, for example, between age groups or socioeconomic groups.

The four responses selected fall roughly into two groups. The first two start from the idea that the degree or frequency of generalization across behaviors may be limited unless some cultural demand intervenes. The second two start more from the expectation that generalization or consistency is likely to be the normal state.

The four are given unequal space in the discussion below, not because of variations in value but because I have given more thought to some, the fourth especially, than others.

## SOME MODELS FOR BEHAVIOR

### Generalization as a Cultural Value

Cole and his colleagues found marked context effects in the performance of the Kpelle, i.e., marked changes depending on the particular materials or instructions used. On some forms of a task, the Kpelle were similar to Western groups, on others they were not (Cole et al., 1968a, b; 1971).

The findings led first to the hypothesis that "cultural differences reside more in the situations to which particular cognitive processes are applied than in the existence of a process in one group and its absence in another" (Cole et al., 1971, p. 233). This hypothesis accounts for part of the data. It does not account, however, for the fact that context effects were less marked among Western groups than among the Kpelle. The tasks, one should note, were derived from Western experimental psychology (for example, tasks of classification, number judgment, discrimination learning), but the processes involved would appear to be part of the learning that all cultures demand.

To account for the Western consistency, Cole (1972) has asked whether the occurrence of generalization may reflect a cultural value, that is, a high value placed on a search for universals, for principles that cover all events. In our culture, for instance, efforts towards generalization are usually regarded as "good," and we may easily slide into regarding generalization as something to be expected in the course of normal development, something intrinsic to the nature of thinking itself. From this point of view, it may be no accident that Bruner (1957) describes thinking as "going beyond the information given," and Bartlett (1958) describes it as "gap filling."

Cole's (1972) question fits with some other cross-cultural observations. One such observation from a colleague of mine (J. Mosel) who knew Thailand well suggests that no Thai would develop a theory of cognitive dissonance, i.e., a theory based on the idea that one would feel uncomfortable and expend a great deal of effort in ironing out discrepancies between actions or ideas. The other is a note by Gladwin (1970) on the navigational system developed by a Pacific group, the Puluwat. Their system is intricate and meets many of the criteria we would use for abstract thought, for example, it contains a large number of variables and it involves the use of an imagined reference point. Gladwin (1970) was impressed by its sophistication but puzzled by the fact that it contained some internal inconsistencies. The system had apparently been developed to take account of all the events the islanders were likely to meet. Once this goal had been met, no further action seemed called for. On our standards, however, the system would be regarded as unfinished.

If we follow Cole's (1972) suggestion, where does it lead us in terms of ways of describing behavior, experience, or development? One direction is towards a second look at models based on the idea that generalization and response to discrepancy are the sign of or the stimulus to cognitive development (see Berlyne, 1960; Bruner, 1957).

A second direction concerns the description of experience. Different cultures or subcultures may vary a great deal in the extent to which they emphasize working on complete answers, covering both present and possible events, as against the more pragmatic goals of locating only the information needed for the moment. They may also vary in the value and the practice given to finding loose ends or coming up with questions.

In a related direction, Cole's (1972) question leads one to ask: What are the areas that different groups or different individuals specify as "reasonable" areas in which to search for complete answers? I am, for example, only interested in pragmatic information about how my car runs, and the culture I live in accepts my lack of curiosity in this area. In addition, what is it that we teach as worth generalizing, i.e., what are the processes we select as worth extending to other contexts? In Bennett's (1970) work, for instance, many of his series called for counting (Bennett, personal communication). The Fijians, it appears, were prepared to count numbers and to count letters, but not to count shapes. The Indians, however, found it reasonable to count all three. In this respect, the Indians were closer to the Anglo-European practice of extending the operation of counting to any and all material. We might be said to be teaching our children: "When in doubt, count."

One last implication from Cole's (1972) question remains, an implication dealing with task procedures. The traditional choice of unfamiliar material for testing may be based on our assumption that generalization to a new event is not only a sign of ability but also an activity that has been practised before, in one context or another. Even the use of practice items is in itself based on the assumption that individuals will be spontaneously trying to use the practice period to generalize and anticipate subsequent items. Neither assumption may be valid.

## Intelligence as Skill in a Particular Medium

Cole's (1972) hypothesis implies that the extension of an idea or skill from its first context may depend on the extent to which we have been encouraged to actively look for new contexts, to search for limits. Olson (1970) also emphasizes the role of demand, but in more specific terms.

Olson (1970) has analyzed in depth the performance of United States and African children—Logoli and Kipsogi in Kenya—on tasks involving diagonals (drawing, defining verbally, or constructing with checkers). He has been especially concerned with the way skill on one diagonal task fits with skill on another, data that have led him to a particular way of looking at experience and transfer.

Performatory acts, Olson (1970) suggests, such as constructing, defining, drawing, and sorting, spark a search for needed information of a particular kind. "Any performance is a sequential act. As such it involves a continuous set of decisions at each point in time as to how to begin, how to continue . . . and how to terminate it. Each of these decision points requires information [p. 182]," information seen as relevant to a choice between the alternatives considered at each decision point. In effect, given the need to act, individuals take a new and directed look at the world around them.

On this basis, cultural differences may occur in the demands for different actions and in the choices considered as alternatives. Each culture achieves the kind of cognitive development it asks for: "We may infer that the . . . culture determines which elaborated cognitive structures will develop. . . . The lack of some such structure says more about the requirements of the culture than it does about the structure of the primitive mind" (Olson, 1970, p. 115).

Such a demand-oriented view of experience fits very well with some cross-cultural studies. It fits, for example, with the general finding of elaborate, "abstract" spatial systems among people who travel a great deal in country with few landmarks or shifting landmarks: Eskimos, Pacific Islanders, and some desert Arabs. (Brief descriptions of such systems are given in the appendix of Lynch, 1960.)

In addition, Olson's (1970) position offers a way of looking at an issue raised by Wohlwill (1973). The issue is that our descriptions of environment are meagre, to say the least. He suggests that one way of characterizing environments may be in terms of whether learning is expected to take place predominantly through response experience ("learning by doing") or by stimulus experience (e.g., watching *Sesame Street*). Olson (1970) proposes that stimulus and response effects may be part and parcel of the same experience. The effect of a demand for action, he argues, is a change in perceptual information, a change in knowledge about the world rather than purely a change in a specific response. It is the effect on knowledge that then allows for transfer across actions:

> Drawing and making a checker diagonal may share many of the same features; that is, require some of the same information, but not the identical information. . . . This same point is true in regard to the medium of language. The choices indicated . . . are nonidentical. To the extent they overlap and only to that extent, skill in articulating the diagonal in language will have transfer value to performing it on the checkerboard [Olson, 1970, p. 184].

In other terms, either stimulus or response experience may give rise to new information, as long as they embody some demand. And transfer from one demanded act to another depends on the common choices involved and the common information needed, rather than on a common response or a common underlying ability. The overall result should be a greater variation of skill with the particular setting or "medium" of the task than we would expect if a broad general skill were the only factor involved.

## Behavior as Monitoring

The hypotheses proposed by Cole (1972) and by Olson (1970) suggest that the nondisplay of a particular behavior or skill may largely depend on the novelty of a demand. Either the information needed for the task has not been needed before, or it has been needed but remains tied to some other context. The overall result may be the need for new learning—learning that supplies new information, demonstrates a new extension of what is known, or overcomes resistance to an altered way of looking at a problem.

An alternate possibility, one that would especially contribute to the off-and-on appearance of some behaviors, has been suggested by Serpell (1969, 1971) and Shapiro (1960), who have pointed out that several African groups, both schooled and unschooled, make the same types of orientation errors as Anglo-Europeans do on copying and construction tasks. The difference lies in the frequency rather than in the type of error. Serpell (1969, 1971) has used such results to suggest that some cultural differences may reflect a difference in the extent to which people have learned to monitor and inhibit a common tendency. Left to ourselves, for example, we would all display orientation errors of the same type and frequency on a copying task. Some cultural groups, however, provide sharper warnings and more experience in being alert for such errors.

Serpell's approach might be termed a "vigilance" theory of behavior. It suggests first of all that behavior may often be best accounted for not in terms of the strength of a single response but in terms of the relative strengths of competing responses. In addition, it suggests the interesting possibility that one way of specifying differences in skill or in experience may be in terms of the way we monitor events, with events defined as the behavior of objects, of others, or of oneself. Learning to know, for example, where the traps are likely to be in a particular problem or where one's own weaknesses and needs for help occur may be a special form of learning requiring a particular form of experience.

### Behavior as Display or Selection

We have so far considered the possibilities that the nonappearance of a behavior may stem from (a) no prior experience in using the behavior in the specific context of the task; (b) no self-instruction to look for particular extensions from other contexts; or (c) the inhibiting effect of an alternate response, possibly combined with lack of experience in monitoring or balancing alternative responses.

Suppose we turn to the behavior that is displayed. We might well ask: Are there other behaviors that might have occurred? If so, what conditions led to the selection of this behavior rather than others? These questions parallel those that follow from nondisplay, namely: Is the behavior we seek ever displayed by this individual, in this context at other times or in other contexts? If so, why not here?

The double set of questions has led several investigators to suggest that differences between groups may stem either from a difference in the repertoire of behaviors or from a difference in selection from the repertoire (Glick, 1975; Goodnow, 1972; Pick, 1974). The same investigators have also been led to ask: What are the conditions that lead to the selection of a particular behavior for display? One critical condition appears to be the way a task situation is interpreted. This is no new discovery, but one that cross-cultural studies remind us of in forceful terms, bringing out again and again the fact that task situations may be interpreted in more ways than we had thought possible or likely. Glick's (1975) "wise man—stupid man" is one example. Another, very prominent example is the set of studies dealing with the perception of depth in pictures. Almost all of these studies, reviewed by Glick (1975), by Lloyd (1972), and by Miller (1973), use Hudson's (1960) pictures, with the subjects typically asked such questions as: "Which is closer to the man, the antelope or the elephant?" Many unschooled Africans, and some with schooling, take the question literally: if one works strictly from distances on paper, the elephant is closer to the man. If one adopts the interpretation, however, that the question refers to "real" distance, i.e., distance in a portrayed world, then the position on the page and the size of the elephant are cues to the antelope being the correct answer.

In the last 10 years, research in this area has swung from the conviction that unschooled Africans do not perceive depth to the realization that there is more than one way of looking at the pictures—these have been called two-dimensional and three-dimensional interpretations—to wondering what is involved in learning to see only one interpretation or the other. It is difficult for us, some of us, at least, to set aside the three-dimensional interpretation. It was apparently agonizingly difficult for some of Hudson's original subjects to make a choice between the two. Pick (1974) notes, for example, that Hudson reports some subjects taking an hour or more with a single picture, in an agony of indecision as to whether they should base their judgment on one interpretation or the other. Such results lead easily to a conclusion neatly stated by Pick (1974): "Dissimilar performance may have more to do with how tasks get defined for different groups of subjects than with differences in cognitive skills. Questions for study then become why and how tasks get defined in a particular way [p. 15]."

At this point, we have moved from the argument that displayed behavior is often a selection to the argument that a major factor affecting selection is the way the situation is defined. We must now, however, face the question: How are situations defined? What is the difference between one situation and another? This is the question I wish to explore a little further. To do so, I plan to make use of data from cross-cultural work, particularly data where we have found to our surprise that other people do not always share our assumptions about the "obvious" meanings of situations and the "obvious" appropriateness of certain behaviors. I shall be especially concerned with data indicating assumptions that have become incorporated into the way we construct or score tasks and that may be particularly likely to give rise to uneven performance.

## INTERPRETING TASK SITUATIONS

One approach to asking how task situations are interpreted is to look at the goals and the methods judged appropriate by both parties to the testing situation. Tasks that call for common goals and common methods might then be expected to belong together, tasks with discrepant goals and methods to show poor relationships. In particular, the performances that strike us as "oddly poor" in some cultures may be occurring on tasks where the two parties have a different sense of what is appropriate.

In effect, we need to ask: What do people regard as a "good" or "correct" answer? What do they regard as a "good," an "elegant," or a "clumsy" method? More pointedly, what do we ourselves regard as "good" or "more mature," and where do such ideas come from? Are they matters of fact or beliefs about intellectual good manners? Do they really represent a difference in the level of thought or a difference in particular values?

Some answers must inevitably be tied to particular types of tasks. Classification is an example. Glick's "wise man" brings us face to face with the fact that a 4 × 5 classification system is "better," on our standards, than a 10 × 2. We clearly have ideas, as Shipstone (1960) noted in a United States study of classification, about the proper number of classes and the proper distribution of items in categories: three categories with six items each, and a fourth category with one item, leaves us slightly uncomfortable. We also have a number of jokes about people whose "miscellaneous" category contains more than any other, or more than all others combined. Nonetheless, we know very little about these assumptions, and Shipstone's (1960) study is the only one I know of that discusses them explicitly.

Classification also involves expectations about the relative worth of seeing similarities as against differences. We tend to regard similarities as more important, accounting perhaps for the sizeable collection of classification tasks we have developed and our ready use of them as measures of intelligence. In some other cultures, however, the uniqueness of objects and the presence of differences may be more highly valued. Rural Mexicans, in Maccoby and Modiano's (1966) description, are more at home with differences, uncomfortable with generalities, but in no danger of losing "the sense of concreteness of things and becom(ing) buried in a dry nominalism." "Dry nominalism" will be especially appreciated by anyone who has suffered through the similarities subtest of the Wechsler-Bellevue, with its progression of "how are . . . and . . . alike," starting from "orange and banana," moving on to "egg and seed," "poem and statue," and ending with the improbable "fly and tree."

Rural Mexicans, however, are not the only individuals concerned about our passion for finding similarities and our insistence that grouping on "abstract" bases is intrinsically better than on "perceptual" bases. Gaines (1973) has argued that the decline over age in the speed with which one can detect the odd shape in a pattern is a loss encouraged by our culture but probably not by others. In these cultures, a sensitivity to difference apparently remains valued. The most devastating critic, however, is Arnheim (1954). His analyses of classification tasks, and of the values implicit in some new mathematics, e.g., the attitude that all objects can be placed in sets and that the critical attribute of all objects is number, should be required reading for all students of cognition.

What we need, however, is some way of looking at tasks-in-general as well as at specific tasks. Below are some suggestions, dealing with "good" methods and "proper" goals, commenting both on our assumptions and on their possible sources.

### "Proper" Approaches to a Task

Implicit in our expectations about task performance is the idea that people will adopt a particular motivational stance. They may not do so, to the extent that Vernon (1969) has proposed that most cultural and subcultural differences on cognitive tasks are "motivational." What we need now, I suggest, are some ways of breaking "motivation" into some smaller components. What is it that we expect?

*"The idea counts more than the person."* One expectation is that the subject will regard the problem to be solved as resting in the task. Another is that all parties will agree that the "goodness" of an answer is to be judged only in terms

of the value of the ideas produced. The social situation, in our ideal world, is extraneous.

Outside the Western world, many people do not share this value system. In fact, variations occur within the Western world and what we usually learn is some sense of the situations in which it is safe to concentrate only on the idea. When I first came to the United States, for example, I was struck by the politeness with which members of graduate seminars and members of conferences expressed disagreement. Phrases of the type Labov (1970) calls "mitigating terms" seemed very prominent: "I'm no expert, but is it possible . . ." or "This is just off the top of my head, but . . . ." Years later, I was equally amazed at the open thrust and parry, the "aggressiveness" of the Australian discussions I had once taken for granted. In both societies, I suggest, one needs to learn not only the formal rules but also the situations to which they do and do not apply.

*"An honest try."* Puerto Rican children often have difficulty in New York schools because they do not readily accept the set tasks. They may, in fact, evade them altogether rather than making even a token gesture (Hertzig, Birch, Thomas, & Mendez, 1968). African children improve their performances on tasks considerably a second time around—more so than their Western comparison group—as long as they are urged to try hard the second time (Vernon, 1967). It is as if, among well-socialized children in our society, such phrases as "this is a test" or "I have some games for you to play" are sufficient cues to alert the receiver that a certain amount of effort should now be displayed. One should "do one's best" on such occasions or, ideally, at all times. Alternately, one may operate on the maxim that "if a thing is worth doing, it is worth doing well."

Once again, surprise that other people do not approach tasks in one's own way may not be limited to experience in other countries. I was once asked, for instance, why studies I did at Harvard on decision making (probability learning) were based only on males. The reason was that I began the pilot study with both sexes but encountered a number of women students who did not "work hard" at the task, i.e., they spontaneously took the attitude that they would probably not succeed in working out a good system, in large part because it was not their "type of problem." Since the experiment was designed to vary this attitude by the task materials, not by sex, these women were not "good" subjects for my purposes. I can still recall my surprise at the blandness with which they stated, "I never was any good at that type of thing," an exercise in choice that was not part of my belief that one should rise to almost every problem.

Such experiences suggest that one way of filling in the motivational picture is in terms of variations in the choice of problems one gives effort to, in the ways by which one avoids effort without a loss of mutual respect, and in the signals that indicate a need for effort. The gain would not only be theoretical. One would become more alert, for example, to tasks unlikely to elicit the open answer or the honest try we expect. Within our traditions, for instance, "learning by doing" and "learning from one's mistakes" are often acceptable, and guessing is usually expected. These are the traditions that make an early try feasible, and that make it possible to use practice items where the subject learns what is involved by making a trial response and then being given feedback. The same type of practice series, however, might yield a very poor performance among groups such as the Navaho. The latter appear to rely more on "prolonged observation, or 'prelearning'.... A reluctance to try too soon and the accompanying fear of being 'shamed' if one does not succeed may account for the seemingly passive, uninterested, and unresponsive attitude of Indian students" (Ohannessian, 1967, p. 13).

In similar fashion, one might be especially cautious about the use of tasks that call for very direct answers. Tenezakis and Kelly (1973), for example, point out that many aspects of child rearing in rural Greek communities—teasing, deliberate lying and breaking of promises—are based on the idea that children should be alert for unpredictability, especially in human relationships. This background, they suggest, may make conservation tasks difficult to use with Greek children. In their apparent simplicity, the tasks may especially invite "double-think." They may also be anxiety provoking, felt to be "unfair" in their insistence on a bald "yes" or "no" answer with no opportunity provided for a second line of defense or for a display of virtuosity in giving qualified answers.

## Appropriate Methods

Among the tasks we use are some where the method, the route to the goal, is a critical part of scoring, and some where the particular method is irrelevant. The sharpest examples of tasks where the method is critical are those developed by Piaget and his colleagues. On conservation tasks, for example, "true" conservation is defined not simply as the statement that two properties—e.g., amount or weight—remain the same in spite of a surface change, but also as the basing of this statement on a particular kind of reasoning. The child, to be successful in the Genevan sense, must base its answer on a sense of "logical necessity," indicated by the type of reason given and by resistance to suggestions that the answer could be other than the one originally given. Without the realization that success is based on specific methods, Genevan procedures are difficult to understand (Goodnow, 1969), and arguments about behavior indicating "true" conservation or "pseudo" conservation become inevitable.

A contrasting case, success defined independently of method, is provided by the Queensland Test (McElwain & Kearney, 1970). This set of tasks, designed for use in situations where linguistic communication is poor, involves no restrictions on method. What counts is an effective answer, without regard to time, number of moves, or the use of a particular method (the test includes such tasks as Knox Cubes, Passalong, and Kohs Blocks). Used without restrictions,

McElwain and Kearney report, the tasks yield a unimodal distribution and provide a reasonable way of predicting performance in a number of educational and job training situations.

The method-independent type of task should involve the fewest disagreements as to what is required and should allow for relatively even performance across the subtests. It is, however, also the rarer type of task. By and large, we use tasks that call for some attention to method, tagging some methods as better than others or assuming that some methods will be adopted rather than others. What we need to become aware of is those features of method that we especially value and that may not be valued by others. Several such are discussed below.

*Speed.* Rural and nonWestern people may perform well on tasks that carry no time limits but poorly on timed tests (see Havighurst & Hilkevitch, 1944). It is unlikely that such people are slow in everything they do; speed is often critical in some parts of their everyday lives. The question then is: under what conditions is speed really important? When does "slow" mean "stupid" rather than "wise"? A start on this problem has been made by Wober (1972), who points out that "various groups of Ugandans tend to associate their concept of intelligence with slowness, but not with quickness [p. 327]," and presents data indicating that Western education at least by ages 14–16 brings a "move towards dropping the ability-slowness association . . . and . . . the beginning of an ability-quickness identification [p. 328]."

A reluctance to identify faster with better may not always be located in out-of-the-way or rural places. One of the most interesting aspects of a progressive New York school was the poor performance of students on standard IQ measures, not because they failed items, but because they attempted relatively few; they were, in fact, vocally resentful of having to do so many things so quickly. In contrast, their performance on a task calling for group problem solving was better than that of children from several standard schools (Minuchin, Biber, Shapiro, & Zimiles, 1969).

How do such values arise? One of the relevant conditions to a stress on speed may be the belief that "time is money." Another may be what Looft (1973) has called "the psychology of more." Speed depends perhaps on the expectation that one will be given many items, and on the idea that "the best person is the one who comes up with the most answers" (Looft, 1973, p. 26). The "psychology of more," Looft argues, is part of a society that emphasizes the accumulation of goods.

*Minimal moves.* Olson (1966) has described several ways of solving the button-board problem—a task in which people press buttons in order to determine whether the patterns of lights on two boards are identical or not. Philp and Kelly (1974; personal communication) have used the task in New Guinea and have observed: (a) that many of their subjects, even those in high school, press all the buttons on a board, even though the judgment can be made well before this point; and (b) that no subjects adopt by themselves the method of minimal moves. The scarcity of minimal moves was also true for migrant children in Australia, as compared with native Australians. In effect, few subjects outside the Western educated mainstream spontaneously instructed themselves to avoid redundancy. As a result, their performance on the button board appeared far less sophisticated than on tasks in which a high-level score did not call for attention to redundancy.

Why do we expect, however, that redundant moves should be avoided, even when no explicit instructions are given? In many situations, they cost nothing, are less effortful than inferring an effect, and may have a rehearsal function, stamping in the information gained earlier. In some cases, we even consider a double check (e.g., replicating an experiment) as a virtue. Perhaps we regard "minimal moves" as a good device in all situations because the individual will then be more ready for occasions when moves are costly, either in time, effort, or money. A certain form of "mental discipline" will be practiced. In fact, however, students can reduce the number of moves taken once asked to do so (Bruner, Goodnow, & Austin, 1956). A preference for minimal moves on all occasions, it would appear, is a value we expect children to learn, rather than a constant functional need.

*"No hands."* In most of our approaches to cognition, we believe that ideal thought occurs in the absence of objects or, if objects are present, without direct handling of objects. The contemplative life and Rodin's "Thinker" are the ideal. We distinguish between "lower" and "higher" mental processes, and between solutions to problems that come "from above" ("pure" thought) and solutions that come "from below" (moving the stimulus materials around) (Duncker, 1945).

A score based on "no hands," I have come to think, is the basis for the poor performance of unschooled Chinese on the combinatorial task (Goodnow, 1970). The critical instruction on that task comes before asking for combinations of six colors, after practice with two, three and four colors: "Stop for a while and see if you can think of a trick or a system that will make it easy to find all the pairs, without repeating any." Success is scored as starting off with a reasonable system (a softening of the original Genevan criterion of finding all 15 pairs in a systematic manner). The practice items, however, allow one to reshuffle at will. They also contain no warning that one should be trying to figure out a "no hands" system, and the assumptions are made, I certainly made them at the time, that an individual will be expecting the number of colors to become progressively larger and will be spontaneously working on a good method while the numbers are still small.

What are the conditions leading to placing a high value on doing everything in one's head, without regard for whether it is always a useful way of proceeding? One may speculate that the belief goes with a stratified society where manual labour is the province of the lower classes. Certainly, Hanfmann's (1941) results with the Vygotsky task suggest that a tendency to rely exclusively on a "no hands" method goes with increasing years of education, people with PhDs being especially prone.

*"Something of one's own."*   Rohwer (1971) describes differences among U.S. ethnic and class groups in terms of their giving back a list of words in the same order as received versus breaking away from the original order and reporting words by categories. Hodgkin (1973) comments that many students from Southeast Asia may be undervalued in Australia because they have been trained to give back chapter and verse rather than modifying the statements and ideas of others. In contrast, some Western training, especially that of academics, involves learning a delicate balance between "originality," "extending the ideas of others," "flat contradiction," and a "proper sense of the literature." Students from other cultures bring one to the feeling that values are often involved in training of this type. So also do variations in bibliographic preference. My own bias—and I think it is part of an Australian undergraduate training—is for at least one "odd" or "old" reference, and I still find myself surprised at United States articles that are restricted to work that has appeared in the last 5 or 10 years.

The origins of such values are far from clear. Deference to one's elders is one possible factor. So also is the extent to which it is felt that the major part of knowledge has already been discovered or is unlikely to be extended by oneself, attitudes that seem to go with a restriction of attention to the learning and repeating of work by past authorities (Dart, 1972). Whatever the source, however, a variation in such values will clearly alter performance on tasks that allow a choice between repetition and reorganization.

Without doubt, other variations exist in the way "good" or "mature" methods are defined. I have, I hope, given sufficient examples to start others wondering about additional tacit assumptions or values that may not be shared by others and that, incorporated into the presentation or scoring of some tasks, may give rise to uneven cross-cultural differences.


## CONCLUSION

I have suggested that the off-and-on appearance of skill, giving the impression of individuals who sometimes do well and sometimes surprise us by doing poorly on our tasks, may be the result of unspoken assumptions about proper goals and good methods. Where these assumptions are held jointly by both task giver and task taker, performance may not contain such surprises. Where they are not shared, however, performance may be far from what we expect. Given a collection of tasks where assumptions are sometimes shared and sometimes not, the overall effect will be an uneven display of skill and extreme difficulty in making inferences about any "level" of thought achieved.

Awareness of our own values and their reflection in tasks should do more than help interpret uneven performance. It should also help us select or adapt tasks for more effective use in other cultures. We should be better able to anticipate where a task will encounter a lack of understanding or some definite resistance.

I should like to end with two comments. One is that a great deal remains to be learned about assumptions dealing with proper methods, good answers, and reasonable tasks. Perhaps the easiest way is to start with one's own experience, with the occasions where one has decided that a task was "stupid," or has felt some sense of outrage that a performance should be scored as it is.

The second point is that the issues raised by cross-cultural studies are echoed in within-cultural studies. Several investigators, for example, have become concerned with context effects on cognitive performance. One prominent area is language, where the need to collect samples of spontaneous language as well as test-situation language has been strongly argued, especially by Labov (1970). The other prominent area is that of memory, particularly analyses of techniques or strategies used in remembering a set of items (Flavell, 1970; Rohwer, 1971). Age differences occur in the extent to which individuals spontaneously use some sort of mnemonic, e.g., clustering items by type, or combining pairs of items into a single image or verbal unit. A large part of the age differences, however, may be wiped out when subjects are provided with mnemonic aids, either by direct prompting, or by varying the stimulus contexts (e.g., presenting the pair cow–ball in the sentence, "The cow chased the ball").

Outside of cognitive studies, a parallel to cross-cultural studies may be found within the area of personality, where concepts such as "trait" or "dispositional state" also seem to be suffering from the findings of lack of consistency across contexts. Bowers (1973) in fact suggests that a complete specificity of behavior might be avoided by analyzing the common or recurrent meanings given to situations. We have, it appears, a convergence of interest in the behaviors that may lie behind any displayed behavior, and in the extent to which an individual can change the first behavior displayed. We have as well, it seems, an increasing awareness that a large part of developing intelligent behavior, in social and cognitive situations, must consist of learning that most rules apply "usually but not always." The learning of contexts, exceptions, and compromises leaves one with an even stronger respect than usual for the subtlety of learning underlying intelligent behavior.

## ACKNOWLEDGMENTS

The preparation of this paper was aided by support from the National Institute of Child Health and Human Development (1-RI-HD 03105) and from the Research Grant Committee of Macquarie University.

# REFERENCES

Arnheim, R. *Visual thinking*. Berkeley, California: University of California Press, 1954.

Bartlett, F. C. *Thinking*. London: Allen & Unwin, 1958.

Bayley, N. Behavioral correlates of mental growth: Birth to thirty-six years. *American Psychologist*, 1968, **23**, 1–17.

Bennett, M. J. Reasoning test response in urban and rural Fijian and Indian groups in Fiji. *Australian Psychologist*, 1970, **5**, 260–266.

Berlyne, D. E. *Conflict, arousal, and curiosity*. New York: McGraw-Hill, 1960.

Bowers, K. Situationism in psychology: An analysis and a critique. *Psychological Review*, 1973, **80**, 307–336.

Bruner, J. S. Going beyond the information given. In H. Gruber *et al.* (Eds.), *Contemporary approaches to cognition*. Cambridge, Massachusetts: Harvard University Press, 1957.

Bruner, J. S., Goodnow, J. J., & Austin, G. A. *A study of thinking*. New York: Wiley, 1956.

Cole, M. Toward an experimental anthropology of thinking. Paper presented at the meeting of The American Ethnological Society Council on Anthropology and Education, Montreal, April, 1972.

Cole, M., Gay, J., & Glick, J. A cross-cultural investigation of information processing. *International Journal of Psychology*, 1968, **3**, 93–102. (a)

Cole, M., Gay, J., & Glick, J. Some experimental studies of Kpelle quantitative behavior. *Psychonomic Monographs*, 1968, **2**(10, Whole No. 26). (b)

Cole, M., Gay, J., Glick, J., & Sharp, D. *The cultural context of learning and thinking*. New York: Basic Books, 1971.

Dart, F. E. Toward a scientific attitude in developing countries. In M. W. Ward (Ed.), *Change and development in rural Melanesia*. New Guinea: University of Port Moresby Press, 1972 (5th Waigani Seminar).

Dasen, P. R. Cross-cultural Piagetian research: A summary. *Journal of Cross-Cultural Psychology*, 1972, **3**, 23–39.

Dennis, W., & Najarian, P. Infant development under environmental handicap. *Psychological Monographs*, 1957, **71** (7, Whole No. 436).

Deregowski, J. B., & Serpell, R. Performance on a sorting task: A cross-cultural experiment. *International Journal of Psychology*, 1971, **6**, 273–281.

Duncker, K. On problem solving. *Psychological Monographs*, 1945, **58**(5, Whole No. 270).

Feldman, C. F., & Hass, W. A. Controls, conceptualization, and the inter-relation between experimental and correlational research. *American Psychologist*, 1970, **25**, 633–635.

Flavell, J. Developmental studies of mediated memory. In L. Lipsitt & H. Reese (Eds.), *Advances in child development and behavior*. Vol. 5. New York: Academic Press, 1970.

Gaines, R. Matrices and pattern detection by young children. *Developmental Psychology*, 1973, **9**, 143–150.

Gladwin, T. *East is a big bird: Navigation and logic on Pulawat Atoll*. Cambridge, Massachusetts: Harvard University Press, 1970.

Glick, J. Cognitive development in cross-cultural perspective. In F. D. Horowitz (Ed.), *Review of child development research*. Vol. 4. Chicago: University of Chicago Press, 1975.

Gombrich, E. H. *Art and illusion*. Princeton: Princeton University Press, 1960.

Goodnow, J. J., A test of milieu effects with some of Piaget's tasks. *Psychological Monographs*, 1962, **76**(36, Whole No. 555).

Goodnow, J. J. Problems in research on culture and thought. In D. Elkind & J. Flavell (Eds.), *Studies in cognitive development: Essays in honor of Jean Piaget*. New York: Oxford University Press, 1969.

Goodnow, J. J. Cultural variations in cognitive skills. In D. R. Price-Williams (Ed.), *Cross-cultural studies*. New York: Penguin, 1970.

Goodnow, J. J. Rules and repertoires, rituals and tricks of the trade: Social and informational aspects to cognitive and representational development. In S. Farnham-Diggory (Ed.), *Information processing in children*. New York: Academic Press, 1972.

Goodnow, J. J., & Bethon, G. Piaget's tasks: The effects of schooling and intelligence. *Child Development*, 1966, **37**, 573–582.

Grant, C. V. & Schepers, J. M. An exploratory factor analysis of five new cognitive tasks for African mine workers. *Psychologia Africana*, 1969, **12**, 181–192.

Greenfield, P. M., & Bruner, J. S. Culture and cognitive growth. *International Journal of Psychology*, 1966, **1**, 89–107.

Hanfmann, E. A study of personal patterns in an intellectual performance. *Character and Personality*, 1941, **9**, 315–325.

Havighurst, R. J. & Hilkevitch, R. R. The intelligence of Indian children as measured by a performance scale. *Journal of Abnormal and Social Psychology*, 1944, **39**, 419–433.

Heron, A., & Simonsson, M. Weight conservation in Zambian children: A nonverbal approach. *International Journal of Psychology*, 1969, **4**, 281–292.

Hertzig, M. E., Birch, H. G., Thomas, A., & Mendez, O. A. Class and ethnic differences in the responsiveness of preschool children to cognitive demands. *Monographs of the Society for Research in Child Development*, 1968, **33**(Whole No. 117).

Hodgkin, M. C. Cross-cultural education in an anthropological perspective. In F. A. J. Ianni & E. Storey (Eds.), *Cultural relevance and educational issues*. Boston: Little, Brown, 1973.

Hudson, W. Pictorial depth perception in subcultural groups in Africa. *Journal of Social Psychology*, 1960, **52**, 183–208.

Kagan, J., & Klein, R. E. Cross-cultural perspectives on early development. *American Psychologist*, 1973, **28**(11), 947–961.

Labov, W. The logic of nonstandard English. In F. Williams (Ed.), *Language and poverty*. Chicago: Markham, 1970.

Lévi-Strauss, C. *Structural anthropology*. New York: Basic Books, 1963.

Looft, W. R. Conceptions of human nature, educational practice, and individual development. *Human Development*, 1973, **16**, 21–32.

Lloyd, B. B. Perception and cognition: *A cross-cultural perspective*. Middlesex, England: Penguin, 1972.

Lynch, K. *The image of the city*. Cambridge, Massachusetts: MIT Press, 1960.

Maccoby, M., & Modiano, N. On culture and equivalence: I. In J. S. Bruner, R. R. Olver, & P. M. Greenfield (Eds.), *Studies in cognitive growth*. New York: Wiley, 1966.

McElwain, D. W., & Kearney, G. E. *Queensland test handbook: A test of general cognitive ability designed for use under conditions of reduced communication*. Melbourne, Australia: Australian Council for Educational Research, 1970.

Minuchin, P., Biber, B., Shapiro, E., & Zimiles, H. *The psychological impact of school experience*. New York: Basic Books, 1969.

Miller, R. J. Cross-cultural research in the perception of pictorial materials. *Psychological Bulletin*, 1973, **80**, 135–151.

Ohannessian, S. *The study of the problems of teaching English to American Indians*. Washington D.C.: Center for Applied Linguistics, 1967.

Okonji, O. M. A cross-cultural study of the effects of familiarity on classificatory behaviour. *Journal of Cross-Cultural Psychology*, 1971, **2**, 39–49.

Olson, D. On conceptual strategies. In J. S. Bruner, R. R. Olver, & P. M. Greenfield (Eds.), *Studies in cognitive growth*. New York: Wiley, 1966.

Olson, D. *Cognitive development: The acquisition of diagonality*. New York: Academic Press, 1970.

Philp, H., & Kelly, M., Product and process in cognitive development: Some comparative data on the performance of school age children in different cultures, *British Journal of Educational Psychology,* 1974, **44**, 248–265.

Pick, A. D. The games experimenters play: A review of methods and concepts in cross-cultural studies of cognition and development. Unpublished manuscript, University of Minnesota, 1974.

Rohwer, W. D., Jr. Prime time for education: Early childhood or adolescence? *Harvard Educational Review,* 1971, **41**, 316–341.

Serpell, R. Cross-cultural differences in the difficulty of copying orientation: A response-organization hypothesis. *Human Development Research Unit Reports,* University of Zambia, 1969, No. 11.

Serpell, R. Preference for specific orientation of abstract shapes among Zambian children. *Journal of Cross-Cultural Psychology,* 1971, **2**, 225–239.

Shapiro, M. B. The rotation of drawings by illiterate Africans. *Journal of Social Psychology,* 1960, **52**, 17–30.

Shipstone, E. J. Some variables affecting pattern conception. *Psychological Monographs,* 1960, **74**(17, Whole No. 504).

Tenezakis, M. D., & Kelly, M. R. Affect and cognition in Greek migrant children: Reflections on some tentative evidence. Paper presented at the Australian Conference on Cognitive Development, Australian National University, Canberra, Australia, February 1973.

Tolkin, S. R., & Konner, M. J. Alternative conceptions of intellectual functioning. *Human Development,* 1973, **16**, 33–52.

Vernon, P. E. Administration of group intelligence tests to East African pupils. *British Journal of Educational Psychology,* 1967, **37**, 282–291.

Vernon, P. E. *Intelligence and cultural environment.* London: Methuen, 1969.

Wober, M. Culture and the concept of intelligence: A case in Uganda. *Journal of Cross-Cultural Psychology,* 1972, **3**, 327–328.

Wohlwill, J. F. The concept of experience: S or R? *Human Development,* 1973, **16**, 90–107.

# 10
# Culture, Technology, and Intellect

David R. Olson

*The Ontario Institute for Studies in Education,*
*Toronto, Canada*

The range of issues with which any theory of intelligence must deal is bounded on one side by considerations of man as a biological animal and on the other side by those of man as a social or cultural animal. Both of these sets of considerations share some common assumptions about the nature of human intelligence. Goodnow (Chapter 9) and Charlesworth (Chapter 8) both make the clear and convincing case that intelligence has everything to do with successful adaptation. Further, they agree that one cannot discuss adaptation usefully unless one specifies clearly what it is that the system is to adapt to. Neither of them is satisfied with the blindness of traditional theories of intelligence to the cognitive demands of various ecological niches. To answer the question of the demands that the environment makes upon intelligence, Charlesworth urges ethological studies of naturally occurring adaptive behavior on the part of children growing up in our culture. Goodnow argues that the answer to this question may come into focus by comparing the intellectual demands of different cultures. Quite different performances are considered adaptive in different cultures. For example, tests that are found to be correlated indices of intelligence in one culture are unrelated in another. Goodnow's sensitive treatment of these cultural differences gives her chapter some of the features of a field manual for the ethological study of intelligence. Up to this point the chapters of Goodnow and Charlesworth are highly congruent.

But what, if anything, does underlie adaptive performances—what Charlesworth calls "highly generalizable and highly usable, life valuable (cognitive) operations that are responsible for intelligent behavior [p. 158]?" The answers offered to this question show more clearly the differences in underlying theoretical bias—in Charlesworth's case, a bias towards a biological account of intelligence, in Goodnow's case, a bias towards a cultural account of intelligence.

Charlesworth sees intelligence being called upon for personal survival—man against nature. But Goodnow shows that each culture poses different problems for its members. The use of intelligence is less to mediate between man and nature than to mediate between man and his cultural environment, his artifacts—his classification systems, navigational system, language, and mathematics. Culture can be viewed as a set of conventions, institutions, and artifacts that arrange and control man's interactions with nature. The culture minimizes the occurrence of novel or unexpected natural events.

The contrast I am drawing between a biological model and a cultural model may be depicted as in Fig. 1. In the biological model, adaptive intelligence is assumed to be that which mediates between man and nature—man survives by adapting to nature. In the cultural model, it is assumed that the culture has already "worked-up" procedures for dealing with the natural environment, these procedures being embodied in the artifacts, institutions, conventions, and technologies of that culture. Intelligence in this case mediates between man and culture. Intelligence, when considered in terms of underlying abilities is that set of abilities required to master the tools, artifacts and technologies of the culture; when considered in terms of skilled performance, it is the set of competencies achieved by the mastery of those technologies.

This latter cultural conception of intelligence has been suggested by several writers including Bruner (1966), Medawar (1973) and Popper (1972). McLuhan (1964) has stated the issue in its most succinct form in his celebrated claim that

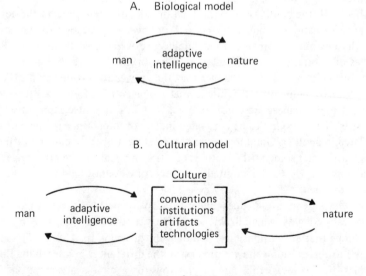

FIG. 1   Two models of adaptive intelligence.

media are the extensions of man. The remainder of this chapter is an attempt to articulate a cultural view of intelligence and to consider some of the evidence that bears on it.

## CULTURE AND INTELLIGENCE

It is a commonplace that the mental activities that have occupied man have altered with the changes in his cultural environment. Western man's current concern with reflective intelligence, the formulation and criticism of theories and the like are of relatively recent origin. Yet these changing demands to which the human mind must adapt have yet to make their impression on theories of intelligence. Neither Piaget's theory of intelligence nor that theory associated with the testing movement make allowance for the possibility that intelligence is largely culturally determined, that what the mind can do depends upon the devices provided by the culture. An examination of some of the ways in which the media, technologies and artifacts of a culture extend or otherwise interact with human psychological resources to produce an intelligent performance is the necessary focus of such a theory. As the impetus for the construction of such a theory comes more from the study of the roots of Western culture than from empirical research, I shall defend the argument with cultural–historical evidence even though I intend it as a psychological theory of intelligence.

Is it possible to show in any clear way just how the invention of any particular technique or technology has altered the structure of performances that one would call intelligent? As Goodnow points out, gross correlations between technology and cognition can be quite misleading. Hence, I propose to examine one such cultural–technological change, namely, the invention of writing systems, and to sketch the biasing effect of that technology on the mental processes that were relevant or constituent to intelligent performances.

My more general purpose is to elaborate the claim that a conception of intelligence must specify, as a major constituent, the structure of various technologies and the demands they put on the cognitive processes. It is therefore reasonable to begin with a more general look at the relation between technology, technique, and competent performance. For example, it should be obvious that a judgement of man's strength was altered by the domestication of "beasts of burden." What a man can haul when he has an animal to help him is not well indicated by the size of his biceps. It is not that one cannot make some assessment of the strength of the man's biceps, it is merely that such an assessment is of little interest. A similar effect would be produced by the invention of machines having mechanical advantage or by the invention of power sources like engines and electricity. The important point to notice is that when you consider the man's strength or power, you must look at the man–machine system; the underlying processes that go into an act of strength differ depending on the machine that the man is "hooked" to.

But technologies are not only a means of modifying motor activities. They are also a means of modifying cognitive activities. They alter what we can do and the psychological processes that are constituent to that activity. According to Socrates in *Phaedrus,* the Egyptian god Thoth boasted that his invention of a writing system would greatly improve on memory, while the other gods claimed that it would destroy memory. I would say it made memory a luxury just as machines (or slaves) made his biceps a luxury; memory became something relegated to the decorative, bizarre or occult, the memory feats performed brilliantly in the circus and mundanely in the psychological laboratory.

The idea that adaptation could be cultural as well as biological is over a century old. Samuel Butler, author of *Erewhon* (1872), developed the conception that there is a parallel between the evolution of organs and the evolution of tools or machines. Animal evolution proceeds primarily by *endosomatic* evolution, the biological modification of organs. Human evolution proceeds primarily by *exosomatic* evolution, the development of new organs outside of our own bodies. Popper (1972) adds: "But man, instead of growing better eyes and ears, grows spectacles, microscopes, telescopes, telephones, and hearing aids. And instead of growing swifter and swifter legs, he grows swifter and swifter motor cars. . . . Instead of growing better memories and brains, we grow paper, pens, pencils, typewriters, dictaphones, the printing press, and libraries [pp. 238–239]." Exosomatic organs are transmitted from generation to generation just as surely as endosomatic organs. While it is easy to see that technologies have altered the input and output systems, it is less obvious that they have altered the higher mental processes that we call intelligence. The Whorfian hypothesis to the effect that spoken languages which differ from culture to culture produce different conceptions of reality has yielded disappointingly little. Yet it may be noted that while the acquisition of a spoken language is universal and its consequences are inextricably tied to human cognition, the acquisition of a written language is not universal and its consequences are only now becoming apparent. Thus writing, as a technology, may have particularly obvious cognitive effects.

## THE INVENTION OF A PHONETIC WRITING SYSTEM

Havelock's (1973) account of the origins of written language describes a cultural invention that radically altered not only human culture but also human cognition. In McLuhan's aphorism, man changed an ear for an eye. Havelock's contribution to the study of the consequences of literacy consists in part in contrasting the ways in which knowledge is organized and preserved in the absence of a written language with the ways in which it is organized by means of a written language.

The codification of the knowledge of procedures and traditions of a culture in the absence of a writing system is called an "oral tradition." An oral culture, as Frye (1971) points out, "depends upon memory, and consequently it also depends heavily on verse, the simplest and most memorable way of conventionalizing the rhythm of speech [p. 38]." The possibility of such a tradition was completely overlooked until relatively modern times. In 1928, Milman Parry drew the conclusion that the *Illiad* and the *Odyssey,* usually attributed to a literate Homer, were in fact examples of oral composition, composed over centuries by bards who were nonliterate for audiences who could not read (Parry, 1971). Homer may have recorded them, but he most certainly did not "write" them.

Speech that has been shaped by the requirements of auditory memory Havelock calls *poetized* speech. But these requirements put a considerable bias on the sorts of things that can be said and remembered. The syntax of memorized rhythmic speech permits some kinds of statements and discourages others. Definitions, logical principles, causes and the like are not readily memorized; even now, children who are required to memorize such things adopt alphabetic mnemonics to handle them. Rather, oral tradition is compatible with the type of statements we call "sayings"—proverbs, adages, aphorisms, riddles, commandments and the like which find their way now-a-days into the remnants of rhetoric—"Unaccustomed as I am to public speaking . . ." etc. Havelock (1973) says:

> Neither principles nor laws nor formulas are amenable to a syntax which is orally memorizable. But persons and events that act or happen are amenable. . . . Orally memorized verse (including the epics) is couched in the contingent: it deals in a panorama of happenings, not a program of principles [p. 51].

Havelock goes on to argue that the sudden blossoming of classical Greece is to be attributed largely to the invention of an explicit writing system, namely, the phonetic alphabet.

> For the first time the governing word ceases to be a vibration heard by the ear and nourished in the memory. It becomes a visible artifact. . . . The documented statement, persisting through time unchanged, is to release the human brain from certain formidable burdens of memorization while releasing the energies available for conceptual thought. The results as they are to be observed in the intellectual history of Greece and of Europe were profound [p. 60].

The invention of a phonetic alphabet was a remarkable achievement, the consequences of which have been brilliantly analyzed by Havelock. Basically, alphabets prior to the Greek alphabet were attempts at transcription of actual sound systems. But it is impossible to create a one-to-one correspondence between a written character and a speech sound because there are thousands of recognizable speech sounds; to provide one character for each sound would require thousands of written characters. An extremely large number of characters were employed before the invention of the phonetic alphabet, with the result that the written language was so complicated that only a few professional scribes could master it. Any reduction in the number of written characters, such that several sounds were represented by the same character, increased the ambiguity of the character. To illustrate, an alphabet that had characters only for consonants could not provide differential representations for such words as *bell, ball, bill;* they would all have to be represented by *bll.* The writing systems prior to the phonetic alphabet can therefore be described as nonexplicit.

The consequences of such a writing system are important. Havelock (1973) states:

> ... when it came to transcribing discursive speech, difficulties of interpretation would discourage the practice of using the script for novel or freely-invented discourse. The practice that would be encouraged would be to use the system as a reminder of something already familiar, so that recollecting of its familiarity would aid the reader in getting the right interpretation.... It would in short tend to be something—tale, proverb, parable, fable and the like—which already existed in oral form and had been composed according to oral rules.... The syllabic (writing) system, in short, provided techniques for recall of what was already familiar, *not instruments for formulating novel statements which could further the exploration of new experience* [p. 8; italics mine].

The invention of the phonetic alphabet, therefore, was a significant step towards rendering language explicit, of putting the meaning into the text. In a single step it became less dependent upon context of the utterance or upon shared or prior knowledge. Language became an instrument for formulating original statements—statements that contradicted common sense. Under the impact of writing, the structure and the content of language changed. Havelock (1967) elsewhere has shown that Plato's *Republic* is to a large extent an attack upon the oral poetic tradition. Socrates demanded the sort of statement that today we call logical or rational, a statement that "prefers its subject to be a concept rather than a person, and its verb to be an 'is' verb rather than a 'doing' verb" (Havelock, 1973, p. 51). Poeticized speech came to be considered a deceitful luxury; logical prose, epitomized by the syllogism and the dialogues, was a truthful necessity. It is to this logical, if prosaic, use of language that we, even today, attach the label "rational."

The implication to be drawn from this analysis of the relation between oral and written language for the study of human cognition is obvious. First, the nature of an intelligent performance changed dramatically with the invention of a technological device. What was intelligent in an oral culture was considered maladaptive in a literate one, and Plato set out to eradicate it. Second, the demands placed upon the central nervous system changed. A powerful acoustic memory, once a necessity, became a luxury. In its place came logically connected prose statements, which, because they were preserved as a visible artifact, could be reflected on analytically. The conclusion toward which I am pointing is that the functioning of intelligence cannot be specified outside of the technology with which it is interacting. Intelligence is a quality of a performance, and performances we call intelligent necessarily imply the employment of one technology or another.

Similarly, all tasks or performances that we require from children on intelligence tests reflect competence with our technologies. They assess the level of competence of a child or an adult in using some artifact that we find important in our culture. If children come from a different culture or subculture, they do poorly. If we assessed our own performance on some technological device evolved in another culture, such as the navigational system of the Puluwat (Gladwin, 1970) we would also do poorly. In sum, according to our current conception of intelligence, the types of performances that we take as evidence of intelligence are those that rely on a type of symbolic competence that we have been unaware of. Not knowing that these performances reflect heavily the level of competence with these devices or technologies, we have assumed that they are the consequence of some underlying general "ability." Now, if it is agreed that our measures of intelligence reflect different kinds of symbolic competencies, it is perfectly legitimate to measure this level of competence to determine, for example, if a child requires more practice, but it is illegitimate to draw any inferences about so-called underlying abilities.

The concept of intelligence remains an intriguing one. But now the question becomes one of characterizing the nature of human competence. The analysis of the invention of writing systems has shown the origins of one type of human competence, a type of competence that underlies Western cultures. Let us now consider another, more recent but equally important one.

## THE INVENTION OF EXTENDED PROSE STATEMENTS: THE ESSAYIST TECHNIQUE

To this point I have argued that the invention of an artifact, the phonetic alphabet, has altered both human culture and human cognition. I want now to consider the possibility that a particular use of a technology, what I shall call a technique, may also alter the nature of human competence. Again, this argument is only partly my own. It relys heavily upon the work of Havelock, McLuhan, and Ong.

The use of extended prose statements which are logically interdependent is a technique of relatively recent origin—a technique that was closely, though not exclusively tied to the invention of printing. The changing use of language was indicated by several contemporaneous events: the changing conception of poetry of the Romantic movement, the decline of rhetoric, the rise of the British essayists and the Protestant attitude to scripture (Olson, in press). All of these features are a consequence of a new respect for the autonomy of printed texts, the search for the logical implications of printed statements on the part of the readers, and an attempt to formulate original statements from which true implications could be derived on the part of the writer.

Ong's (1971) major contribution is to show that the Romantic movement coincided with the codification of knowledge in printed form—for example, the encyclopedia of d'Alembert and Diderot, published in 1751. With print taking over the role previously served by human memory, formulaic poetry was no longer useful for preserving cultural information. As a result, poetry shifted to a concern with originality. In Ong's (1971) words: "When truths needed no longer to be constantly reiterated orally in order to remain available, virtuosity, that is, superlative skill in manipulating well-worked material, was displaced by 'creativity' as an ideal [p. 294]."

The changing role of prose was no less dramatic, as documented by Ong (1961) in his analysis of the work of Peter Ramus, a sixteenth century educational reformer. Ramus' work was devoted largely to an attempt to substitute the logical analysis of written text for the rhetoric which had been dominant since antiquity. The Middle Ages had preserved great quantities of "florilegia," collections of wise and pithy sayings in which school boys were indoctrinated. These sayings were still utilized up to the time of Erasmus' *Adagia*. But with Ramus, the emphasis shifted from the rhetorical virtuosity of manipulating formulaic *sayings* to the logical analysis of *statements*. While Ramus, in his day, was regarded as a pedant, the technique of logical analysis of statements became a dominant feature in the use of language.

It is just such a shift in attitude toward language that had, a century earlier, led to Luther's claim: "The meaning of Scripture depends not upon the dogma of the church but upon a deeper reading of the text." For the first time in history it was assumed, whether correctly or not, that the meaning was given by the text, not by the prior knowledge coded in the dogma, nor in the perceptual context in which the sentence was uttered, but rather in the structure of the discourse itself. The text had to stand on its own. Written material was now read in a manner in which it had not been read before—what is the text asserting and what are the necessary implications of that assertion?

The more fundamental effect was on the writer: How could something new be written such that the implications of that assertion are correct? This concern ushered in the use of the form of extended statement I have called the "essayist technique," with its bias towards abstract general statements from which series of true implications could be drawn. This development has had dramatic consequences for our current conception of knowledge in general, and of our language in particular.

The reliance on logically connected prose statements as the instrument of certain knowledge was the distinguishing feature of the British empiricist tradition. John Locke (1632–1704), whose *Essay Concerning Human Understanding* was an early attempt at extended prose statement, well represents the intellectual bias which originated at that time and which characterizes our present use of language. Knowledge was an extended logical essay—an assertion examined and re-examined to determine all of its implications, in a single coherent text. It was the nonfiction equivalent of a farce, and it is interesting to note that when Locke began his criticism of human understanding he thought that he could write it on one sheet of paper in an evening. By the time he had exhausted the possibilities of the subject utilizing this new technique, the essay had taken twenty years and hundreds of pages. Locke's technique differed notably from the predominant writing style of the time. Ellul (1964) says:

> An uninitiated reader who opens a scientific treatise on law, economy, medicine, or history published between the sixteenth and eighteenth centuries is struck most forcibly by the complete absence of logical order [p. 39].... It was more a question of personal exchange than of taking an objective position [p. 41].

The use of the essay served as an "exploratory device" for examining an old problem and in the course of that examination producing new knowledge.

While *oral* discussion biases statements in the direction of proverbs, metaphors and witty sayings, *written* statements are uniquely adapted to an analysis of the implications of those statements. If one's mental resources are utilized in remembering a statement, there are no residual resources to reflect on the logical implications of that statement. Writing the statement down releases mental resources for other activities. But the use of writing not only has the consequence of making the logical implications of statements more detectable; it also has the effect of altering the statements themselves. The tendency to look at statements to see what could be deduced from them yields implications— implications which are often out of phase with experience. The detection of such false implications could serve as an occasion for reformulating the original statement. If one considers the sort of statements that would survive the analysis of their implications, one arrives at the criteria of statements of (1) great generality that are (2) not easily falsifiable. These criteria are in fact those of general theories.

The use of the essay method, therefore, was the occasion for the creation of such theories. This is not to imply that oral language and oral tradition had no theories but merely that their theories were generated and validated by different means. A proverb is not the same as a premise. The process of formulating statements and deriving their implications, testing or examining the truth value of those implications and using the results to revise or generalize the original assertion, is not only a characterization of the philosophical methods of the empiricist philosophers, but also a characterization of the methods of deductive empirical science. In science, one can see more clearly the process of making assertions, deriving implications and verifying or falsifying them by empirical means. The result is the same, namely, the formulation of a small set of connected statements of great generality. My claim is that general theories are the necessary consequence of the utilization of a particular technique, that of trying to construct statements from which other true statements can be derived as implications. Newton's laws and Locke's theory of understanding can be seen as manifestations of the utilization of the same genre of literature. The establishment of the Royal Society in 1662 buttressed this use of language by devoting itself not only to the advancement of science, but also to "the improvement of the English language as a medium of prose" (Innis, 1951, p. 56).

Consider the implications of the repeated application of this technique to our knowledge of, for example, cows. One feature of cows, that they give milk, may be called concrete; another feature, that they are mammals, may be called abstract. The question is this: What is the occasion for the "detection" of these different features? As long as one's purpose is simply to competently perform practical actions, the "give milk" feature is critical, the "mammal" feature is a luxury. However, as soon as one's purpose is to formulate statements from which true implications can be drawn, one is forced to detect or create features which bear a class inclusion relation to the event in question. That is, the only necessarily true implication that can be drawn from the sentence, "This is a cow," is that "It must be a mammal," that is, some feature that is necessarily a constituent of the meaning of the concrete noun. In contrast, notice that the other implication, "It must give milk," is not necessarily true. The application of this technique of formulating more abstract categories from which true implications can be drawn, when applied to objects, would yield the superordinate taxonomic schemes that Aristotle took to be an "unbiased" picture of reality. I would prefer to say that taxonomic structures are the picture of reality that results from the repeated application of a *particular technology*—it is not a natural or unbiased or objective view of reality.

Although these comments simply introduce a line of examination, they have been offered to indicate the aspects of language that come to be developed (discovered or invented) under the impact of a particular technological device. The essayist technique and written language generally, in the process of formulating general statements from which true implications can be drawn, have as a by-product created the abstract logical concepts that we who are so habituated to a literate culture tend to view as part of nature herself. Modern science, like "rationality," is an indirect consequence of the invention of a particular technology.

## TECHNOLOGY AND INTELLIGENCE

I have discussed the invention of one technology, writing systems, and one technique, the formulation of true statements from which implications which are true can be drawn, and I have tried to show that these devices are responsible for the cognitive characteristics of abstraction and rationality that we currently characterize as being indicative of intelligence. Our culture has invented two devices of extraordinary power—written statements and extended prose statements. Their consequence is the formulation of statements of exceedingly wide generality. I would offer this as an explanation of Goodnow's (Chapter 9), Greenfield's (1972), and Scribner and Cole's (1973) important findings regarding the lack of generalizability of problem solutions in traditional cultures. Lacking written prose, they are less concerned with the formulation of general statements than Western cultures are. It is these general statements which permit or induce generalizations.

Until now, however, the reliance on these technologies of writing has never been visible to their users. We, as psychologists, have never fully realized our dependence on a single, itself biased, technique. Plato attacked the oral tradition without realizing his commitment to prose; Luther never realized his commitment to printed scripture; Locke, and for that matter Popper, never realized their dependence on the essayist technique. Now we are beginning to see the way in which our achievements reflect the reliance on technique. Intelligence is not something we have that is immutable; it is something we cultivate by operating with a technology, or something we create by inventing new technology. Intellectual achievements in our own time depend critically both on hooking our human resources to the most powerful technologies available and, more importantly, *on creating technologies that bring worthwhile goals within the reach of every man.* There are as many ways of being intelligent as there are technologies; invention of new technologies will create new ways of being intelligent.

The measurement of "abilities" is founded on a gross misapprehension of human intelligent performance. Tests may indicate level of competence in any of the symbol systems or technologies that make up our culture; poor performance may suggest the necessity for education or for inventing new technologies. But test performance never reflects directly the basic cognitive abilities; rather, it reflects those abilities as amplified by the technologies of the culture. Further, the invention of new technologies or the alteration of our environment may call upon radically new kinds of basic human abilities; those highly valued in a mechanical culture of even a half century ago have become somewhat obsolete because of technological change.

The primary qualities of mind are, therefore, not simply biological in nature. They are the achievement of the coupling of very limited human resources with the technologies which, by and large, have been invented to circumvent those limitations. The technologies have the effect of making some particular underlying abilities critical, or at least relevant, to intelligent performance. To illustrate, oral memory, which was absolutely critical to intelligent performance in the oral Homeric world, became largely irrelevant with the invention of writing since writing reduced the demands placed upon oral memory. But writing created a new set of possibilities for the culture and a new set of demands on the users. I have tried to detail one set of these in my treatment of what I have called the essayist technique—the statement of a conjecture which is then stuffed with its own implications, and the subsequent revision of that conjecture. To be intelligent as an essayist calls upon a different set of underlying capacities than to be intelligent as an oral poet or rhetorician.

The question remains as to whether these "underlying abilities" can be examined or specified. Intelligence is necessarily the mastery and utilization of the technological system—verbal abilities reflect competence with the technology of language, probably written rather than oral, reflecting the bias of our current "prose" culture; numerical abilities involve competence with the number system. It may not be possible to assess the abilities that underlie the mastery of skills or competencies in general, because abilities tend to take the shape offered by the culture for the deployment of those abilities. Measures of level of competence in various cultural skills may be useful for guiding educational decisions, but the conception of a general quality of mind that so intrigued the nineteenth century Darwinists is dead.


## INTELLIGENCE TESTS

The conception of intelligence that is dominant in our culture may be characterized by the terms "abstractness" and "rationality." Abstraction refers to the fact that an event is treated not in terms of its functional or perceptual qualities but rather in terms of its membership in some class-inclusive category. Thus, a pen is "a writing instrument" but not "to write with" or "for school." An apple and a peach are alike because they are both "fruit" but not because they are both "to eat" or both "round"—or so our Binet norms claim. Classification at the level of function is universal, while classification by means of superordinates is unique to a literate culture; only the latter is taken as an index of intelligence.

Rationality refers to the quality of arguments. Thus, if a conclusion "follows logically" from its premises, it is rational. If you prefer steak to goulash and lobster to steak, you should prefer lobster to goulash. Standard IQ tests rely on such logical problems. But I have assembled an array of evidence based on Havelock and Ong and McLuhan and Frye that "abstraction" as defined by superordinate categories is a direct consequence of the invention of a writing system—statements given the permanence of writing become subject to criticism as opposed to simple misinterpretation. It becomes possible to differentiate what is intended from what is said. What is said is explicit and replicable in phonetic writing systems. Rationality, I have argued, is the direct consequence of the development of the extended logical prose, what I have called the essayist technique, which demands both the analysis of the necessary implications of abstract statements *and* the formulation of abstract statements from which true implications can be drawn. Abstraction and rationality, then, are to a large extent the necessary but unintended consequences of technological developments. Hence, intelligence tests reflect simply the extent to which children in our society and/or members of other cultures have mastered these very special techniques.

This conclusion helps explain some otherwise puzzling facts. First, the dramatic change in "intelligence" correlated with the onset or mastery of reading and/or schooling (White, 1965) presumably reflects an adjustment to the newly encountered permanence of statements. Second, the important effects of formal schooling found by Scribner and Cole (1973) are presumably related to the development of the use of language for formulating general statements. This is, in fact, their hypothesis. Third, social class differences are presumed to reflect the utilization of these different linguistic forms. Highly literate parents may be expected to communicate the explicit logical structure of printed texts in at least two ways, through their own abstract language and, probably more importantly, through reading printed stories. Intellectual differences, then, are to some extent linguistic differences, not so much in spoken as in written language. Why, then, are they not more easily altered? Perhaps it is because the structure of such devices and the competencies built upon them are implicit and hence not easily changed, a problem I have considered elsewhere (Olson, 1973).

If these arguments hold up, intelligence as it is conventionally studied is trivial. Yet intelligence as human competence is both interesting and important. What, then, can we say about the relation between mind and technology? Once we have seen that what we have conventionally dignified by calling intelligence is simply the consequence of exploiting technology or technique, we can rephrase the question of intelligence by asking a set of new questions: First, what are limiting features of mind that set boundary conditions to all techniques, a question which H. Simon has interestingly set for himself (Simon, 1969). Second, what are the qualities that a technology gives to mind? The alphabet permits us to use alphabetic mnemonics; the number system permits us to do mental arithmetic; writing gives us a larger working memory. More important, it may be the case that problem solving, constructing theories, and thinking generally are not simply things that go on in our minds so much as they are something we construct on paper, much as an artist constructs an image on a canvass. Once constructed externally they can be "run off" internally as mental skills. A third question that requires radical reformulation is the nature–nurture issue. Intelligence is not the simple interaction of genes with the environment. We "inherit" both our endosomatic organs and our exosomatic organs and these together are involved in the assimilation of our personal environmental experiences. Environment is not "of a piece"; hence, the question is poorly formed. Fourth, as educators, our concern should be with the possibility of "design," the invention and refinement of technologies that will bring a set of worthwhile personal and social goals within the reach of every member of the culture.

A better understanding of all of these issues is likely to be advanced both by the cross-cultural studies pursued by Goodnow and by the ethological studies pursued by Charlesworth. Both are necessary for even a limited understanding of how the cognitive resources of the child are linked to the accumulated resources of the culture to yield adaptive behavior.

The expressions of a culture—its technologies, techniques, symbols and artifacts—mediate between man and nature. They provide the means for the achievement of practical ends, they serve as instruments for the exploration of reality, and perhaps most importantly, they provide the mental apparatus for intelligently transcending the limitations and bias of personal, private experience.

## REFERENCES

Bruner, J. S., Olver, R. R., & Greenfield, P. M. (Eds.), *Studies in cognitive growth.* New York: Wiley, 1966.

Ellul, J. *The technological society.* New York: Vintage Books, 1964.

Frye, N. *The critical path.* Bloomington: Indiana University Press, 1971.

Gladwin, T. *East is a big bird: Navigation and logic on Pulawat Atoll.* Cambridge, Massachusetts: Harvard University Press, 1970.

Greenfield, P. M. Oral or written language: The consequences for cognitive development in Africa, the United States and England. *Language and Speech,* 1972, **15,** 169–178.

Havelock, E. A. *Preface to Plato.* New York: Grosset & Dunlap, 1967.

Havelock, E. A. Prologue to Greek literacy. In C. Boulter (Ed.), *Lectures in memory of Louise Taft Semple, second series, 1966–1971.* Cincinnati: University of Oklahoma Press for the University of Cincinnati, 1973.

Innis, H. A. *The bias of communication.* Toronto: University of Toronto Press, 1951.

McLuhan, M. *Understanding media: The extensions of man.* New York and Toronto: McGraw-Hill, 1964.

Medawar, P. Man: The technological animal. *Smithsonian Magazine,* May, 1973.

Olson, D. R. What is worth knowing and what can be taught? *School Review,* 1973, **82,** 27–43.

Olson, D. R. From utterance to text: The bias of language in speech and writing. In R. Diez Guerrero & H. Fisher (Eds.), *Logic and language in personality and society.* New York: Academic Press, in press.

Ong, W. J. Ramist classroom procedure and the nature of reality. *Studies in English literature, 1500–1900.* Winter, 1961, **1**(1).

Ong, W. J. *Rhetoric, romance, and technology: Studies in the interaction of expression and culture.* Ithaca: Cornell University Press, 1971.

Parry, A. *The making of Homeric verse: The collected papers of Milman Parry.* Oxford: Clarendon Press, 1971.

Popper, K. R. *Objective knowledge: An evoluationary approach.* Oxford: Clarendon Press, 1972.

Scribner, S., & Cole, M. Cognitive consequences of formal and informal education. *Science,* 1973, **182,** 553–559.

Simon, H. *The sciences of the artificial.* Cambridge, Massachusetts: MIT Press, 1969.

White, S. Evidence for a hierarchical arrangement of learning processes. In L. P. Lipsitt & C. C. Spiker (Eds.), *Advances in child development and behavior.* Vol. 2. New York: Academic Press, 1965.

# Part IV

## BASIC PROCESSES
## IN INTELLIGENCE

# 11
# Problem Solving and Intelligence

Lauren B. Resnick and Robert Glaser

*University of Pittsburgh*

We will argue in this chapter that a major aspect of intelligence is ability to solve problems, and that careful analysis of problem-solving behavior constitutes a means of specifying many of the psychological processes that intelligence comprises. To build the argument for this approach, we will first consider some general issues surrounding the term intelligence, and then suggest why problem solving provides fertile ground for the experimental study of intelligence.

We begin by accepting, provisionally, the layman's quite general definition of intelligence as "the ability to learn," and assume that this means the ability to learn things important in one's environment. We next note that much, perhaps most, learning occurs without formal instruction, that is, out of the context of established teaching institutions. Virtually all of the learning that children manage prior to the age of five or six occurs without such formal instruction. Even during the school years, much of what is learned is outside of any formal curriculum, and during most of one's adult life little formal instruction is engaged in, yet learning certainly continues. Even where deliberate instruction is provided, it is rarely "complete" in terms of assuring that the learner experiences or attends to every aspect of what is to be learned, or that he or she is systematically taught every skill in exactly the form used by experts.

This incompleteness of instruction, even in school, is an important point with respect to the definition of intelligence. In traditional forms of schooling (including those most prevalent today), children are exposed about equally to instruction, but some children learn more of whatever is offered than others. It is precisely this difference in amount learned under approximately equivalent conditions of exposure that makes intelligence tests work as predictive instruments. The actual items on most intelligence tests are tests of what one already knows. Whoever knows more (of the kind of thing being tested), and knows how to use that information under test-like conditions, will do better on the tests. Thus, the tests measure what the individual has managed to learn from past exposure, relative to other individuals. Presumably, if someone has been good in the past at acquiring knowledge, and if conditions of instruction remain more or less the same, then he or she will be good at acquiring knowledge in the future. In other words, although the test items are usually measures of learning already achieved, intelligence tests are indirectly measures of how well one can learn on one's own.

The import of these observations is that if we are to account for intelligence, we must account for the ability to learn on one's own in the absence of direct or complete instruction. To put it another way, we must account for the processes involved when an individual, under conditions of limited or less than explicit instruction, makes a transition from one state of competence to another. More broadly, we must seek a characterization of processes that are involved, or that an individual employs, in the acquisition of a new capability.

## ATTEMPTS TO ACCOUNT FOR TRANSITIONS IN INTELLECTUAL COMPETENCE

Where can we turn in modern psychology for serious study and elucidation of this problem of cognitive transition? An obvious first candidate is cognitive–developmental theory of the Piagetian and neo-Piagetian variety. Cognitive–developmental theory has been centrally concerned with charting changes in intellectual ability, and further, has stressed the "working from within" nature of cognitive growth. The child "constructs" cognitive reality and these constructions define his intellectual competence. In accounting for transitions in competence, emphasis is placed on what the child does, not on what he is taught.

Although the concern for internally produced structural transition is indeed strong, actual research on cognitive development in the Piagetian tradition has focused largely on description of the resulting state differences—differences in cognitive performances and inferred "deep" competence—at different points in development. This work has left the problem of accounting for transition between these states, or stages, almost completely uninvestigated and unspecified. The problem is considered only in the most general terms. When a child is in a given stage, he or she assimilates new information and experience into existing cognitive structures. From time to time however, "accommodations" occur, like miniature scientific revolutions. New structures are formed to account for the new experience and these then become the organizing structures for future encounters with the environment. Transition, then, occurs via accommodation. But on closer look, all of the important questions remain. When and why do accommodations take place? What tips the balance in favor of accommodation over assimilation? What actually *happens* during the process of accommodation? These questions are posed by cognitive–developmental theory, but not answered by it.

A recent monograph by Flavell (1972) underscores the absence of a strong theory of transitions within the Piagetian stage theory tradition. Flavell is concerned with how two "cognitive items" that are sequentially ordered in terms of temporal development are related to one another, that is, how acquisition of one item influences or determines acquisition of another. Flavell suggests that, of several kinds of transition relationships, "inclusion" sequences—cases where items are combined to form new items—are particularly amenable to clear explanation in terms of processes called upon in performance and transition.

Inclusion relationships have also been proposed as a means of accounting for growth in intellectual capability by Gagné (1962; 1968), in what has come to be known as cumulative learning theory. Gagné argues that complex abilities can be analyzed into simpler components, prerequisites, that are combined during acquisition of the complex ability. Since each prerequisite task can also be analyzed into its component abilities, and since each complex task can be combined with others to produce a still higher level of performance, it is possible to specify a hierarchy of tasks that cumulate through successive layers of positive transfer to greater and greater levels of cognitive competence. With respect to cognitive development, cumulative learning theory suggests that small changes in ability cumulate across tasks and over time to create an apparently large and qualitative shift in competence.

Although at one level of analysis cumulative learning theory seems to function as a potential explanation of stage changes in development, at another and deeper level a learning hierarchy represents no more than a collection of ordered but discrete state descriptions, albeit at a finer grain of description than Piagetian stages. A hierarchy of tasks does not explain the combinatory processes or transfer mechanisms by which new competence is actually produced. It is probably not too extreme to argue that the most interesting events, in terms of a theory of intelligence, happen between the specified points in a hierarchy. Yet cumulative learning theory, like Piagetian theory, is largely silent as to what goes on.

David Klahr (see Chapter 6) reports on work that can be thought of as an attempt to formalize through simulation an essentially cumulative learning hypothesis concerning cognitive development. The aim is to characterize increasingly complex performances on Piagetian tasks in terms of a limited set of processes defined by computer programs. These processes, in various combinations, are shown to be sufficient to perform a variety of tasks. As more processes enter the system, more complex and developmentally more advanced tasks can be performed. As Klahr points out, current formulations offer no really satisfactory (or "well-modeled") explanations for how a process enters the repertoire.

Further, there is, at present, no way to answer the question of how available processes are assembled (i.e., combined) to solve new problems.

This important question of assembly is partially masked by the use of production systems in current modeling attempts.[1] Production systems appear to solve the assembly problem by embedding it in the matching of current short-term memory contents (data structures) with production rule conditions. An action is carried out whenever the proper conditions are met; thus, within a production system formulation there is no need to postulate a separate assembly mechanism. However, as increasingly complex levels of performance are reached, new production rules are required if actions previously carried out under one set of conditions are to be used under new conditions. Thus, the essential problem of assembly—the use of available actions in new contexts—remains. This point should become clearer as we move to some specific examples later in this chapter.

## ASSEMBLY AS A MECHANISM OF TRANSITION IN COGNITIVE COMPETENCE

The problem before us is accounting for intelligence as a process wherein individuals develop new cognitive competence without direct or complete instruction. The question is one of transition between states of competence. We have argued that neither cognitive—developmental nor cumulative learning theory have as yet adequately addressed the problem of transition, nor have beginning attempts at an information processing theory of development. Further, we have suggested that a useful way of thinking about the problem of

---

[1] A production system, as defined by Newell (1973) is a scheme for specifying an information-processing system:

It consists of a set of productions, each production consisting of a condition and an action. It has also a collection of data structures; expressions that encode the information upon which the production system works—on which the actions operate and on which the conditions can be determined to be true or false. A production system, starting with an initially given set of data structures, operates as follows. That production whose condition is true of the current data (assume there is only one) is executed, that is, the action is taken. The result is to modify the current data structures. This leads in the next instant to another (possibly the same) production being executed, leading to still further modification. So it goes, action after action being taken to carry out an entire program of processing, each evoked by its condition becoming true of the momentarily current collection of data structures. The entire process halts either when no condition is true (hence, nothing is evoked) or when an action containing a stop operation occurs [p. 463].

transition is to attempt to account for the combination or assembly of existing processes into more complex ones.

## Assembly as Problem Solving

If one scans the psychological literature for places where the question of assembly has actually been experimentally addressed, one is drawn to the literature on "problem solving." We are drawn there with some reluctance because problem solving is at least as disorganized a topic in experimental psychology as intelligence—and it has not even had its share of psychometricians to provide it with a working operational definition. Problem solving has been studied in one form or another virtually throughout the history of scientific psychology, and proponents of various theories of psychology have attempted to explain problem-solving phenomena in terms of their own theoretical constructs. Despite the theoretical diversity, there exists a surprising consensus concerning what constitutes a "problem" in psychological terms, and a review of some of the classical literature on problem solving suggests a number of working hypotheses relevant to our present question of assembly and cognitive transition.

Psychologists agree that the term "problem" refers to a situation in which an individual is called upon to perform a task not previously encountered and for which externally provided instructions do not specify completely the mode of solution. The particular task, in other words, is new for the individual, although processes or knowledge already available can be called upon for solution. Associationist psychologists working in the Hullian tradition, such as Maltzman (1955; Maltzman, Brooks, Bogartz, & Summers, 1958), interpret problem solving in terms of the position of the appropriate response in a habit-family hierarchy. The emphasis is on accessing responses already available, but not dominant. Other definitions, too, stress calling up of available responses, but focus on processes of assembling them to form a new solution. Maier (1933), for example, gives this definition: "The solution of a problem . . . is a pattern consisting of parts of past experience which have become integrated. These parts of experience need never have been previously associated [p. 144]."

Wertheimer (1959), the spokesman for the Gestalt psychology of insight, defines problem solving in the following way: "[A] discovery does not merely mean that a result is reached which was not known before . . . but rather that a situation is grasped in a new and deeper fashion. . . . These changes of the situation as a whole imply changes in the structural meaning of part items, changes in their place, role and function, which often lead to important consequences [p. 169–170]." Wertheimer thus stresses the prior existence of components of the "solution" but focuses on the processes of restructuring and insight that lead to recognition of the solution as relevant.

Problem Solving as Invention

The classical literature on problem solving has directed much of its attention to tasks that require the invention or construction of a new strategy or material object. In these tasks a tool, physical or intellectual, is produced. Materials or processes are combined to make available something that had not existed before. The behavioral and/or technological repertoire is enlarged through processes of cognitive and physical assembly of prior elements.

The general characteristics of these "invention" tasks can best be conveyed by considering some examples. By far the largest set of such tasks has been studied under the label of "functional fixedness." The most familiar of these include the two-string, hat-rack, pendulum, and blowing-out-the candle problems introduced by Maier (1970), and the gimlet and candle-on-the-wall problems originally studied by Duncker (1945). In each of these problems, the subject is asked to build an object or to perform some action. An array of objects is provided, one or more of which *can* be used in solving the problem, but none of which are *typically* used that way. Thus, there are clamps and poles for the hat-rack problem but no wall hooks. There are various items that can serve as pendulum bobs in the two-string problem, but, at least in some versions of the problem, no extra piece of string or elastic. There are a box and matches in the candle-on-the-wall problem, but the box is filled with tacks and there is no recognizable candleholder.

In all of these tasks objects are combined or assembled in many ways to produce new and (at least temporarily) useful objects. They are inventions in the same sense that the telephone, the Bessemer furnace, and the airplane are inventions. Other invention problems are more cognitive in nature, with the problem solver not necessarily engaging in physical manipulation, but with the same combinatorial processes at work, based on past experience and knowledge as well as current task demands. One such problem is the radiation problem, studied and discussed at some length by Duncker (1945). Another is the parallelogram problem studied by Wertheimer (1959) and his students (Luchins & Luchins, 1970).

Invention problems address in a particularly direct way the question of transition in competence without direct instruction—the question with which this chapter opened. In invention problems individuals who are successful solvers have gained a new competence. They can do or make something they were unable to do or make before. They have learned something new. Further, they have managed this on their own, or with minimal external help. Thus, they have engaged in learning in the absence of instruction. Finally, in all of the problems the solutions are built out of information or partial solution routines already in the individuals' repertoires. In this way invention problems highlight the assembly process which we have suggested may be central to an understanding of the nature of intelligence.

A Model for Solving Invention Problems

Using commonly current information-processing constructs, it is possible to characterize invention/problem solving as a process of encoding a problem, i.e., building a representation in working memory (WM), and then searching long-term memory (LTM) for a stored routine (whole or partial) relevant to the problem as formulated. If a routine that works under present conditions of the task environment (TE) is not found, further features of the TE may be noted or the immediate goal of problem-solving activity redefined so that routines not previously recognized as relevant or useable will become so. We describe this general set of processes in terms of three aspects: (1) problem detection, (2) feature scanning, and (3) goal analysis.

*1. Problem detection.* Consider Fig. 1. Actions A through F define a problem detection routine. The process assumes an individual who has already encoded the problem as verbally stated. This has established in WM a goal (Box A). The first step in solving the problem consists of searching LTM for a routine that is encoded as relevant to the goal (Box B). If such an item is found, a test is made for whether the conditions required for carrying out the routine are present (C). If the answer is yes, the routine can be performed (D), and then tested for success in meeting the goal (E). If successful, the problem is "solved"–in fact, it was not really a problem since it had useable routines already available. The right-hand branches from B, C, and E, by contrast, set a "true" problem. If at B no solution routine relevant to the goal is found in LTM, a problem is automatically recognized (Box F). Alternatively, a candidate solution may have been found at B, but the necessary conditions for running it not met (C), or the action may not be successful (E). In each case, a problem would be defined. This definition constitutes, in effect, a new goal, or a new encoding of the situation.

Wertheimer's (1959) descriptions of initial reactions to the parallelogram problem provide some examples of problem detection. In some of Wertheimer's experiments children who knew an algorithm for finding the area of a parallelogram presented in a horizontal display, as in Fig. 2 at the top, were then given a vertically presented figure (as at the bottom of the Fig.). Some children immediately recognized the figure as one they had not "had yet" and refused to proceed. These children in effect failed to find a candidate solution routine. Others attempted to apply the standard routine. They dropped perpendiculars and then recognized an unfamiliar situation. These children apparently recalled the standard routine for finding area (at B of Fig. 1), failed to note that it was inapplicable (C), tried it (D), and then found it unsuccessful (at E).

*2. Feature scanning.* Assume now that, by one route or the other, a problem has been detected; no immediately applicable or successful routine for the goal as initially represented has been found. It is characteristic of individuals who have detected problems to begin to scan the environment, apparently searching

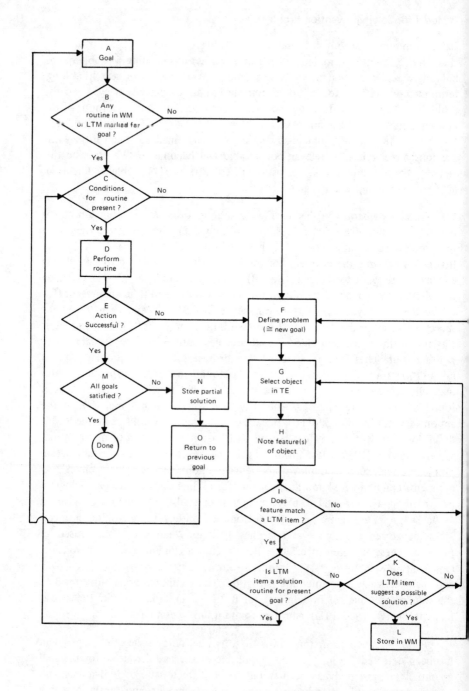

FIG. 1  A model for solving invention problems.

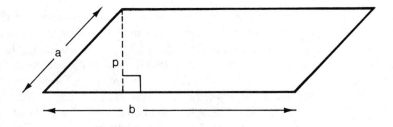

Area = b x p

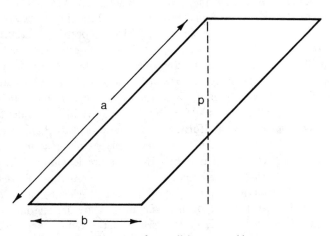

FIG. 2     Area of a parallelogram problem.

for clues. In functional fixedness problems, they typically attend to one after another of the objects available, apparently noting features of the objects. There is no evidence that there is an attempt to do an exhaustive scan, or to list all possible uses of the objects, as might seem to be suggested by theories of problem solving and creativity that stress fluency in producing many "unusual uses." Rather, this seems to be an idea-getting phase, a mapping of the environment, a highly heuristic, and possibly partly random activity, much influenced by what first falls to hand or eye. Coupled with this scanning of the physical environment, there is frequently a questioning of the experimenter concerning the nature of the task requirements and restrictions on what can be done.

Boxes F through L of Fig. 1 represent a sequence of events occurring during this feature-scanning phase. The opening conditions (F) are set up by the results of the problem detection phase. Problem detection has resulted in a new definition of the goal. This condition initiates search of the task environment. The first action in this search is to select an object in the task environment (G). The term "object" is used to refer to both physical and symbolic objects, including verbal information from the experimenter. Feature detection activities can now begin (H). The noting of some feature in the external environment activates a new look at the contents of LTM (I). LTM is scanned for any item that "matches" or is linked to the feature noted. If an LTM item is found, the model suggests an evaluation of relevance to the goal as presently formulated (J). Essentially, the question is asked whether the item retrieved suggests (or constitutes) a solution. If an already organized solution is found, it is tested for applicability under present conditions (C) and, if possible, run (D) and tested for success (E). (Note that these actions return to a problem detection phase, thus signifying the constant interplay between problem detection and feature scanning activities in problem solving). More typically, however, not a full but a possible or partial solution is found (K) and this information is "kept in mind," that is, stored temporarily in working memory (L) as processing continues.

Although it leaves the inner workings of many processes unspecified, this general model directs attention to important characteristics of the problem-solving process. First, the process is extremely sensitive to the task environment. An initially empty WM is modified by a scanning of actually present objects or verbal instructions. What enters WM in this way may vitally affect the outcome of continuing problem-solving efforts. Second, the process is characterized by a working back and forth between the current task environment and previously acquired knowledge (the "contents" of LTM). Feature detection leads to recall; recalled items are tested for relevance to the current situation. What actually enters WM is the result of this interaction. Finally, it is evident that the capacity of WM will vitally affect the problem-solving process, by limiting how much of the information noticed in TE or accessed in LTM can be kept accessible. Selective rehearsal strategies of some kind are thus likely to be crucial to successful problem solution.

*3. Goal analysis.* Note that the success or failure of the routines just described is dependent on finding an LTM item that matches the current definition of the problem. If the initial goal (at A) does not produce a match, it is only by creating a new goal (at F)—thus in effect defining a new problem—that feature-scanning activities can be initiated. Further, feature scanning alone does not ensure finding a routine. Successive redefinitions of the problem may be needed if either noted features or routines available in the individual's repertoire are to be recognized as relevant.

Much of the classical problem-solving literature, particularly that drawn from the Gestalt tradition, focuses on this "restructuring" of the problem so that it becomes soluble. Emphasis in the Gestalt analyses is on the "insightful" nature of the process; the *aha!* nature of the experience, the way in which solution follows almost immediately upon recognition of a new form of the problem. Wertheimer's examples of this are familiar and dramatic. But Duncker is more explicit in suggesting the way in which analysis of the demands of a problem can lead to a solution. Examining the way in which one solution, considered and rejected, may lead to the next, Duncker (1945) speaks of the "process of solution as development of the problem [p. 7]." To quote him:

> The final form of an individual solution is, in general, not reached by a single step from the original setting of the problem; on the contrary, the principle, the functional value of the solution, typically arises first, and the final form of the solution in question develops only as this principle becomes successively more and more concrete. In other words, the general or "essential" properties of a solution ... precede the specific properties; the latter are developed out of the former [pp. 7–8].

Duncker illustrates this process by presenting a "family tree" of solutions for the radiation problem (see Fig. 3), each more specific than the one above it, but more general than those below. More modern terms for this redefinition process include identifying "differences" to be reduced as in Newell and Simon's General Problem Solver (see Ernst & Newell, 1969) or "relating givens to unknowns" as in Greeno's (1973) discussion of problem solving. In Duncker's family tree it is possible to think of each solution possibility as a goal, directing search for a particular process. Each goal has subgoals that are explored until what Duncker calls a "block" is found (i.e., no productive ideas emerge). There is then a return to a higher level in the tree for a new start.

The important point concerning goal analysis is that goals are continually being redefined as a function either of memory search, usefulness of recalled routines, or noticed features of the environment. However a goal is generated, the contents of WM will eventually be modified. In addition, the task environment itself may be modified if actions performed result in a physical change in the presented stimuli. It is in both these senses that goal analysis can be thought to yield a "restructured" problem that permits use of already accessed routines or redirects the search for appropriate routines.

## SOME STUDIES ON INVENTION AND ASSEMBLY

In the rest of this chapter, we will briefly describe and discuss some of our own research on assembly processes in invention problems. The tasks we work with are invention tasks of a particular kind. First, they are chosen so as to be relatively easily analyzed in terms of component routines that are subject to instruction. It is thus possible to assure, via instruction, that all subjects who enter the invention phase of an experiment are capable of calling upon and using these routines as separate processes, the assembly of which we can then observe.

Two tasks of this kind have been experimentally studied to date. One is a variant of Wertheimer's parallelogram problem. The second is derived from the task of multidigit addition involving carrying. The two problems share a com-

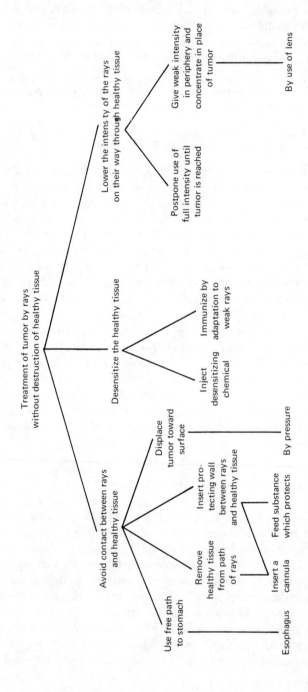

FIG. 3 Tree of solutions to radiation problem. (From "On Problem-Solving" by Karl Duncker. *Psychological Monographs*, 1945, 58(5, Whole No. 270), pp. 1–112. Copyright 1945 by the American Psychological Association. Reprinted by permission.)

216

mon structure. In both cases the task as presented during the invention session has clear surface similarities to tasks encountered and successfully performed earlier in training. Thus, a "usual routine" for the class of problems exists in the subject's repertoire, and his or her first response is normally to attempt to apply this routine. However, in our problems, some aspect of the new invention task makes the usual routine inapplicable. The individual faced with the new task must, therefore, recognize that the usual routine is not applicable to the present case, thus detecting a problem, and then somehow construct a new routine by combining components in his or her repertoire. In each of the tasks the construction of the new routine is accomplished by applying a transformation routine that has the effect of changing the stimulus presented in the problem situation into one to which the usual routine does apply.

For the parallelogram problem, the usual routine is finding the area of rectangular figures by superimposing 1-inch cubes on the figures and then counting the cubes. Areas of two figures can be compared by putting cubes on both, counting both, and then comparing the numbers. This routine is simply an operationalizing, in a form suitable for young children, of the formula for area: Area = Length × Width. The routine is not applicable to nonrectangular figures, because the blocks cannot be fit over them without hanging over the edges. The transformation routine that makes it possible to solve the problem is to cut the nonrectangle and rearrange the pieces into a rectangle. This must be done without adding or throwing away any pieces, thus maintaining equivalence between the presented and transformed stimuli.

The carrying problem involves the use of special materials that have been designed to represent the decimal and place value notation system for children just learning the number system. The materials (shown in Fig. 4) consist of blocks: unit cubes, ten–bars, hundreds–squares. These blocks can be assigned to certain positions in a columnar array, and thus display the value of the different columns in decimal notation. Any three-digit numeral can be represented in blocks on a three-column board. Conversely, any display of blocks that has nine or fewer blocks per column can be written as a numeral. Thus, in Fig. 4, the display in row (a) stands for 275 and the display in row (b) stands for 409. Representing blocks with numerals 1 through 9 is taught to children as a "notation routine." If there are more blocks than nine in any column, however [as in row (c)], the notation routine would not be applicable, since only one digit is permitted in each column. To solve such a problem it is necessary to first transform the stimuli. This can be accomplished by exchanging the blocks (ten ones for a ten-bar, for example), and placing the new block in its appropriate column. This is a concrete representation of the process we actually engage in when we carry in addition.

Figure 5 schematizes the task structure common to these two problems. A task stimulus and instructions are presented (A), and the subject tests the usual routine (B). Finding it inapplicable, the solution is to transform the task stimuli

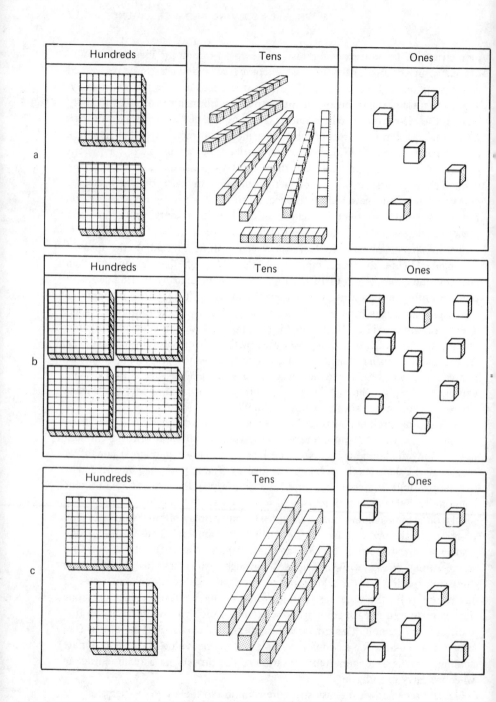

FIG. 4  Block displays for notation problem.

(D) while preserving important equivalences between the presented and transformed stimuli (E and F). Once the transformation has been made, it is now found possible to apply the usual routine (B). This is done (C), and the problem is solved. Note that the arrow between B and D in the figure is dotted. This represents the fact that the B–D connection is the invention that must be made by the individual. In our experiments the links A–B and B–C are typically taught directly; so are the links D–E–F–E. But B–D is not taught, and the subject's solution of a problem consists of recognizing that when the usual routine is not applicable, the transformation routine can be applied. This invention consists of assembling two sets of routines, each well learned separately, but not previously used in combination.

## Problem Detection

Our initial studies were concerned with problem detection. Most of the classical physical invention problems studied in the past contained clear environmental cues as to when the problem was solved. The strings were or were not tied together; the candle was stuck on the wall or not; there was or was not a place to hang one's hat. In our problems, by contrast, the criteria for an adequate problem solution are not as self-evident. Problem-detection activity (indicated by the recognition of nonsolution) as a component of problem solving is thus more important.

An early exploratory study highlighted the effects of initial problem-detection activity on later parts of the problem-solving process. The task was the notation (carrying) problem described earlier. First-grade children were divided into two training groups. In one group, the notation routine was taught by a series of games and practice exercises in which there were never more than nine blocks in any column. The children learned to write a three-digit numeral to represent the array without ever encountering the question of applicability of the routine. This was called the No-Detection group. The Detection group, by contrast, had notation routine training in which ten or more blocks occasionally appeared in either the tens or the ones column. When the child attempted to notate such a column, the experimenter stopped him, saying, "That column has more than nine blocks. You are only allowed to put one numeral in each column; so you do not have a way to do that column yet." Training on the exchange routine was identical for both groups.

Following training on the separate components, notation and exchange, there were ten invention trials. In these trials the children were presented arrays in which one column contained more than nine blocks and were asked to write the numeral that represented the display. Any child who did not spontaneously engage in exchange when encountering a notation problem with more than nine blocks in a column was prompted, using an increasingly explicit series of

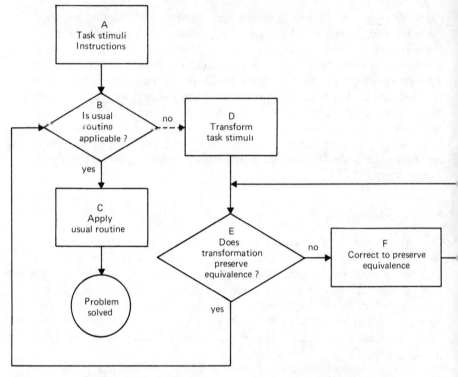

FIG. 5   Schematic diagram of successful problem solving.

prompts. *None* of the children in the Detection group attempted to write two digits within a column—the typical "illegal" response made by untrained children. Thus, it was clear that Detection training quite clearly established a self-regulated problem-detection routine that prevented the child's accepting a false solution. *All* children in the No-Detection group did attempt incorrect notation. These attempts were interrupted by the experimenter, who pointed out that only one digit per column was permitted, and that there were too many blocks in the column.

To determine the effects of self-regulated problem detection as opposed to external pointing out of the problem, we counted the number of trials on which a prompt to exchange was needed, and also noted the specificity of the prompt that finally did produce exchange behavior. There was no clear difference between the groups in either measure. Thus, establishment of a strong problem-detection routine may prevent acceptance of incorrect solutions; but it does not of itself make invention of new solutions any more or less likely. Instead, the strong effect of an established problem-detection routine emerged in the way in which the exchange operations were carried out. *Every* child in the No-Detection group made what we called an "exchange error." An exchange error is essentially an incomplete exchange, one that does not preserve equivalence. Typically, ten unit-cubes are counted out and returned to the pool; but instead of picking up a ten-bar and adding it to the tens column, the child notates the ones column and goes on to the tens column as originally presented. *No* child in the Detection group made such an error. Thus, a well-established problem-detection routine appears, on first look, to have its effect not so much in facilitating accessing of the transformation routine, but in carrying it out smoothly once accessed.

We have considered several possible explanations for this effect. Our currently favored hypothesis is that the problem-detection routine leads to the establishment of a goal structure that calls on the exchange routine intact, while the lack of self-initiated problem detection sets up a goal structure that calls on pieces of the exchange routine, but not on the full routine itself. Figure 6 schematizes this hypothesis in terms of nested "stacks" of goals that activate and interrupt each other. There are two stacks, one for subjects in the Detection group, one for subjects in the No-Detection group. Movement through the stack is downward when new subgoals are being formulated, upward when subgoals are satisfied. Movement is always one goal down, or one up, at a time.

The two stacks share some goals (i.e., Notate and Reduce), but not all. Both groups begin with an active goal of Notate. For the Detection group, this activates a new goal, Test Applicability of Notate. When the Notate routine is found not to be applicable, new goals are formulated (the next two down in the list) that search for a routine that will solve the problem. This successive formulation of subgoals eventually produces the Exchange goal. Exchange will be satisfied only when *both* Reduce (a reduction of blocks in one column of the display board) *and* Replace (a corresponding replacement in the next column)

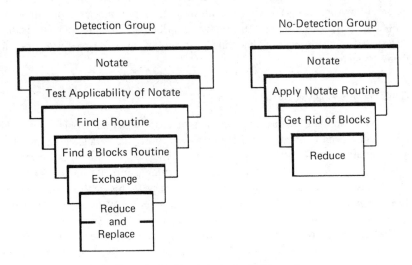

FIG. 6    Hypothesized goal stacks for two invention groups.

have been satisfied. Thus, incomplete exchanges will not satisfy the Exchange goal. Only when Exchange *is* satisfied will the next goal up in the stack be reactivated. Successive goals will then be satisfied until Notate itself is again active.

The right side of Fig. 6 shows the hypothesized goal stack for subjects who did not detect the problem, the No-Detection group in the experiment. Starting with the Notate goal, these subjects are hypothesized to immediately activate the goal Apply Notate Routine, which leads to an action of attempting to notate one of the columns. Our model assumes that, when stopped by the experimenter, these subjects encode the interruption as something like "Can't do it; too many blocks." A reasonable subgoal to establish given this encoding is Get Rid of Blocks, which interrupts the Apply Notate goal. This new goal produces a further subgoal, Reduce, a goal shared with the Detection group. The Reduce goal is satisfied once 10 blocks are eliminated from a column, but for the No-Detection subjects the interrupted goal for Reduce is not Exchange, but Get Rid of Blocks. Get Rid of Blocks is therefore reactivated, shown to be satisfied, and Apply Notate Routine is in turn reactivated. Replace—the second half of a complete exchange—is never generated as a goal by No-Detection subjects, because Exchange was never an active goal.

Our data suggest that problem detection is indeed an important part of the invention process in that the way problems are initially detected, and therefore encoded, will probably affect the quality of the observed solution behavior. Specifically, the present analysis proposes a relation between problem detection and the way the initial goal is analyzed. This suggests that any inclusive attempt to elucidate the nature of problem-solving behavior must deal with questions regarding problem detection: To what extent is problem detection built into the external environment? To what extent are detection strategies common across problems, and to what extent are they task-specific? Are there stable individual differences in likelihood of detecting problems; if so, what processes underlie these differences?

## Goals and the Analysis of the Problem

We next examined details of invention behavior when a problem-detection routine had been explicitly taught. For this purpose, the parallelogram problem was presented to fifth-grade students in a study conducted by Lynn Morris (Morris & Resnick, 1974). Morris began by writing a formal simulation analysis of the problem, using production-system language. This analysis then guided development of a training procedure in which children were taught the conditions and actions that made up each task component.

The basic structure of the task, shown in Fig. 7, is expressed in a production system (FIND AREA) that serves to organize and call on other production systems. These latter production systems define the separate "routines" that are taught to subjects. Three routines are called on by FIND AREA. These are TEST

APPLICABILITY, USE BLOCKS, and TRANSFORM. Each was taught separately. The FIND AREA production rules were taught, with the exception of FA4, the rule that calls on TRANSFORM when a nonrectangle ("no-figure") has been detected. FA4 corresponds to the B–D link in Fig. 5. Construction and use of this rule constituted the invention that was sought.

Figure 8 summarizes the physical stimuli present and the experimenter's instructions for training each of the three routines and for the invention test. Twenty-four children were trained, each individually over a period of several weeks. On the invention test, three classes of subjects emerged. Five *Inventors* spontaneously and with relatively short latencies announced that the thing to do with the nonrectangle was cut it and then use the blocks. All other children began placing blocks on the nonrectangle. As the figure began to fill up with blocks, the experimenter intervened. She said, simply, "That's wrong, you can't do that." Two strikingly different responses to this feedback appeared. One group of seven children immediately cleared the figure of blocks. Another group (12 children) did not clear the blocks but instead tried to rearrange them on the figure, apparently trying to make them "fit" better. Of the seven who cleared the figure, all subsequently thought of cutting the figure to produce a rectangle without any external prompting to do so. We call these children *Assisted Inventors* because, while they needed some feedback to distract them from the

FA 1: ((GOAL: FIND AREA) ⟶ LOOK AT.FIG)

If you want to find how big a figure is, look at the figure.

FA 2: ((GOAL: FIND.AREA) AND (FIG) ⟶ (GOAL:
     TEST.APPLICABILITY.OF.BLOCKS))

If you want to find how big a figure is, and you have a
figure, then test to see if the blocks routine is applicable.

FA 3: ((GOAL: FIND.AREA) AND (YES.FIG) ⟶ (USE.BLOCKS
     (SATISFY GOAL))

If you want to find how big a figure is and it is a figure
to which the blocks routine is applicable (i.e, a 'yes-fig')
then use the blocks routine and the goal will be satisfied.

FA 4: ((GOAL FIND.AREA) AND (NO.FIG) ⟶ (GOAL:
     TRANSFORM))

If you want to find how big a figure is and it is a figure
to which the blocks routine is not applicable (i.e, a 'no-fig')
then try to transform the figure.

FIG. 7   Production system for FIND AREA.

blocks routine, they in fact constructed and inserted FA4 for themselves. Equally striking, of the 12 who did not clear the figure, but instead rearranged the blocks, *none* ever mentioned cutting or tried to cut without direct prompting to do so by the experimenter. They failed to call on TRANSFORM on their own (i.e., they did not construct FA4), although they used the routine perfectly smoothly once prompted to do so. These children, half of our sample, must be termed *Noninventors*.

The Assisted Inventors and the Noninventors provide two clearly contrasting behavior patterns: When told "That's wrong" by the experimenter, those who were to invent cleared the figure; those who would not invent rearranged the blocks. What might have caused the different responses? And what differential effect did the responses have on the remainder of the solution process? With respect to the first question, a difference in currently active goals at the time of the experimenter's interruption might well account for the different responses. Given the same starting goal, Find Area, assume that some children take seriously the Test for Applicability of Blocks goal. When they place blocks on the nonrectangular figure, these children are really carrying out a concrete test, seeing if the blocks will fit. When the experimenter interrupts these children, they interpret her "Wrong" in terms of their current goal. Since they are testing to see if the blocks fit, they conclude that "wrong" means they do not fit, and therefore clear the figure. Assume now that some other children actually establish immediately a Use Blocks goal, and this is what they are doing when they put the blocks in the nonrectangle. The experimenter's interruption is interpreted by these children in terms of the current goal, Use Blocks. Her "Wrong" is taken to mean that the blocks are placed incorrectly; thus the blocks are rearranged rather than removed.

With respect to the second question, the effect of clearing the blocks on the remainder of the solution process is to make visible again the nonrectangular figure. This allows the child to notice its features, and probably to detect the "extra" piece at one end and the lack of it at the other, thus generating the idea of reconstructing the figure. Thus a new goal (Transform) would be formulated as a result of scanning the task environment. While this interpretation is not documented with clear-cut protocols or other data, it suggests further experiments in which periodic reconstruction of the physical display is a variable manipulated in order to determine the effects of a "return to an initial position."

## The Task Environment: Effects of External Cues on Accessibility of Routines

We have discussed the role of problem detection and goal analysis in promoting invention, suggesting at several points that these processes interact with feature detection and scanning of the task environment (TE) in the solution process. We

now turn to a more direct consideration of the way in which the task-environ-
ment features may affect problem solution.

Examination of Fig. 8 reveals close similarity in several features between the
cue conditions present for the training of the Use Blocks routine and for the
invention test. In both cases there are two figures present; in both, the child is
asked to "Find which is bigger." Thus, the invention task was presented in the
context of TE cues very similar to the Use Blocks training task, and very
different from the Transform training task, where only one figure was present
and where the instructions were to cut it and make it into a rectangle. A recent
study conducted by Tim Mulholland (1974) examined the effects of modifying
the invention situation so that the cues were not so similar to those of block
training. Half of 24 fourth-graders were given an invention task in which only a
single figure (a parallelogram) was presented (thus more similar to transformation
than to block training), and the instructions were simply "Find how big this is."
The other half received the invention problem of the prior experiment where
two figures, a rectangle and a parallelogram, were present. It was reasoned that
the modified invention condition, with only a single figure that was not a
rectangle, would not preemptively call the blocks routine. Rather, it would
invite inspection of the situation and thus promote problem detection and a
resultant goal analysis. Thus, conditions for accessing the transformation routine
were thought to be stronger in the modified task. Mulholland's data suggest that
the revised problem presentation does facilitate invention. Of the 12 children
receiving the original two figures, only two invented, whereas six of the 12
children invented in the modified single-figure condition, and average time to
solution was shorter for the latter group.

## Optimizing Invention

We mention briefly one last study conducted by James Pellegrino and Margaret
Schadler (1974). It represents an attempt to use everything we then knew or
suspected concerning invention processes in designing a set of task conditions that
would maximize the likelihood of invention. Pellegrino and Schadler's study again
utilized the parallelogram task. Training on the Use Blocks, Test for Applicability,
and Transform routines proceeded as in the prior experiments, but modifications
were made in the invention phase. The most important change was designed to
foster goal analysis by making children more self-conscious about the reasons
for their actions. When the invention task was presented, the children were
required to "look ahead" by verbalizing possible goals and strategies for
meeting them before taking any action. Thus, in the invention situation the
children were presented with two figures (either two parallelograms or a parallelogram and a rectangle) along with scissors and blocks, but the experimenter
said only "What do you think I want you to do?" This forced the child to
verbalize a goal for the problem. The experimenter elicited as many goal

| Routine | Physical Array | E's Instruction |
|---|---|---|
| USE BLOCKS | | "Find which is bigger." |
| TEST FOR APPLICABILITY | <br>or | "Does this figure have four right angles ?" |
| TRANSFORM | Various non-rectangular figures presented one at a time. Scissors handed to or pointed out to child. Booklet to paste figures into. | "To make this into a rectangle, you have to cut a part off and paste it on somewhere else. You must use all pieces and have four right angles." |
| INVENTION | <br>or | "Find which is bigger." |

FIG. 8   Summary of stimulus conditions in the Morris experiment.

statements as the child was able to give. Only then was the next question asked: "Tell me how you would find which is bigger." The child was then required to state a plan of action and to tell how the planned action would help achieve the goal. Once the child had given one plan and a justification for that plan, he was allowed to proceed whether or not the experimenter thought it a good plan.

Under these "look ahead" conditions, 14 out of 16 children solved the problem, regardless of whether they were presented with two parallelograms or a parallelogram and a rectangle. Of the children who were not asked to verbalize goals and look ahead, but instead were asked simply to "Find which is bigger," only six out of 16 were able to solve the invention problem. In the latter group, there was slightly more invention on the part of those who were presented the two parallelograms, indicating that the task environment did have a facilitating effect in cueing the solution strategy, but the major conclusion drawn from the experiment was that "although the stimulus array (TE) is an important factor, the most powerful determinant of performance was the look-ahead verbalization activity, which effectively maximized solution for both arrays" (Pellegrino & Schadler, 1974, p. 19).

The results of this experiment suggest that the general strategy of planning ahead and considering alternative goals may be a very powerful component of problem solving. The looking ahead strategy appears to be both simple to use and easy to teach. It seems, in fact, that all that may be necessary is to remind people that they ought to consider their goals and possible actions; once reminded, they can access what they already have learned to do. Furthermore, it seems likely that the looking ahead strategy is generalizable across a variety of tasks, although this remains to be established experimentally. Such a strategy appears to be worth pursuing in instructional work designed to improve the ability to learn on one's own, and thus, by the definition adopted at the beginning of this chapter, improve one's intelligence.

## IMPLICATIONS FOR THE STUDY OF INTELLIGENCE

To recapitulate, we have argued that intelligence can be viewed as the ability to acquire new behavior in the absence of direct or complete instruction, and that this ability involves processes that can facilitate the transition from simpler to more complex cognitive performance. Posing the question in this way, we have used problem-solving behavior of the special kind we call invention as a window through which to examine the way in which individuals make transitions in competence on their own. Our strategy has been to present a model of this kind of problem solving which suggests the classes of processes that underly the ability to learn without direct instruction, that is, to invent. Our obligation now is to suggest what this model implies for intelligence. We have argued that intelligence, defined as a transition process involving the assembly of components already in an individual's repertoire of competence, can be characterized in terms of three general kinds of activity: problem detection, feature scanning (noticing features in the environment), and analysis of goals. It is the way in which these activities are carried out that distinguishes good from poor solution of invention problems. The potential of an individual as a problem solver is a function of three things: (a) existing competence in task-specific subskills or components which need to be assembled in a solution; (b) general strategies with respect to problem detection, feature scanning, and goal analysis—i.e., the assembly processes themselves; and (c) the features of the particular task environment.

In our studies we have consistently assured the presence of the component subskills, thus allowing attention to be focused on assembly processes and task environment features. We have in some cases directly manipulated certain features of the task environment, and have shown (at least suggestively at this point) that task conditions that draw attention to certain features of the situation foster the finding of good solutions. One might say that "well-arranged" problem presentations lessen the demand on feature-detection strategies and thus raise the probability of many individuals' finding solutions. Somewhat more indirectly, we have manipulated the likelihood of problem-detection behavior, by teaching task-specific problem-detection routines (that is, the Tests for Applicability of the usual routines) that serve to focus the individual's attention on certain key features of the particular invention task environment to be encountered. These problem-detection routines, too, have been shown to facilitate solution, probably by organizing subsequent search behavior in terms of an optimal goal structure that enables features of the task environment to be matched with available routines stored in memory.

It would appear, then, that if one wanted to help people perform as good problem solvers, one thing to do would be to put them into optimally designed environments—that is, environments that highlight relevant stimulus features and that directly suggest the locus of the problem. We might, if we became very intelligent about designing such environments, be able to create situations in which all of our subjects seemed to be highly intelligent. But such a feat of engineering would miss the point of our concern. As we said at the outset of this chapter, intelligence is precisely the ability to acquire new abilities under less than optimal environmental conditions, conditions where the appropriate solution routines are not directly prompted or specifically taught. Under such conditions, which are quite general in the normal course of life, the burden of detecting relevant features, analyzing problems, and establishing appropriate goals rests with the individual. This implies that to account for intelligence, we have to address problem-detection strategies, feature-scanning strategies, and goal-analysis strategies as generalized competencies of the individual and as competencies in which individuals differ.

The heart of our effort lies in our attempt to develop a model for a pervasive kind of human behavior. In so doing, we purposely have used concepts drawn from current information-processing theories, in the hope that many of the unanalyzed components of our model will be opened for inspection by others, and thus perhaps give more explicitness to the preliminary notions presented here. In our own experimental work a key tactic is to use instruction in the hypothesized processes as a means of verifying the reality of those processes. In the studies reported in this chapter, the instructional efforts were for the most part limited to routines specific to the particular tasks involved. A job now ahead is to devise means of instructing people in the processes we have hypothesized as general to problem solution, and to evaluate the effects of such instruction across a variety of task environments. We have made a pilot attempt in this direction, with respect to the goal-analysis component of our model—namely, the requirement in the Pellegrino—Schadler study that children engage in goal analysis by verbalizing plans of action and predicting expected outcomes. The effect across tasks of such self-consciousness about goals and probable outcomes remains to be examined. Similar efforts with respect to teaching generalized strategies of problem detection and heuristics of feature scanning are also required next steps. To the extent that such a research program, based on instruction, proves tractable, we hope at a later date to be able to point with more certainty to one critical set of the processes that constitute intelligence and perhaps to give increased operational meaning to the possibilities for increasing intelligence via instruction.

## ACKNOWLEDGMENTS

The research reported herein was supported by the Learning Research and Development Center, supported in part by funds from the National Institute of Education (NIE), United States Department of Health, Education, and Welfare. The opinions expressed do not necessarily reflect the position or policy of NIE and no official endorsement should be inferred.

## REFERENCES

Duncker, K. On problem solving. *Psychological Monographs,* 1945, 58(5, Whole No. 270), 1–112.

Ernst, G. W., & Newell, A. *GPS: A case study in generality and problem solving.* New York: Academic Press, 1969.

Flavell, J. H. An analysis of cognitive–developmental sequences. *Genetic Psychology Monographs,* 1972, 86(2), 279–350.

Gagné, R. M. The acquisition of knowledge. *Psychological Review,* 1962, **69,** 355–365.

Gagné, R. M. Learning hierarchies. *Educational Psychologist,* 1968, **6,** 1–9.

Greeno, J. G. The structure of memory and the process of solving problems. In R. L. Solso (Ed.), *Contemporary issues in cognitive psychology.* Washington D.C.: Winston, 1973.

Luchins, A. S., & Luchins, E. H. *Wertheimer's seminars revisited: Problem solving and thinking.* Albany: Faculty-Student Association, State University of New York, 1970.

Maier, N. R. F. An aspect of human reasoning. *British Journal of Psychology,* 1933, **24,** 144–155.

Maier, N. R. F. *Problem solving and creativity in individuals and groups.* Belmont, California: Brooks/Cole Publishing Company, 1970.

Maltzman, I. Thinking: From a behaviorist point of view. *Psychological Review,* 1955, **62,** 275–286.

Maltzman, I., Brooks, L. O., Bogartz, W., & Summers, S. S. The facilitation of problem solving by prior exposure to uncommon responses. *Journal of Experimental Psychology,* 1958, **56,** 399–406.

Morris, L., & Resnick, L. B. *Assembling component processes in problem solving.* Paper presented at the meeting of the Midwestern Psychological Association, Chicago, May 1974.

Mulholland, T. M. *Availability versus accessibility of a subroutine in problem solving.* Unpublished masters thesis, University of Pittsburgh, 1974.

Newell, A. Production systems: Models of control structures. In W. G. Chase (Ed.), *Visual information processing.* New York: Academic Press, 1973.

Pellegrino, J. W., & Schadler, M. *Maximizing performance in a problem solving task.* Unpublished manuscript, University of Pittsburgh, Learning Research and Development Center, 1974.

Wertheimer, M. *Productive thinking.* (Enlarged ed.) New York: Harper & Row, 1959. (Originally published in 1945.)

# 12
## Metacognitive Aspects of Problem Solving

John H. Flavell

*Institute of Child Development*
*University of Minnesota*

The theory and research presented in Chapter 11 have several very commendable features. First, they deal with problem-solving performance in children. This is a topic which, somewhat surprisingly, has not been much studied in recent years. Resnick and Glaser interpret "intelligence" as the ability to solve problems, and of course some people may not agree with that definition. It would be hard, however, for anyone to disagree with the proposition that children's problem solving is a worthwhile and currently understudied object of research.

A second and particularly praiseworthy feature of their research is their strategy of first training or building in the necessary problem-solving components, and then testing to see if the child actually utilizes them when solving the problem. This strategy obviously permits Resnick and Glaser to control out one obvious and usually important source of a child's problem-solving failure. They also propose to make the actual behavioral solution of each problem a trivially easy matter, providing only (a very *big* "only," it turns out) that the child "thinks to" retrieve the solution procedure from his repertoire. Thus, this strategy sensibly puts in certain competences at one end and takes out certain "noisy" performance obstacles at the other.

Finally, the authors' approach keys on what many of us think to be perhaps *the* central problem in learning and development, namely, how and under what conditions the individual assembles, coordinates, or integrates his already existing knowledge and skills into new functional organizations. Piaget, Gagné, Bruner, and numerous other students of learning and development have pointed up the crucial importance of this assembly or integration process as a vehicle or mechanism of cognitive progress. As Resnick and Glaser rightly note, however, existing descriptions tend to be "largely silent as to what goes on [page 207]" in the actual process itself. I believe that Benson Schaeffer of the University of Oregon has been a little less silent about it than many, and suggest that Resnick and Glaser might find his recent work of some interest (Schaeffer, 1973; Schaeffer, Eggleston, & Scott, 1974). They could also of course consult even more easily on this problem with their many assembly-oriented neighbors at Carnegie–Mellon University.

Resnick and Glaser's research provides us with some striking examples of children failing to solve problems for which they possess the necessary solution procedures. They *ought* to solve these problems, we think, and yet they do not. Why not? What problem-adaptive things might they be failing to do, or what problem-maladaptive things might they be doing instead? My own guesses on the matter originate in the expected place, namely, the area in which I have done most of my recent research and thinking. This area is the development of "metacognition," and especially of a subspecies of it called "metamemory" (Kreutzer, Leonard, & Flavell, 1975). "Metacognition" refers to one's knowledge concerning one's own cognitive processes and products or anything related to them, e.g., the learning-relevant properties of information or data. For example, I am engaging in metacognition (metamemory, metalearning, metattention, metalanguage, or whatever) if I notice that I am having more trouble learning $A$ than $B$; if it strikes me that I should double-check $C$ before accepting it as a fact; if it occurs to me that I had better scrutinize each and every alternative in any multiple-choice type task situation before deciding which is the best one; if I become aware that I am not sure what the experimenter really wants me to do; if I sense that I had better make a note of $D$ because I may forget it; if I think to ask someone about $E$ to see if I have it right. Such examples could be multiplied endlessly. In any kind of cognitive transaction with the human or nonhuman environment, a variety of information processing activities may go on. Metacognition refers, among other things, to the active monitoring and consequent regulation and orchestration of these processes in relation to the cognitive objects or data on which they bear, usually in the service of some concrete goal or objective.

With respect to the storage and retrieval of information in particular, there are a number of "metas" that the child may gradually acquire. He may learn to become sensitive to those situations in which deliberate storage of selected information now would likely prove useful subsequently, e.g., in solving some problem or performing effectively on some task at a later time. He may similarly learn to keep what he knows is going to be problem-relevant information updated and ready to retrieve at a moment's notice. Likewise, in cases in which the need to do such planful storage and maintenance of information could not have been foreseen, he may acquire the very adaptive habit of making a deliberate, systematic search for whatever problem-relevant information happens to be available for retrieval. I have used the terms "storage" and "retrieval" in this paragraph, but have deliberately avoided prefacing them with "memory."

The reason is that purely internal, in-the-head storage and retrieval processes are only part of what we should be concerned with here. In real, extralaboratory life situations, people make extensive use of external storage and retrieval resources, both human and nonhuman. In the outside world, people take notes on things and make notes of things; they exploit the capacious and leakproof memories of books, tape recorders, videotapes, films, and computers; they get other people to help them store and retrieve information, both internally (i.e., in other peoples' heads) and externally. The real world's tasks generally have the properties of an open-book, take-home exam, even if the memory researcher's tasks do not.

We might say that the growing child has much to learn about how, where, and when to store information and how, where, and when to retrieve it, as means to a variety of real life goals. The "how" includes a variety of storage and retrieval strategies. The "where" refers to a variety of storage and retrieval resources (the child's head, the heads of others, and numerous nonhuman resources). The "when" has already been alluded to, and may be pertinent to Resnick and Glaser's findings. It refers to the child's growing sense that such and such situations call for active, deliberate attempts to learn and store, and that so and so situations call for active, deliberate attempts to retrieve and apply what is in store. There is already considerable research evidence that young children have much to learn about the "how" aspect (e.g., see references cited in Ritter, Kaprove, Fitch, & Flavell, 1973). I believe that developmental studies directed towards the "where" and "when" aspects would be equally productive and revealing. I predict, in fact, that they will loom large in future research on children's learning and memory development. A term like "production deficiency" (Flavell, 1970) will no longer be unnaturally confined to a child's failure to use spontaneously some in-the-head mnemonic he has the basic competence to use. If the term is used at all, it will as readily be applied to similarly-based failures to utilize external sources of storage and retrieval ("where"), and indeed to think of storing or retrieving at all, however or wherever ("when"). I believe many of Resnick and Glaser's subjects could be described as having some sort of retrieval production deficiency of this very general, "when" variety.

Is there anything along these lines that children could be taught that would improve their ability to assemble effective problem-solving procedures from already available cognitive components? Perhaps they could somehow (I do not know how) be taught to produce and respond to some very general imperatives and questions when solving problems. Here are some possible candidates. Examine task features carefully. Is there a problem here? Is the problem I just solved the one I originally had in mind to solve, or is it only a subproblem or even an irrelevant problem? If I don't initially succeed in solving the problem, I should keep trying. When trying to solve a problem, search *both* internal *and* external sources for solution-relevant information and procedures unless—shades of Jacqueline Goodnow's astute characterization of our culture—part of the problem is some adult who inexplicably insists that you do it all in your head.

Keep track of past solution efforts, their outcomes, and the information they yielded, using external records if it makes sense to do so (and if that perverse adult will let you); actively "remember" to remember, monitor, and update information and actively bring this information to bear on the problem. If children and other fallible organisms (e.g., adults) could somehow be induced to produce and react appropriately to the functional equivalents of such imperatives and questions, I believe they would be far better problem solvers. Resnick and Glaser seem to make a similar point· "A job now ahead is to devise means of instructing people in the processes we have hypothesized as general to problem solution, and to evaluate the effects of such instruction across a variety of task environments [page 229]."

Finally, some priceless suggestions to Resnick and Glaser about the conduct of future research. Nothing is more conducive to a self-righteous sense of scientific altruism than to make sage, *ex cathedra* pronouncements as to how *others* should do *their* research; it also takes remarkably little effort and "intelligence."

First, follow your own prescriptions about how to solve problems. Make your research goals as clear and specific as possible and try to make each experiment tell you something you really wanted to know concerning these goals. I think some of the research moves reported have been at least a bit tangential to the main objective.

Second, don't be quite so exclusively oriented toward external behaviors and external environments. Try to find out what is running through the child's mind as he or she wends his or her way through the task. I have found that one can sometimes get good leads simply by asking them what they are trying to do at various points. Interrogation procedures are likelier to be productive with older than with younger subjects, of course.

Third, don't overestimate the correspondence between your information-processing type flow diagrams (e.g., Fig. 1) and cognitive reality. While I realize you are well aware of the dangers of doing this, models do have a way of taking on an air of reality through sheer use and familiarity. I suspect that a lot of human thought, even in problem-solving situations, may be erratic and inconsistent in direction, subject to multiply embedded interruptions and detours, and generally replete with vague, difficult-to-model ideas.

Fourth, consider trying to devise problem situations which are still more naturalistic, even more "ethological–ecological" than the school-type tasks you have been working with. For example, children are constantly solving social–interactional as well as nonsocial problems; indeed, some of your subjects were apparently trying to solve a social problem when you thought they were trying to solve a nonsocial one (page 224). Similarly—my *idée fixe* again—it would be interesting to see how children would handle problems when given free access to external stores of relevant information. One possibility that combines your inclinations with mine would be to study the way children do homework problems. The investigator's role in relation to the child in such a study would of course be problematic; some blend of a Socratic and Rogerian role might yield useful data on the child's plans and their enactments. I suspect that children's study strategies may change quite a bit as a function of cognitive–developmental level and other variables. This suspicion leads naturally and innocently to a suggestion I have wanted to make all along: Consider the possibility of doing developmental studies of children's problem solving as well as the essentially adevelopmental studies with child subjects that you have done so far.

Finally, I would certainly encourage the line of research represented by the Pellegrino and Schadler (1974) study (pages 225–227), in which children were encouraged to become self-conscious about their strategies and objectives. I began this critique by commending you for building in the prerequisite bricks. I will close by commending you for now trying to supply the integrating mortar as well.

## REFERENCES

Flavell, J. H. Developmental studies of mediated memory. In H. W. Reese & L. P. Lipsitt (Eds.), *Advances in child development and behavior.* Vol. 5. New York: Academic Press, 1970.

Kreutzer, M. A., Leonard, C., & Flavell, J. H. An interview study of children's knowledge about memory. *Monographs of the Society for Research in Child Development,* 1975, 40(4, Serial No. 112).

Pellegrino, J. W., & Schadler, M. Maximizing performance on a problem solving task. Unpublished manuscript, University of Pittsburgh, Learning Research and Development Center, 1974.

Ritter, K., Kaprove, B. H., Fitch, J. P., & Flavell, J. H. The development of retrieval strategies in young children. *Cognitive Psychology,* 1973, 5, 310–321.

Schaeffer, B. Skill integration during cognitive development. Paper presented at the Conference on Current Research in Long-Term Memory, University of Dundee, Scotland, July, 1973.

Schaeffer, B., Eggleston, V. H., & Scott, J. L. Number development in young children. *Cognitive Psychology,* 1974, 6, 357–359.

# 13
# Varieties of Cognitive Power

Earl Hunt

*University of Washington*

People differ in the way they think, how much they think, and how well they think. To put the case mildly, there are debates about how such differences should be described. My belief is that questions about intelligence can only be discussed within the broader topic of cognition. In this chapter I shall describe several recent empirical studies which have convinced me that such an approach is possible. Before presenting them, I want to offer a discussion of the broad philosophic approach followed by our group, for I feel that many of the debates about intelligence have suffered from the failure of the debaters to make clear their philosophic assumptions.

A *world view* is a cognitive framework within which one seeks certain types of explanations for phenomena. For instance, in the Middle Ages most people assumed that what they experienced was an expression of the will of God, and explanations were sought by interpretation of the scriptures. The same approach can be found today on certain radio stations. Tyler (Chapter 2) has made it clear that intelligence, as the term is commonly used, is a concept that was introduced to cope with problems that could only exist within a world view stemming from democracy (all citizens should have equal opportunity to develop their talents) and Darwinism (variation of the species). Some way had to be found to relieve the state of the burden of opening doors to people who could not pass through them. The way chosen was to produce an objective ordering of the citizenry. In abstract theory each citizen was to be described relative to the other citizens, and the description would be used to determine how the state should support the individual's personal development. This abstract and really quite benign idea of ordering is stated in its extreme form in Huxley's *Brave New World*, where each person is assigned to an intellectual class and offered appropriate opportunities and duties.

Modern cognitive psychology operates from a different world view. We want to explain how things work. Specifically, we want to know what sort of information processing machinery would produce the phenomenon we call thinking. Then when we look at a particular individual we want to describe that person in terms of the absolute functioning of mental machinery, and not by contrasting the person at hand with the last ten or last ten thousand people seen previously. This world view leads us to investigate mental ability in a way different from the method that Binet and his followers used. To understand the difference, an analogy to physical ability may be useful.

Most people accept the idea that differences in physical ability exist. We agree that it is expressed in sports, and then are uncomfortable when we realize that sports can vary from basketball to soccer to golf. If we consider the "far out" cultures of ballet and the equestrian events, the picture is even more confusing. Still, most observers claim that the concept of physical ability is a reasonable one.

Now, how would the psychometrician's world view dictate an investigation of physical ability? We could correlate measures taken of performance in various activities said to require the ability. There is more than a hint of Binet here. We would measure and correlate accuracy of placement of a tennis ball, distance a football could be kicked, and the like. We would find that such measures had some generality. Measures of tennis skill, for instance, could be used to predict performance in squash and badminton. On the other hand, the generalization would not be perfect. It would also be possible to attack our measures on theoretical grounds as not measuring "true physical ability," but only skill in a particular sport. In other words, the measures would have high predictive value (sometimes) but little construct validity.

To refine our measures, but not abandon the world view of ordering, we could apply more sophisticated statistical techniques, such as factor analysis. This would identify common components which seemed to be running through a variety of individual measures. Given a small amount of ingenuity, we could define some Primary Physical Abilities, such as sprinting, stamina, motor reaction time, and the like. It would not be hard to construct tests whose items had high loadings on only one of these primary abilities. No doubt someone would market such a test, with greatly improved construct validity. Construct validity, though, would still not be perfect because the primary abilities would be taxonomic abstractions from observations, rather than dimensions dictated by any theory of how the body is actually moved. Sadly, in the process of improving construct validity we would find that our predictive validity had deteriorated. The great boxers do not always have the fastest reaction times.[1] Finally, we would find that many of our "pure" tests were indeed not even

---

[1] Muhammed Ali, a heavyweight boxer who, in his prime, was lauded for his "cat-like reflexes" had a quite average motor reaction time (Keele, 1973).

applicable to some of the situations which clearly involved control of the body. Imagine testing ballet dancers to see which of them could run across the stage fastest!

We could proceed at a third level of analysis. Body movements are, after all, produced by physical reactions in a machine that has been studied by the more reductive disciplines of anatomy and physiology. We could describe an individual's athletic potential in terms of power and control over various muscle groups in the body, sense of equilibrium, keeness of vision, and many other theoretically justified measures. Such a description would have high construct validity even though, for a variety of reasons, it might have very low predictive validity, i.e., the test could not predict current performance in almost any sport.

The world view about cognition which I espouse is an almost exact analogy to this view of athletic ability. On occasion, we develop intellectual aptitude measures whose purpose is to locate individuals who, without very much added training, are capable of performance at a given level of ability. Predictive validity is then a must; construct validity is a secondary concern if it is a concern at all. Predictive validity is the province of the personnel officer, as correctly identified by the Supreme Court in the now-famous Griggs vs. Duke Power case. On other occasions we want to know who can be trained, i.e., who possesses the basic skills to be brought to an adequate level of performance within reasonable time limits. In still other situations we do not have a very clear idea of what the target performance task is, and therefore we are more concerned with the measurement of transferable underlying skills. These are the province of the psychometrician, who properly develops tests which blend construct and predictive ability. Finally, we are just now beginning to return to Galton's theoretically oriented measurement of individual differences. Carroll's work (Chapter 3) represents an explicit attempt to establish a connection between existing psychometric instruments and modern cognitive theory. What I shall report are some additional findings at the basic measurement level. My argument is that certain types of individual differences are logical consequences of a particular model of cognition, and furthermore, these differences can be shown to be actual dimensions of variation in human performance.

## THE THEORETICAL BASIS

The foregoing remarks demand a model. The one which has (provisionally) guided our work is the *distributed memory* model of cognition. It has been described in detail elsewhere (Hunt, 1971, 1973; Hunt & Poltrock, 1974), so only a brief description will be given here. The model is a variant of the "box in the head" approach some cognitive psychologists have adopted from computer science. Its central idea is that information storage and transformation occur in three separate stages, which we can label informally as "preconscious thought," "conscious thought," and "long-term memory." There are a number of substages within each stage. The way the stages are organized is shown in Fig. 1. When information first enters the sensorium it is passed "upwards," toward short-term memory (STM), in a series of progressively higher order codes. These codes are based upon recognition of the sensory input as an example of a pattern stored in long-term memory (LTM). When information in a buffer is recognized as a known pattern, the appropriate pattern name is placed in the next higher buffer. The process continues until information is placed in STM, at which time it reaches the level of "conscious thought."

Active information processing occurs in the two boxes labeled STM and intermediate-term memory (ITM). Roughly, STM contains an echoic memory of recognized stimuli (e.g., the words just read) while ITM contains an information structure capturing the internal meaning of the current situation. STM is thought of as holding information for seconds, while ITM may hold information for minutes or hours. Therefore, ITM takes the role of "long-term memory" as this phrase is used in most discussions of psychological experiments, especially those taking place over the course of an hour or so of time. LTM, by contrast, contains permanent information.

Thought is conceived of as a sequence of transformations of information in the STM–ITM system. The transformations allowable are described by *production rules* (Newell & Simon, 1972; see also Klahr, Chapter 6 of this volume). A production rule consists of a left-hand side and a right-hand side. The left-hand side is, functionally, a pattern recognition rule describing a class of states into which the joint STM–ITM system may fall. When a left-hand pattern is recognized, the corresponding right-hand rule is activated. The right-hand rule is an action rule, which may order a change in STM or ITM, storage of information in LTM, or an overt response. When these actions are completed, the contents of the STM–ITM system are again matched to left-hand patterns, initiating a new cycle of thought.

Clearly the system is driven by pattern recognition based upon information stored in LTM. The availability of this information may affect system action. In particular, we wish to make a distinction between speech and nonspeech information. At least some speech information is assumed to be stored in the left brain portion of LTM, and at least some nonspeech information in the right brain portion. This will be important, because certain buffer memories are assumed to have direct access to only one side of the brain. Access to the other must come indirectly, via a rebroadcast method, where information is transferred from one side of the brain to the other only if pattern recognition does not occur on the initial receiving side. This assumption is based upon the extensive recent work on speech perception and hemispheric specialization (Gazzaniga, 1970). The assumptions as stated are obviously too broad (for instance they do not consider what happens to left handers) but they will serve for the discussion at hand.

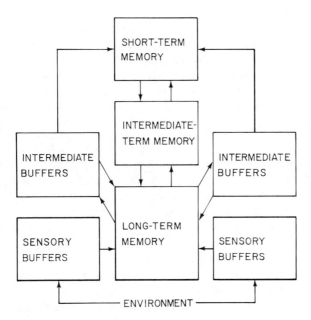

FIG. 1    The distributed memory model.

Within this model there are many places where we expect to find individual differences. A by no means exhaustive list is the following:

1. The distributed memory model must be able to perform what, in a computer system, would be called lexical recognition. Borrowing a term from Morton (1969), we may call the concept associated with a particular pattern a *logogen*. Do people differ in the speed with which logogens can be aroused? Even a small difference in arousal speed would be important, since the arousal of a lexical code is something we do many times. For example, I have made a crude estimate that there are 500,000 morphemes to be recognized in a pocket novel. A small saving in an operation that is to be done half a million times in two hours produces a considerable gain in cognitive efficiency.

2. Do people differ in the rapidity with which they can manipulate information in STM? Such manipulation is central in active problem solving, since the successive activations of productions are, essentially, successive exchanges of information in the STM–ITM system.

3. Is storage in the STM–ITM system a separate ability, distinct from storage in the LTM system? This question is not only interesting from the individual difference viewpoint, it is also central to the controversy over whether memory is to be represented by a "box in the head" model, which implies separate storage areas, or whether it is better represented by progressively more complex codings in a unitary storage system (Craik & Lockhart, 1972).

4. Is there any evidence for significant differences in the speed with which individuals transmit information from place to place within the total system?

5. To what extent can individuals alter their performance by the use of "differential programming," which shifts the burden of information processing on a fixed task from one component of the distributed memory system to another? Can this be related to some other significant dimension of individual differences?

Granted that all these types of individual differences could exist, how should we go about illustrating the fact? The theory is of little help here, for the theory states what type of differences might underly performance variation, but does not state what identifiable individuals will display these differences. Eventually a theory of the genesis of individual differences may be developed to tell us where to look for differences in cognition, much as a theory of cognition tells us what to look for. In the absence of such a theory we must proceed in a cruder manner: by comparing individuals who differ in gross measures of mental performance, in the hopes that they will display differences in tasks designed to give a finer picture of their information processing capacity.

Where are we to find populations of individuals likely to differ in the ways we have described? Several sources are available. One possibility, which I and my colleagues have utilized in our own research, is to contrast the performances of individuals who differ in their conventional psychometric test scores (Hunt, Frost, & Lunneborg, 1973; Hunt, Lunneborg, & Lewis, 1975). This approach has a practical advantage. If people with different psychometric intelligence profiles display different capacities on more basic memory tasks, then we shall be a step further along in establishing the construct validity of conventional tests. This is enormously important. Conventional intelligence tests are inexpensive personnel screening devices which often have good predictive ability, but have been challenged because of their lack of construct validity. Establishing a connection between cognitive psychology and present psychometric test theory would, in itself, be a useful thing. Any such finding, however, will be a byproduct of our current effort to determine the existence of postulated dimensions of intellectual variation.

Another place we might look in a search for individual differences is at the contrast between normal individuals and those who are either unusually gifted or unusually dull. There is, of course, a monumental literature on the mentally handicapped. Although we shall make reference to it, we have not attempted any research and have completed only the most casual literature searches in this area. In part this is due to the heterogeneous nature of the "mentally retarded," which could confuse the issue.

The special study of superior individuals has proven somewhat more rewarding. By superior we mean normal individuals (i.e., not different in any obviously organic way) who do unusually well at a given task. For example, Simon and his colleagues at Carnegie-Mellon University have spent a great deal of time contrasting good and excellent chess players (see Simon, Chapter 5). At the University of Washington, Tom Love and I have obtained a good deal of success in studying excellent memorizers, or mnemonists (Hunt & Love, 1972a, b; Love, 1973). From this work I have abstracted some general hypotheses about individual differences in memory.

There is one major source of biological variant we have yet to explore—age. Regardless of whether one accepts or rejects the Piagetian argument, it is clear that mental functioning displays a reasonably ordered sequence of development. Studies of the nature of this sequence should be of assistance in producing a complete model of adult cognition. Although I shall say very little about developmental aspects of cognition in this particular article, it certainly is not because I feel that the topic is unimportant.

## AROUSING LONG-TERM MEMORY CODES

A complicated way of saying that we recognize something is to say that a stimulus arouses conceptual codes stored in long-term memory (Atkinson & Westcourt, 1974). For example, the type characters $A$ and $a$, although not physically identical, share a common name. The act of recognizing highly over-learned codes occurs literally thousands of times every hour of our waking life. My colleagues and I have found that there are substantial individual differences in the speed with which the codes can be accessed. Our studies contrasted the performance of college students in the upper or lower quartile of the distribution of scores on a conventional verbal intelligence test. We will refer to these two groups as "high verbals" and "low verbals," although it is important to remember that these terms are defined relative to the norm for students at a major university. The subjects in our low-verbal group still have sufficient verbal ability to attend college.

Several experiments (Hunt, Frost, & Lunneborg, 1973; Hunt, Lunneborg, & Lewis, 1975) have used an adaptation of the "name versus physical identification" paradigm originally developed by Posner, Boies, Eichelman, and Taylor (1969). Observers are shown two letter pairs which may vary in name (e.g., $A\ B$) or type case ($A\ a$). In the physical identity condition the letters are to be judged "same" only if they are physically identical. In the name identity condition letters are to be judged identical if they name the same letter. The physical identity task can thus be accomplished without determining the name of the letters involved, while the name identity task requires retrieval of the conceptual code associated with the visual patterns. The time required for name retrieval can be found by subtracting reaction time (RT) in the physical identification task from RT in the name identification task. Table 1 contrasts data obtained from high and low verbal university students, using two quite different means of obtaining RTs. In one study the stimuli were presented on a computer control-led display screen and subjects responded by pressing a key, as in many conventional RT studies. In the other, subjects sorted 3 x 5 inch index cards with letter pairs typed on them. In both situations low verbal students required significantly more time to retrieve a conceptual code, but not to judge physical identity.

The same point has been addressed in a somewhat different way in a Bachelor of Science Honors thesis by H. Brunner (reported in Hunt, Lunneborg, & Lewis, 1975). Brunner was interested in seeing if high verbal subjects would be differ-entially sensitive to a conceptual cue in an incidental learning situation. The ostensible task was free recall of lists of "meaningless" syllables of varying length. In fact, some of the lists contained pairs of consecutive syllables which, taken together, made up a word. An example is *prob lem*. Figure 2 illustrates the results. High-verbal subjects were not more accurate in their ability to recall syllables that did not combine to make words, but were much more able to recall those syllables which did make up a word. The effect was most pro-nounced if the individual syllables were presented rapidly.

A third line of evidence for differential sensitivity to conceptual cues can be found in a series of studies on the release from proactive inhibition (PI release) phenomenon. In a PI release study subjects are given several trials in which they observe a short list of stimuli (usually three or four words), engage in an overtly interfering task for about 30 sec, and then attempt serial recall of the stimulus list. On each trial the stimulus list is drawn from words containing some feature

Table 1

Time Required to Make Name and Physical Identification as a Function of Psychometrically Defined Verbal Ability

Means of median time to
recognize letters (msec).

|  | Name Identification | Physical Identification | Difference |
|---|---|---|---|
| High verbals | 588 | 524 | 64 |
| Low verbals | 632 | 543 | 89 |

Mean time to sort I6 cards (seconds).

|  | Name Identification | Physical Identification | Difference |
|---|---|---|---|
| High verbals | 14.74 | 13.68 | 1.06 |
| Low verbals | 16.07 | 14.35 | 1.72 |

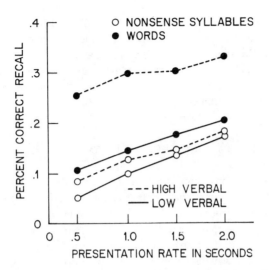

FIG. 2  Proportion of word syllables or nonsense syllables recalled as a function of verbal ability and presentation rate. (From Hunt, Lunneborg, & Lewis, 1975.)

in common, such as nouns from the same category. Recall is usually quite accurate on the first trial, then drops rapidly, providing that the successive stimulus lists are from the same category. On the *release trial* the stimulus category is changed. For example, the first three trials might use animal names as stimuli, and the fourth (release) trial use vegetable names. Typically performance returns to its original high level (*release from PI*) and then deteriorates again if trials are continued with the new stimulus class. Wickens (1972) has reviewed the types of changes that seem to be effective in producing PI release. It appears that the most important feature in PI release in adults is the change of a conceptual rather than a physical feature.

There are several studies indicating that there are individual differences in sensitivity to PI release. All the studies used "extreme" groups in one sense or another. Korsakoff's syndrome is a severe memory disorder associated with senile psychoses and chronic alcoholism. Cermak, Butters, and Moreines (1974) have reported that Korsakoff syndrome patients do not display PI release for taxonomic categories. Pender (1969; reported in Wickens, 1972) has found that there are qualitatively different changes in the PI release phenomenon over the age range from grade school to college. In general, changes in acoustic cues were relatively more effective in producing PI release in children. This suggests a progression toward more exclusive reliance on semantic coding as children progress toward adulthood, which is certainly reasonable. It is not the case, though, that all adults complete this shift. In our own laboratory we have found marked differences in proactive inhibition phenomena associated with verbal ability. A Bachelor of Science Honors thesis by Susan Nix (reported in Hunt,

Frost, & Lunneborg, 1973) contrasted release from PI in high- and low-verbal subjects. The results are shown in Fig. 3. The high-verbal subjects were clearly much more sensitive to a change in semantic category.

In summary, it appears that there are reliable and important individual differences in the ability to recognize and assign meaning to arbitrary physical stimuli. This is a very important dimension of human performance.

## REPRESENTATION IN LONG-TERM MEMORY

Any number of situations require that we solve a problem by consulting the data stored in long-term memory. The fact that people will differ in their answers to a long-term memory problem is obvious. The more interesting question is why? Is it because two people may have different data in their memories, or because they organize that data in a different fashion? To give content to this question we must consider the way data may be held in memory.

There are two sharply contrasting theoretical representations of how long-term memory may be structured. One is the *Euclidean space* model first proposed by Osgood, Suci, and Tannenbaum (1957) to account for psycholinguistic observations, and developed more recently by a number of experimenters who have benefited from the availability of mathematical techniques which were unknown when Osgood began his work. The second is the *network* model, variants of

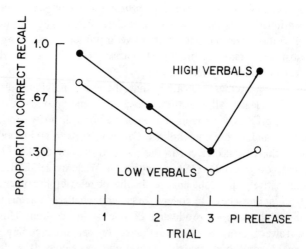

FIG. 3   Release from PI as a function of verbal ability. (From "Individual Differences in Cognition: A New Approach to Intelligence" by E. Hunt, N. Frost, and C. Lunneborg, in G. H. Bower (Ed.), *Psychology of Learning and Motivation.* Vol. 7. New York: Academic Press, 1973.)

which have been proposed by several current experimenters (e.g., Anderson & Bower, 1973; Quillian, 1968; Rumelhart, Lindsay, & Norman, 1972).

Henley's (1969) study of animal names illustrates the Euclidean space line of research. She found that subjects treated animal names as if they were points in a three-dimensional space defined by the perceived size, predacity, and "humaneness" of the creature in question. A gorilla, for instance, would be high on size and humaneness and low on predacity. Certain types of problem solving can be thought of as operating in this space. Rumelhart and Abrahamson (1973) applied a Euclidean model to the solving of analogies problems. Each problem had the form "$A$ is to $B$ as $C$ is to ... $D1, D2, D3, D3$." They reasoned that such problems can be solved by defining the relation between two terms to be the directed vector from one to the other. Therefore, to solve an analogy the subject should locate the vector from the $A$ term to the $B$ term, and then extend it from the $C$ term. The probability of choice of any $D$ term as an answer should then depend upon its distance from the end of the vector with base at $C$. These steps are illustrated in the sample problem shown in Fig. 4. Rips, Shoben, and Smith (1973) and Rumelhart and Abrahamson (1973) have been able to muster a substantial amount of empirical evidence in favor of this model of problem solving.

Now what does this have to do with individual differences? First, analogies problems are themselves examples of a more general class of problems in which the problem solver searches first for an ideal solution, conceptualized as a point in an appropriately defined Euclidean space, and then casts around for a feasible

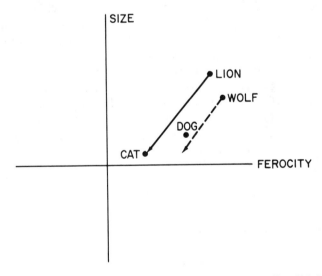

FIG. 4    Example of analogical problem solving in a semantic space. "Dog" is in approximately the same position relative to "wolf" as "cat" is to "lion."

solution by finding an occupied point near the ideal point. The choice of political candidates (or spouses) may be conceptualized this way. The sort of solutions obtained will depend both upon the dimensions used to define the semantic space and the assignment of objects of points in the space. I suggest that individual differences in solving certain types of problems may come from two qualitatively different sources: disagreement about the location of points in the space and disagreement about the space itself.

In the network formulation of semantic space the concepts of thought are represented by nodes, and the relations between them by labeled arcs. Obviously any problem solving using long-term memory will be affected by the precise structure of the graph. A series of studies by E. Loftus (1973) can be used to illustrate this point. She has developed a "memory-production paradigm," in which subjects are given a class term and one or more qualifiers, and then asked to produce a member of the class satisfying the restrictions of the qualifiers. An example is "Think of a fruit . . . (pause) . . . that begins with P." The time to do this can be contrasted to the time required for a control task, in which the qualifier is presented first, that is, "Think of something that beings with P . . . that is a fruit." Loftus argues that, if presenting a term first (as in the fruit–P case) reduces the reaction time in producing an example, then this is evidence that the first term serves as an index entry into a person's semantic net. If this reasoning is accepted, then it ought to be possible to use Loftus' technique to initiate a systematic exploration of the terms a given individual uses to organize long-term memory. Only a very little data has yet been obtained using this method. Loftus and Loftus (1974) used the method to provide some evidence that advanced psychology graduate students have a more differentiated system of labels for categorizing well-known psychologists than do beginning students. Similar, but only anecdotal, evidence has been obtained in my own laboratory in contrasting history professors and their students. At this time all one can say is that this is the sort of theoretically oriented study of individual differences which ought to be done. A similar statement could be made about the techniques used to determine the dimensions of a Euclidean semantic space. What are needed are studies that distinguish between differences in how individuals structure semantic knowledge and differences in how concepts are assigned to locations in a different structure.

## HOLDING DATA IN DIFFERENT MEMORY AREAS

Writing information into long-term memory is as important as retrieving information from it. Most current theories assert that writing information into long-term memory involves coding the current situation into some representation in *working memory,* and then storing this representation. I will now sketch some evidence for the existence of a differential ability to deal with working memory.

A first order question is whether the ability to manipulate working memory is any more than a general memorizing ability. Apparently it is, for people who do well on short-term memory tasks may not do well when recall is measured over longer retention intervals. In cooperation with Thomas Nelson, who has been interested in the study of long-term episodic memory, Clifford Lunneborg and I looked at individual differences in original learning and relearning of paired associates over a period of several weeks (see Hunt, Frost, & Lunneborg, 1973). Nelson's experiment used three groups. One group learned a list of noun–number pairs to a criterion of one perfect recital, and then attempted to recall it about six weeks later. Relearning to the original criterion followed recall. The second and third groups learned verb–number or adjective–number pairs. Otherwise they were treated identically. The correlation between number of errors to criterion in original learning and number of items recalled six weeks later was −.15 for the group learning noun–number pairs, −.66 for the verb group, and −.03 for the adjective group. These results certainly do not lend strong support to the proposition that there is a unitary memorizing ability.

An even more dramatic illustration of the difference between short-term and long-term memory for arbitrary material has been obtained by Tom Love (1973) in a series of experiments on extremely good memorizers, or mnemonists. Love's subjects were selected, after very rigorous screening, for their ability to memorize information ranging from an arbitrary number matrix to a text passage of several hundred words. The screening tests were not "short-term memory" tests in the sense that this term is used in most of the psychological literature, but neither did they involve retention of information for periods of an hour or more. Thus they fell into what I have referred to as the intermediate-memory range (Hunt, 1971). Two of Love's experiments are especially useful in making the point that is to be made here. The mnemonists served as subjects in the Atkinson and Shiffrin (1968) continuous paired-associates task. This task involves more than 100 trials in which numbers are paired with letters. Only a few letters are used, so the pairings are continuously being changed. The subject's task is to keep track of the numbers currently paired with each of the letters. Performance is measured by determining the proportion of correct responses as a function of *lag*, the number of trials intervening between the trial on which a response is paired with a stimulus and the trial on which the pair is tested. Figure 5 shows the results for Love's mnemonists (Ms) and some control subjects, "normal" university undergraduates. Clearly the mnemonists do better. This superiority vanishes when the task involves paired-associate recall over weeks. Love also compared mnemonists to the "normal Stanford undergraduates" who served as subjects in another long-term paired-associates task used by Nelson (1971 a, b). The subjects learned a list of number–letter pairs to a criterion of one correct

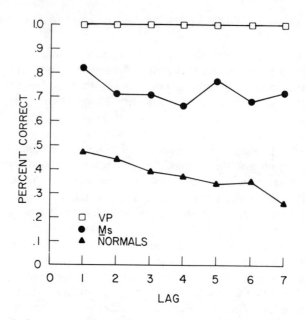

FIG. 5    Performance of mnemonists and normals in continuous paired associates.

recall, then recalled and relearned the list six weeks later. The mean values for the mnemonists were almost identical to those obtained by Nelson.

Love's results are illustrated more dramatically by the data from an exceptional mnemonist, VP, who had previously been found to be very much superior even to the subjects Love selected. His data are also shown in Fig. 5. The subject VP performed the running paired-associates task on five different occasions, for a total of 750 trials. He made six errors! Normal performance on this task is about 30–40% correct, averaged over lags. By contrast, VP's ability to retain paired associates for a period of weeks exactly matched the mean performance of Nelson's subjects (Hunt & Love, 1972a, b).

Love's work illustrates another important distinction in memory abilities, the distinction between "motivated" and "unmotivated" long-term retention. The results just cited argue that *when original learning is constant* there is essentially no correlation between acquisition and long-term retention. Also, in each study care was taken to reduce the role of meaning. If individuals with unusually good short-term memory abilities are given the same time as normal individuals to encode material, then it is quite possible that the encoding schemes (and subsequent retrieval performance) of the talented individuals will be superior. For example, Hunt and Love (1972b) found that the mnemonist VP could produce an unusual number of semantic associations to "meaningless" nonsense syllables in a very short time. Similar, though less well controlled reports have been made of the capabilities of other "great memorizers." It is certainly clear that mnemonists can retain arbitrary associations for long periods of time if they are given the opportunity to develop an encoding scheme. One of Love's subjects had, as a child, been obsessed with baseball statistics. When challenged in 1973, he correctly recalled Willie Mays' 1966 batting average. This is a feat typical of those demonstrated by stage memorizers (Barlow, 1952). VP was able to recall as much or more of Bartlett's tersely written *War of the Ghosts* after one year than control subjects could recall after one hour. Since meaningful material lends itself to encoding, it is not surprising that mnemonists are particularly good at recalling such stimuli.

## SPEED OF MANIPULATION OF DATA AS NECESSARY IN SHORT-TERM MEMORY

Our studies of students with high and low verbal ability have also shed some light on the nature of the short-term memory capability. In general, high-verbal subjects do better than low-verbal subjects on (often nonverbal) tests involving short-term memory. Their superiority has two forms. One is the capacity to manipulate data more rapidly in short-term memory. The other is a superior ability to retain information about the order in which items enter into short-term memory.

Differences in speed of information processing in short-term memory can be illustrated by the study of simple problem-solving situations which require the manipulation of information held in memory for brief periods of time. We (Hunt, Lunneborg, & Lewis, 1975) have completed two experiments illustrating an interaction between individual differences and problem complexity. The first of these experiments used a paradigm for reasoning about sentences and pictures attributable to Clark and Chase (1972). The subject is shown a sentence, and then a picture. The task is to determine whether the sentence accurately describes the picture. The pictures were all either of an asterisk above a plus, $\overset{*}{+}$, or of a plus above an asterisk, $\overset{+}{*}$. The sentences referred to "stars" and "pluses." They were constructed by combining words from the following choices:

(star, plus)   (blank, not)   (above, below)   (plus, star).

Thus typical sentences were "star above plus" or "plus not below star." A substantial body of evidence has been gathered to support the following performance model (Trabasso, 1972) for this task:

1. The sentence is encoded into an internal representation which depends upon the complexity of the sentence structure. The internal representation is more complicated if "not" is present.
2. The picture is coded into an internal representation.
3. The two are compared.
4. A response is chosen.

Both the sentence encoding and the comparison processes are assumed to be more complicated if the sentence representation is complex. Therefore the time required to complete either Stage 1 or Stage 3 should be greater for sentences containing "not" than for comparable sentences and pictures without "not." Indeed, this is the case (Clark & Chase, 1972). Now consider the situation in which two groups of subjects with presumed differences in speed of information processing attack these problems. A constant difference in complexity ought to lead to a smaller absolute change in RT in the faster group. In fact, this is what we found. We repeated the Clark and Chase study with two modifications: first, we used subjects with high and low verbal intelligence scores; second, the sentence appeared and was displayed until the subject indicated that he had comprehended it. This provided a measure of Stage 1, encoding of the sentence. The picture was then displayed and the subject compared the picture to the sentence and chose a response, thus completing Stages 2 through 4.

Figure 6 shows our estimates of time to process negations in the Clark and Chase task, displayed separately for high- and low-verbal subjects and for encoding and comparison stages. "High verbals" are substantially faster. To obtain further evidence as to whether this represents a single operation, we[2] conducted a study in which times for encoding and decision on negation items were computed for a single group of subjects, not selected for their verbal ability. The correlation between the two negation measures was .86, which strongly indicates a reliable dimension of individual difference.

Mental arithmetic is a second task which can be used to make the same point. For adults, adding two digits is trivial and may often be done by direct reference to memory. Simple addition is much more complicated if we change base and code. For example, if Sunday is zero and Saturday is six, with the other numbers distributed appropriately, then what is Monday plus Thursday? The answer, Friday, may be obtained by determining the number corresponding to Monday, and then advancing the appropriate number of day names beyond Thursday. We presented addition problems based on day names, month names, and letters. All three lists are obviously highly overlearned by college students! Nevertheless, the problems created from them vary markedly in difficulty. Difficulty, or at least problem complexity, springs from two different sources: the size of the base (7 for day names, 12 for month names, and 26 for letters); and the presence or absence of a carry in the problem. We found that the difference between high- and low-verbal subjects in RT on mental arithmetic tasks increased with increased problem complexity in either form. This is what would be expected if the high verbals are more rapid processors of short-term memory information; increasing the amount of computation required should spread the two groups further apart.

Many tasks require that we keep track of the order in which information enters short-term memory. This could be done either by tagging each stimulus

[2] These data were collected by Philip Bitar.

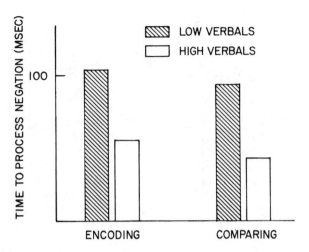

FIG. 6    Time required to process negation as a function of verbal ability. Time plotted is reaction time to a sentence containing "not" minus reaction time to the logically equivalent affirmative sentence. (From Hunt, Lunneborg, & Lewis, 1975.)

representation with order information directly, or by tagging the representation with "time of entry" markers. Whatever the mechanism that they use, we have found that high-verbal subjects have an unusual ability to record stimulus order. Hunt, Lunneborg, and Lewis (1975) found that one of the best information processing measures for discriminating between high- and low-verbal subjects was a measure of the number of stimulus transpositions made in a variation of the Peterson and Peterson (1959) short-term memory paradigm, in which subjects have to retain a short stimulus list while accomplishing an interfering task for several seconds.

Poltrock has conducted another experiment in our laboratory which illustrates individual differences in order retention even more dramatically. The task was to judge the temporal order of two dichotically presented stimuli which actually differed in interstimulus arrival time by only 50 msec. This is an extremely difficult task. The stimuli used were either stop consonants or nonspeech sounds. Previous work (Day, Cutting, & Copeland, 1971) has shown that right handed subjects have a bias toward reporting speech stimuli received in the right ear as "first," but are biased toward reporting the stimulus received in the left ear as first in the case of nonspeech stimuli. Poltrock tested the extent of this bias in subjects of varying verbal ability. His results are shown in Fig. 7. High-verbal subjects were more accurate overall. Even more interesting, high-verbal subjects did not display a bias, which is consistent with the hypothesis that they more accurately perceive order information.

These results argue that there is a short-term memory ability and suggest that it has two separate components, speed of information processing and ability to retain order. The experiments cited do not provide any information as to

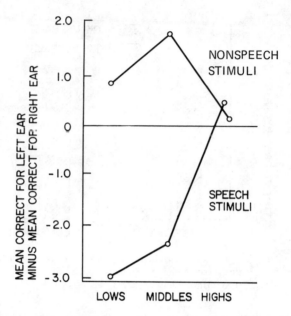

FIG. 7   Mean number of correct judgments of temporal order of presentation (ordinate) as a function of verbal ability (abcissa) and type of stimulus. (From Hunt, Lunneborg, & Lewis, 1975.)

whether the two components of STM are independent or whether they are correlated expressions of some general STM facility. The answer to this question will have to await further research.

## EFFECTS OF MODALITY DIFFERENCES ON STIMULUS PROCESSING

Another question which we have not yet addressed in any systematic way is the question of modality differences. To what extent does the input modality of a stimulus determine its later processing? There are clearly some effects. Snyder (1973) has shown that the speed with which subjects can solve mental rotation tasks, such as those developed by Shepard and Metzler (1971), is a reliable parameter of the individual and, furthermore, that it can be related to conventional psychometric tests of imaging ability. This ability may be very different from any of those we have tested in our work with verbal material. Virtually every theory of memory stresses the importance of rehearsal of verbal material (Atkinson & Westcourt, 1974). By contrast, the absence of any serial position effects in memory for strictly visual material (G. Loftus, 1974; Potter & Levy, 1969) is strong evidence for qualitatively different STM mechanisms for nonauditory material. This suggests that people who are good at one type of short-term memorization may not necessarily be good at the other.

This hypothesis was tested in an exploratory study by Michelle Ellis and myself. Eighteen subjects were shown three "lists." The first list was a sequence of eight gestures, the second a list of ten words, and the third eight gestures paired with words. (Lists are numbered for convenience, order of presentation was balanced over subjects.) Following the presentation of a list the subject attempted to recall it. The correlation between word recall and gesture recall was .09, which is hardly striking evidence for a unitary short-term memory capacity. Recall on the combined words and gestures task, however, could be predicted from performance in recalling gestures or words separately (multiple $r = .65$).

## THE RELATION BETWEEN LEARNING AND INTELLIGENCE

Virtually all the tasks studied in modern cognition have some element of learning. Numerous reviews and experimental studies have concluded that "There is no relationship between learning and intelligence." Why, then, are we trying, once again, to show one? I shall present two arguments for the position that the earlier studies were faulted. One line of argument can best be referred to as the arrogance line of argument. If there is no relationship between learning and one's measure of intelligence, then it is time to change the measure. I honestly believe this. This still leaves me with the problem of reconciling our experimental results, which have shown relationships between conventional intelligence test scores and learning measures, with the reasonably large body of literature indicating that there is no such relation. Two hypotheses are advanced for the previous negative results. One is that the experiments simply lacked power in the statistical sense. Intelligence tests show a substantial correlation with school grades, which are an (admittedly imperfect) measure of learning over a period of months or years. The reliability of a measure of learning ability taken from a one hour sample of behavior is suspect. This is especially true when the learning is of material from which meaning has largely been removed, since a more modern view of memory as a coding process suggests that a great deal of learning depends on one's ability to see relations between old knowledge and current stimuli.

A second reason for being suspicious of the previous studies is the sophistication argument. Virtually all the early work used "raw" measures of learning (e.g., errors, trials to criterion). By contrast, our studies have used parameter estimates derived from the raw measures. The relation between the observable responses in a learning situation and the parameter estimates derived from them is often nonlinear. This could obscure a straightforward attempt to relate response measures of learning to intelligence.

## RELATION OF THE MODEL TO PSYCHOMETRICS

A concluding word is in order on the relation of the approach taken here to some of the current psychometric views of intelligence. At a general level, what we have tried to do is develop a process model of cognition, whereas psychometric models display abilities in a static structure relation to each other. In theory, it should be possible to define the process components underlying any structurally defined ability. Carroll (Chapter 3) has made an excellent start toward this goal in his analysis of the process demands implied by the tests in the Educational Testing Service's "Reference kit for mental factors." A somewhat similar analysis has been conducted for the Raven Progressive Matrix Test (Hunt, 1974). These sorts of analyses are needed in order to tie our very considerable knowledge of correlational evidence about psychometric tests to the theory of individual differences propounded here.

We may also look at the philosophy of this approach to individual differences in the light of the theories based on psychometric studies. The parametric approach is similar to Guilford's (1967) *structure of intellect* model in emphasizing specific, rather than hierarchically ordered, abilities. The major difference is that in Guilford's approach the place where an ability ought to be found is determined by a static model of the things people do and the operations used to do them, rather than by reference to a dynamic model of cognition.

The distinction between information processing machinery and control programs may be seen by some as paralleling Cattell's distinction between fluid and crystallized intelligence (Cattell, 1971; Horn, 1968). The obvious correlation is between structural parameters and fluid intelligence on the one hand, and control processes and crystallized intelligence on the other. Empirically, though, there is a discrepancy. Cattell and Horn regard verbal tests primarily as measures of crystallized intelligence, whereas in our work we have found that high scorers on verbal tests are characterized by exceptional short-term memory ability—which should be related more to fluid intelligence. There are a number of points about this finding that should be cleared up. For one thing, the relationships we have found between verbal intelligence and memory, although significant, are certainly not so high that one would want to say the two terms referred to the same ability. For another, most of our studies have dealt with a particular population, young adults, in which we would expect to find substantial variation in both fluid and crystallized intelligence. It would be of interest to see if the same relations would be found in younger children, where Cattell's theory asserts that most of the individual differences will be due to fluid intelligence, and in the elderly, where most of the individual differences should be associated with crystallized intelligence.

Finally, the approach given here is philosophically opposed to Humphreys' (1970) incremental theory of intelligence. Humphreys argues that intelligence at any time is the sum of previously acquired intellectual capacities, and that the increment to these capacities in a unit of time is independent of the level of capacity. I have argued that cognitive power is determined by structural parameters which also partly determine the ability to acquire new information. Therefore the amount of information acquired in a fixed time should be correlated with the amount acquired thus far.

A comparison of this approach to psychometric theories on a piecemeal basis is apt to obscure a very basic fact. This approach has far more in common with Galton than Thurstone! Psychometric theories regard both individuals and tasks as points in a Euclidean space of basic abilities, thus defined by a linear combination of those abilities. My argument is that an individual is a highly nonlinear combination of basic abilities. In fact, by choosing different control strategies, two individuals may make their performances on the same task depend upon different nonlinear combinations of their structural capacities. If this is correct, then a psychology of individual differences cannot possibly be recovered from data analyses based upon linear models, no matter how sophisticated the analyses. The psychology of intelligence must be part of the psychology of cognition.

## ACKNOWLEDGMENTS

The preparation of this report was supported by the National Institute of Mental Health, Grant MH 21795, to the University of Washington. I would like to thank my colleagues Martha Holland, Tom Love, Clifford Lunneborg, and Steven Poltrock, for their comments on a number of the issues discussed here. Geoffery Loftus' careful criticisms of an earlier draft have, hopefully, made the current effort more direct and understandable. Finally, I have been greatly assisted by the conference participants on the verbal presentation of some of the information contained here. Lauren Resnick's editorial work has been of special assistance.

## REFERENCES

Anderson, J. R. & Bower, G. H. *Human associative memory.* New York: Halsted Press, 1973.

Atkinson, R., & Shiffrin, R. Human memory: A proposed system and its control processes. In K. Spence & J. Spence (Eds.), *Advances in the psychology of learning and motivation.* Vol. 2. New York: Academic Press, 1968.

Atkinson, R., & Westcourt, K. Some remarks on a theory of memory. In P. Rabbit & S. Dornic (Eds.), *Attention and performance V.* New York: Academic Press, 1974.

Barlow, F. *Mental prodigies.* New York: Philosophical Library, 1952.

Cattell, R. B. *Abilities: Their structure, growth, and action.* Boston: Houghton-Mifflin, 1971.

Cermak, L. S., Butters, N., & Moreines, J. Some analyses of the verbal encoding deficit of alchoholic Korsakoff patients. *Brain and Language,* 1974, 1, 141–150.

Clark, H., & Chase, W. On the process of comparing sentences against pictures. *Cognitive Psychology*, 1972, 3, 472–517.

Craik, F., & Lockhart, R. Levels of processing: A framework for memory research. *Journal of Verbal Learning & Verbal Behavior*, 1972, 11, 671–684.

Day, R., Cutting, J., & Copeland, P. Perception of linguistic and nonlinguistic dimensions of dichotic stimuli. Paper presented at the 12th Annual meeting of Psychonomic Society, St. Louis, 1971.

Gazzaniga, M. *The bisected brain.* New York: Appleton-Century-Crofts, 1970.

Guilford, J. P. *The nature of human intelligence.* New York: McGraw-Hill, 1967.

Henley, N. A psychological study of the semantics of animal terms. *Journal of Verbal Learning & Verbal Behavior*, 1969, 8, 176–184.

Horn, J. Organization of abilities and the development of intelligence. *Psychological Review*, 1968, 75, 242–259.

Humphreys, L. Theory of intelligence. University of Illinois Psychology Department Technical Report, 1970.

Hunt, E. What kind of computer is man? *Cognitive Psychology*, 1971, 2, 57–98.

Hunt, E. The memory we must have. In R. Schank & K. Colby (Eds.), *Computer models of thought and language.* San Francisco: Freeman, 1973.

Hunt, E. Quote the Raven? Nevermore! In L. Gregg, (Ed.), *Knowledge and cognition.* Hillsdale, New Jersey: Lawrence Erlbaum Assoc., 1974.

Hunt, E., Frost, N., & Lunneborg, C. Individual differences in cognition: A new approach to intelligence. In G. H. Bower (Ed.), *Psychology of learning and motivation.* Vol. 7. New York: Academic Press, 1973.

Hunt, E., & Love, T. How good can memory be? In A. Melton & E. Martin (Eds.), *Coding processes in human memory.* Washington: Winston, 1972. (a)

Hunt, E., & Love, T. The second mnemonist. Paper presented at American Psychological Association meetings, Honolulu, 1972. (b)

Hunt, E., Lunneborg, C., & Lewis, J. What does it mean to be high verbal? *Cognitive Psychology*, 1975, 7(2), 194–227.

Hunt, E., & Poltrock, S. The mechanics of thought. In B. Kantowitz (Ed.), *Human information processing: Tutorials in performance and cognition.* Hillsdale, New Jersey: Lawrence Erlbaum Assoc., 1974.

Keele, S. W. Attention and human performance. Pacific Palisades, California: Goodyear, 1973.

Loftus, E. How to catch a zebra in semantic memory. Paper presented at the Minnesota Conference on Cognition, Minneapolis, 1973.

Loftus, E., & Loftus, G. Changes in memory structure and retrieval over the course of instruction. *Journal of Educational Psychology*, 1974, 66(3), 315–318.

Loftus, G. Acquisition of information from rapidly presented verbal and nonverbal stimuli. *Memory and Cognition*, 1974, 2, 545–548.

Love, T. Information processing characteristics of good memorizers. Unpublished Masters thesis, University of Washington Psychology Department, 1973.

Morton, J. Interaction of information in word recognition. *Psychological Review*, 1969, 76(2), 165–178.

Nelson, T. O. Recognition and savings in long-term memory: Related or independent? *Proceedings of the 79th Annual Convention of the American Psychological Association*, 1971, 6, 15–16. (Summary) (a)

Nelson, T. O. Savings and forgetting from long-term memory. *Journal of Verbal Learning & Verbal Behavior*, 1971, 10, 568–576. (b)

Newell, A., & Simon, H. *Human problem solving.* Englewood Cliffs, New Jersey: Prentice-Hall, 1972.

Osgood, C., Suci, G., & Tannenbaum, P. *The measurement of meaning*. Urbana, Illinois: University of Illinois Press, 1957.

Pender, N. J. A developmental study of conceptual, semantic differential, and acoustical dimensions as encoding categories in short-term memory. Final Report of Project #9-E-070, U.S. Department of Health, Education, and Welfare, Northwestern University, 1969.

Peterson, L., & Peterson, M. Short-term retention of individual verbal items. *Journal of Experimental Psychology*, 1959, 58, 193–198.

Posner, M., Boies, S., Eichelman, W., & Taylor, R. Retention of visual and name codes of single letters. *Journal of Experimental Psychology*, 1969, 79(1, Pt. 2), 1–16.

Potter, M., & Levy, C. Recognition memory for rapid sequences of pictures. *Journal of Experimental Psychology*, 1969, 81, 10–15.

Quillian, M. R. Semantic memory. In M. Minsky (Ed.), *Semantic information processing*. Cambridge, Massachusetts: MIT Press, 1968.

Rips, L., Shoben, E., & Smith, E. Semantic distance and the verification of semantic relations. *Journal of Verbal Learning & Verbal Behavior*, 1973, 12, 1–20.

Rumelhart, D., & Abrahamson, A. A model for analogical reasoning. *Cognitive Psychology*, 1973, 5, 1–28.

Rumelhart, D., Lindsay, P., & Norman, D. A process model of long-term memory. In E. Tulving & W. Donaldson (Eds.). *Organization of memory*. New York: Academic Press, 1972.

Seamon, J. G., & Gazzaniga, M.S. Coding strategies and cerebral laterality effects. *Cognitive Psychology*, 1973, 5, 249–256.

Shepard, R., & Metzler, J. Mental rotation of three-dimensional objects. *Science*, 1971, 171, 701–703.

Snyder, C. Individual differences in imagery and thought. Unpublished doctoral dissertation, University of Oregon, 1973.

Trabasso, T. Mental operations in language comprehension. In J. Carroll & R. Freedle (Eds.), *Language comprehension and the acquisition of knowledge*. Washington: Winston, 1972.

Tulving, E., & Donaldson, W. (Eds.), *Organization of memory*. New York: Academic Press, 1972.

Wickens, D. Characteristics of word encoding. In A. Melton & E. Martin (Eds.), *Coding processes in human memory*. Washington: Winston, 1972.

# 14
# Language and Intelligence

Janellen Huttenlocher

*University of Chicago*


## INTRODUCTION

This chapter concerns the relation of linguistic ability to other aspects of cognitive ability. I will consider this issue in the context of the more general problem of the relation of language to thought, because the nature of this relation determines how these abilities may vary with respect to one another. The issue is one which has concerned investigators from many disciplines.

Various theorists have linked thought to language in a manner which seems to imply that linguistic ability and other aspects of intelligence must necessarily vary in a one-to-one fashion. Some have argued that thought is basically linguistic in nature. This includes, among others, philosophers who have said that genuine knowledge—"knowing that" as opposed to "knowing how"—is linguistic in nature; behaviorists who have identified thought with internal speech; and cultural anthropologists who have proposed that language molds thought, and that different languages may give rise to different world views. Others have argued that language and thought arise from common underlying intellectual capacities, such as the ability to abstract or to formulate rules. In addition to these long-standing general arguments, certain current models of language comprehension and of thought processes which I will discuss below also assume a close link between language and thought.

An opposing tradition has treated thought and language as separate. In a recent chapter, Brewer (1974) reviews some of the arguments which have been presented. The most salient are, first, that language can differ while thought remains the same, as in paraphrase, and that language can be the same while thought differs, as in ambiguity; and, second, that the introspections of humans and evidence from nonverbal organisms suggest that certain mental processes, such as those involved in visual recognition and in complex motor tasks, do not require language.

In evaluating arguments about the relation of language to thought one must be careful to specify the sense in which the term "language" is employed. In the context of the "language and thought" problem, the term usually refers to the role of natural language, namely of the linguistic code itself, in thought. Sometimes, however, it is used to refer to the role of symbolization in thought. These, I suggest below, are two very different issues. In this chapter, I use the term "language" in the former sense, and take the "language and thought" problem to refer to the problem of how natural language is involved in conceptualization and thought.

Even in this context, the linguistic code, of course, derives its importance in human affairs from the fact that it bears a systematic relation to conceptualization and thought. However, as implied in the familiar claim that language is conventional and arbitrary, knowledge of the code and conceptual knowledge are fundamentally different in kind. The linguistic code includes the sound patterns of its lexical elements and the rules for combining these elements into grammatical sequences but by itself does not preserve information about events. The preservation of information about events comes about because the code constitutes a symbolic scheme which is mapped onto aspects of nonlinguistic experience.

Certain anatomical areas of the brain are specialized for perceiving and producing speech, so that it seems reasonable to argue with Geschwind (1966) and other neurologists before him, that the speech code is represented in different parts of the brain than those where conceptual information is stored. Indeed, certain pathological conditions affect linguistic ability differentially from other aspects of intellectual ability. Furthermore, even in normal populations, tests of mental abilities reveal two distinct factors, which are generally referred to as "spatial" and "verbal" factors. "Verbal" tasks test not just knowledge of the code, but ability to use it meaningfully; yet even this ability is to some extent separate from "spatial" ability. For all of these reasons, it seems that it would be mistaken to link natural language too closely to thought in its most general sense.

This chapter develops the position that while thinking does involve symbolic processes, it does not always involve the symbols of natural language. Such a notion is at least implicit in the writings of many cognitive theorists. In this chapter I will examine the general role of symbols in memory and thought and attempt to clarify the particular role of linguistic symbols. Within the framework developed below there is no reason to expect that individual differences in the adequacy of thought processes need be closely related to individual differences in the ability to aptly use the linguistic code.

## SYMBOLS

While natural language provides a means by which people symbolize their experiences, it is not the only means. Let us examine the linguistic code in the broader context of symbolic systems. I will adopt Goodman's (1968) terminology, using the expression "symbol scheme" to refer to a set of symbols and to rules for combining them, and the expression "symbol system" to indicate such a symbol scheme when it is taken together with a correlated field of reference. Thus, for example, the printed alphabet of English is a symbol scheme that forms a symbol system when taken together with the reference field of "sound English." The words of "sound English" and the rules for their combination are a symbol scheme that forms a symbol system when taken together with its reference field of objects, events, etc., which make up "object English." As Goodman points out, the correlation of a symbol scheme with a field of reference normally involves not only a correlation of individual symbols, which he calls "characters," with objects from the field of reference, but also a correlation of the relations among individual characters with relations among objects within the field of reference—for example, the left–right spatial relation of words in written English is correlated with the before–after temporal relation of words in sound English.

For the elements or operations of a symbol scheme to represent the elements or operations in another domain, the former must be systematically mapped onto the latter. There need be no physical resemblance between the elements or operations in the two domains; thus the sounds of the words of natural language do not typically resemble what the words denote, nor do the different arabic numerals resemble different degrees of numerosity. There are certain obvious restrictions on the nature of a symbol scheme which may be used to represent particular sorts of information from another domain, and no doubt there are many other restrictions which are not so obvious. For example, to represent ten different objects or events one must employ a symbol scheme in which elements can be designated in ten different ways, and so on. Not only must a scheme be rich enough in principle to represent a situation, but the symbol user must retain how that scheme is mapped onto various aspects of that target situation.

Goodman (1968) distinguishes symbol systems like those we have just considered from others which lack "disjointness and finite differentiation." Pictures and devices like the ungraduated thermometer are in the latter category in that they involve an infinite number of elements. Such depictions may be distinguished from diagrams or maps in that for these, as opposed to pictures, one knows exactly which features are representationally relevant: "The only relevant features of the diagram are the ordinate and abscissa of each of the points the center passes through. The thickness of the line, its color and intensity, and absolute size of the diagram, etc., do not matter" (Goodman, 1968, p. 122).

Whether a particular schema is a depiction versus a diagram may be a matter of degree.

I have argued earlier that the internal representations of events involved in thinking are in many ways comparable to the observable symbolic activities involved in talking, map making, etc. (Huttenlocher, 1973). That is, the same considerations which hold for representing information in words or maps seem just as applicable to representing information in thought. The mental representation of a problem situation and of the operations involved in its solution can only be successful if the symbolic scheme is sufficiently rich, and if correspondences between the target situation and the scheme are established and maintained. If these conditions are met, a solution achieved in thought may be applied to a target situation. We will return to this issue later in this chapter.

## THE LINGUISTIC CODE IN RELATION TO EVENTS

Let us consider what cognitive structure must be postulated to account for the ability to use language consistently in relation to events, given that the linguistic code is a conventional symbol scheme, and that knowledge of the code is separate from knowledge of the world. I take as an example the ability to judge whether simple descriptions of spatial relations are appropriate to particular pictures of object arrays because this type of example has been used recently by various investigators (e.g., Chase & Clark, 1972; Trabasso, Rollins, & Shaughnessy, 1971) in presenting models of the comprehension process. These models are potentially misleading in that they fail to stress the implications of the fact that language is a conventional code and thus might lead one to conclude that conceptual knowledge and knowledge of the linguistic code are not in any important sense distinct from one another.

The "picture–sentence verification" models postulate that comprehension involves a matching process whereby the picture and the sentence are made to assume a common format. If the two "match," the sentence is judged true; otherwise it is judged false. This matching process has been thought of either as a conversion of one input into the form of the other (encoding of the picture into a linguistic format or of the sentence into a pictorial format) or as the encoding of both inputs into a third common format, often called an "abstract proposition," so that the listener can determine whether sentence and picture "match." I will deal only with the latter because it is the one currently regarded most seriously.

Apart from the conceptual difficulties with matching models, empirical support for them has been obtained in highly constrained experimental tasks which do not model the critical elements involved in ordinary cases of language comprehension. For example, Chase and Clark (1972) use sentences all of which describe the vertical relation between two objects in schematic drawings. [Star is (is not) above (below) cross.] The pattern of latencies for judging the truth and falsity of such sentences against pictures (which show either a star above a cross or a cross above a star) is consistent with the hypothesis that subjects "encode" the picture in a form which parallels a positive description and list whether this encoding "matches" that presented in the sentence (although this is not the only possible interpretation of the data). For these tasks, subjects can simply focus on the vertical relation between the objects in the schematic drawing, making it plausible to argue that they generate an appropriate proposition from the picture which can later be matched against the proposition from an incoming sentence. However, a model based on such tasks may reflect task-specific strategies and not be at all generalizable to comprehension in ordinary settings.

A person cannot usually predict how an event will later be described. Even for simple outline drawings, people would normally retain sufficient information to allow them to judge the truth of many assertions, concerning not only spatial relations but also characteristics of the individual objects. They might also retain information which is not easily describable, such as the fact that a line varies in thickness at different points in the drawing. If comprehension is studied under conditions where subjects can build up expectations concerning which sentences will be used, or where the situations being described involve schematic drawings with only a few easily nameable objects, properties, and relations, the investigator may too hastily conclude that people's experiences with objects and events are always "encoded" into some format that bears a straightforward relation to natural language descriptions.

In this context, let us note that some current investigators postulate that conceptual information in general should be regarded as "propositional" (e.g., Anderson & Bower, 1973; Kintsch, 1974; Rumelhart, Lindsay, & Norman, 1972), which seems compatible with one form of storage of conceptual knowledge posited by matching models of comprehension. However, certain points should be kept in mind with respect to these models of conceptual memory. First, there has not been any explicit specification of what might constitute empirical evidence that conceptual knowledge is stored in "propositional" form as opposed to being stored in some alternative form. Second, there is not yet sufficient empirical data to support any particular claims concerning the form in which conceptual information is retained.

These "propositional" models examine conceptual knowledge from the vantage point of a theory of linguistic meaning. Thus, Rumelhart et al. (1972) explicitly choose to represent the entirety of conceptual knowledge in terms of Fillmore's case grammar, a linguistic model of the underlying conceptual relations which are directly encoded in the syntax of natural languages. If one takes seriously the argument that the linguistic code is separate from conceptual information, and that certain aspects of conceptual information may not be easily encodable in language, one should not start with linguistic theories in examining the forms of conceptual knowledge.

In any case, insofar as current models assert that conceptual knowledge is "propositional," they must be careful about assuming that these propositions are in any sense linguistic, even in the sense of involving linguistic deep structures. The linguistic code only preserves information when correlated with nonlinguistic experience. Therefore, models of comprehension must posit the occurrence of an underlying *mapping* process which relates the linguistic code to perceived events. The necessity for a mapping process is a logical consequence of the assumption that the linguistic code is a conventional, or arbitrary, symbol scheme.

Let us explicitly outline what sort of cognitive structure would be necessary to account for people's ability to use language systematically in relation to events.[1] To know how a name applies to an object class, a person must possess an *object schema*—stored information about how a class of objects looks, feels, and functions—and must be able to recognize objects as instances of the object class. He or she must also possess a *word-sound schema*—namely, stored information about the sound of a particular word—and must be able to recognize incoming words as instances of the word-sound class. Finally, he or she must have stored a *mapping of the sound schema onto the object schema* to know where the word is appropriately applied. With respect to descriptions of perceptible relations, for example, for the relation "above," a person must possess a *perceptual relation schema* for vertical arrays and must be able to recognize vertical arrays involving pairs of objects as belonging to the category of vertical relations. In addition, he or she must have stored an ordered relation among the words in a sentence, which we call a *syntactic schema*. He or she must be able to recognize an incoming sentence as an instance of the *syntactic schema*. Finally, he or she must have stored a *mapping of the ordered relation among words onto the ordered relation among objects.*

Consider then what "abstract proposition" matching models must claim about the "encoding" of linguistic and perceptual inputs into the postulated abstract format, given that the relation of the code to perceptual experience is conventional. Two mapping operations would seem to be involved, one that maps perceptual input into the abstract format and another that maps linguistic input onto this abstract form. It is essential to note that the two inputs cannot both be "encoded" via natural nonarbitrary processes into the same abstract format. Conventional mapping operations must be postulated to avoid the false assumption that there is an inherent non-arbitrary relation between the mental representations of events and the linguistic code.

The linguistic code bears a conventional relation to the material it encodes for abstract as well as for perceptual aspects of experience, even though not much is

---

[1] These same points are made in Huttenlocher and Higgins (1972), Huttenlocher (1973), and Huttenlocher (1975). An extensive discussion of the model, which is merely sketched in these papers, will appear in Higgins and Huttenlocher, *Symbols and Other Signs,* in preparation.

yet known about how to characterize such conceptual knowledge. One frequently encounters expressions like "verbal information" or "verbal concepts." Indeed, much of people's information about events and even certain of their conceptual categories are acquired either from general verbal context or directly by explicit definition, and it may be that certain conceptual notions can *only* be acquired through verbal context or definition. For example, the concept "density" may have been presented as "weight per unit volume." However, the concept of density concerns the nature of material objects and the definition would be vacuous unless the notions of *weight, volume,* and so forth, were already anchored in some conceptual structure.

In summary, I have considered certain implications of the conventional nature of the language code for the form that models of language comprehension must assume. I indicated that one must take care to avoid the potentially misleading implications of certain current models of comprehension, particularly of "matching models." I have not proposed an alternative model, but have simply indicated the minimal structure requirements for such models, namely, that they must postulate the existence of stored information about the code, stored information about events, and rules of relation between them. Not much is currently known about the form in which people's knowledge of events is stored, and I have suggested that one should not start from theories of linguistic meaning in examining the forms which conceptual knowledge assumes in memory and thought.

## SPATIAL REASONING

Prior to examining the representation of information in thought, I want to consider certain studies of problem solving. These studies will be important to the discussion in that they suggest that certain problem situations may be represented in the individual by spatial images, and that the operations involved in solving such problems may be represented by imaginary sensory-motor acts.

First consider a set of studies by Shepard and his colleagues. Shepard and Feng (1972) presented diagrams of flattened-out cubes and asked people to judge whether two arrows drawn on these diagrams would meet if one actually made the cubes. The time required to make judgments of this sort varied with the number of folds required to get the two arrows into position on the cube, suggesting that the mental operations in imaginary paper folding are analogous to those in *actual* paper folding. In another set of studies (e.g., Shepard & Metzler, 1971; Metzler & Shepard, 1974), people were asked to judge the identity of two visual forms, each of which involved a major axis with two arms mounted at its ends. These forms were either the same, or differed in the angles at which the arms were mounted to the major axis. The time it took subjects to judge whether the two forms were identical was found to vary linearly with the angle of separation between their major axes. This finding suggests that the mental operations involved in making these judgments are analogous to actual operations with real objects where one figure is rotated until its major axis is parallel to that of the other.

In tasks where people must infer the appearance of arrays of objects from different vantage points there is evidence that they mentally rotate the array, as they do in Shepard's tasks (Huttenlocher & Presson, 1973; Huttenlocher & Presson, in preparation). People apparently code arrays by assigning elements to particular spatial locations and transform those arrays by tracing the paths of focal elements as they change relative to the subject. The coding of arrays is diagrammatic in the sense that only certain aspects of the array are represented in consciousness. Elements are typically described as relations among points in space; their locations are claimed to be separated by no particular distances, and the elements are not represented as to color or size.

Let us turn to a rather different type of problem, namely, to ordering syllogisms. These are verbal problems in which information about the order of a set of items along some dimension is given in a series of premises—for example, "Tom is taller than Harry. Joe is shorter than Harry. Who is the tallest?" Each premise in such problems describes the order of two adjacent items. Subjects must order the entire set of items by combining the information from the separate premises. DeSoto, London, and Handel (1965) proposed that people solve such problems by representing the order of items as a spatial array. Their proposal was based on subjects' introspections. Subjects agreed as to how various dimensions should be laid out spatially, for example, that the dimension of "goodness" should be arranged vertically with the better items to the top.

The spatial ordering hypothesis was extended by Huttenlocher (1968) to explain the relative difficulty of different forms of the syllogism. Subjects' introspections suggest not only that they represent ordered item information spatially, but also how they combine information from the separate premises. Subjects claimed that they first arranged the two items from the first premise, and then treated later premises as instructions about how to place successive items into that spatial array. In support of these claims, a parallel was found between the difficulty of adding a new item to an array of real objects according to particular instructions and the difficulty of ordering a new item in a syllogism from a comparable premise; it is easier when the new item is grammatical subject of the premise.

Further evidence that subjects represent item order by using the mental equivalents of spatial arrays comes from studies of ordering problems with more than two premises (see Potts, 1972, 1974; Potts & Scholz, in press; Trabasso, Riley, & Wilson, 1975). These investigators found that even though each premise in such problems specifies the order of adjacent items, the ease of answering questions such as "Is Tom taller than Harry?" increases as the positions of two items in the set are further apart. Thus the difficulty of answering particular questions about item order does not reflect the way that information was presented, but rather reflects the distance between items in the final ordered series, just as for real arrays. Further, questions are easier to answer if they involve items from the ends of the series, just as for actual arrays.

## REPRESENTING INFORMATION IN THOUGHT

In the problems above, people report that images and the manipulation of images are integral to their problem-solving processes, and there is behavioral evidence to support their claims. Further, there is evidence that such imagery may involve specifically visual processes. Thus, Brooks (1968) found that visual distraction can interfere with problem solving which involves spatial imagery. Nevertheless, the imagery of problem solving clearly is not analogous to after-images or eidetic images, nor to the percepts arising from direct encounters with objects or events. First, problem-solving imagery does not bear a straightforward relation to people's stored information about events. For example, people's images of object arrays in our perspective tasks do not, introspectively, involve fully perceived objects but rather colorless, shapeless points in space with no metric information about the distances between them. There would be no reason to expect faded percepts to be incomplete in these ways. I examine the relation of this problem-solving imagery to perception and memory later on.

The imagery of problem solving involves just those elements of experience regarded as critical by the problem solver and seems best described as diagrammatic in Goodman's sense. As I suggested, such images can provide symbolic schemes by which to represent problem situations and the mental operations involved in the solution process. In this sense, such mental representations are equivalent to physically realized diagrams, models, etc. For example, just as one might represent information about an automobile accident by using any small objects to demonstrate the direction and angle of impact of the vehicles, one might use symbolic elements in thought in an analagous fashion to represent these aspects of the accident.

In contrast to the position that various symbolic schemes can be used in thinking, some investigators argue that thought processes should be identified with linguistic deep structures. Thus, Newell and Simon (1972) discuss the mental representation of problem situations as follows:

> To the extent that the problem representations we shall postulate do, in fact, explain the problem solving behavior of human beings, the claim that the structures embodying these representations are linguistic deep structures gains strong support. For if this were not so, *and* if language is implicated in thinking, then we would have to postulate a distinct set of deep structures, holding the meanings of the surface structures, carried along . . . in parallel with the "nonlinguistic" problem representations. But this is an

unnecessary and unparsimonious multiplication of hypothetical entities that has no evidential support. We prefer the simpler course that identifies deep structures closely with semantics, hence with the internal symbol structures that are the media of thought [p. 66].

This argument is consistent with empirical research by these investigators that uses verbal protocols of subjects to index their mental processes.[2]

Rather than it being "an unnecessary and unparsimonious multiplication of hypothetical entities" to separate problem representations from linguistic deep structures, I would argue that it is important to make such a distinction. The mental representations we have examined seem less like linguistic deep structures than like concrete models; they involve neither the types of conceptual information encoded in lexical elements, nor the conceptual relations encoded in syntax. Symbol schemes surely can be directly mapped onto the situations they represent without natural language intervening, as, for example, in the relation of musical notation to a melody it represents, or in the relation of an engineer's model plane and simulated windtunnel to the actual plane and wind conditions they are used to stand for. Surely, the information represented in thought can also involve various symbol schemes without natural language intervening.

In fact, there seems no end to the types of symbolic schemes that people may use in thinking. Familiar activities from one domain may serve as symbolic schemes which provide heuristics for solving problems in another domain. As we have seen, the verbal problem of ordering items along an abstract dimension can be mapped onto the familiar activity of spatially ordering actual objects; this provides the problem solver with a symbol scheme whereby he imagines himself to be physically arranging actual objects, later replacing the elements and operations from this symbol scheme with those from the domain of the problem. Such symbol schemes may be employed only temporarily, creating heuristics for problem solving. Thus, a symbol scheme need not bear a permanent relation to the domain it is used to represent as is the case in the words and syntax of natural language (excepting metaphorical extensions, etc.).

In evaluating the apparent differences among symbol systems, such as natural languages versus diagrams, some investigators have focused on the question of whether these different schemes are, in principle, translatable. Goodman (1968) argues that analog schemes such as pictures and maps are fundamentally different from categorical schemes such as natural language. In this context, the question has been raised as to whether maps or pictures can be translated in terms of a digital code. Certainly digital codes can approximate pictorial depic-

---

[2] These authors themselves deal with problem representations that bear no obvious relation to "linguistic deep structures" and, indeed, this quote from them does not do justice to their own excellent work. Nevertheless, the statement itself is theoretically misleading in the consideration of thought processes.

tions, as in computer representations of faces. Not only that, but continuous functions may be represented by algebraic formulas involving discrete symbols, as in $y = 2x^2 + 3$.

What seems critical is not so much whether different symbol schemes are in principle translatable, but that different schemes are normally used to encode different types of information. The information encoded by the lexical elements in natural language differs from that encoded by musical notes or by particular points on graphs, and the types of relations designated by the syntactic relations among words differ from those designated by the relation among musical notes or by the relations among points on a graph. A person may be able to use one symbol scheme but not another to represent certain information; for example, one may be familiar enough with a person's face to be able to produce a recognizable sketch, and yet be unable to formulate a description such that someone else could recognize that face. Even if the speech code can, in principle, be used to represent the same information as a graph, with lexical elements designating particular spatial points and the relation among lexical elements designating spatial relations among points, this is not how it is ordinarily used. Natural language has evolved as a symbol system for encoding certain aspects of people's experience.

It is possible that natural language is not suited for encoding particular sorts of information, either because of its inherent properties such as being categorical rather than analog or because it has not been used in certain cognitive realms. However, this possibility has not been systematically explored. The problem is complicated since, in one sense, any information can be encoded in language. That is, people who have shared a target experience can always agree to use a particular word or expression to designate it, even if they could not have described it to someone who had not had that experience. Thus words can be used to retrieve information about target experiences, such as the appearance of particular faces, even in cases where words cannot easily be used to create that experience as new information for a listener.

## THOUGHT AND MEMORY

I suggested above that in problem solving people may use various symbol schemes to represent selected aspects of their experience. Introspectively, this also seems true of thought processes in situations where directed problem solving is not involved. Consider, for example, a person imagining a possible meeting with three colleagues to discuss his future plans. He may represent only certain aspects of the physical environs of the meeting as, for example, his own position relative to a door, etc. The people in the imagined encounter may be represented only as points in particular spatial locations, much as in the three-term series problem. Thus, just as only selected features of situations are represented in problem solving, only selected features of the information in long-term memory may be represented in thinking generally, or in reminiscing (that is, in active memory).

The ability to reminisce about events in their absence has long been treated as being closely related to the symbolic abilities involved in language use. Thus Aristotle said that only humans can reminisce about events in their absence, even though animals as well as humans can recognize events experienced earlier. Certain investigators have been concerned with whether various accomplishments of animals necessarily involve the ability to represent information in active memory, for example, when an animal shows surprise at finding a pellet at a place where he had seen lettuce being hidden earlier. The issue is whether the ability to consider the properties of absent objects is a specifically human (symbolic?) ability.

In this context, Piaget (1962) argues that the shift from the "sensory-motor" intellectual stage of the child's first two years of life to the succeeding stages of "representational thought" involves the appearance of the ability to use symbols mentally. During the transition between stages, the child can symbolize his experiences in terms of actual overt behavior, as in deferred imitation where he demonstrates recall of various elements of an earlier experience by representing them in his own actions. Piaget proposes that the use of such overt representational behavior precedes the child's use of internal symbols, which he regards as essential for representational thought.

The notion that symbolic processes are involved in active memory also seems consistent with the constructivist view that recall of material from long-term memory cannot be accurately described simply as a transfer or "lighting up" of stored information. That is, "reconstruction" of stored information during recall may involve symbolic representation of that information. Neisser (1967) describes the process of bringing information from long-term memory into active memory metaphorically as the building on and fleshing out of the bones of a dinosaur. One way to interpret this metaphor is that "bones" designates the data base of stored information, and that the "building" process designates the representation of aspects of that information via symbol schemes in active memory.[3]

Piaget and Inhelder (1973) similarly stress the distinction between the data base of long-term memory and the symbolization of information in active memory in their discussion of developmental aspects of memory. They report the following phenomenon. Young children were shown an array of sticks ordered by size, at an age when they were unable to order a set of sticks to match that array. Some months later, these children were asked to arrange the

---

[3] Note, however, that to treat images as symbolic schemes for representing certain sorts of information in active memory differs from Neisser's position that imagery is a "cognitive luxury," a mere accompaniment of thought.

sticks as they had seen them earlier, and they did better than they had done initially. While these findings have been disputed because of lack of proper controls (e.g., Finkel & Crowley, 1973), our concern here is with the theoretical claim. It is suggested that information may be entered in long-term memory that will only be fully appreciated later when new intellectual capacities develop, allowing the child to represent aspects of that information effectively in active memory; in particular, the order of the sticks in the ensemble.

While the notion that information can be entered in long-term memory before it can be effectively represented in active memory may seem odd, it is plausible insofar as the information which the child comes to be able to represent is implicit in or deducible from information which has already been stored. Indeed, it was noted above that an animal or very young child apparently can recognize objects or events without being able to reminisce about them, that is, without being able to consider the properties of those objects and events in active memory when they are not present. Yet for someone to be able to recognize particular objects or events and discriminate them from others, he must have retained information about those objects or events. Thus, a person can enter certain types of information in long-term memory and use it in recognition without necessarily being able to actively represent that information in reminiscence or thought.

In the context of such a view, one might ask whether the content and organization of stored information could be similar across individuals, with individual differences in ability arising from how well aspects of that information can be actively represented during thinking. This is not plausible, however, because the representations a person uses in active memory can have a major effect in forming concepts which become stored in his long-term memory, and much of the material in long-term memory is a result of the symbolic representation of earlier material. For instance, it would seem that "abstract" concepts may require active symbolic representation to be formed in the first place. To take an example, consider a notion like "justice," which designates interactions of the individual with the state, etc. Such a notion may arise out of childhood encounters where toys were shared, etc. In first applying the notion of "justice" to social institutions, the symbol scheme used in active memory may involve a concrete situation which provides a model for representing the interactions of larger social units. If the court is represented by an adult and the accused by a child, the decision processes of the court may be interpreted by representing them in terms of concrete notions of bad behavior, punishment, etc. Insofar as notions are actively represented in thought before entering long-term memory, individuals who differ in their ability to think would also differ in the contents of their long-term memories.

In certain respects, however, the content and organization of long-term memory may be similar in individuals of different ability. Young children and retarded individuals act like normal adults on certain tests of meaning relatedness. For example, among adults, presentation of successive lists of words of similar meaning followed by a list of different meanings leads to decline in recall followed by improvement following meaning shifts (Wickens, 1970, 1972). We found parallel results in three-year-olds with shifts of categories from animals to clothing, to body parts, etc. (Huttenlocher & Lui, in preparation). We also obtained increases in the memory spans of four-year-olds by blocking words according to taxonomic category (Huttenlocher & Newcombe, in preparation). In a study of pathological children with difficulties in understanding connected discourse, Yudkowitz (1975) found better free recall for words from the same taxonomic category than for unrelated words. Thus, long-term memory may be similarly organized in all people with respect to concepts designated by concrete nouns, perhaps indicating that symbolic processes are not involved in their formation.

Finally, let us consider another aspect of the relation between long-term memory and thought, namely, why words and images only sometimes arise during thinking if those symbol schemes are *used* in thinking. However, the physical characteristics of symbol schemes, for example, the sound schemas of words or the color and width of the lines in a map or its scale, would not seem to have a function in thought. Indeed, people frequently report mental diagrams or maps involving shapeless, colorless points, lines of no particular length, etc. If symbolic schemes in thought involve only those elements which serve a symbolic function in preserving or transforming information, then there is no reason why words or pictorial detail need not appear more than fleetingly in consciousness during thought. In this sense, the symbol schemes in thought would differ from those used in communication, much as Vygotsky suggested years ago.

In summary, I have considered the relation of problem solving to active memory (reminiscence), and the relation of both of these to long-term memory. I suggested that symbol schemes may be used in active memory to represent aspects of information stored in long-term memory, and that in this context one can interpret some of the intuitions of both animal psychologists and cognitive theorists about the processes involved in active memory. I also suggested that the symbol schemes used in active memory generally, like those in directed problem solving, need not involve the symbols of natural language.

## LANGUAGE USE

Language use involves the perception and production of speech itself as well as encoding and decoding messages about the world of objects and events. With respect to its information coding functions, I suggested that there may be differences in how directly information from different cognitive realms can be coded in linguistic form. The target information that people want to communicate verbally, like thought in general, no doubt may be far removed from natural language meanings, for example, when it concerns how to work a particular machine or what route to follow to get a particular location.

When the mental representation of target information is, for example, maplike in form, interesting problems may arise in coding it verbally. In a study of people's descriptions of their apartments, Linde (1974) found that they began with the entrance and proceeded as in an actual tour, without jumps through space or retracings. She postulated that the immediate input to such descriptions consisted of tree structures with apartment entries as the top nodes. While not much is known about the form in which spatial information is stored (see Downs & Stea, 1973), one might expect a person's knowledge of his own apartment, which he traverses in various ways, to be flexible in perspective rather than invariably oriented from the entrance. The postulated tree structures may not directly reflect the spatial knowledge in long-term memory, but rather may be constructed for the particular purpose of creating a representation that will be appropriate input to a verbal description that can be comprehended.

There are many circumstances when the target information a speaker wishes his listener to consider may be far removed from the literal meanings of the verbal messages he uses. For example, he may know that some or all of that information is already familiar to that listener, so that he can say, for example, "Remember the view from Route 2 near the hairpin turn after Hicksville?" Perhaps the classic example of this sort is from Tolstoy, cited by Vygotsky (1962), where a successful communication between lovers is based on the first letters of a sequence of words. The device of leading one's listener to previously stored information is also used in conveying new information, as in "The view from Joe's room is like the one after Hicksville on Route 2, but on a larger scale."

There has been considerable concern recently with the psychological processes involved in language use. Initially, investigators focused on the literal meanings of sentences, but a number of studies, notably those by Bransford and his colleagues (e.g., Bransford, Barclay, & Franks, 1972; Bransford & Franks, 1971) have led to a fairly general consensus that sentence comprehension can only be meaningfully examined in its larger linguistic and nonlinguistic context, and in terms of a listener's general conceptual knowledge. This may be true even for the simplest and most literal of descriptions. Consider these simple sentences: "The toddler is running," "The dog is running," "Roger Bannister is running." There is not a simple single notion of "run" occurring in the particular syntactic combination which specifies the relation of actor–action; rather, the notion of running itself depends on what the listener knows about the characteristics of the described actor.

A satisfactory framework in which to examine the psychological processes involved in language use remains to be worked out. Several investigators have pointed out that the role of general conceptual knowledge must be made explicit and incorporated into psychological models. I have pointed out that, in addition, the representation of the target information which people wish to communicate may involve symbol systems different from natural language. In this case, verbal encoding may require translation among symbol systems. When such translation is difficult or impossible, the speaker may use metaphor, liken the target information to other information assumed to be familiar to the listener, etc.

## THE RELATION OF LANGUAGE TO THOUGHT:
## INDIVIDUAL DIFFERENCES IN COGNITIVE FUNCTION

Let us consider what the discussion above suggests about the relation of linguistic ability to general intelligence. A person's ability to speak meaningfully obviously depends on his nonlinguistic knowledge. However, a person may be able to represent certain information in thought and to solve problems involving that information without necessarily being able to formulate verbal messages that could convey that information to others. Especially when the representation of information in thought involves symbol systems different from those of language, the ability to think and the ability to describe may be quite separate. This seems clear in the case of spatial information which is most easily represented diagrammatically or in maps. In addition, when a person forms a representation involving some new heuristic in thought, it may be difficult for him to encode it in terms of the symbol system of natural language, of his usual ways of making diagrams, etc. In such cases a person may create some new symbolic system, perhaps initially drawing upon some familiar nonlinguistic domain to provide a model (symbol scheme) to use in communication and then maybe evolving some new symbolic scheme.

Not only may the ability to deal with information in certain cognitive domains be relatively independent of the ability to describe it well, but, in general, the ability to encode information aptly or even understandably in verbal form may be relatively independent of competence in thinking. Various special skills seem to be involved in verbal fluency. Speakers may differ in the extent to which they have developed programs for mapping various aspects of their experience into discourse. Even more removed from general cognitive competence would be differences in the ease with which a person can access the code itself; for example, in how quickly word schemas themselves can be recalled.

Decoding as well as encoding skills might vary somewhat independently of other aspects of intellectual ability, although there is no empirical evidence that this is actually the case. The ability to construct mental representations of target information from incoming verbal messages might differ from the ability to construct comparable mental representations from diagrams or maps, or spontaneously from direct encounters with events. There might also be factors related only to processing of the code itself and not to other aspects of cognitive ability, for example, differences in the speed or accuracy of segmenting sequences of speech sounds into separate lexical elements, or of identifying sound-patterns as instances of particular word-sound schemas, which, at least in the extreme case, might hamper the listener in constructing, at the same time, mental representations of the information being described.

Factor analytic studies of mental abilities repeatedly show verbal and spatial abilities as separate factors. As we have seen, there are many facets to "verbal ability" and these might vary somewhat independently from one another among different individuals. The aspects of verbal ability that have been examined in standardized tests and found to contrast with spatial ability include vocabulary, comprehension of passages, verbal reasoning, and verbal fluency. Spatial ability has many facets as well; standardized tests include matching of designs, finding hidden figures, and rotation tasks similar to those of Shepard and his colleagues. Interestingly, even though ordering syllogisms are in one sense "verbal" reasoning problems, the ability to solve them correlates with spatial rather than verbal ability (Thurstone & Thurstone, 1941), as one would expect from the experimental studies described above.

Not only have verbal and spatial abilities been found to vary quite independently among individuals in the population at large, certain studies also report that these abilities are differentially distributed in different population groups (Lesser, Fifer, & Clark, 1965), and between the sexes (see Jacklin & Maccoby, 1972, for a review). Sex differences in spatial ability have been found to be large and consistent, with only about 25% of women scoring above the median for men (O'Connor, 1943). Intrafamily correlations in spatial reasoning skills have suggested to some investigators that observed differences in ability may have a genetic basis. These correlations are high for mother–son and for father–daughter, but zero for father–son; further, for siblings, sister–sister correlations are higher than brother–brother correlations, which in turn are greater than sister–brother correlations (Bock & Kolakowski, 1973; Stafford, 1961). These investigators note that such a pattern is consistent with the hypothesis that spatial ability is sex linked and carried on the X chromosome.

In certain aspects of verbal ability, women have been found to be superior to men, notably in tests of fluency where one gives as many words as possible which meet certain criteria—which begin with M, which designate foods, etc. Sex differences have not been found in tests of comprehension or verbal reasoning (Thurstone & Thurstone, 1941), or in verbal communicative accuracy (cf. Higgins, 1975). There may be sex differences in language development as well as in adult performance on verbal tests (Harris, in press). Girls tend to talk earlier than boys and have less difficulty learning to read (Jacklin & Maccoby, 1972). One study reports that comprehension, as indicated by the Peabody Picture Vocabulary test, does not show sex differences in childhood (Brimer, 1969). However, the Peabody only tests familiarity with object names, not the comprehension of either more abstract words or syntax.

In addition to findings showing distinct spatial and verbal factors in normal populations, it is well known that certain pathological conditions differentially affect verbal and spatial abilities. Spatial abilities may be relatively intact in people with left-hemisphere damage who show considerable aphasic difficulties. Aphasia itself varies as to whether it is predominantly receptive or predominantly productive. In contrast, spatial abilities may be seriously impaired in people with right-hemisphere damage whose receptive and productive language seem relatively intact (e.g., Milner, 1971; Warrington & Taylor, 1973).

In certain developmental disorders one finds a discrepancy between conceptual and language development. In some cases of autism, there is considerable syntactically well-formed speech, but it tends to be echolalic, and when not obviously echolalic, tends to be inappropriate or only loosely related to its context. Such children may have good short-term verbal memories and may easily learn to read, in the sense of sounding out words, while showing marked comprehension deficits (e.g., Hermelin & O'Connor, 1971; Huttenlocher & Huttenlocher, 1973). Processing of the speech code itself seems to be intact in these children; the defect lies either in the connections of the linguistic code to conceptual knowledge or in the nature of the conceptual knowledge itself. In contrast, children with developmental aphasia may perform well on nonverbal tasks, but be unable to use the linguistic code in either comprehension or production. These children seem to have difficulty in learning the linguistic code itself, but the nature of their receptive problem is not well understood. One hypothesis is that they are unable to encode the sequential order of speech sounds (e.g., Stark, 1967); another is that they are unable to discriminate among the consonants which are basic units in the linguistic code (e.g., Tallal & Piercy, 1974).

In conclusion, let us consider what the relative independence of verbal and spatial abilities within the individual suggests about the relation of language to thought. Standardized tests have focused chiefly on the ability to construct mental representations and draw inferences based on linguistic input, as seen in tasks of verbal reasoning and comprehension of passages, rather than on perception or production of the code or decoding or encoding ability per se. To a very limited extent, encoding ability has been tested; some verbal fluency tests require the subjects to find words that meet a particular meaning criterion. Vocabulary tests require an ability to produce language, but verbal definitions are a very special sort of encoding task. These tests suggest that the ability to represent and transform information from linguistic input is quite separate from the ability to represent and transform spatial information. This is consistent with the notion that at least two distinguishable types of symbolic processes are involved in thinking. Surely more information concerning the nature of thought processes and their relation to various aspects of linguistic ability will emerge as individual differences in normal populations and of pathological phenomena affecting thinking and language use are examined more systematically. Especially this should be the case if these efforts are coordinated with the theoretical and empirical investigation of mental process within experimental psychology.

## ACKNOWLEDGMENTS

The author thanks Deborah Burke, E. Tory Higgins, and Mary C. Potter for their helpful comments on this chapter.

## REFERENCES

Anderson, J., & Bower, G. *Human associative memory.* New York: Halsted Press, 1973.

Bock, R. D., & Kolakowski, D. Further evidence of sex-linked major-gene influence on human spatial visualizing ability. *The American Journal of Human Genetics,* 1973, **25,** 1–14.

Bransford, J., Barclay, J., & Franks, J. Sentence memory: A constructive versus interpretive approach. *Cognitive Psychology,* 1972, **3,** 193–209.

Bransford, J., & Franks, J. The abstraction of linguistic ideas. *Cognitive Psychology,* 1971, **2,** 331–350.

Brewer, W. F. The problem of meaning and the interrelation of the higher mental processes. In W. B. Weimer & D. S. Palermo (Eds.), *Cognition and the symbolic processes.* Hillsdale, New Jersey: Lawrence Erlbaum Assoc., 1974.

Brimer, M. Sex differences in listening comprehension. *Journal of Research and Development in Education,* 1969, **3,** 72–79.

Brooks, L. R. Spatial and verbal components of the act of recall. *Canadian Journal of Psychology,* 1968, **22,** 349–368.

Chase, W. G., & Clark, H. H. Mental operations in the comparison of sentences and pictures. In L. Gregg (Ed.), *Cognition in learning and memory.* New York: Wiley, 1972.

DeSoto, C., London, M., & Handel, S. Social reasoning and spatial paralogic. *Journal of Personality and Social Psychology,* 1965, **2,** 513–521.

Downs, R., & Stea, D. *Image and environment: Cognitive mapping and spatial behavior.* Chicago: Aldine, 1973.

Finkel, D. & Crowley, C. Improvement in children's long-term memory for seriated sticks: Change in memory storage or coding rules? Paper presented at the Society for Research and Child Development meetings in Philadelphia, 1973.

Geshwind, N. Disconnection syndromes in animals and man. *Brain,* 1966, 88, 585–642.

Goodman, N. *Languages of art.* New York: Bobbs-Merrill, 1968.

Harris, J. Sex and language. In E. Donelson & G. Gullahorn (Eds.), *Women: Psychological perspective.* New York: Wiley, in press.

Hermelin, D., & O'Connor, N. *Psychological experiments with autistic children.* New York: Pergamon, 1971.

Higgins, E. T. *Social class differences in verbal communicative accuracy?: A question of "Which question?"* Princeton University, Psychology Department Record Reports Series, No. 11, Princeton, New Jersey, 1975.

Higgins, E. T., & Huttenlocher, J. *Symbols and other signs.* Manuscript, in preparation.

Huttenlocher, J. Constructing spatial images: A strategy in reasoning. *Psychological Review,* 1968, 75, 550–560.

Huttenlocher, J. Language and thought. In G. Miller (Ed.), *Language and communication.* New York: Basic Books, 1973.

Huttenlocher, J. Encoding spatial information in sign language. In J. Kavanagh & J. Cutting (Eds.), *The role of speech in language.* Cambridge, Massachusetts: MIT Press, 1975.

Huttenlocher, J., & Higgins, E. On reasoning, congruence and other matters. *Psychological Review,* 1972, 79, 420–427.

Huttenlocher, J., & Huttenlocher, P. A study of children with "hyperlexia." *Neurology,* 1973, **23**(10), 1107–1116.

Huttenlocher, J., & Lui, F. Conceptual organization in young children: A demonstration involving a release from proactive inhibition. Manuscript, in preparation.

Huttenlocher, J., & Newcombe, N. Span of recall for semantically related words. Manuscript, in preparation.

Huttenlocher, J. & Presson, C. Mental rotation and the perspective problem. *Cognitive Psychology*, 1973, **4**, 277–299.

Huttenlocher, J., & Presson, C. The encoding and transformation of spatial information. Manuscript, in preparation.

Jacklin, C., & Maccoby, E. *Sex differences in intellectual abilities: A reassessment and a look at some new explanations*. Paper presented at the meeting of American Educational Research Association, 1972.

Kintsch, W. *The representation of meaning in memory*. Hillsdale, New Jersey: Lawrence Erlbaum Assoc., 1974.

Lesser, G. S., Fifer, G., & Clark, D. Mental abilities of children from different social class and cultural groups. *Monographs of the Society for Research in Child Development*, 1965, **30**, No. 4.

Linde, C. The linguistic encoding of spatial information. Unpublished doctoral dissertation, Columbia University, 1974.

Metzler, J., & Shepard, R. Transformational studies of the internal representation of three-dimensional objects. In R. Solso (Ed.), *Theories of cognitive psychology*. Hillsdale, New Jersey: Lawrence Erlbaum Assoc., 1974.

Milner, B. Interhemispheric differences in the localization of psychological processes in men. *British Medical Journal*, 1971, **27**, 272–277.

Neisser, U. *Cognitive psychology*. New York: Appleton-Century-Crofts, 1967.

Newell, A., & Simon, H. *Human problem solving*. Englewood Cliffs, New Jersey: Prentice-Hall, 1972.

O'Connor, J. *Structural visualization*. Boston: Human Engineering Laboratory, 1943.

Piaget, J. *Play dreams and imitations in childhood*. New York: Norton, 1962.

Piaget, J., & Inhelder, B. *Memory and intelligence*. New York: Basic Books, 1973.

Potts, G. Information processing strategies used in the encoding of linear orderings. *Journal of Verbal Learning and Verbal Behavior*, 1972, **11**, 127–240.

Potts, G. Storing and retrieving information about ordered relationships, *Journal of Experimental Psychology*, 1974, **103**(3), 431–439.

Potts, G., & Scholz, K. The internal representation of a three-term series problem, *Journal of Verbal Learning and Verbal Behavior*, in press.

Rumelhart, D., Lindsay, P., & Norman, D. A process model for long-term memory. In E. Tulving & W. Donaldson (Eds.), *Organization of memory*. New York: Academic Press, 1972.

Shepard, R., & Feng, C. A chronometric study of mental paper folding. *Cognitive Psychology*, 1972, **3**, 288–293.

Shepard, R., & Metzler, S. Mental rotation of three-dimensional objects. *Science*, 1971, **171**, 701–703.

Stafford, R. E. Sex differences in spatial visualization as evidence of sex-linked inheritance. *Perceptual and Motor Skills*, 1961, **13**, 428.

Stark, J. A comparison of the performance of aphasic children on three sequencing tests. *Journal of Communication Disorders*, 1967, **1**, 31.

Tallal, P., & Piercy, M. Developmental aphasia: Rate of auditory processing and selective impairment of consonant perception. *Neuropsychologia*, 1974, **12**, 317.

Thurstone, L., & Thurstone, T. *Factorial studies of intelligence*. Psychometric Monographs, No. 2. Chicago: University of Chicago Press, 1941.

Trabasso, T., Riley, C., & Wilson, E. The representation of linear order and spatial strategies in reasoning: A developmental study. In R. J. Falmagne (Ed.), *Reasoning: Representation and process in children and adults.* Hillsdale, New Jersey: Lawrence Erlbaum Assoc., 1975.

Trabasso, T., Rollins, H., & Shaughnessey, E. Storage and verification stages in processing concepts. *Cognitive Psychology,* 1971, **2**, 239–289.

Vygotsky, L. *Thought and language.* Cambridge, Massachusetts: MIT Press, 1962.

Warrington, E., & Taylor, A. The contribution of the right parietal lobe to object recognition. *Cortex,* 1973, **9**, 152–164.

Wickens, D. Encoding categories of words: An empirical approach to meaning. *Psychological Review,* 1970, **77**, 1–15.

Wickens, D. Characteristics of word encoding. In A. Melton & E. Martin (Eds.), *Coding processes in human memory.* Washington: Winston, 1972.

Yudkowitz, E. The effect of prior contextual information on the free recall of normal and schizophrenic children. Unpublished doctoral dissertation, Columbia University, 1975.

# 15

# Language Comprehension and the Deverbalization of Intelligence

Charles A. Perfetti

*University of Pittsburgh*

There are two complementary perspectives on intelligence developed in the preceding chapters. One is the notion that memory is part of intelligence (Hunt, Chapter 13). The other is that language is not part of intelligence, or at least not an important part (Huttenlocher, Chapter 14).

Hunt's hypothesis, in my oversimplified expression of it, reflects the great increase in status gained by the concept of memory in recent years. Or possibly it reflects the depths to which the concept of intelligence has fallen. In either case it is a bit distant from the common sense idea that intelligence and memory are very different things.

On the other hand, the claim that intelligence and language are not closely related is a recurrent theme that takes on different forms in different disciplines and theoretical frameworks. The counterpoint, that intelligence and language are closely interdependent, perhaps has enjoyed slightly more support, although not enough to weaken debate. The debate is permitted to flourish largely because of the high degree of abstraction involved in the principal concepts. Language and intelligence (or cognition) are both abstractions, but participants in the controversy often appear to treat only intelligence as an abstraction while treating language as something more concrete. This inevitably leads to the claim that intelligence or cognition is the more "basic" concept, not dependent on language. Huttenlocher's argument that a nonlinguistic intelligence is fundamental reflects awareness of this abstraction dilemma. By assuming that language is as much an abstraction as thought, her argument takes on considerable interest.

In the remainder of this chapter, I will attempt first to raise some general points concerning intelligence and language in the abstract and then turn to a discussion of basic individual differences in intelligence and memory which I shall extend to comprehension.

283

## THE DEVERBALIZATION OF INTELLIGENCE

The basic issue involved in Huttenlocher's claim that language and intelligence are not the same is the representation of knowledge. To put the issue this way is a considerable improvement in the language–thought debate, since it does not suggest that language is merely speech, as Piaget, for example, seems to imply in claiming cognition is basic and language is secondary. The possibility that knowledge has more than one form of representation seems well taken. However, whether the forms of representation are mutually translatable or mapped to a common format does not impress me as a basic psychological issue. Since people can and do match messages that originate in different forms, some operation that allows comparisons of information is essential. This can be done, as Huttenlocher has suggested, by at least any of the following: (a) mapping language information onto a nonlanguage format; (b) mapping nonlanguage information onto a language format; and (c) mapping both onto a third format. Exactly how this is done is something that can be decided for any particular purpose. For example, for a computer program to perform comparisons from different inputs requires translation to a common format, and this format is similar to an abstract semantic deep structure of some sort. Notice this is not a linguistic problem, but a general problem of information structure. For example, I can draw a map that indicates the best street route from my office to my house. I also can drive my car along the same route. In neither case is there a need to talk about a linguistic representation, but there must be a means of translating the two representations into a common format. This single representation allows two nonlinguistic activities. It is the basis both for drawing the map and for driving the car along the selected route. The formating requirement is not a linguistic issue; it is simply a requirement for representing an intelligent problem solution.

There is a less abstract but equally persistent component to the language and intelligence issue that needs some comment in the context of intelligence testing. The role of language comprehension is seen prominently in verbal abilities tests which require the examinee to solve verbal analogies, identify antonyms, complete sentences, etc. For example, the Scholastic Aptitude Test includes each of these tasks and also occupies about half of the examinee's time with a reading comprehension task which requires a wide range of vocabulary, syntactic, and inferential skills.

However, as we know too well, the relationship between language abilities and intelligence testing has been a source of some distress. Attempts to make first culture-free and then culture-fair tests have largely been efforts to *deverbalize* intelligence. It may be that IQ tests owe their predictive success to their large verbal component, because of the value verbal skills have for social and financial success in Western societies—a point that has been made before, for example in the fictional but plausible rise of the meritocracy described by Michael Young

(1961). Young's meritocracy represents a parody of the democratic ideal implemented by intelligence tests. Status is determined not by title or inherited wealth, but by scores on verbal intelligence tests. Thus, the meritocracy needs verbal intelligence. Correlations between currently valued measures of success and a completely deverbalized IQ test would probably be drastically reduced. A reduction in the predictive value of IQ tests might not be an entirely negative event and might even be useful for focusing attention on other relevant sources of success. But in any case, perhaps we should be concerned with the relationship between criterion achievements and basic process differences, including the sort of basic processes identified by Hunt, as well as some others that might be identified. Such relationships are just as basic from a cognitive process point of view and potentially just as useful from an instructional point of view.

## INDIVIDUAL DIFFERENCES IN COMPREHENSION AND INTELLIGENCE

Turning now to individual differences in cognition as this question is approached by Hunt, I believe it is sufficiently challenging to try to discover relationships between intelligence measures and basic processes without introducing additional factors such as language comprehension. However, the role of language comprehension is important in such an endeavor because of its intimate involvement with basic processes and its high correlation with verbal intelligence measures. In this sense, language comprehension is the source of verbal intelligence.

The comprehension of written as well as oral language is significant in the basic process analysis of verbal intelligence. For example, much of the information that is used by an adult in taking a verbal aptitude test has been obtained through reading. This is probably especially true of the sorts of individuals who are among Hunt's high verbals. In a testing conference, Carroll (1966) concluded that there is ample evidence that listening comprehension and reading comprehension depend on somewhat different skills. At the same time it is clear that there are systems of intelligence operating in language comprehension of both types.

Correlations between standard tests of intelligence and standard tests of reading comprehension tend to be positive and moderately large. (For example, in the third- and fifth-grade samples we have worked with, we have observed correlations of .5–.7 between Otis–Lennon Intelligence Measures and Metropolitan Achievement Tests of Reading Comprehension.) Such correlations suggest that reading achievement and IQ tests are measuring some of the same things. Thus, quite aside from the merits of the assertion that the place to look for intelligence is in language comprehension, we have grounds for asking about the relationships between comprehension scores and basic processes. In our research we are using tasks which are derivable from more or less fundamental psycholinguistic tasks that have developed within the context of experimental work, and the parallel with Hunt's approach is worth mentioning. Hunt has taken basic experimental tasks such as continuous paired associates, free recall of nouns, letter-matching experiments, and release from proactive inhibition and compared the performance of adult subjects who differ in verbal ability scores. Using tasks such as word decoding, probing memory for elements of sentences and clauses, phoneme monitoring, and a few others, we are comparing the performance on these tasks of children who differ on reading comprehension scores.[1]

In two of these tasks, we have measured the speed with which children can identify single words presented in isolation. Whereas one task requires word production and the other requires same–different judgments, the converging interest is in single word decoding. One class of words is composed of very common English words whose meaning all children presumably know. A second class is composed of relatively common English words some of which are unknown to most children. Interest in these words is focused on a comparison between the child's decoding performance on known and unknown words, as determined by a vocabulary test. The third class of words is composed of pseudowords, that is, nonwords that conform to permissible English spelling patterns. Thus, we have three classes of words that vary in the extent to which they are semantically developed entries in the child's lexicon.

The results contain something of interest, I believe, for a consideration of relationships between basic skills and verbal achievement. Considering latencies only for correctly produced words, we found that skilled comprehenders, whom we can call "high verbals" to emphasize the likelihood that they have something in common with Hunt's group, are faster than poor comprehenders ("low verbals"). However, while the difference between high and low verbals is significant over all word classes, the difference is greatest for the class of nonwords and smallest for the class of very common words. This is true for both third- and fifth-graders.[2] In other words, high verbals are *somewhat* faster than low verbals at reading words which are highly familiar to both groups and *very much* faster at true decoding, that is, at breaking the orthographic code of a never-before-seen word. Consistent with this is the finding that decoding differences between words for which the child knew the meaning and words for which he did not occurred only for the *less* skilled reading group.

This seems to suggest that lexical "look-up," presumably what is involved in reading a highly familiar word, is *less* significant as a source of individual variation than the "lower-level" process involved in matching a sequence of

---

[1] Thomas Hogaboam, Susan Goldman, and Laura Bell have been working with me on various aspects of this research.

[2] Our data suggest that for college students separated on the basis of the Davis Reading Test, high scores continue to have shorter vocalization latencies.

letters to a stored sequence of sounds and producing them. The fast coding that Hunt notes as characteristic of high verbals may be a necessary component of efficient reading comprehension. Just as individuals differ in speed of letter name matching, but not in physical matching, so they also differ in speed of word coding. In the case of low verbals, the cumulated processing demands produced by meaningful text may exceed their capacities.

We have also found some memory differences between our two groups. In a running discourse task similar to one investigated by Jarvella (1971), children listen to a story composed of simple vocabulary. Their listening is occasionally interrupted by the occurrence of a probe word from a sentence recently heard in the story, and they are to provide the word that followed it. While there is practically no difference between skilled and less skilled readers for a word from the last clause heard, the skilled group (high verbals) are substantially better than the less skilled for a target from the preceding clause. Moreover, the two groups do *not* differ on probe digit memory performance. The probe digit task is nearly identical to the discourse task, except numbers are probed instead of words.

Finally, a third task in which we have found differences is phoneme detection. IQ-matched skilled readers are faster in responding to the word-initial target phoneme /d/ in a sentence such as "The small white *d*oll in the suitcase belonged to the red haired girl." Since subjects are required to comprehend the sentence as well as to react to the target phoneme, one might take such a result as reflecting differences in syntactic skills or immediate memory capacity. However, the advantage of skilled readers on this task was at least as large when the target phoneme occurred in a word list that subjects were expected to recall. While understanding such results requires more work, it is tempting to note again the implication of a basic verbal process connected with word analysis.

The view emerging from this research is that there are certain specific language-related abilities that distinguish skilled and less skilled reading comprehension. Code access is one such difference, as E. Hunt found with the letter name matching task. However, in our results the memory differences seem only to involve language and not some general short-term memory difference. The phoneme detection results may suggest a possible source for this difference at the level of word analysis. Of course, there is not strong support for any particular interpretation of this pattern of results as yet. For the moment I tend to believe that rapid automatic coding and recoding operations that interfere minimally with working memory are important sources of cognitive difference.

## MEMORY AS A FOUNDATION FOR INTELLECT AND COMPREHENSION

In the case of E. Hunt's cognitive model, and Carroll's use of it (Chapter 3) there is an issue concerning memory and memories. Frankly, I am not sure whether there are immediate significant implications of this issue for developing a cognitively based theory of intelligence, but in the long run there may be. Hunt has identified cognitive process differences that are of considerable significance for the goal of establishing a scientific basis for intelligence, or at least for verbal intelligence.

With respect to verbal intelligence, we may want to ask about the properties of memory, if memory is to be the scientific base on which to attach the concept of verbal intelligence. Is it a well-defined system with well-understood components? Is it a system with functionally distributed components, such as sensory registers, short-term stores, and long-term stores? Of course, this is a question concerning an entire class of models (e.g., Atkinson & Shiffrin, 1968; Waugh & Norman, 1965), not a particular instance of it. The question is whether this class of component memory models provides the most useful metaphor for the salient facts of memory.

There is a surprising consensus on what the salient features of memory are and, except for occasional voices in the dark, there is even agreement on what its parts are, if not on exactly how it works. In fact, one of the remarkable accomplishments of human experimental psychology has been the elevation of the concept of "memory" from an earlier position in which it was synonymous with "*just* memory" or "rote memory" to a lofty position as a fundamental human intellectual achievement. Not exactly equal to "thinking" perhaps, but in the form of "working memory" at least the workshop of thought.

However, there have always been competing metaphors for memory, and we are occasionally reminded that some of these are plausible alternatives to the component approach. Recent reminders of this have come from Craik and Lockhart (1972) and Cermak (1972), who have argued that memory can be better understood as a product of processing level than as a location of information storage. This argument belongs to the general class of theories that see memory as a more or less continuous process (e.g., Melton, 1963) and seems to include coding theories that emphasize the coding of stimuli in successive stages (Posner, 1969). Another perspective on the role of memory is provided by Flavell's hypothesis (Flavell, Friedrichs, & Hoyt, 1970) that intentional memory is a developmental process distinct from normal everyday perceptual processing, which only incidentally makes available a memory representation. Since all or nearly all of the data that have been taken as support for the component memory models have been data for college students, it is at least possible that different metaphors of memory are required at different developmental stages, even if the component models are the best metaphors for adult information processing. Of course, if one accepts the argument of Craik and Lockhart (1972), component models are not the best model even of adult memory.

The general properties of the depth-of-processing approach include the following:

1. Information is retained in different codes processed roughly in stages. These stages are levels of processing.

2. The information from any code is available as a memory.

3. The quality of a memory, for example, whether it is primarily "phonemic" or primarily "semantic," depends upon which processing level has been involved, *not* upon which memory store it is in.

4. Central processes under individual control and highly influenced by task demands determine which level of processing is reached.

This last feature, of course, has the potential for rendering this an untestable system. But, provided some more precise notions of the processor can be developed, this is not inevitable.

Of course there are many aspects to the memory-models issue and a wealth of data can be interpreted according to one or both models. However, there is merit to the depth-of-processing approach not only for experimental memory research, but also for comprehension research. This is true partly because, unlike memory and intelligence, comprehension has not been a well-defined psychological idea. Comprehension is usually defined by contrasting it with "production" or "memory" or "interpretation" according to the purpose. The depth-of-processing framework provides a means for describing comprehension in terms of a cognitive system perhaps more congenial to it than a component model of memory. In this view, the processing of natural language input occurs to different levels that can be roughly characterized as (a) phonemic, (b) syntactic, (c) semantic, (d) interpretive, and (e) thematic. The operation of these comprehension levels can be observed experimentally to be dependent upon task demands, ranging through the levels of processing required to judge the meaningfulness of sentences, to remember the words of a sentence, or to determine whether the sentence follows from a particular context (e.g., Dooling, 1972). In general, each level of comprehension leaves a characteristic memory trace. It is possible that individual differences in intellectual functioning, including especially language comprehension, may be systematically investigated and described in terms of levels of comprehension. Individual differences become a question of what levels are characteristically reached under what conditions for different individuals.


## SO WHAT?

Regardless of details concerning cognitive models, I think the approach carried out thus far by Hunt is a valuable one. I also believe that the approach may be valuable for language comprehension as well as for intelligence. However, there are a few remaining criticisms that can be anticipated.

One is that cognitive power has been identified with receptive verbal processes or with comprehension, and there is more to intelligence than that. In general, Hunt has not gone beyond verbal memory except in some digit memory tasks. Thus, it is true that we are dealing either with short-term or low-level processes or with verbal long-term memory. Indeed there is much significant intelligence omitted. However, to be able to even scratch the surface of the verbal component of intelligence and to pin it to an interesting and plausible, if not ultimate, cognitive theory will be a major achievement. Carroll (see Chapter 3), in fact, carries the idea beyond the verbal domain.

A second issue is more problematical in my opinion. That is, if someone is interested in how to boost achievement in general or verbal achievement in particular, will he or she be in a position to do it any better after having tied verbal intelligence to basic processes? The main question is whether the discovery of basic processes can be extended to the discovery of ways to improve them by instruction. This is an open question; but I see, on the one hand, no reason why this should be an automatic consequence of validating the cognitive model, nor, on the other hand, any reason why it should be impossible. At the risk of appearing overly optimistic, I think there is a reasonable chance that the careful pursuit of such an approach could pay off with increased verbal achievement scores. Such increases are occasionally obtainable even in the absence of knowledge as to why certain procedures are effective (e.g., Bereiter & Englemann, 1966). However, efforts along this line would not be mere application of principles that fall out of the cognitive theory. Presumably we would not do something like train children to show release from proactive inhibition; but we might invent ways to strengthen short-term coding operations by intensive practice with name codes, words, classes, etc. It may be that vocabulary enrichment programs are helpful, where they are helpful at all, in increasing the efficiency of semantic memory and, at the same time, short-term processing speed, insofar as the latter is in part dependent on how semantic codes are formed and transformed. In fact it may be true that in general, although both long-term memory (or higher-level processes) and short-term memory (or lower-level processes) produce intelligence-related differences, both employ the language system, especially its semantics. Well-developed, quickly accessible word meanings may be a single unifying part of the verbal intelligence system. Despite attempts to deverbalize intelligence, vocabulary-like tests have remained components of many intelligence tests, and vocabulary tests correlate highly even with deverbalized tests.

## CONCLUSION

Finally, I would like to conclude by making a few more or less bald assertions that constitute a summary of previous points and include some points that have not been made in the previous discussion.

1. Language comprehension and verbal intelligence are closely interrelated. There are, however, intellectual abilities that are not dependent on language, as

Huttenlocher has reminded us. A coherent theory of intellect must take this into consideration. However, for that rather large component of intellectual functioning that is cognitively and psychometrically related to language, the ability to comprehend language structures may form the link.

2. Memory is an essential component of language comprehension and verbal intelligence. Memory is a foundation for intellectual functioning, but whether it is best understood as a system of discrete components may be an open question.

3. The search for individual differences in parameters of basic processes is a welcome program. Notwithstanding past failures to discover learning or memory factors associated with intelligence, the development of memory models and more precise experimental measurement methods improves somewhat the chances for success of a program such as Hunt's in the area of intelligence.

4. Not just standard intelligence tests, but tests of other functions important to schools and to other cultural and individual purposes might be investigated in terms of specific models of cognition, no matter how tentative. I have mentioned one example, that of reading comprehension.

5. There are several admonishments relevant for such enterprises:

(a) Standardized tests should not be used exclusively in the research program, especially when instructional strategies are drawn from the research. If we restrict our measures to, say, standard tests of verbal ability, we may fail to discover important individual differences in basic cognitive processes. This is especially true if a cognitive parameter is irrelevant for performance on a certain test.

(b) All tests, whether standard or not, should be chosen with some care. Experimental psychologists interested in building a convergent view of intellect will need measures that converge, or at least measures for which nonconvergences are reasonably well described.

(c) We must be able to look critically at this enterprise from a broader social viewpoint. We should not use the identification of basic cognitive differences to further entangle heredity–environment questions and related issues connected with IQ testing. To identify individual differences in the rate of retrieving a name code or in the speed of memory search that are related to IQ scores is not to discover innate capacity differences. To us this is an obvious point, but to others, less pure of heart, it may be tempting to cite such differences as "hereditary" since they are more "basic" than previous measures related to IQ.

(d) Related to this last caveat is a more general one, perhaps more problematical. The discovery of basic cognitive differences that are related to verbal intelligence tests will have the effect of providing construct validation to these tests. As long as such process relationships were lacking, we could say, "Well, these tests perhaps don't *really* measure intelligence. Their only use is that they *predict success* in schools." At some point in the forseeable future, we may instead be hearing, "These tests are valid measures of true intelligence. Not only do they have predictable and consensual validity, they measure basic intellectual functioning." Even if "basic" is not distorted to "innate," there is a bit of a problem. We need to be reminded that it is not the two-link correlation that matters, that is, the correlational chain of (a) basic abilities with IQ scores, and (b) IQ scores with school achievement. Why not focus on the real functional relation of interest, between basic abilities and school achievement, or some other index of success for that matter? Despite the best intentions of professional testers and perhaps the neutral intentions of experimental psychologists, there remains a mystique associated with the IQ test that adds nothing to the fundamental relationship of interest, namely, that between basic cognitive functioning and criterion-measured intellectual achievement. From this perspective, IQ tests are merely prestigious intervening observations and perhaps experimental psychology should be somewhat cautious about adding to their prestige.

## REFERENCES

Atkinson, R. C., & Shiffrin, R. M. Human memory: A proposed system and its control processes. In K. W. Spence & J. T. Spence (Eds.), *Advances in the psychology of learning and motivation research and theory, VII.* New York: Academic Press, 1968.

Bereiter, C., & Englemann, S. *Teaching disadvantaged children in the preschool.* Englewood Cliffs, New Jersey: Prentice-Hall, 1966.

Carroll, J. B. Factors of verbal achievement. In A. Anastasi (Ed.), *Testing problems in perspective.* Washington, D.C.: American Council on Education, 1966.

Cermak, L. S. *Human memory: Research and theory.* New York: Ronald Press, 1972.

Craik, F. I. M., & Lockhart, R. S. Levels of processing: A framework for memory research. *Journal of Verbal Learning and Verbal Behavior,* 1972, **11,** 671–685.

Dooling, D. J. Some context effects in the speeded comprehension of sentences. *Journal of Experimental Psychology,* 1972, **93,** 56–62.

Flavell, J. H., Friedrichs, A. G., & Hoyt, J. D. Developmental changes in memorization processes. *Cognitive Psychology,* 1970, **1,** 324–340.

Jarvella, R. J. Syntactic processing of connected speech. *Journal of Verbal Learning and Verbal Behavior,* 1971, **10,** 409–416.

Melton, A. W. Implications of short-term memory for a general theory of memory. *Journal of Verbal Learning and Verbal Behavior,* 1963, **2,** 1–21.

Posner, M. I. Abstraction and the process of recognition. In G. Bower (Ed.), *Advances in learning and motivation.* New York: Academic Press, 1969.

Waugh, N. C., & Norman, D. A. Primary memory. *Psychological Review,* 1965, **72,** 89–104.

Young, M. *The rise of the meritocracy.* Baltimore: Penguin Books, 1961.

# Part V

## GENERAL CONSIDERATIONS FOR THE NATURE OF INTELLIGENCE

# 16
# Intelligence and Cognitive Psychology

W. K. Estes

*Rockefeller University*

The concept of intelligence has always been a source of paradoxes. It has been one of the most robust concepts of psychology, but at the same time one of the most elusive.

Whatever it is, intelligence can be measured with high reliability and considerable validity. To be sure, one can emphasize the limited predictive value of intelligence tests which do not reflect equally the abilities needed to deal with all aspects of everyday life. In this book Neisser (Chapter 7), for example, has suggested the qualification "academic intelligence" to circumscribe the applicability of standard intelligence tests. Nonetheless, if one has only a short time in which to gain information about an individual and needs to appraise the likelihood that he or she can be trained to function as a soldier or to become a doctor or an accountant or a programmer or to manage a small business, one can scarcely do better than to utilize a standard intelligence scale.

But this robustness at a heuristic level has been known for a half century or more. The elusiveness becomes manifest whenever attempts are made to go beyond the problem of selecting elements of a test battery on the basis of external criteria in order to reformulate or purify the tests on the basis of rational considerations. The perennial efforts to analyze intelligence tests in terms of theoretically based ideas, and thus to arrive at purer measures of capacities, have never proven strikingly successful. Neither have the many attempts (see, e.g., McNemar, 1942; Thorndike, 1926; Woodrow, 1946) to relate test scores to functioning in simple laboratory tasks involving learning and memory. One of the principal emphases of this book is a new round of attempts to rationalize the concept of intelligence, this time primarily in terms of problem solving. What is new about the present attempts, and what grounds do we have to expect more fruitful outcomes than have characterized similar efforts in the past?

295

## RELATING INTELLIGENCE TO COGNITIVE PROCESSES

One reason for the limited fruitfulness of earlier efforts may have been the inadequacy of the available learning theories; another, the lack of laboratory research on tasks of the type involved in intelligence tests. Now we stand better in both respects.

  The first really substantial effort to relate intelligence to learning processes was that of Thorndike (1926), but the association theory available to him was too limited in conceptual resources to make the task at all feasible. Thorndike defended ingeniously his idea that intelligence is simply a function of the total number of effective associative connections available in an individual's nervous system. The influence of his effort may perhaps be seen in a continuing tendency for some psychologists to be intrigued with correlations between brain weight and intelligence, but it did not lead to theoretically directed research.

  The next generation of learning theories, in which the traditions of association theory and conditioning were combined, generated considerably richer conceptual structures and did begin to lead to systematic, theoretically directed research on problems of intellectual development and disabilities (for a review, see Estes, 1970). Still more recently we have seen the emergence of information processing models and a proliferation of new techniques for the analysis of information storage, retrieval, and organization in memory.

  Several of the chapters in this volume present variations on themes growing out of these developments. Carroll, for example, undertakes systematically to identify concepts or processes arising in current theories of memory which one would expect to be reflected in performance predicted by the various factors extracted from intelligence test batteries. The characterization of factors in terms of concepts having to do with short- and long-term memory and the like is, of course, only a first step. The present effort can be expected to be enlightening only if it is followed by actual research in which predictions concerning test performance that follow from the analysis in terms of cognitive functions are generated and tested.

  A concrete example of the kind of follow-up I have in mind would be the prediction concerning sex differences on the digit-symbol scale of the Wechsler–Bellevue test which follows from an analysis of the task in terms of scanning and coding processes. This scale has customarily been classified as nonverbal on the basis of its content and the spatial manipulation involved. Consequently, it has appeared anomalous in that girls are found to score higher than boys, whereas boys generally score higher than girls on subtests involving spatial manipulation and lower on verbal subtests (McNemar, 1942). However, an experimental analysis of the digit-symbol task by Royer (1971) lends support to the assumption that the symbols are recoded in terms of verbal labels (Estes, 1974). On this interpretation, the superior performance by girls no longer constitutes an exception to the general rule concerning sex differences.

E. Hunt (Chapter 13) presents a somewhat different approach. Hunt begins with theories of memory and then attempts to deduce situations in which individual differences in performance should be observed. His analysis leads, for example, to the demonstration of large individual differences in a simple comparison task. The next step is to show that these differences are related to scores on standard tests of verbal intelligence. This interesting correlational result sets the stage for research which is now needed in order to close the gap and show through what chain of events, or through what sequence of processes, individual differences in simple tasks that were predicted on the basis of cognitive theory come to be reflected also in test performance.

## EXPLAINING COMMUNALITIES IN TEST SCORES

Throughout the entire history of research on intelligence the central problem which has shaped the course of investigation has been that of explaining communalities in test performance. The almost ubiquitous occurrence of positive correlations among scores on various tests and scales led early to various conceptions of general ability, ranging from Spearman's *g* to various systems of multiple factors. However, extensive and prolonged research efforts have not led to clear convergence on any one of these systems, and on the whole there seems to be increasing disillusion with the original idea that intercorrelations and factor analyses would lead to uncovering the basic structure of the mind as determined by the underlying neural organization (see, e.g., Tuddenham, 1962).

Disaffection with the naive idea of a uniform basic structure underlying mental organization in all individuals has not by any means dampened the search for the sources of communality in test scores. These sources might reasonably be sought for in brain structures and their genotypic determinants, in properties of mental tests themselves, in psychological processes presumably operating in test behavior, and in the varieties of behavior outside the laboratory that provide the ultimate criterion for measures of ability.

With regard to the first of these alternatives, recent work which might have been, but is not, reviewed in this volume provides some encouragement. Substantial increases in the sophistication of genetic analysis, and in the combination of psychological and neurological techniques needed for the localization of aspects of verbal and nonverbal information processing in the two hemispheres, keep open the possibility that we may find the explanation of some small part of the observed variance and covariance of test scores in biological and genetic factors (Bock, 1973). All indications are that this route is a long one, and at present we cannot foresee anything but slow and costly progress toward limited objectives.

The most sustained and systematic analysis of the content of intelligence tests and the behaviors involved in responding to test questions is perhaps that of J. P.

Guilford, culminating in his structure of intellect model (Guilford, 1967). He characterizes intellect in terms of three principal dimensions: the content of tests used to measure intelligence; the operations that must be utilized by an individual in responding to the test; and the products of past learning which are required to make these operations possible. Though this systematization must provide a useful basis for many lines of related research, its direct relevance to the explanation of individual differences in intellect is limited, in that Guilford concentrates upon the mental operations that are required for success on various scales and tests rather than upon the operations actually utilized by individuals as they generate mixed patterns of success and failure. Thus, it is not surprising that the dominant emphasis in current research, characterizing in particular nearly all of the contributions to this volume, is directed less toward the requirements of successful test performance and more toward the processes actually involved in intellectual behavior.

It is an attractive possibility, and one motivating the efforts of the many investigators who are taking current theoretical developments in cognitive psychology as their starting point, that the varied tests involved in the appraisal of intelligence may tap a relatively small number of basic mental processes which combine in various ways to determine performance in specific situations. I have reviewed elsewhere the evidence from a wide spectrum of current research in cognitive psychology which suggests that this approach is timely and likely to be productive (Estes, 1974). But productivity will require more than the mapping of psychological concepts onto test factors. As has recently been pointedly reemphasized by an experienced investigator working on the factor side of this interdisciplinary boundary (Bock, 1973), we cannot rest with intuitive characterizations of test factors in terms of psychological processes, for these identifications may continue to be seriously misleading in spite of increasing methodological sophistication on both sides.

I believe that a type of research that is critically needed but in short supply would involve systematic experimental analyses of the behaviors involved in mental tests, conducted within the same theoretical and methodological frameworks as current research on other aspects of learning and memory. One of the few clear-cut examples of this type of analysis in the recent literature is the study by Royer (1971) of processes involved in the digit—symbol substitution test.

Increasing concern with processes rather than capacities has the effect of bringing research on intelligence into closer interaction with research in other aspects of cognitive psychology. In particular, current work on stimulus coding, on the functions of retrieval cues in recall, and on the hierarchical organization of information in memory is serving to delineate specific factors that are responsible for large differences in levels of intellectual functioning in situations similar to those utilized for the assessment of intelligence.

We cannot, however, afford to be satisfied with the goal of simply identifying cognitive processes involved in intellectual tasks, on the supposition that these processes are automatically called forth in the presence of tests or other situations requiring intellectual activity. Major attention will need to be given to the ways in which processes become organized to make for efficient performance, the kinds of sequencing of experience which lead to the development of habits of encoding information, chunking, grouping, utilizing of retrieval cues— the specific strategies which make the difference between lower and higher levels of performance on intellectual tasks.

## INTELLIGENCE AND COGNITIVE DEVELOPMENT

Furthermore we need to keep in mind the possibility that the answers to the problem of communality may not lie entirely in direct inferential relationships between performance and the underlying capacities or organization of cognitive processes in the individual. Consideration of the relationships between intellectual performance and its cultural setting (see, e.g., Goodnow, Chapter 9, and Olson, Chapter 10) raises the possibility that observed communalities in intellectual performance, in test situations or elsewhere, may be reflections of communalities in the developmental history of the individuals studied rather than direct indicators of individual differences in capacity or processes.

To illustrate this notion by means of an analogy, imagine that we are engaged in observing the output of a color television factory with the specific task of predicting the time that particular sets can be expected to remain in service before being returned for major repairs. In the course of this study we note that as sets come off the assembly line, they are labeled with various tags; in particular, each set has attached a colored tag and a label bearing a number. Through followup observations we discover significant correlations between the properties of these tags and performance of the TV sets as measured by time before major repairs. Let us say that we find that the combination of information from the two tags is quite a reliable predictor, that both the colors of the colored tags and the numbers on the numbered tags individually correlate less highly than the combinations, but still significantly, with performance and that the two measures correlate positively with each other. In order to explain our observations we would then presumably proceed to attempt to find correlations between the tag measures and various properties of the electronic components of the TV sets. However, in this example all such efforts would come to naught, for it happens that the tags are not related in any direct causal way to any of the components but rather identify the inspectors who pass on the acceptability of the set at two different stages in the assembly process. It happens that some inspectors are more careful and conscientious than others, and it is the individual differences among inspectors that lead to the predictability of the tag measures with respect to TV set performance. Returning to the problem of intelligence, I would like to suggest that communalities in test performance may in some cases prove to be explainable not by communalities in capacity but rather by communalities in developmental history.

If any area of research on intelligence has been underrepresented in this volume it is that related to cognitive development. The reason may well be that theory has not moved ahead as fast with regard to development as with regard to the end result of development. Studies of mental retardation from the standpoint of learning theory (Estes, 1970) and studies of the development of discriminative and mnemonic abilities in different cultural settings (Cole, Gay, Glick, & Sharp, 1971; Cole & Scribner, 1974; Goodnow, Chapter 9) point to the overwhelming importance of the occurrence and proper sequencing of relevant learning experiences as a prerequisite to efficient intellectual performance. We cannot, however, assume that major advances in this area will come automatically as a function simply of increased industry on the part of empirical investigators. Rather, they may wait upon innovations at a theoretical level comparable to those attendant upon the application of computer simulation models to human problem solving.

## APPROACHES TO INTELLIGENCE VIA COMPUTER SIMULATION MODELS

The difficult and largely unsolved problem of relating performance on laboratory tasks to test scores is bypassed in the approach of Simon, who simply ignores intelligence tests, identifies intelligence with the ability to solve problems, and looks for generality by sampling a variety of problem situations. His strategy is to concentrate on the development of computer simulation models for performance in various problem-solving situations, assuming that success in this task will lead to the identification of the basic abilities involved in the various tasks. The work already reported by Simon and his associates has certainly led to valuable new insights concerning activities in problem solving. However, there is room for some skepticism as to whether this approach will necessarily lead to the identification of basic abilities.

Simon (Chapter 5) notes, for example, that short-term and long-term memory systems are represented in the simulation models for all of the problem-solving tasks and therefore one might conclude that short-term and long-term capacities must fall in the class of basic abilities sought for. However, the extent to which these capacities are actually necessary for the performance of an individual engaged in solving problems depends to a major extent upon constraints imposed by the experimenter. If the subject is denied the use of paper and pencil or access to reference sources, then demands on both short- and long-term memory may be very great. But these are artificial constraints from the standpoint of problem solving outside of the laboratory, and it is clear that demands on both aspects of memory can be greatly reduced in practice by the use of recording devices and references. Similarly, we can see already that many other of the specific operations involved in the performance of an individual solving a problem can be replaced by auxiliary devices.

Should we, then, assume that the abilities associated with various aspects of the task that can be taken over by technical aids are not "basic," but that once we have identified all of these there will remain a core of aspects of performance which do depend upon basic abilities? Conceivably so, but there seems also grave danger of falling into the same type of fallacy that led some of the earlier investigators of brain extirpation techniques virtually to the conclusion that the physical basis for memory of an experience lies nowhere in the brain. It may well turn out that basic abilities cannot be identified or set in one-to-one correspondence with any of the boxes in flowchart representations of simulation models but rather must be sought at a more abstract level.

Another thought which occurs to me in connection with the approach exemplified particularly by Klahr (Chapter 6) and Simon (Chapter 5) is the need for more explicit consideration of the extent to which we should depend on computer simulation models as the primary basis for theory construction. There is some danger of being dazzled by the virtuosity of the individuals working with these models and failing to appreciate that the approaches exemplified may need to be complemented by other techniques of theory construction. With respect to research in cognitive psychology during the past decade, it appears to me that research on perception has not been greatly facilitated by computer simulation models, that work on rote memory (especially paired associate learning) has been advanced both by computer simulation and by other types of mathematical models, whereas work on human problem solving has been virtually revolutionized by the computer simulation approach. What the situation will prove to be with regard to cognitive development seems at present an open question. Relatively direct extension of the types of computer simulation models now being developed in connection with problem solving may prove to be just what is needed, but the possibility remains that some of the theoretical insights we require may come through other avenues.

In the case of classical scientific problems that are now well understood, it is in many instances not at all clear that the approaches actually followed could have been replaced by computer simulation methods without loss. Take, for example, the matter of understanding the behavior of a gyroscope. If one had bypassed the study of physics but had become a skillful programmer, there is little doubt but that one could have proceeded directly from observations of the behavior of a gyroscope to the writing of a program that would provide an excellent simulation. Once he had demonstrated the ability to simulate the behavior of a gyroscope, this hypothetical researcher might claim that he had an adequate theoretical understanding of the phenomenon, just as does the investigator who demonstrates his ability to simulate the performance of a human problem solver dealing with the tower of Hanoi problem. But clearly the understanding would be of a quite different kind than that of one who approached the problem by way of classical physics. The latter, though he could not simulate the meanderings of any particular gyroscope, could provide an explanation of the behavior characteristic of gyroscopes as a class in terms of ideas that apply also to bicycles, spinning tops, and a variety of other phenomena that are related only at the level of rather abstract theoretical concepts.

To follow the illustration one more step, we might note that the two approaches could be combined. An investigator who had mastered the principles of kinematics, conservation of momentum, and the like, could take these into account in developing a program which would simulate the behavior, not only of gyroscopes, but of a variety of other devices which depend on the same principles. He thus would have a means of demonstrating the predictive value of his theoretical scheme even for situations too complex to allow explicit predictions from the equations of classical mechanics. I do not mean at all to depreciate the obvious values and power of simulation techniques, but I do wish to emphasize that investigators of human intellectual functioning should expect that they will have to combine a variety of techniques at both the empirical and theoretical levels in order to advance our understanding of the almost uncharted complexities of human problem solving and cognitive development.

## PRODUCING INTELLIGENT BEHAVIOR

Psychological research on intelligence has perhaps been less productive than we would like as a source of ideas and methods relevant to problems of education. Looking through the lines of research activity represented in this volume for signs of increasing relevance, I find some encouragement in the studies dealing with conditions of effective intellectual functioning. A new concern with the problem of producing intelligent behavior is well exemplified in the program of Resnick and Glaser (Chapter 11). These investigators take as their starting point not measurements of intellect, but rather a commonsense view of intelligence as the ability to learn ways of solving problems. Their next step is a systematic empirical analysis of procedures for teaching children to solve a particular type of problem, conducted within the general framework of current models for information processing. This approach manifests a welcome shift in emphasis from the study of intelligence for the purpose of prediction to the analysis of intellectual performance for the purpose of creating more effective educational settings for the development of intelligent behavior. It seems to me that both theory and practice are bound to gain from increased emphasis on this strategy of concentrating on the problem of coming to understand how efficient intellectual performance can be produced, rather than taking as a starting point extensive study of the differences in performance manifest at a particular time by individuals with varied and unknown learning histories. In this approach, attention to individual differences does not consitute a separate topic but emerges naturally as the investigators begin to consider the ways in which different individuals respond to specific aspects of training.

With regard to the identification of intelligence with problem-solving ability, a minor qualification that might merit consideration is that of avoiding too narrow a definition of problem solving. In both the experimental and the theoretical studies reported to date, problem solving is identified with the solution of preset problems—that is, with situations in which a goal can be defined in advance and then the problem-solving activity of the individual described in terms of the selection of tactics and strategies that bear varying degrees of relevance to the goal. However, we should perhaps not pass over lightly the observation of Charlesworth (Chapter 8), that children appear to spend a very small proportion of their time in solving problems—at least problems that are definable by adult observers. Further, it is not obvious that observations of adults would yield a much different picture. To be sure, we conceive of some individuals—doctors, automobile mechanics, chess players, and perhaps even politicians—as functioning primarily in problem-solving activities which may differ only in complexity from those customarily studied in the laboratory. But it is by no means obvious that the creative activity of scientists, artists, novelists, or mathematicians falls in the same category. Much of the behavior that we identify with the highest levels of intellectual functioning appears not so much to be directed toward the solution of preset problems as simply to be an exercise of the individual's capacities for producing new organizations of information.

## TRENDS AND PROJECTIONS

What can we say in general concerning the place of the concept of intelligence in cognitive psychology? One might, a priori, expect the relationship between intelligence and cognition to be close, especially in the light of developments reported in this volume, but the expectation would not be borne out by a survey of recent literature in either field. The term "intelligence" does not so much as make an appearance in the index of Neisser's *Cognitive Psychology* (1967), and it fares little better in the journal of the same name.

Doubtless one reason for this absence of the interconnectedness that would be expected on rational grounds is a certain aloofness from practical affairs on the part of investigators of learning and cognition. Research on intelligence had its origin primarily in practical problems of predicting school success and has retained close connections with problems of assessment and prediction in education, the military, and industry. Research in cognitive psychology, except perhaps for computer simulation approaches to problem solving, has been oriented primarily toward the development of general models for processes assumed to characterize all individuals, and toward the testing of these models in experiments dictated almost exclusively by theoretical considerations.

One major point of contact between the study of intelligence and the study of learning has centered in the recent research on aspects of mental retardation having to do with learning and learning disabilities (see, e.g., Ellis, 1970; Estes, 1970). But in the nature of things, a focus on mental retardation leaves little scope for practical application of research bearing on higher mental processes. This lack may be remedied in the future by the currently increasing concern with problem solving and organization in memory (as, for example, in Resnick and Glaser, Chapter 11, and Simon, Chapter 5).

A closer relationship between the two disciplines need not and probably will not entail any great increase in frequency of references to intelligence in the literature of cognitive psychology. Rather, present trends suggest a receding of the term intelligence as a dominant psychological concept, concurrent with a shift of research emphasis away from the goal of refining the definitions of abilities in order to further their measurement, and toward that of understanding intellectual behavior. It does not necessarily follow, however, that we must expect a continuing lack of attention to individual differences on the part of investigators in cognitive psychology. On the contrary, a salutary development manifest in the present volume (e.g., E. Hunt, Chapter 13) has been the emergence of new interest in individual differences as a direct consequence of findings emanating from theoretically oriented research on cognitive functions.

# REFERENCES

Bock, R. D. Word and image: Sources of the verbal and spatial factors in mental test scores. *Psychometrika,* 1973, **38,** 437–457.

Cole, M., Gay, J., Glick, J., & Sharp, D. W. *The cultural context of learning and thinking.* New York: Basic Books, 1971.

Cole, M., & Scribner, S. *Culture and thought: A psychological introduction.* New York: Wiley, 1974.

Ellis, N. R. Memory processes in retardates and normals. In N. R. Ellis (Ed.), *International review of research in mental retardation.* New York: Academic Press, 1970.

Estes, W. K. *Learning theory and mental development.* New York: Academic Press, 1970.

Estes, W. K. Learning theory and intelligence. *American Psychologist,* 1974, 29(10), 740–749.

Guilford, J. P. *The nature of human intelligence.* New York: McGraw-Hill, 1967.

McNemar, Q. *The revision of the Stanford–Binet scale.* New York: Houghton-Mifflin, 1942.

Neisser, U. *Cognitive psychology.* New York: Appleton-Century-Crofts, 1967.

Royer, F. L. Information processing of visual figures in the digit symbol substitution test. *Journal of Experimental Psychology*, 1971, **87**, 335–342.

Thorndike, E. L. *Measurement of intelligence.* New York: Teacher's College, Columbia University, 1926.

Tuddenham, R. D. The nature and measurement of intelligence. In L. Postman (Ed.), *Psychology in the making.* New York: Knopf, 1962.

Woodrow, H. The ability to learn. *Psychological Review,* 1946, **53**, 147–158.

# 17
# The Nature of
# "The Nature of Intelligence"

James F. Voss

*University of Pittsburgh*

## INTELLIGENCE AS A SAMPLE OF BEHAVIOR

As a general discussant of the chapters in this volume, I begin my task by noting those aspects of the respective presentations that appear to me to make special contributions to the understanding of the nature of intelligence. Thus, I have sampled the writings of the other contributors, using as my criterion of selection those observations made which I thought to be of special significance to the theme of this volume. I am particularly impressed with Tyler's (Chapter 2) lucid summary of what psychometric research on intelligence testing has told us to the present time. Her comments showing the parallel aspects of compulsory education and the testing movement are noteworthy. I view with interest Carroll's (Chapter 3) attempts to take a broadly stated cognitive theory and relate the processes of the theory to mental test factors. Even though the data are somewhat cumbersome, and the classification somewhat arbitrary, the fact that such an attempt has been made is, I believe, of importance.

In the next section of the volume, Simon's discussion (Chapter 5) is of interest in a number of ways. First, in his description of the Tower of Hanoi task, his ability to distinguish strategies is, I feel, quite important, not because of the strategies per se, but because he demonstrates a specific technique that provides for the study of individual differences in the strategies used in a problem-solving task. Also it is important to note that at the outset, Simon defines intelligent behavior, not intelligence, and his analysis pursues the problems related to this type of behavior. Klahr (Chapter 6) presents an interesting exposition of simulation, as applied to developmental problems, although a question may be raised regarding how Klahr's model is related to intelligence as the term is defined in the traditional psychometric sense.

The primary contribution of Charlesworth (Chapter 8), I believe, is his emphasis upon a number of issues we often have disregarded or avoided. In particular, the need to understand man in relation to his adaptation to his environment is a point worth repeating. An interesting question he has raised is whether man's intelligence is all it is purported to be when viewed in terms of biological adaptation. Indeed, as Charlesworth notes, this question does challenge one of our basic assumptions about intellect. Finally, Charlesworth's statement suggesting that the mental-testing movement is out of touch with reality constitutes a challenge for the justification of testing. A similar point is made in Neisser's comments (Chapter 7). Tyler's rejoinder, at least as implied by her contribution, would likely be that testing *does* do certain things well and that relationships between test performance and environmental events have been obtained.

Goodnow (Chapter 9) has extended the concern about the environmental-testing relationship into the cultural realm. Goodnow tends to emphasize that there may be a need for the development of culture-*centered* rather than culture-*free* tests. Furthermore, in my opinion, she calls for a rather sobering reevaluation of each phase of test content and procedure, because apparently nothing may be taken for granted regarding cross-cultural testing. Of perhaps even greater significance is Goodnow's indication that the same principle may hold for tests in our subcultures. Finally, on the issue of intelligence measurement and the environment, the notion set forth by Olson (Chapter 10), i.e., the concept that intelligence as we know it is highly related to the technological development of written language, is extremely provocative. Certainly the development of an historical–environmental approach may help to provide a different type of perspective on the nature and measurement of intelligence.

With respect to the chapters on "basic processes" in intelligence, E. Hunt's (Chapter 13) discussion of his attempts to study *which* task performances are correlated with verbal test performance constitutes a clear effort to relate test performance to a particular aspect of cognitive performance, a goal worthy of commendation. I believe that Hunt's model, as of now, has little relation to his data; yet, Hunt's objectives are of considerable potential significance. Perhaps of greater interest is the question of how verbal performance as found on particular tests may be related to other areas of behavior and to development, especially when children who demonstrate verbal skill at an early age may be reinforced for verbal activity as they develop. Such a procedure probably works extensively in verbal behavior, as it apparently does in the development of such talents as musical ability.

Huttenlocher's contribution (Chapter 14) on language development raises at least two issues of note. First, what may be termed verbal skill may of necessity require careful delineation of a comprehension and a production component. This distinction suggests that the measurement of verbal skills via the usual tests may be tapping the comprehension component and neglecting the production component. Second, Huttenlocher raises the issue of the relation of spatial or dimensional encoding processes and verbal processes. It is only fitting, with the emphasis upon cognition shown here, that this issue be raised, since it has been such a concern in recent years in cognitive psychology—as found, for example, in the study of imagery-related and verbal memory components.

The comments by Perfetti (Chapter 15) should be noted both in a general and in a specific way: generally, because his comments point to how cognitive processes have dominated the content of this volume and because he articulates the interrelationships one may find among memory, intelligence, and comprehension; specifically, because Perfetti considers the question of how a "level of processing" model may be a reasonable alternative to the short-term, long-term type of model most prevalent here. Finally, Perfetti is to be commended for providing a clear statement of the question of the relationship of comprehension as a verbal skill to the issue of measuring verbal intelligence.

Resnick and Glaser (Chapter 11) describe intelligence in terms of problem solving, as they relate it to invention tasks. Of special interest is their emphasis upon the notion of assembly; and, although not specifying how the relationships are formed that hold experiences together, they at least focus on the problem. Flavell's comments (Chapter 12) I find of interest especially with respect to what he calls "metacognition."

My remarks up to this point constitute selected themes and items of interest from the various chapters in this volume. Viewing these points as a whole, one is impressed with the extremely broad range of behavior that has been referred to here as intelligence or intelligent behavior. We may note, however, that Bayley (1955) has demonstrated that variability of intelligence test performance increases with age. Perhaps the variability of opinion expressed here regarding definitions of intelligent behavior may be interpreted in terms of the age of the contributors, or perhaps it may be interpreted in terms of the age of the field of intelligence. In any event, the variability in the material presented leads me to conclude that, with respect to "the nature of intelligence" found in this volume, *intelligence may be defined as what the participants report that they measure.* This diversity of definitions, however, leads me to try to reduce this variation. To accomplish this objective, my next step in promoting an understanding of the nature of intelligence is to perform a factor analysis of the various chapters in this book.

## A FACTOR ANALYSIS OF "THE NATURE OF INTELLIGENCE"

The method of factor analysis employed here is what may be called an egocentric method, which essentially means that the method is completely subjective. In performing such an analysis, the first question to which I addressed myself was whether there is a *g* component in the chapters of this volume. Is there, in other words, some general factor that one may single out in the presentations made here? My initial reaction was that there was not; however, in reviewing the participants' contributions, I have concluded that there is a quite general $g$ factor. I would label this factor one of attitude or orienting—or task set, if you will—and to me it essentially is the position that the study of intelligence, in order to be meaningful, must relate testing behavior to psychologically important processes. *Which* psychological processes are involved and *how* one relates the processes to intelligence may vary; but basically, the $g$ factor as found here is the position that the understanding of intelligence must proceed via the relating of intelligence to psychologically meaningful processes.

Next, I went on to delineate classes of factors that could be extracted from the outputs of the contributors. The first class of factors I arrived at may be termed Definitional, i.e., factors related to the definition of intelligence, either explicitly or implicitly. The first and probably strongest Definitional factor is that intelligence involves problem solving in some type of a *specific task situation.* Those chapters having an extremely substantial loading of this factor are of course those of Simon and of Resnick and Glaser. Both of these chapters essentially consist of an approach which says that intelligence is problem solving and to understand problem solving will help us to understand intelligence. Klahr has a reasonably substantial loading of this factor, although in his case it is problem solving within a general Piagetian context. Huttenlocher's chapter, I believe, has a small loading, as do the comments by Flavell.

The second Definitional factor involves the position that intelligence is problem solving, but problem solving *in relation to the environment* as well as in relation to task factors. Having strong loadings on this factor are the chapters by Charlesworth and by Goodnow, and the discussions by Olson and Neisser. Charlesworth's chapter is of course biologically oriented, whereas the others are cultural or historical—cultural in perspective, but both approaches stress the need to study environmental aspects of problem solving.

A third Definitional factor is intelligence as test performance. This factor is found to a reasonable degree in the chapters by Tyler, Carroll, E. Hunt, Cooley, and to a lesser degree, Goodnow. I believe one would also find the Huttenlocher and Perfetti chapters loaded on this factor, although they considered primarily verbal intelligence.

The fourth and last Definitional factor is that of the ability to learn. Although this factor is found in the contributions by Tyler, Resnick and Glaser, and, to some extent, in Carroll's chapter and Cooley's comments, it may nevertheless be observed that no chapter has a really marked loading of this factor. Klahr pointed to the need for a learning component in his system, but his $D$ factor is an objective not yet incorporated into the system. Indeed, with respect to this factor, Tyler's comment should be noted, namely, that intelligence test performance is related to the ability to learn in altitude, not width.

The second class of factors that I extracted from the material presented here may be termed factors related to Method and Approach. The first of these factors involves the use of computer simulation and in particular the use of production systems to program the more implicit aspects of intellectual performance. Chapters highly loaded with this factor include of course those of Simon and Klahr. To a lesser degree are the loadings found in the chapters by Carroll and by Resnick and Glaser, who employed the concept of a production system but not to the degree of the Simon and the Klahr work. Evidently, the use of the production system is regarded by a number of people to be useful, potentially or actually. Perhaps one aspect of the study of intelligence may involve what the assumptions of production systems may imply about intelligent behavior.

The second Method-and-Approach factor may be termed a task-correlate factor. By this I mean that a number of chapters involved an attempt to take a given task or a series of task situations and relate the task performance to intelligence test performance. The contributions espousing this approach, in one way or another, are those by E. Hunt and Carroll. I also believe that Perfetti's chapter implies a need to relate comprehension performance and intelligence test performance. The approaches in these chapters are by no means identical, with for example E. Hunt approaching the problem by relating high- and low-verbal performers to performance on various tasks and Carroll attempting to describe the cognitive processes that are found in a particular set of mental factors. But the various individuals approaching the matter in this way do share the common goal of relating test performance to task performance, and by this approach they endeavor to get at the processes related to and possibly involved in intelligence test performance.

A third Method-and-Approach factor may be termed interactive. This approach stresses the study of man in relation to his environment, with emphasis placed upon the effect of environmental processes. Charlesworth's position is strongly loaded on this factor, and Goodnow implies the existence of this factor, although less obviously than Charlesworth. Olson is clearly in this realm, if one admits to a historical approach.

A fourth Method-and-Approach factor is the approach which seeks to understand intelligence by studying intellectual development. A few chapters advocate that we approach the study of intelligent behavior by determining how a child goes from, for example, Stage 1 to Stage 2. By studying the transitions between these stages, we may ultimately gain an integrated knowledge of how the transitions yield more learning. The Klahr chapter and Resnick and Glaser presentation, along with Flavell's comments regarding their work, are obviously heavily loaded with this factor.

A fifth factor of Method and Approach may be termed the analysis of verbal skills in relation to intelligence, with loadings in the contributions by Perfetti, Huttenlocher, Carroll, and E. Hunt. It should be noted that this factor includes the phonemic, syntactic, and semantic analysis of cognitive processes and how they relate to intellectual behavior.

The third class of factors that is derivable from the contributions I have elected to call the Mechanism factors. This class of factors refers to those writings which postulated some form of process or mechanism that is involved in intellectual behavior. One Mechanism factor that permeates the presentations is of course the existence of long-term memory. Many of the presentations assume the existence of a long-term memory store; thus, this factor may be regarded as a rather general Mechanism factor, even though Perfetti pointed out an alternative interpretation of it, and Olson regarded memory as possibly archaic.

The next Mechanism factor is the postulation of a short-term, working memory that processes input information and obtains information from long-term memory. Essentially, it is a central control-like mechanism which may be found in one form or another in the chapters by Carroll, Simon, Klahr, E. Hunt, and Resnick and Glaser.

The third and most pervasive Mechanism factor is probably some form of attentional factor dealing with sensory recognition processes. This is a factor recognizing the existence of processes which process input selectively, although Neisser did point out that this process may be related to other mechanisms. E. Hunt implies this selective mechanism, as do Klahr and Simon.

The fourth Mechanism factor is one implicit in most chapters, but made explicit in Goodnow's, namely, a mechanism called "cultural set." This factor represents the processes that provide certain individuals within a cultural or technological setting with predispositions to respond in certain ways.

The above classes of factors are the major components of the participant behavior of this volume, at least from my point of view. Of course, I would readily grant that each person present may have arrived at a somewhat different classification system, but I do believe the above factors provide a reasonable description of the presentations. I also would acknowledge that there is a good chance that at least some of the factors would change with different participants. Thus, as happens with factor analyses of this type, one tends to be limited by the data he puts into the analysis—in this case the particular participants. But this is not the major concern with the factor-analytic approach to the volume's content; the primary problem is that the study of the intellectual behavior of this volume via factor analysis does not show how these factors are related to the broader theoretical issues involved in the study of intelligence. To follow this line of inquiry, we now turn to the third part of this discussion.

## THE NATURE OF "THE NATURE OF INTELLIGENCE"

First and foremost, one detects evidence within the chapters to support Tyler's assertion that the testing movement, in terms of how one person stands relative to a group, may have run its course. There is little discussion of test construction and little mention of distributions of test scores. There are no factor-analytic models presented and nothing new is derived from test scores per se. Instead, two themes recur throughout the volume: the first, that we should apply the modern developments of cognitive theory, especially as related to information processing, to the study of intellectual behavior, so that we may understand the processes underlying such behaviors; the second, that we should be aware that our tests, or at least our performances on tests, are the products of interactions of man with his environment—his cultural environment, his biological environment, and his intellectual heritage, especially as it is related to his written language. The reasons for these two trends are not completely understood, but neither are they completely obscure. One reason for these trends is that interest in man's higher processes has advanced tremendously in the past decades, to the point where it can now come to grips with intellectual behavior. A second reason, in all likelihood, is that the racial and other cultural problems within our society have clearly called for a reevaluation of what the mental test and intelligence testing are all about.

But how should these two needs—the need to explain intellectual behavior via cognitive theory and the need for greater understanding of environmental factors—be handled? What do the participants advocate, either explicitly or implicitly?

As one would expect, there are, as usual, individual differences. Tyler speaks of a few approaches, the one she closely relates to being the need to study the individual's skill bank or repertoire and, by implication, how a person selects and utilizes the skills he or she has. Goodnow advocates a similar approach, with an emphasis on studying instructional or task factors. Carroll makes probably the most obvious attempt to salvage the mental test as a real source of psychological worth by trying to find how mental factors may be related to cognitive processes. E. Hunt follows a tack that is somewhat similar, for he advocates the salvaging of test behavior by finding how certain task performances are related to test behavior. The computer simulation people, although not necessarily admitting it overtly, have already left the intelligence test behind them. The intelligence test scores of people solving the Tower of Hanoi problem by Strategy 1 rather than Strategy 3 may be of interest for some reason, but it is not clear why they should be. Indeed, intelligence has essentially been redefined by Simon in terms of intelligent behavior, by Resnick and Glaser in terms of process, and by Klahr in terms of development. What about Charlesworth and Goodnow? Goodnow demonstrates the extreme difficulty of cross-cultural testing; for Charlesworth, the position is to go out and observe, and incorporate your observations into the behavioral indices you may want to develop—a procedure that I am sure will have many problems.

The deep structure of these comments, it seems to me, is that one may keep mental testing, but if it is kept, it must be redefined—perhaps beyond recognition (and possibly in the long run beyond recall)—or, at least it must be reevaluated in the light of the advancements of experimental psychology and of the concerns regarding cultural interactions. So, we find that this volume in a sense reflects a transition from $S_1$ to $S_2$, where $S_1$ represents the state of intelligence as a test and $S_2$ represents a study of processes that are involved in intelligent behavior. But where does that leave us for the future? Let us now examine that issue.

## THE FUTURE OF "THE NATURE OF INTELLIGENCE"

Parenthetically, it may be noted that since at least four contributors to this volume have worked in the area of probability learning, prediction seems to be an appropriate venture for this volume. It seems to me that the next step in the evaluation of mental testing, perhaps barely discernible at the present time but nevertheless alluded to by Perfetti, is that for the first time we are in a position to construct tests that are based upon process. More specifically, in the future I believe tests will be developed that will provide reasonably precise measures of an individual's performance on a given process that is considered psychologically important. The processes tested may be letter recognition, short-term memory ordering behavior, ability to retrieve and perhaps relate semantic long-term memory information, and many others, dependent upon the ingenuity of the theorists and skill of the test developers. This movement, which I think is inevitable, has many implications, and I would like to mention only a few.

First, it means that intelligence tests will be developed so that the questions or sets of questions will be diagnostic in nature, with the results of the test giving not primarily a global score but a scoring profile based upon the processes related to the test categories. The next step, developing training procedures to improve an individual's ability to perform particular process-related tasks, would likely then be forthcoming. Second, the predicted development means that cognitive theorists and test developers will of necessity work more closely together. Third, the hypothesized development of tests related to practice means *not* that psychometricians will be out of business but that psychometricians will have a better idea of criteria of intelligent behavior. Fourth, it means that problems of testing such as those mentioned by Charlesworth and by Goodnow can be taken into account because of a better understanding of the theoretical processes involved in the environmental–individual interactions, and tests can be developed in relation to these processes. Thus, it seems reasonable to predict that tests related to specific processes will be the wave of the future, although such a development is not of course without its own problems. Such a movement will, furthermore, be successful only to the degree that basic research and theory are successful and that the tests are successfully developed. However, I think putting identified processes into testing form is in a sense secondary. Indeed, it may be asserted that if one can write a program for a process, one should be able to develop a test for it. It is the theory that will be complicated.

Finally, I believe that issues such as those presented in this volume will no longer be relevant in one or two decades. Why? Because by that time it will be acknowledged that the concept of intelligence is a remnant of faculty psychology, and the concept will eventually disappear through disuse. In its place there will be process-related test batteries in the school that will be much more diagnostic than intelligence tests currently are. Indeed, I believe that, at a minimum, the tests will include extensive physiological components related to visual, auditory, speech, and memory factors. I also suspect that if theory really develops, motivational processes also will be measured. No doubt, whether or not tests related to various processes have a $g$ factor may still be the object of someone's inquiry, but a more likely basis for a discussion will be whether or not the knowledge available at that time does a sufficient job of describing intelligent behavior.

## ACKNOWLEDGMENTS

The research reported herein was supported by the Learning Research and Development Center, supported in part by funds from the National Institute of Education (NIE), United States Department of Health, Education and Welfare. The opinions expressed do not necessarily reflect the position or policy of NIE and no official endorsement should be inferred.

## REFERENCES

Bayley, N. On the growth of intelligence. *American Psychologist,* 1955, **10,** 805–818.

# 18
## Ordinal Scales of Infant Development and the Nature of Intelligence

J. McVicker Hunt

*University of Illinois*

First, let me say that I am delighted to have an opportunity to learn more about the work on the process and informational aspects of problem solving in intelligence that has been presented by the various authors here. This is the one group where I find in vogue a view of intelligence highly consonant with that I presented in *Intelligence and Experience* (Hunt, 1961). The new approach to the structure of intellect that Carroll (Chapter 3) has been working on, the strategies of information processing that Simon (Chapter 5) and Klahr (Chapter 6) are coming up with, E. Hunt's (Chapter 13) search for variations in the strategies of information processing in people who differ in intelligence as now measured—all of these are very interesting to me.

Part of what has been presented is new to me. The cultural clusterings that Goodnow (Chapter 9) has described are new despite the fact that I once taught social psychology. In recent years, I have not been reading the cross-cultural literature. I have been somewhat familiar with the search of Resnick and Glaser (Chapter 11) for the conditions that foster creativity—that is, their process of invention. I think their idea of focusing on the conditions that foster inventiveness is excellent. Inasmuch as the work of Charlesworth (Chapter 8) and Huttenlocher (Chapter 14) concerns very young children, even infants, it has a ring of familiarity because it involves the age range with which I have recently been working. Although I have heard of it for the first time, Huttenlocher's work is not unrelated to my own.

What I want to do is less a matter of discussing these various contributions than describing work of my own that I believe is relevant. What I want to say hardly fits the role of a discussant, even though Lauren Resnick suggested I present it, so I want to acknowledge the dissonance that I feel. Nevertheless, I believe what I have to present of my own work will have something to say about some of the work reported here by others.

## MEASURING DEVELOPMENT AND LEARNING

Earl Hunt urged us to utilize the existing technology of intelligence testing even while searching for the variations in information processing associated with individual differences in intelligence as now measured. From adolescence on, this may be a fruitful tactic. I do not see it working for early development. In fact, despite the brilliance of Binet's invention of the metric of mental ages, I believe this invention has interfered with understanding early psychological development. Incidentally, I learned only here, from Leona Tyler, that Binet himself used the term "mental levels" instead of "mental ages."

Actually, it makes little difference whether the metric concerns mental levels or mental ages. Either way, it involves a kind of substitutive averaging process which enables each test to stand for every other one in defining the individual's age or level. In that averaging process, what Binet did was to throw a blanket over the details of the consecutive structural organizations that constitute early psychological development. Wilhelm Stern's invention of the IQ was another such blanket. Furthermore, the IQ was conceived as a permanent, static dimension of a person. It served to make a static process out of psychological development, which is actually highly dynamic. The IQ also tended to fix in our minds the concept of a static rate of development, when the actual rate is highly plastic. The implausibility of this quotient shows in its failure to predict learning scores, a fact first noted by Woodrow (1938, 1939). More recently, Guilford (1967, pp. 14–20) has reviewed other studies confirming this failure and still more recently, as background for an application for research support, John L. Horn has summarized a substantial list of new studies in which neither intelligence-test scores nor intelligence-test factors predict how much different people will learn in given situations. As a matter of fact, the best predictors of how much people will learn in one situation are instances of how much they have learned in other similar situations. This finding comes independently from Feuerstein (1972a, b), and his Learning Potential Assessment Device, in Israel, and from Sullivan (1964) at the Memorial University at St. John's, Newfoundland.

Despite the fact that John Carroll finds the information and the information-processing skills that are assessed by tests of intelligence related to performance in school, I believe norm-referenced testing has been very injurious to the educational enterprise. First, it has tended to separate testing from the teaching–learning process. Second, it has tended to take the attention of both student and teacher away from the specific-achievement goals of learning tasks. Criterion-referenced testing (Glaser, 1963) represents an attempt to return to these goals. Third, because norm-referenced tests serve chiefly a selective function, their use in education has brought selection into the educational process where it has served no good purpose. In fact, it has been injurious in that it has exaggerated the role of comparative status and injured the self esteem of many. As predictors, moreover, the norm-referenced tests have had the artifactual defect of producing self-fulfilling prophecies. Fourth, these predictions or prophecies have tended to reduce the motivation for ingenious teaching. One gets from a teacher the fact that the child is doing "as well as could be expected." Finally, as Humphreys (1959, 1962) has noted, the IQ is often treated as a measure of potential rather than a measure of achievement.

## ORDINAL SCALES: AN ALTERNATIVE

Now I would like to come to the alternative approach of ordinal scales in the assessment of psychological development. I was led to this approach through a round-about process. In the middle 1950s, I set out to write a book on behavioral science and child rearing. The idea was to put together from the behavioral and social sciences the evidence relevant to what we believe about fostering intellectual and motivational development in infancy and early childhood. At that time, I was looking at the matter pretty much from the standpoints of psychoanalysis and Hullian learning theory. In the process, I examined much of the existing literature. This may be a mistake for anyone set on writing a book. What I read served to change my mind so radically that I have never written that book. I had always presumed, as I was taught, that intelligence is largely fixed by heredity, and that the emotional aspect of personality is the one modifiable by experience. As I examined the evidence in the literature, it looked as if experience were at least as important if not more important for the intellectual side of development than for the emotional side. The literature that I reviewed included the work of Piaget. His idea of hierarchical organization of intellect in successive stages of development suggested an alternative mode of assessment based on sequential orders in the structures achieved. His notion of a hierarchy of stages got reinforced through the work of Gagné (1966a, b; Gagné & Paradise, 1961). Ina Uzgiris, one of my students at the University of Illinois, was also interested in this inspiration from Piaget's work, so we decided to collaborate on the development of a set of ordinal scales of infant development (Uzgiris & Hunt, 1975).

What we did (it was actually Ina Uzgiris who did most of it) was to go through Piaget's descriptions of the development in his own three children and pull out as many of the progressive landmarks in their informational interaction with their environments as we could identify. From these, we developed some others and then we chose for continued work those that different people could readily identify with high levels of agreement. In our tests of intersubjective agreement, we went out of our way to get examiners with differing characteristics. We were able to find a substantial number of these landmarks in behavioral development showing 95% agreement. Some few show levels of agreement just under 80%.

After several false starts, we divided these landmarks into six series, with a series on imitation actually consisting of two: one gestural, the other vocal. From these series, a cross-sectional scalogram analysis resulted in seven ordinal scales. You will recall that Piaget identified six stages in the sensorimotor phase of psychological development. We found it feasible to have high levels of intersubjective agreement on more than six steps in the scale for each branch of development. Time will not permit me to take you through these scales in detail, but I can at least name the nature of each of the seven, give you the number of steps, and give you also the measure of ordinality provided by Green's (1956) index of consistency.

The first of these scales concerns "visual following and object permanence." It has 14 steps, and Green's index of consistency for these 14 steps is .97 for the 84 infants who served in this portion of the study. The second scale concerns "the development of means for obtaining desired environmental events," and has 13 steps for which Green's index of consistency is .81. The third scale concerns "development of gestural imitation," and has 9 steps for which the index of consistency is .95. The fourth concerns "the development of vocal imitation"; it also has 9 steps with an index of consistency of .89. The fifth scale concerns the "construction of operational causality," and it has 7 steps with an index of consistency of .99. The sixth scale concerns the "construction of object relations in space," and consists of 11 steps with an index of consistency of .91. The seventh scale concerns "the development of schemas for relating to objects," and consists of 10 steps with an index of consistency of .80. These indices of consistency are all based upon our cross-sectional scaling study (Uzgiris & Hunt, 1975).

It is beginning to appear from the evidence available thus far that the sequential order in actual development confirms for the most part the ordinal relationships derived from this cross-sectional scaling. Uzgiris (1973) has found the sequential orders prevailing in a longitudinal study of 12 infants from predominately middle-class families confirming for the most part the ordinality from the cross-sectional scaling. These 12 infants have had experience similar to those who served as subjects in our scaling study. From longitudinal data on infants being reared from birth in an Iranian orphanage, still incompletely analyzed, I can say also that the sequential order of achieving all but one of the 14 steps in the scale of visual following and object permanence confirms the ordinality of the cross-sectional scaling study. From inspection, I glean, moreover, that nearly perfect confirmation holds for the scales of object relations in space and of operational causality. This is less true for the scale on the development of means for achieving various environmental events, and for the scale on the development of schemas for relating to objects. These data from the orphanage study say nothing about the development of vocal imitation because vocal imitation fails to develop under orphanage conditions.

Once a number of sequential ordinal scales are available, they provide opportunity for several fortunate modifications in the strategy for assessing early psychological development and for studying its structure. First, ordinal scales permit one to get quantitative meaning directly from a child's performance. In traditional norm-referenced tests, the meaning of a performance comes from the interpersonal comparisons implicit in such statistics as percentile ranks or standard scores. On an ordinal scale, the fact that an infant succeeds with one step and fails the next one on a give scale defines his level of development on that scale. Second, measures of development in terms of mental age and IQ implicitly make age the key independent variable in development. Ordinal scales serve to disentangle psychological development from age. They thereby permit one to use age of achieving levels on the various scales as a dependent variable, and with it to assess the impact of various independent variables on development. Third, whereas the substitutive averaging involved in determining mental ages and IQs serves to hide the structural details in psychological development, having an ordinal scale for each of several branches of development invites the investigation of organizational structures. Moreover, having more than six steps in each scale permits testing the validity of those organizational structures described by Piaget as stages. Let me, however, make a disclaimer: We have not covered all domains of psychological development in these scales. At best we have made but a healthy start.

## NOVEL FINDINGS FROM STUDIES USING ORDINAL SCALES

Let me summarize some of the results from investigations in which we have used these scales. In one study, John Paraskevopoulos and I have compared the ages of children living in orphanages with differing child-rearing practices who are at the various levels of development for object construction and vocal imitation (Paraskevopoulos & Hunt, 1971). At the Municipal Orphanage in Athens, where there are approximately 10 infants per caretaker, the children at the top level of object permanence average 45 months of age. At Metera Center in Athens, where the infant–caretaker ratio is approximately 3 to 1, they average 35 months. Home-reared children from working parents who are at this same top level of object permanence averaged 30 months of age. Such comparison of the ages of children at a given level of development permits one to assess the effects of environmental circumstances in a cross-sectional study.

In a newly completed study at an orphanage in Tehran, we have used a longitudinal strategy in what I like to call "wave design." For a baseline control, we started with a sample of infants developing under the customary practices of the institution. The only intervention was a regular examination of each infant with the ordinal scales: biweekly during the first year and every fourth week thereafter. In successive waves, we intervened with various environmental enrichments calculated to hasten development. Uzgiris also used this same longitudinal strategy with a sample of 12 infants from predominantly middle-class families of Worcester, Massachusetts. In the Parent and Child Center of Mt. Carmel, Illinois, David Schickedanz and I used three of the scales (object construction, development of means, and vocal imitation) to evaluate the effects of an intervention. Eight consecutive infants born to parents who were participating in the program of this Center got the same schedule of examinations as that used by Uzgiris in Worcester (see Hunt *et al.*, 1976).

It is of interest that the Mt. Carmel infants from families of poverty who received this intervention achieved top-level object permanence at a mean age of 73 weeks, whereas those from predominantly middle-class, professional families in Worcester did not achieve this level of object permanence until an average age of 98 weeks. Thus, the intervention served to hasten the achievement of top-level object permanence in infants from families of poverty enough to put them approximately six months ahead of those from families of middle class. Yet, that same intervention failed to hasten the development of vocal imitation. These same infants at Mt. Carmel failed to achieve top-level vocal imitation until their average age was about six months older than the average age at which the Worcester infants achieved top-level vocal imitation (Hunt, Paraskevopoulos, Schickedanz, & Uzgiris, 1975). This was a surprise to us. Note that it would be essentially impossible to get such structural information from comparisons of mental ages of developmental quotients.

Consider two more findings of such a structural nature. I was led to the orphanage in Tehran by a study made there by Dennis (1960). To get a quick assessment of the development of the children in the Tehran orphanages, Dennis used postural and locomotor performances. Approximately two-thirds of those infants in their second year who had been in the orphanage from birth were not yet sitting up. Moreover, approximately 80% of those in their fourth year were not yet walking. Since then, the program of Iranian orphanages has been greatly improved. Yet, until recently, I have never seen an infant who developed from birth in the Tehran orphanage who sat up until near the end of his first year of life, unless he happened to become a pet of a caretaker. Never had I seen but one such infant standing and cruising at less than 18 months of age. In our first wave of human enrichment, we simply decreased the infant–caretaker ratio to about 3 to 1 and had some student nurses visit the children five days a week. Caretakers and student nurses did what came naturally with the children; they got no instruction on the kind of experiences to provide. What they appear from clinical impressions to have done was to carry the children about and to put them in scooters and push them around the floor. What changed in these infants was the age at which they began to sit up, to stand, and to cruise around their cribs. All but one of the 10 in this wave were not only sitting up, but were also up on their feet and cruising about their cribs at between 11 and 13 months of age. It is interesting but humanly unfortunate that these infants were substantially advanced in no other branch.

The other example concerns gestural and vocal imitation. From reading Piaget's reports on the development of his own three children, I got the impression that imitation is a unitary process and that infants achieve what amount to corresponding steps in the development of gestural and vocal imitation at the same ages. This was quite the contrary for the children developing in this Tehran orphanage. Gestural imitation develops with relatively little retardation, but vocal imitation is either greatly retarded or it fails to develop at all. Three-year-old children who have lived in the orphanage from birth neither understand spoken language nor speak. It would appear that visual observation plus the experience of repeated examinations is enough to keep the development of gestural imitation going, but the repeated examinations fail utterly to foster vocal imitation. Where gestural imitation comes through visual experience, vocal imitation comes through auditory experience, and development in the two branches of imitation appears to be quite independent.

## RELATION TO CHAPTERS IN THIS VOLUME

These findings may help to explain Goodnow's culture based clusters. They demonstrate, I believe, that there is not only plasticity in the rate of development in general; there is also a great deal of independent plasticity in the rates of development along the several branches. The rate of development in each branch depends much upon the kinds of environmental circumstances encountered. Presumably the cultures Goodnow has investigated differ in the kinds of circumstances they provide for infants and young children.

Perhaps these findings are relevant also to Huttenlocher's findings concerning children who are highly verbal but lack understanding of their verbalizations. Before I try to make this point, however, I should make explicit my belief that the language function emerges out of a coordination of object construction, the accumulated sensorimotor knowledge that comes to be symbolized in language, and vocal imitation, the source of the vocal signs for this knowledge of objects and actions. The vocal patterns that become the signs of early language are, I believe, acquired through vocal imitation. Vocal imitation is both cognitive and motivational in character. This coordination of object construction with vocal imitation calls for a level of each that I cannot now specify. It takes place at the point in development where infants get the learning set that "things have names." The existence of this set is manifest, I believe, in such behavior as asking or asserting, "that?" Such behaviors are repeated until someone gives the infant a name of that thing.

Now to the possible relevance of our findings to Huttenlocher's. The fact that the intervention used at the Parent and Child Center in Mt. Carmel advanced the average age (73 weeks) at which infants from families of the poverty sector achieved top-level object permanence to approximately 6 months ahead of the average age (98 weeks) of this achievement by children of predominantly middle-class parents in Worcester illustrates how object construction can be advanced ahead of vocal imitation. In fact, the range of reaction, defined as the difference between the estimated mean age (182 weeks) at which the children at the Municipal Orphanage of Athens achieved top-level object construction and that (73 weeks) at which the Mt. Carmel children achieved this same level of object permanence, is over two years (Hunt et al., 1975). In the light of this finding, it is conceivable to me that Huttenlocher's verbally fluent but noncomprehending children may well have lived under conditions which pushed language achievement, consisting of vocal imitation, the acquisition of word sounds, of the rules of syntax, and of knowledge of language, well ahead of their achievement of concrete knowledge of the collective meanings of the language they were vocalizing.

From several considerations, we have gleaned a hypothesis concerning the experiences that fostered object construction in Mt. Carmel. First, the intervention was heavily loaded with opportunities to manipulate responsive materials. For about half of the children, the intervention was limited to the period of daycare because their mothers failed to participate in the Mothers' Training. One of the toys in which the infants took a great interest over an extended period of time was a shapebox. Objects thrust through the holes in the top would disappear, but could readily be retrieved by lifting the top of the box. Although the intervention also contained instructions designed to foster vocal imitation, the fact that over half of the mothers failed to participate and that during the period of daycare only one or two of the participating mothers were serving as caretakers left little opportunity for fostering vocal imitation. I can only speculate about what special circumstances would foster language achievements without fostering object construction and knowledge of reality. Perhaps a useful empirical hypothesis could be gleaned from investigating the circumstances under which Huttenlocher's verbally fluent but noncomprehending children have developed.

Charlesworth suggested that something happens to change children during their second, third, and fourth years—yes, indeed, several kinds of things. First, a genetically dictated program of maturation is underway. Epstein (1974a, b) has assembled evidence from the world's literature that spurts in brain growth, unassociated with the long-observed spurts in muscle and bone growth, are associated with IQ spurts in potential for learning. There may be such a spurt between the ages of 2 and 4 years, and there is substantial evidence for others between 6 and 8, 10 and 12, and 14 and 16. These surely can be modified by both nutritional and informational interaction with the environmental circumstances encountered. Through their informational interaction with circumstances, children gain knowledge. They cannot tell you about this knowledge, but they give you evidence of it in their actions. Some of these actions appear among the various kinds that provide evidence for object construction. Evidence of acquisitions in cognitive knowledge shows also in the means used by infants to obtain desired environmental events, in an infant's knowledge of objects in space, and in his or her grasp of causality. An infant gains not only information from his informational interactions; he also achieves transitions to new levels of operation for information processing. These transitional learnings also show in his actions. Consider one example from the development of object construction. At one level, when a desired object is placed within a container and the container made to disappear under a cover where the desired object is dumped out and the container is brought back empty, the infant looks into the container, finds it empty, and gives up. At the next level, when the container comes back empty, the child notes the emptiness, darts directly to the cover where the container was made to disappear, and retrieves the desired object.

Consider another example, this one from the scale on the development of means for achieving desired environmental events. When an infant in a playpen is presented with a stick within his reach, he typically grasps the stick midway between the ends and pulls it horizontally against the bars of the playpen. Only after he has tugged and pulled does he accidentally get hold of one end and draw the stick to him between the vertical bars. At a later point, the child reaches immediately for one end of the stick in a fashion clearly indicating that he has anticipated what was required by a mental combination. Such are the implications of new levels of information processing implicit in the nature of the transitions in early cognitive development.

Transitions are also prominent in the development of intrinsic motivation, that is, that kind of motivation inherent in information processing and action (Hunt, 1963, 1965, 1971). In the first weeks following birth, it appears that change in the nature of on-going receptor input is what attracts and arouses infants. Repeated exposures to given patterns of such change lead to recognitive familiarity which is a basis for attraction (Greenberg, Uzgiris, & Hunt, 1970; Weizmann, Cohen, & Pratt, 1971). Later, it is what is novel and challenging, on either the perceptual or motor level, that becomes attractive. Henceforth, in development, there is an optimum in the relationship between level of development in a child and the complexity, and novelty of the environmental circumstances or the challenge in the situation encountered that attracts and interests him. Finding this optimum constitutes for parents and teachers what I like to call "the problem of the match." Too little in the way of challenge, novelty, or complexity is boring. Too much becomes threatening (see Hunt, 1965, 1966).

From the standpoint of this "problem of the match," I find myself interested in Charlesworth's finding that only about 2% of the interactions of the children that he has been observing involved problem solving, as usually defined. This does not surprise me, because an optimum level of challenge or novelty would almost never be perceived by psychologists as either a frustrating or a problem-solving situation. Toddlers would tend to avoid such situations as threatening, yet the materials and models that interest them appear to foster a continuing process of enjoyable accommodative change that probably realizes what approaches the infant's maximum potential for psychological development. I am also interested in the fact that Klahr knows of no computer simulation for achieving the transition from level to level, and thus far has been unable to produce one. If and when computers can be made to simulate such developmental transitions, we shall have moved a major step in understanding psychological development. Creating computer simulations comes only after a high level of understanding of a phenomenon exists.

In the meantime, I believe it is important for the understanding of development during the preschool years to extend the construction of sequential ordinal scales from the sensorimotor phase to the phase of concrete operations. The nature of the essential branches in behavioral development during this phase is still unclear to me, but I see the possibility of at least two extensions. One of them, being conducted in our own laboratory by Ruth Harper, involves haptic perception. In the examination, the child must reach through holes in an opaque barrier to feel a thing that is out of sight in order to identify it. In our approach, the child is provided with five things in each given category. One set of these is within view. The examiner then hands the child one example of a category at a time. When the child thinks he can tell which of those in view he is feeling, he indicates it. If he can identify all five, the betting odds that he is unable to identify the whole category concerned become very low. Our subjects extend from two-year-olds, who are able to identify only such highly familiar objects as a spoon and a hairbrush, up to eight- or nine-year-olds who become able to identify plastic circles with 5, 6, 8, 10, or 12 little knobs equally spaced around circles of plexiglass. Such identification demands that the child look at the models, count the numbers of knobs, and then planfully go through the manipulation of counting the knobs on the plastic circle in his hand. I believe intuitively that an ordinal scale is also implied in Roger Brown's (1973) descriptions of a child's first language.

Such scales for the later preschool years would go a long way toward providing a solid descriptive base for investigating the nature of transitions, the development of structural combinations, and the nature of the kinds of experience important for the development of each transition. Not only would we have thereby a better understanding of development, but I believe such understanding might have the additional value of permitting a kind of synthesis in early education between the demands that cultures make on children, on the one hand, and the developmental needs of the children, on the other.

## REFERENCES

Brown, R. W. The development of the first language in the human species. *American Psychologist*, 1973, **28**, 97–106.

Dennis, W. Causes of retardation among institutional children: Iran. *Journal of Genetic Psychology*, 1960, **96**, 47–59.

Epstein, H. T. Phrenoblysis: Special brain and mind growth periods: I. Human brain and skull development. *Developmental Psychobiology*, 1974, 7, 207–216. (a)

Epstein, H. T. Phrenoblysis: Special brain and mind growth periods: II. Human mental development. *Developmental Psychobiology*, 1974, 7, 217–224. (b)

Feuerstein, R. *Studies in cognitive modifiability: The dynamic assessment of retarded performers.* Vol. 1: *The clinical LPAD battery.* Jerusalem, Israel: Hadassah Wizo Canada Research Institute, 1972. (Mimeographed preliminary report) (a)

Feuerstein, R. *Studies in cognitive modifiability: The dynamic assessment of retarded performers.* Vol. 2: *The LPAD analogies group test experiment.* Jerusalem, Israel: Hadassah Wizo Canada Research Institute, 1972. (Mimeographed preliminary report) (b)

Gagné, R. M. Contributions of learning to human development. Vice-presidential address of Section I, American Association for the Advancement of Science Meeting, Washington, D. C., 1966. (a)

Gagné, R. M. Elementary science: A new scheme of instruction. *Science*, 1966, **151**(3706), 49–53. (b)

Gagné, R. M., & Paradise, N. E. Abilities and learning sets in knowledge acquisition. *Psychological Monographs*, 1961, 75(14, Whole No. 518).

Glaser, R. Instructional technology and the measurement of learning outcomes: Some questions. *American Psychologist*, 1963, **18**, 519–521.

Green, B. F. A method of scalogram analysis using summary statistics. *Psychometrika*, 1956, **21**, 79–88.

Greenberg, D. J., Uzgiris, I. C., & Hunt, J. McV. Attentional preference and experience: III. Visual familiarity and looking time. *Journal of Genetic Psychology*, 1970, **117**, 123–135.

Guilford, J. P. *The nature of human intelligence.* New York: McGraw-Hill, 1967.

Humphreys, L. G. Discussion of Dr . Ferguson's paper. In P. H. Dubois, W. H. Manning, & C. J. Spies (Eds.), *Factor analysis and related techniques in the study of learning.* (Technical Report No. 7) ONR Contract No. 816(02), pp. 183–187, 1959.

Humphreys, L. G. The nature and organization of human abilities. In M. Katz (Ed.), *The 19th Yearbook of the National Council on Measurement in Education.* Ames, Iowa: National Council on Measurement in Education, 1962.

Hunt, J. McV. *Intelligence and experience.* New York: Ronald Press, 1961.

Hunt, J. McV. Piaget's observations as a source of hypotheses concerning motivation. *Merrill-Palmer Quarterly*, 1963, 9, 263–275.

Hunt, J. McV. Intrinsic motivation and its role in psychological development. In D. Levine (Ed.), *Nebraska symposium on motivation.* Vol. 17. Lincoln: University of Nebraska Press, 1965. Pp. 189–282.

Hunt, J. McV. Toward a theory of guided learning in development. In R. H. Ojemann & K. Pritchett (Eds.), *Giving emphasis to guided learning.* Cleveland, Ohio: Educational Research Council, 1966.

Hunt, J. McV. Intrinsic motivation: Information and circumstance. In H. M. Schroder & P. Suedfeld (Eds.), *Personality theory and information processing.* New York: Ronald Press, 1971.

Hunt, J. McV., Mohandessi, K., Ghodssi, Mehri, & Akiyama, M. Development of orphanage-reared infants (Tehran): Interventions and outcomes, *Genetic Psychology Monographs,* 1976, **94**, 177-226.

Hunt, J. McV., Paraskevopoulos, J., Schickedanz, D., & Uzgiris, C. Variations in the mean ages of achieving object permanence under diverse conditions of rearing. In B. L. Friedlander, G. E. Kirk, G. M. Sterritt (Eds.), *The Exceptional Infant,* Vol. 3: *Assessment and Intervention.* New York: Bruner/Maezel, 1975.

Paraskevopoulos, J., & Hunt, J. McV. Object construction and imitation under differing conditions of rearing. *Journal of Genetic Psychology,* 1971, **119**, 301–321.

Sullivan, A. M. The relation between intelligence and transfer. Unpublished doctoral thesis, McGill University, 1964.

Uzgiris, I. C. Patterns of cognitive development in infancy. *Merrill-Palmer Quarterly,* 1973, **19**, 181–204.

Uzgiris, I. C., & Hunt, J. McV. *Assessment in infancy: Ordinal scales of psychological development.* Urbana: University of Illinois Press, 1975.

Weizmann, F., Cohen, L. B., & Pratt, R. J. Novelty, familiarity, and the development of infant attention. *Developmental Psychology,* 1971, **4**, 149–154.

Woodrow, H. The relation between abilities and improvement with practice. *Journal of Educational Psychology,* 1938, **29**, 215–230.

Woodrow, H. Factors in improvement in practice. *Journal of Psychology,* 1939, 7, 55–70.

# 19

# A Factor Model For Research on Intelligence and Problem Solving

Lloyd G. Humphreys

*University of Illinois, Urbana-Champaign*

A recent issue of the New York Times carried a story about the low level of reading achievement in schools in New York City and compared that city's record with results in several other large cities. Children in the cities reviewed have below average performance in reading comprehension with about three-quarters reading below grade level. The story also commented on the very considerable differences among the schools within a given city.

Relationships between these reading records and intelligence test scores may perhaps furnish a little perspective on criticisms that have been levelled against intelligence tests by many lay persons and a not inconsiderable number of psychologists in recent years. Some of the criticisms are justified, but many are not. Consider the following. A carefully administered individual test of intelligence, either the Wechsler or the Binet, at age 5, will predict mean reading comprehension scores of students in grade 12, whether for cities or for separate schools within cities, with high accuracy. Those same intelligence test scores will predict individual reading comprehension scores in grade 12 with much more modest, though considerably better than chance, accuracy. These predictions are not contingent, within quite wide limits, on the type of instruction children are receiving, on the training of their teachers, or on the level of economic support of the schools. The principal contingencies are the availability of an intelligence test in the child's native language and attendance at schools that use the language of the 12th-grade test.

While I confidently expect that the experimental psychology of cognitive processes will throw considerable light on the nature of the tests and the nature of reading in the next 20 years, I also confidently expect that intellectual assessment 20 years hence will be more similar to present test procedures than to any laboratory-derived procedure. I shall attempt to lay a groundwork for these assertions and to relate this groundwork to the content of several of the other chapters presented.

## FACTOR MODELS

It is highly desirable, no matter what the nature of the independent variables may be, to think about dependent variables in terms of a factor model. In experimentation in which the independent variables are not attributes of the person and in which subjects are assigned to treatment groups at random, the factor model supplements the linear model of the analysis of variance for the dependent variable. For example, if there are two independent variables, the components of variance model of the analysis of variance breaks down the variance of the dependent variable into components associated with variable $A$, variable $B$, their interaction, and error. The factor model typically breaks down the variance of the same dependent variable into the attribute of the subject that is measured, a nonerror specific, and measurement error. (Note that "error" in the components of variance model and in the factor model are not identical. The former typically includes more than measurement error.)

If the independent variables are themselves attributes of the subject, it is impossible for the investigator to assign subjects at random to treatment groups. Under these circumstances the components of variance model is not applicable (see Humphreys & Fleishman, 1974). Underwood (1957) has also discussed this same problem though in a different context. In all such experimentation some sort of factor model is essential for both the independent variables and the dependent variable. While this limitation has not been widely accepted by investigators, the major defect of the components of variance model can be stated quite simply. An investigator typically obtains experimental groups defined by the level of their scores on one or more attributes. Groups so formed, however, also differ from each other on every attribute correlated with the one or ones used in defining the groups. Therefore, it is impossible to assign a component of variance in the dependent variable that is unequivocally associated with a particular independent variable. Such assignment depends directly on the experimenter's ability to assign subjects at random to treatments.

Classical measurement theory analyzes a score into true and error components. This is inadequate since the question of the nature of the true score is begged. The name that a particular psychologist attaches to the score is a very fallible guide. If one is dealing with the total score on a test, factor thinking must be applied to the items. If one is dealing with measurement in the physical system (centimeters, grams, seconds—cgs), factor thinking is applied to the components of a composite measure (cgs scale).

## Factorial Components of Variance

I start with the premise that any single behavioral measurement, whether by a test item or by a cgs scale, is composed of three components which are similar to those suggested by Loevinger (1954). These are the attributes that the psychologist wants to measure ($a$), nonrandom noise specificity or bias ($b$), and random noise or error ($e$); that is, the classical true score is divided into two components ($a$ and $b$). Loevinger used the classical measurement term "constant error" for the second component, but this is misleading. Most bias is intrinsic to the behavioral measurement operation. Reasoning requires both content (words, numbers, figures) and some type of operation (analogies, series, classification). Knowledge of word meanings requires some type of operation and some definition of the universe of words from which the test items will be drawn. The universe can only be sampled, and examinees will have had differential experiences with different subsets. The multitrait-multimethod paper of Campbell and Fiske (1959) discusses the same basic issue, although method variance is only one, albeit an important, source of bias. Note that method variance is intrinsic to the measurement operation and cannot be controlled.

If the score is composed of $a$, $b$, and $e$ components, when scores are obtained on a sample of people, the variance of the scores, making assumptions about independence of the components, is the following:

$$S_x^2 = S_a^2 + S_b^2 + S_e^2.$$

## Reduction of Bias Variance

The experience of many psychologists working in many different areas is that the bias variance is likely to be very large in any single behavioral measurement. This is especially true of test items but applies to measurement in the experimental laboratory as well. The attribute variance may be very small relative to the other components. An effective way to reduce the variance of error is to obtain several independent measures under carefully standardized conditions. The only way to reduce bias variance is to obtain several measures in which the bias factors are as independent as possible from one measure to another, and to compute a composite score for the several components. The rule is to maximize heterogeneity of the several measures within the limits of the definition of the attribute. Small contributions to variance of the attribute in a single measure build up in the total score when each element measures the same attribute but different biases. The total contribution to variance of the bias factors as a group is decreased in the composite score, while the contribution of any one bias factor becomes very small indeed (see Humphreys, 1960).

Although Cronbach and his co-workers (1972) use a different terminology, generalizability theory has a great deal in common with the present analysis of score variance into attribute, bias, and error components. The manipulations required to increase generalizability are precisely those required to build up attribute variance at the expense of bias variance. It is unfortunate that the Cronbach approach has become primarily associated with the concept of reliability in classical measurement theory; the theory has more generality than its association with reliability suggests.

## COMMON APPLICATIONS OF THE MEASUREMENT MODEL

Just as one man's flower is another man's weed, one man's bias is another man's attribute. If one is interested in the number of four-letter words beginning with "s" that examinees can produce in a given amount of time, so be it—but this test should not be called word fluency. The latter attribute is more general than the measure proposed and can only be measured by introducing heterogeneity with respect to word size, starting letter, etc.

### Tests of Human Abilities

General intelligence is a broad attribute. Thus, the test items should be quite heterogeneous and the contribution of any one aspect should not be emphasized at the expense of other aspects. A vocabulary test is not a test of general intelligence, but neither is a test composed entirely of Raven's matrices.

Although an intelligence test is quite broad, a standard test is not as broad as could be justified statistically. There are potential test items correlated with those in an intelligence test that are not now included. Mechanical information and mechanical problem solving constitute obvious examples. On the assumption that mechanical items do correlate positively with those currently chosen for inclusion in intelligence tests, and that these correlations are of about the same magnitude as those among present items, there is only one criterion of whether a broader test should be constructed: its usefulness theoretically or practically. Neither factor analysis nor a priori reasoning that mechanical reasoning is not intellectual is an important consideration. The rule is that it is always legitimate for research purposes to add together items that are positively and homogeneously intercorrelated. Only in this way can the attribute or attributes that the items have in common be investigated. Attribute variance in the single item is typically much smaller than bias variance, which makes research with items at least difficult if not impossible. The total score for the composite measure reflects the causes that produced the intercorrelations, and the investigator is now in a position to determine whether these causes have enough in common with each other to produce psychologically interesting relationships with other phenomena.

Some form of a hierarchical structure of abilities is a natural accompaniment of analyzing the components of a score into attribute, bias, and error factors.

One moves from general intelligence down in the hierarchy to the lowest subdivision by shifting components from attribute to bias. This does not mean, however, that the lowest levels represent the "purest" measures of psychological functions. In a very real sense Guilford's elements are psychologically very complex since these elements consist of contributions inextricably intertwined from each one of his three facets or dimensions.

Critics have described the content of intelligence tests as a hodgepodge of items. In doing so they are being neither very statistical nor psychological. Heterogeneity is the necessary consequence of measuring attributes by means of their manifestations in behavior. The greater the breadth of the trait, the greater must be the heterogeneity of the items. Thus, laboratory assessment of intellectual functioning by the experimental psychologist would be an unfeasible enterprise for widespread use at best; and for the present, having too few laboratory tasks to define the attribute, it is an enterprise of low validity.

## Experimental Cognitive Psychology

The tasks used in the research that stems from Piaget can be analyzed in terms of this factorial model. There is every reason to expect a large concentration of bias variance in any one task. The result is that the intercorrelations of tasks set for children, all of which supposedly measure the same attribute, are low. The best measure of conservation is a composite of several conservation tasks. Thus, the data of Tuddenham and Ward quoted by Tyler (Chapter 2) are not at all surprising.

In the light of the preceding discussion it is understandable why I get a little nervous when an experimental psychologist claims that he is studying problem solving, but uses a single experimental situation which provides only a single score. Bias variance may be quite high. When he obtains relationships between his independent variables and his dependent variable, these relationships may not involve the attribute. If they do not, the error in interpretation is a very serious one. Even if they do involve the attribute, the relationships would be larger and clearer if the bias factors were reduced in size. Such difficulties can be avoided. A desirable methodology is to use more than one dependent variable wherever possible and to analyze the data by means of a multivariate analysis of variance.

## Strength of Conditioned Responses

I showed many years ago (Humphreys, 1940) that no single attribute of strength of human conditioned eyelid responses could be found in the intercorrelations of the several measures of strength traditionally used in acquisition and extinction. At least two independent attributes are involved. Even though all of these traditional measures, and thus both attributes, vary with the independent variable of number of paired presentations of conditioned stimulus and unconditioned stimulus, the logical inference from the individual differences data is that some other independent variable would have differential effects on them. When continuous and partial reinforcement effects are compared, the differential effect is found. Only one of the two attributes, that measured by latency and extinction frequency, shows the increased resistance to extinction following partial reinforcement.

## Some Current Examples

I now turn to some applications of this sort of thinking to three of the chapters presented here. The attempt to observe adaptive behavior, as described by Charlesworth (Chapter 8), in the everyday behavior of children may furnish some useful insights, but it has many pitfalls. It is almost certainly doomed to failure for measurement purposes. This conclusion is based upon the presence in everyday behavior of a high degree of specificity. It is not improbable that systematic noise will overload the observational capabilities of the investigator and bury the attribute in a wealth of trivia.

The present definition of specificity or bias is unrelated to that used by Goodnow (Chapter 9). She discussed the specificity of cultural effects within a group in terms of depression of means of certain measures relative to the means of other measures. Specificity, when defined as a component of variance, affects the size of correlations within a given group. For that group the mean of a test can be depressed without changing its relationships with other tests and with social criteria. High and low scores within the group that has the depressed mean may still reflect differences on the same function or factor as high and low scores in groups with higher means.

Other terms used by Goodnow for the same phenomenon are "unevenness" of mean performance and the "hanging together" of tasks. These terms suggest correlation coefficients, but as used by her apply only to group means. Such effects become related to the intercorrelations of measures only when several different groups are combined in computing intercorrelations for a total group. In the latter case variances and covariances can be analyzed into within-group and between-group components, but it is a completely independent question whether the analysis of within-group variance into attribute, bias (specificity), and error differs from group to group. It is probable that means are more sensitive to cultural effects than are correlations.

Certain aspects of E. Hunt's research program (Chapter 13) can also be discussed in the light of this factorial thinking. Intercorrelations of the same parameters from different experimental contexts should be positive, but probably will not turn out to be high. It is quite possible, even probable, that the correlation of each with a measure of general intelligence will be higher than its average correlation with the other parameters. If this is true, then a composite formed from several parameters should be more highly correlated with the hypothesized attribute than any one of them individually.

## THE CONSTRUCT OF GENERAL INTELLIGENCE

Cooley commented with respect to Carroll's presentation (Chapter 3) concerning the usual evidence for general intelligence. Positive intercorrelations are indeed found among a wide variety of intellectual tasks. These positive intercorrelations constitute a necessary basis for the construct. Let me now add other evidence that is less widely known and quoted.

### Intercorrelations of Means

In one of the publications arising from Project TALENT (1962), means for a random sample of schools are intercorrelated. The correlations among the means of cognitive variables are very high, being largely in the high eighties or low nineties. For example, reading comprehension and mechanical information, in a random sample of schools, show a correlation greater than .90, whereas in a sample of individual students this same correlation is about .35. There is nothing in the process of computing means as such that can produce an increase of this magnitude. (Means are more reliable than individual scores, but this accounts for only a tiny part of the difference.) The only explanation that makes sense is that the selective factors that place children in schools in a nonrandom fashion are operating primarily on a general factor. There is little evidence in the correlations of means for the presence of group factors.

### Heritability of General Intelligence

A second set of data involves heritability estimates (Humphreys, 1974). I compared cross-twin correlations with within-twin correlations for 40 heterogeneous cognitive variables for male and female monozygotic and dizygotic twins from Project TALENT (for definitions and methodology, see Humphreys, 1970). If a trait is highly heritable, the mean cross-twin correlation for monozygotic twins should approach very closely the mean within-twin correlation for those twins. For dizygotic twins under conditions of zero selectivity in mating, the ratio should be .50. Assortative mating pushes this ratio to some unknown amount over .50. Rather than trying to assess degree of heritability, however, I used the ratios to search for differential degrees of heritability among the traits measured by the 40 measures. For the entire set of 40 measures, including academic and nonacademic information, academic achievement, and aptitude measures, the distributions of the cross-twin to within-twin ratios appear to vary only at random from one measure to another. There is as much evidence for heritability of information about the Bible as for heritability of abstract reasoning. My interpretation of these data is that the general factor is very general indeed, that it is involved in all cognitive measures, that the genetic contribution to human abilities, whatever its size may be, is to the general factor, and that the differentiation of cognitive abilities into group factors, as in Thurstone and Guilford, proceeds largely through learning.

## Explanations of the General Factor

To acknowledge the reality of general ability is one thing, but an explanation that suggests an entity or faculty within the person does not necessarily follow. There is every reason to disavow the theoretical tradition associated with Spearman (1927) who described the general factor as mental energy. Cattell (1971), Guilford (1967), and Thurstone (1938), although they stress group factors of varying degrees of breadth in their theorizing, follow Spearman's example in discussing explanations for factors as faculties, entities, or unitary powers of the organism. There is a second tradition in ability theory, however, which I find more attractive. Thomson (1951), E. L. Thorndike (1926), Tryon (1935), and Ferguson (1954) discuss abilities quite differently. Thomson, for example, was able to explain the existence of a general factor in terms of overlapping neural mechanisms and overlapping stimulus–response "bonds" required by the variety of tasks set for examinees by psychological tests. Perhaps the genetic basis for intelligence is in the multitude of structures in the central nervous system in its entirety. One can also assume without fear of contradiction that any genetically determined structures will show a wide range of individual differences.

   Simon (Chapter 5) and others who are programming cognitive theories are operating more nearly in the Thomson than in the Spearman tradition. Thomson, certainly, would have no problem in integrating Simon's work into his thinking, while Spearman would find it very difficult to understand. Similarly, I find Carroll's analyses (Chapter 3) to be well within the Thomson tradition.

## THE DYNAMIC NATURE OF INTELLIGENCE

One important basis for preferring the Thomson sort of explanation for general intelligence, in addition perhaps to a reluctance of long standing to place anything more inside the organism than absolutely essential, is the instability of intellectual performance over time. This instability is most marked during childhood development.

## Instability within the Person

Anderson (1939) suggested almost 35 years ago that the famed stability of IQs could arise from the characteristics of part–whole correlations. Even if the gain in mental age during a given year were uncorrelated with the mental age base at the beginning of the year, correlations from one year to the next would be high.

Over an extended period of time, however, correlations would gradually decrease in size. A short while later, Roff (1941) computed correlations between gains and initial bases and published correlations that varied around zero. Since his correlations were between fallible bases and fallible gains, measurement error provides a spurious negative component to these correlations. With that component removed, the correlations are undoubtedly small positive ones. Nevertheless, their size is far removed from the size one would expect from the reliabilities of initial bases and gains. There may well be some small constant factor in general intelligence during development, but there is a larger degree of unpredictability of gains from initial bases.

By allowing myself a little poetic license, and putting together data from several sources, the table of intercorrelations of IQs computed annually from age 2 to 22 could be described as follows. Correlations just off the principal diagonal (between adjacent years) would be quite high, with their size increasing from age 2 to 22. This means, of course, that intelligence test scores become increasingly stable from test to retest with increasing age at the time of administration of the first test. This increasing degree of stability is a function of the relative variabilities of the initial base and the gain. Although gains have relatively low correlations with initial bases, the size of the base and its variability increases more rapidly with chronological age than the size of the gain and its variability. In the upper diagonal matrix of this table of intercorrelations, the correlations would decrease in size gradually and smoothly from the principal diagonal across the rows and up the columns, indicating a decreasing degree of stability of intelligence test scores as the amount of time between test and retest increases. This decreasing degree of stability is a function of the low correlations between initial bases and gains. These low correlations may produce relatively little instability over the course of a single year, but over many years the low correlations have a cumulative effect. The lowest correlation would be found in the upper right-hand corner of this upper diagonal matrix, the one between intelligence at 2 and at 22, and would probably be below .50 after correcting for measurement error. In contrast the correlation between 2 and 3 might be .80 and the one between 21 and 22 might be .95. Thus, the data suggest a good deal of intraindividual variability in intelligence during development.

## Generality of Individual Instability

Concerning the above, a critic can always argue that the functions measured by the tests change gradually from one age to another. The only answer to this argument at present is the ubiquity with which this particular pattern of correlations is found. One finds a very similar pattern in the intercorrelations of a simple learning task which is acquired to asymptotic levels in the course of a few hours. One also finds completely similar patterns in the intercorrelations during maturation of height and weight, for which the change in function argument cannot hold.

It should also be noted that finding this pattern in both learning data and maturational data means that there is no easy explanation for the similar pattern in the intercorrelations of intelligence tests. The pattern may be caused by differences from one time period to another in opportunities and stimulation, producing unevenness in learning rate; it may be caused by genetically determined unevenness in rate of maturation; or both maturation and learning may be involved. The Thomson theoretical position, utilizing both overlapping stimulus—response bonds and neural structures, appears to provide for a more reasonable interpretation of intraindividual variability than does a position which assumes a fixed, unitary capacity of the organism.

## Subgroup Stability

In spite of the relatively large amount of intraindividual variability present in intellectual performance, subgroup means from different levels of the total distributions of academic grades, intelligence test scores, and occupational performance scores can and do remain stable with respect to each other over time. For example, mean differences among races and social classes seemingly remain constant for the same groups of children as those children move through the public schools. Although individual children tend to regress, in many cases at least they regress toward their subgroup means and not toward the total population mean.

## A Dilemma for Theory

If subgroup means frequently do not regress toward the population mean, but individuals within groups regress toward the subgroup mean, a problem is posed for theory. Low within-group correlations over long time spans can not be overinterpreted to mean, of necessity, lack of psychological communality between functions measured early and those measured late. Low correlations between early intelligence test scores and later occupational success represent a case in point. Logic alone dictates that the success of any selection program can only be measured directly by comparing the mean proficiency of the selected group with that of an appropriate control group or groups. Low stability of relationships within groups is, at best, only indirect evidence; low within-group stability is necessary but not sufficient evidence for lack of psychological communality early and late.

The phenomena of intraindividual variability and subgroup stability over time are ones with which the theoretician, whether he be experimentalist or mental tester, must come to grips. Offhand, this does seem to be one area in which the experimentally trained person may have the advantage over many factor analysts. Reification of factors is all too easy and, as a result, all too common. Although I have tended to use attribute, bias, and error in the singular, these are no more than convenient shorthand expressions and, psychologically, the plural should be used for all three. Among psychometricians Thomson was the first, and among the most persuasive, to see this. Unfortunately, faculty thinking is strongly ingrained in most of us by our language and by our philosophical and religious heritage, so that in spite of persuasive arguments all too few are persuaded. Perhaps a combination of experimentalists and psychometricians can be more persuasive than either group alone.

# REFERENCES

Anderson, J. E. The limitations of infant and preschool tests in the measurement of intelligence. *Journal of Psychology,* 1939, **3,** 351–379.

Campbell, D. T., & Fiske, D. W. Convergent and discriminant validation by the multitrait–multimethod matrix. *Psychological Bulletin,* 1959, **56,** 81–105.

Cattell, R. B. *Abilities: Their structure, growth, and action.* Boston: Houghton Mifflin, 1971.

Cronbach, L., Gleser, G., Nanda, H., & Rajaratnam, N. *The dependability of behavioral measurements: Theory of generalizability for scores and profiles.* New York: Wiley, 1972.

Ferguson, G. A. On learning and human ability. *Canadian Journal of Psychology,* 1954, **8,** 95–112.

Guilford, J. P. *The nature of human intelligence.* New York: McGraw-Hill, 1967.

Humphreys, L. G. Distributed practice in the development of conditioned eyelid reaction. *Journal of General Psychology,* 1940, **22,** 379–383.

Humphreys, L. G. Note on the multitrait–multimethod matrix. *Psychological Bulletin,* 1960, **57,** 86–88.

Humphreys, L. G. Analytical approach to the correlation between related pairs of subjects on psychological tests. *Psychological Bulletin,* 1970, **74,** 149–152.

Humphreys, L. G. & Fleishman, A. Pseudo-orthogonal and other analysis of variance designs involving individual differences variables. *Journal of Educational Psychology,* 1974, **66,** 464–472.

Humphreys, L. G. The misleading distinction between aptitude and achievement tests. In Green, D. R. (Ed.), *The aptitude–achievement distinction.* New York: McGraw-Hill, 1974.

Loevinger, J. Effect of distortion of measurement on item selection. *Educational and Psychological Measurement,* 1954, **14,** 441–448.

Project TALENT Staff. *Studies of the American High School.* Pittsburgh, Project TALENT Office, 1962.

Roff, M. A statistical study of the development of intelligence test performance. *The Journal of Psychology,* 1941, **11,** 371–386.

Spearman, C. *The abilities of man.* New York: MacMillan, 1927.

Thomson, G. *The factor analysis of human abilities.* (5th ed.) New York: Houghton Mifflin, 1951.

Thorndike, E. L. *The measurement of intelligence.* New York: Bureau of Publications, Teachers College, Columbia University, 1926.

Thurstone, L. L. *Primary mental abilities.* Chicago: University of Chicago Press, 1938. (Psychometric Monograph No. 1)

Tryon, R. C. A theory of psychological components—an alternative to "mathematical factors." *Psychological Review,* 1935, **42,** 425–454.

Underwood, B. J. *Psychological research.* New York: Appleton-Century-Crofts, 1957.

# 20

# The Processes of Intelligence and Education

Robert Glaser

University of Pittsburgh

The implications of this volume for education can be considered by examining the relationships between measured intelligence and the task environment provided by schooling. It seems clear that intelligence tests, when examined in terms of their use in the educational enterprise, take on a rather particular meaning—a meaning derived from the way in which the tests are validated for the purpose of predicting or enhancing school achievement. I shall elaborate upon this statement by describing and discussing several models of an educational enterprise. The models are written as flow diagrams, which are only sterile skeletal structures of the process of education, but they do serve, I hope, to make clear the focus of my remarks.

## MODEL ONE: A SELECTIVE, FIXED-TRACK MODEL

Consider the first model in Fig. 1. Before entering the system, individuals exist in some state of initial competence, Box $A$. The characteristics of this initial state are tested in $B$, and then a decision is made either to place an individual in standard task environment $D$, in which particular learning and performance state are tested in $B$, and then a decision is made either to place an individual in the standard task environment $D$, in which particular learning and performance assessment is made of a state of attained competence, with the resulting consequences available at $F$ and $G$—repeat or drop out or award credential. Of course, in practice this stark model may be overlaid with less drastic routines; but for the moment, consider it as given here. The activity carried out in $D$ is generally limited in the alternative modes of learning that it provides, so that the

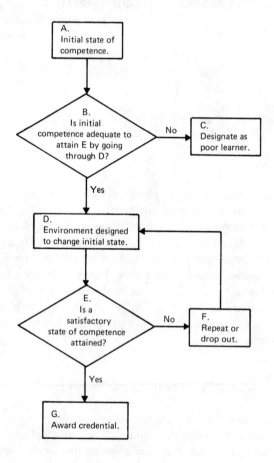

FIG. 1  Model One:  A selective, fixed-track model.

particular abilities selected in $B$ are emphasized and fostered to the exclusion of other possible abilities.

At $B$, monitoring takes place with respect to those abilities that are required for learning in the environment provided for attaining the competence assessed at $E$. The success of the system at $E$, that is, maximizing the number receiving credentials, is realized by admitting those individuals who display relatively high abilities at $B$, abilities that are required to succeed in the educational environment provided. Because only those individuals who have a reasonable probability of success in achieving an award at $G$ are admitted into the system, the particular educational environment provided, $D$, can be maintained. The abilities of individuals that become important to measure are those that predict success in this special environment.

## MODEL TWO: DEVELOPMENT OF INITIAL COMPETENCE

Consider a second model, Fig. 2. It has the same components as the first: an entering test gate, an environment for learning, and measures of attainment. In this second model, however, individuals at $B$ are not only assessed with respect to the presence or absence of abilities that allow them to pass through the entering gate, but some diagnosis is also made of the nature of the abilities tested upon entry. For those individuals whose state of initial competence at the moment does not allow them to pass through the gate, an educational environment is instituted so that this competence is developed to a point where individuals do pass through the gate. It is reasonable to assume that these entering abilities are influenced throughout a span of time before and after gate entry. In this way, through some combination of prior and continued training, entry gate abilities are influenced so that the number of individuals that succeed at $E$ is maximized. It is an obvious hypothesis that the abilities influenced are processes of cognitive performance such as have been discussed in the preceding chapters—for example, memory capabilities, problem solving, and developmental processes in children.

## MODEL THREE: ACCOMMODATION TO DIFFERENT STYLES OF LEARNING

A third model shown in Fig. 3 provides a variety of educational environments and instructional methods. In this model, procedures for passing through the entering gate are different from the previous models in which there was a fixed environment. In this educational setting, the attempt is made to match or to allow individuals to match their abilities to one or more of the environments provided. Individuals who can initially succeed *in any one* of the environments

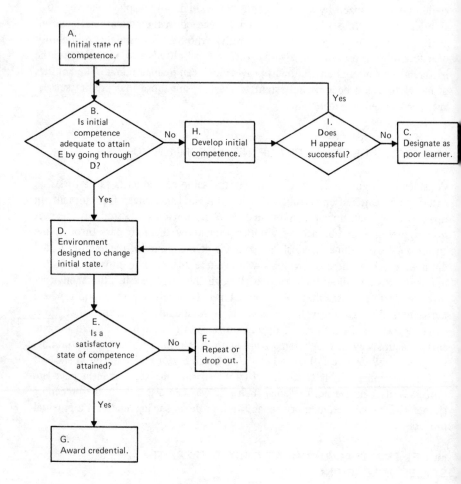

FIG. 2  Model Two: Development of initial competence.

pass through the entering gate. This model assumes that alternative means of learning are adaptive to, and in some way matched to, the abilities of different individuals. It can be assumed that this matching process occurs not only at the entering gate, but that it also takes place continuously during the course of learning. As information is obtained about the learner, this information is used to enhance probabilities of success in alternate learning opportunities and instructional environments.

A significant property of this third flow model is the interaction between a learner's performance and the subsequent nature of the educational setting. An adaptive interaction occurs, the success of which is determined by the extent to which an individual experiences a match between his or her abilities and the activities in which he or she engages.

## MODEL FOUR: DEVELOPMENT OF INITIAL COMPETENCE AND ACCOMMODATION TO STYLES OF LEARNING

A fourth model that can be considered is some combination of the second and third models; this is shown in Fig. 4. In this case, attainment is maximized both by improving abilities required by the entering gate and by providing multiple environments so that matching can occur. This combined model is probably necessary in practice because in the actual realization of the third model, one could only assume a reasonably small number of alternate environments; and the abilities required for these different environments would be the ones that would be developed. At different points in time, as a function of various subject matters to be learned and individual stages of development, there could be movement across the alternate environments.

## MODEL FIVE: ALTERNATE TERMINAL ATTAINMENTS

It is also possible to consider simple versus complex terminal attainment models—a complex model would contain a number of attained states of competence ($E_1$ through $E_3$) as shown in Fig. 5. Simple attainment systems might represent the case in elementary schools, where the educational goal is to teach the basic literacies to all students. Complex terminal attainment systems would be more predominant in higher education. In general, throughout the educational span, complex attainment systems can encourage the potential of different constellations of human abilities and reflect the fact that many different ways of succeeding in the educational system can receive equally recognized credentials.

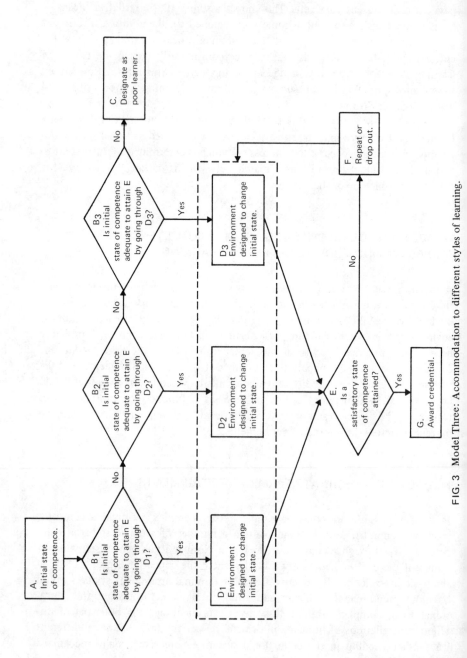

FIG. 3 Model Three: Accommodation to different styles of learning.

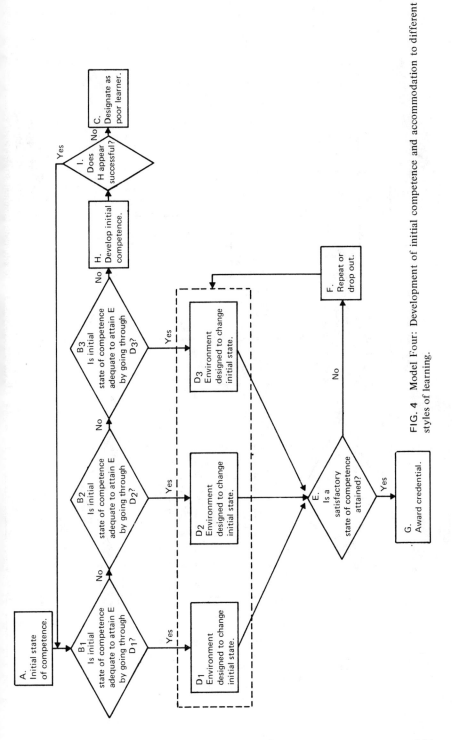

FIG. 4 Model Four: Development of initial competence and accommodation to different styles of learning.

347

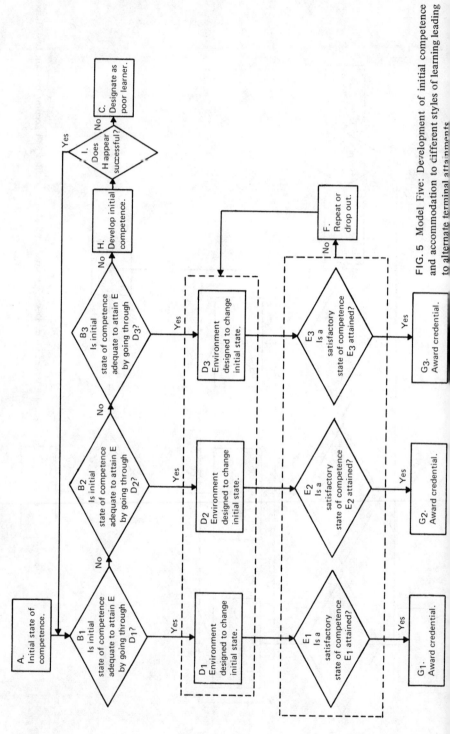

FIG. 5 Model Five: Development of initial competence and accommodation to different styles of learning leading to alternate terminal attainments.

348

## COGNITIVE PROCESSES AND EDUCATIONAL ENVIRONMENTS

It is not unreasonable to equate model one with the prevailing educational system. A particular characteristic of this model (as well as the others) is that the individual differences that become important to assess are those that maximize success in the system, that is, that have predictive validity for success or failure in the system. In the task environment provided by our prevailing system, the present concepts of measured intelligence and aptitude have emerged as entering-gate assessments. The history of selection testing in higher and early education paints the picture clearly. College entrance examinations have taken on the properties of intelligence tests, and a strong determinant of what primary and secondary education is like is the character of the entrance requirements to prestigious institutions of higher learning. Binet's work, the basic model for scholastic intelligence tests, was especially designed to determine which children were unable to profit from instruction as given in ordinary schooling. Until recently, a law in my own state of Pennsylvania relieved the school system of the obligation to educate children certified as "uneducable."

This history is to be interpreted in light of the fact that the validation of a test is a very specific procedure; tests are valid for a specific purpose in a specific situation. As a result, if we base our conclusions about what intelligence tests measure on their most prevalent and effective use, that is, on their validity in our present environments for learning, then we must say they measure those abilities that contribute to success in the particular environment provided in our schools. These tests predict, to some extent, the outcomes of learning in the uniform educational environment provided in model one. They are not especially designed to determine different ways in which students learn best, nor are they designed to measure the specific processes that underlie the learning of various kinds of school tasks. Thus, they may not measure those abilities related to the possibilities inherent in the other models. This state of affairs is attested to by the studies on aptitude-treatment interaction mentioned briefly by Tyler (Chapter 2). These studies have contributed very little information about the relationships between aptitudes, as measured by current tests, and learning variables extracted from experimental psychology. As has been underlined in the papers by Carroll (Chapter 3) and Hunt (Chapter 13), aptitude measures, learning variables, and performance processes have not drawn on the same theoretical base; no general model of the underlying processes involved has guided systematic study (see Glaser & Resnick, 1972).

In the future, we should be in a position to test the power of the concepts and methodologies coming from work in cognitive psychology and cross-cultural research, such as have been described in this volume, in the context of research and development required to design and evaluate the educational models that go beyond model one. If we analyze the cognitive processes necessary for the performance requirements of various scholastic settings, and then analyze the processes that individuals bring to these task environments, we should be able, in the long run, to match the two and thus change the model of our educational system from the first model to the second or third or other models. The second model provides for assistance in the modification of cognitive processes so that individuals can meet the demands of the learning environment provided. The third model provides for identification of the processes in which different individuals are especially talented and for the design of learning environments that utilize these talents. A combination of both of these tactics (as in model four) appears to be a reasonable way to think about a basis for providing educational environments that are adaptive to individual differences and that maximize educational outcomes.

The chapters in this book provide a display of possibilities for the kinds of cognitive processes to be considered in research oriented toward the design and development of new educational models. Perhaps, analysis of abilities that comprise the initial states of competence of individuals on entering an educational system can be related to the characteristics of long-term memory and the underlying dimensions of its semantic space. Perhaps, in assessing individual differences to be considered in individualizing instruction, contact can be made with such cognitive processes as: the properties of short-term memory (such as retrieval time, speed of release from proactive inhibition, chunking size, rapidity of manipulation, and effective retention of input order); the nature of the perceptual system for attending to, recognizing and discriminating stimuli, and for scanning features of a task environment; and, as suggested in the chapter by Resnick and myself (Chapter 11), the processes that underlie the assembly of previously learned repertoires into more complex performance.

Individual difference processes that appear to be related to the matching of talents and cognitive styles with learning environments are suggested by the interesting cross-cultural findings described by Goodnow (Chapter 9) and Olson (Chapter 10). Different cultural backgrounds influence such individual characteristics as the capacity for monitoring one's own behavior, the value associated with generalizing from practice, and the competence in specific skills related to the media most prevalent in one's background and culture. Individuals from different backgrounds interpret problem-solving situations in different ways, and this phenomenon raises several questions relevant to the design of educational environments: Is working quickly and efficiently a cultural value? Is physical manipulation encouraged or is it more distinguished to work out things in one's head? Is it appropriate to even begin a task if one cannot succeed? Is it of value to work on what appears to be a significant problem even though one might not meet with success?

The individual differences in cognitive processes that underlie the concepts of intelligence and aptitude, that underlie facility in problem solving, and that are involved in the differential development, acquisition, and performance of complex behavior are what I have come to call the "new aptitudes" (see Glaser, 1972). These new aptitudes, because they provide clues about how cognitive processes might be modified or employed for learning, appear to have more significant implications for education than do the present correlationally derived relations between aptitude tests and school success. As a result of adaptation to individual cognitive abilities, educational enterprises could be less narrowly selective than model one and could provide alternatives that are adaptive to a wider range of human experiences and talent, as envisioned in models four and five. As E. Hunt and his colleagues have previously written (Hunt, Frost, & Lunneborg, 1973):

"Training of short-term memory processing efficiency, for example, seems more directly approachable than increasing verbal ability. It appears probable to us that a set of new, theoretically based measures of intelligence will move many psychometric predictions from static statements about the probability of success to dynamic statements about what can be done to increase the likelihood of success [p. 118]." And further: "Hopefully the new viewpoint on intelligence will lead to measuring instruments which are diagnostic, in the sense that they tell us how the institution should adjust to the person, instead of simply telling us which people already are adjusted to the institution [p. 120]."

As I have indicated, the essential strategy for the kind of adaptive education dimly seen in models four and five would be to match an individual's abilities to alternate ways of learning and also to attempt to bring the individual's abilities into a range of competence that enhances his or her potential to profit from these available alternatives. Some realization of this kind of thinking is already at hand. Currently under development are individualized, adaptive school programs where children's basic abilities in auditory and spatial analysis and in self-monitoring capabilities have been developed, with subsequent influence upon their success in beginning reading and arithmetic (Rosner, 1972; Wang, 1974). Matching has taken place with respect to children's rate of learning, preference for physical versus verbal manipulation, and preference for many or few instances before coming to a generalization (Glaser & Rosner, 1975; Resnick, Wang & Rosner, 1977). The possibilities for relating cognitive process analysis and educational procedure should be further stimulated by this volume, as should the requirement for much hard work along these lines for some time to come.

## ACKNOWLEDGMENTS

Work on this contribution was carried out under the auspices of the Learning Research and Development Center at the University of Pittsburgh and supported in part by funds from the National Institute of Education, United States Department of Health, Education, and Welfare. The opinions expressed in this paper do not necessarily reflect the position or policy of the sponsoring agency, and no official endorsement should be inferred.

## REFERENCES

Glaser, R. Individuals and learning: The new aptitudes. *Educational Researcher,* 1972, **1**(6), 5–13.

Glaser, R., & Resnick, L. B. Instructional psychology. *Annual Review of Psychology,* 1972, **23**, 207–276.

Glaser, R., & Rosner J. Toward the design of adaptive environments for learning: Curriculum aspects. In H. Talmadge (Ed.), *Systems of individualized education.* Berkeley: McCutchan Publ., 1975.

Hunt, E., Frost, N., & Lunneborg, C. Individual differences in cognition: A new approach to intelligence. In G. H. Bower (Ed.), *The psychology of learning and motivation: Advances in research and theory.* Vol. 7. New York: Academic Press, 1973.

Resnick, L. B., Wang, M. C., & Rosner, J. *Adaptive education for young children: The Primary Education Project.* In M. C. Day, & R. K. Parker (Eds.), *The preschool in action.* (2nd ed.), .Boston: Allyn & Bacon, 1977.
Parker (Eds.), *The preschool in action.* (2nd ed.) Boston: Allyn & Bacon, in press.

Rosner, J. *The development and validation of an individualized perceptual skills curriculum.* Pittsburgh: University of Pittsburgh, Learning Research and Development Center, 1972. (Publication 1972/7)

Wang, M. C. *The rationale and design of the self-schedule system.* Pittsburgh: University of Pittsburgh, Learning Research and Development Center, 1974. (Publication 1974/5)

# Author Index

The numbers in *italics* refer to the pages on which the complete references are listed.

# Subject Index